Political Organizations

PRINCETON STUDIES IN AMERICAN POLITICS:
HISTORICAL, INTERNATIONAL, AND
COMPARATIVE PERSPECTIVES

SERIES EDITORS

IRA KATZNELSON, MARTIN SHEFTER, THEDA SKOCPOL

*Labor Visions and State Power: The Origins of Business
Unionism in the United States*
by Victoria C. Hattam

The Lincoln Persuasion: Remaking American Liberalism
by J. David Greenstone

Politics and Industrialization: Early Railroads in the United States and Prussia
by Colleen A. Dunlavy

Political Parties and the State: The American Historical Experience
by Martin Shefter

Prisoners of Myth: The Leadership of the Tennessee Valley Authority, 1933–1990
by Erwin C. Hargrove

Bound by Our Constitution: Women, Workers, and the Minimum Wage
by Vivien Hart

*Experts and Politicians: Reform Challenges to Machine Politics
in New York, Cleveland, and Chicago*
by Kenneth Finegold

Social Policy in the United States: Future Possibilities in Historical Perspective
by Theda Skocpol

Political Organizations
by James Q. Wilson

POLITICAL ORGANIZATIONS

BY

JAMES Q. WILSON

PRINCETON UNIVERSITY PRESS

PRINCETON, NEW JERSEY

Library of Congress Cataloging-in-Publication Data
Wilson, James Q.
Political organizations / by James Q. Wilson.
p. cm. — (Princeton studies in American politics)
Originally published: New York : Basic Books, 1974.
Includes bibliographical references and index.
ISBN 0-691-04385-X (pbk.)
1. Lobbying—United States. 2. Pressure groups—United States.
I. Title. II. Series.
JK1118.W54 1995
324′.4′0973—dc20   95-14653

1 3 5 7 9 10 8 6 4 2

CONTENTS

INTRODUCTION TO THE PAPERBACK EDITION   vii

ACKNOWLEDGMENTS   XXV

CHAPTER 1 / *Organizations and Politics*   3

PART I
A Theoretical Perspective

CHAPTER 2 / *Rationality and Self-Interest*   19
CHAPTER 3 / *Organizational Maintenance and Incentives*   30
CHAPTER 4 / *Social Structure and Organizations*   56
CHAPTER 5 / *Political Structure and Organizations*   78

PART II
The Perspective Applied

CHAPTER 6 / *Political Parties*   95
CHAPTER 7 / *Labor Unions*   119
CHAPTER 8 / *Business Associations*   143
CHAPTER 9 / *Civil Rights Organizations*   171

PART III
Internal Processes

CHAPTER 10 / *Organizational Creation and Change*   195
CHAPTER 11 / *Authority and Leadership*   215
CHAPTER 12 / *Organizational Democracy*   235

PART IV
External Processes

CHAPTER 13 / *Competition and Coalitions*   *261*

CHAPTER 14 / *Bargaining, Protest, and Violence*   *281*

PART V
Political Roles

CHAPTER 15 / *Organizational Representation*   *305*

CHAPTER 16/ *Organizations and Public Policy*   *327*

INDEX   *347*

INTRODUCTION TO THE PAPERBACK EDITION

When I wrote this book in the early 1970s, my goal was to direct attention to the ways in which the expression of political opinion is shaped by the effort to create and maintain an organization composed of people holding that opinion. Organizations, I argued, are not neutral devices for transmitting citizen preferences to public officials; they are social systems that modify as well as express preferences. Therefore, an increase in the variety and effectiveness of organized interests—that is to say, an increase in the degree to which a political system is pluralistic—is not necessarily equivalent to an increase in the extent to which that system will reflect the views of all of the relevant publics.

I offered examples of this uncertain link between member opinion and organizational activity in the first edition: the AFL-CIO took positions on civil rights that were at variance with the views of members of its constituent unions; the National Council of Churches in Christ pressed causes that were almost surely opposed by most members of many of its affiliated Protestant denominations. Since then more examples have appeared. The American Association of Retired Persons (AARP), which has roughly thirty million members, pressed the federal government to adopt catastrophic health insurance only to discover after the bill was passed that an important part of its own membership was so opposed to the legislation that Congress was forced to repeal it. The Business Roundtable, speaking for the chief executive officers of many of the largest American corporations, has adopted an accommodationist strategy toward many federal tax and regulatory initiatives quite unlike the more oppositional stance once taken by the National Association of Manufacturers; which group speaks for "business"?

My effort to explain the problematic nature of organizational maintenance was shaped by the significance that I and other theorists attached to what is called the collective action paradox or, more commonly, the Olson Problem, named after economist Mancur Olson.[1] The collective action paradox explains why people will not act in concert with others to achieve agreed-upon goals. It has two parts. The first is the free-rider problem: whenever it is possible for a person to enjoy the benefits of collective action without having to contribute to the costs of such action, he or she can ride free on the efforts of others. If I benefit from the efforts of the AARP to protect Social Security or of the Sierra Club to enhance the environment, I will get those benefits whether or not I join either group. Or to say the same thing in other words, since I cannot be excluded from obtaining benefits for which I have not paid, I have no self-interested incentive to join the organization that has caused them to be supplied. The second part is the trivial contribution problem: whenever my prospective contribution to an organization amounts to only a tiny fraction of the resources it needs, I have no incentive to contribute because I cannot improve the ability of the organization to achieve its stated goals. Common Cause seeks to reform campaign finance laws, but its efforts to do so cannot possibly be affected by my check for $25 in annual dues.

Olson discussed two solutions to the collective action paradox. The first is social pressure: in a small group in which members deal with one another face to face, many participants will contribute effort and money in order to avoid criticism from friends or associates. The second is the use of selective benefits that can be given to or withheld from individual members on condition that they supply effort or money to the organization. Such selective benefits include insider information, discounts on purchases, magazine subscriptions, and access to people of power and status.

When this book was first published, I sought to show that the collective action problem could be overcome not only by social pressure and selective benefits but also by appeals to purposes. The problem as posed by Olson and other economists—that rational, self-interested persons will not join voluntary associations simply in order to achieve group interests—was overstated because it failed to take into account the differing ways in which people might define their self-interest. More voluntary associations existed even in 1965, when Olson wrote, than one would have predicted knowing only that people are rationally self-interested. And within a very few years, their number grew exponentially. The dramatic increase in the membership of civil rights, environmental, civil liberties, political reform, and feminist organizations that occurred in the 1970s could not be explained entirely or even largely by the ability of such groups to exert social pressure or supply selective benefits, though these inducements no doubt played a role. To some extent, members were responding to purposive appeals.

I set forth a theory of incentives, first developed by Peter B. Clark and myself, as a way of understanding not only how purposive appeals might work but also, and more importantly, how the kind of incentive employed—material, solidary, or purposive—would affect the goals and tactics of the organization using it.

Purposes as Incentives

While it it is obvious that some people will support a group simply because it claims to serve some larger cause, it is not obvious why that should be.[2] Every mail delivery brings to us worthy appeals; the vast majority get thrown out in the trash. But we act on a few, despite our knowing (if we think about it even for a moment) that we will benefit from the success of a group whether or not we contribute, and that the group's success will not be determined by our modest contribution. Why do some of us respond to such appeals?

The original edition of this book did not supply a very satisfactory answer to that question. Since then, other scholars have examined this problem in much greater detail and I have thought about it a good deal. There are at least four factors that affect our response to purposive appeals.

The first reflects individual differences in temperament. These differences are of two sorts. Some people have a stronger sense of duty than others, leading them to act in a certain way simply because it is "the right thing to do" even if they are aware that their actions will have little practical effect. It is just such a sense of duty that helps explain why people vote even though the chance of one person's vote affecting the outcome of an election is vanishingly small. Owing to some combination of biological endowment and familial experiences, many people feel guilty if they do not vote or do not contribute to a good cause. A different temperamental trait has been identified by Terry Moe. He has suggested that some people display a higher level of "subjective efficacy" than others. This leads them to overestimate the significance of their contributions to collective action so that they are less likely to free ride than one would predict on the assumption that they are both rational and well-informed.[3] Some combination of duty and efficacy explains many forms of political participation. An important research goal is to explore the origins and consequences of these individual differences.

The second factor involves organizational learning. In his account of participation in Common Cause, Lawrence S. Rothenberg has shown that many people will initially join that group because the cost is very low and the purpose seems laudable. Compared with the average citizen, these members tend to be affluent (and so the initial membership fee is not burdensome), highly educated (and so they are exposed to a large amount of political information), politically active (and so they are subjectively efficacious), and politically liberal (and so they are sympathetic to Common Cause's agenda). But initial membership is a relatively casual decision, not driven by a deep attachment to the organization's purposes. By joining, however, they learn more about the group and what it expects of them; those who remain and become active are those who find the group's purposes compelling and its social relations (in my language, its solidary benefits) attractive.[4] Purposive associations attract members in much the same way a magazine gets subscribers: many people are lured by a combination of low cost and general interests; a few people remain because of a learned commitment to purposes and the pleasures of the activity.

A third factor is the perception of a threat. In the years since this book was first published, I have come increasingly to believe that the motive force of any incentive, but especially ideology, is greater when people perceive a threat to remove what they have than when they hear a promise to bestow what they want. Experimental psychology has consistently shown that the prospect of a loss is more likely to motivate action than the expectation of a gain even when the value of the gain and the loss are identical. For example, I predict that it will be easier to induce people to contribute $5 to an organization that tries to protect their retirement benefits from being cut by $50 a month than it will be to get them to contribute the same amount to an association that endeavors to increase their benefits by $50 a month. By the same token, an environmental lobby will get more members by saying that an existing national park faces a reduction in size by 10 percent than it will by saying that the same park might be expanded by 10 percent, even when the probabilities attached to the two outcomes are the same.

There are two bits of evidence that support these predictions. The first is that political associations seeking support rely in their direct-mail advertising more on threats than on promises. I do not need to list studies to confirm this; I only ask the reader to recall the mail that he or she has received requesting donations from political groups. If liberal, they will stress threats to free speech, civil rights, and the environment and refer to the demons responsible for these menaces—big business, Ronald Reagan, and fundamentalist Christians. If conservative, they will stress threats to economic growth, personal safety, and fiscal prudence and refer to a different set of demons—Bill Clinton, Edward M. Kennedy, and the American Civil Liberties Union.

The second bit of evidence can be found in the trends in membership support for various associations. If their members were attracted by the progress the group is making toward achieving its goal, then their numbers would rise as more signs of progress became evident. Thus, the Sierra Club would get more support as a pro-environment administration comes to power in Washington with which the Club has important links. Similarly, an antitax organization would attract more support when a sympathetic administration is in office. Though this sometimes happens, my sense is that these organizations prosper when their enemies are in office. The Sierra Club, for example, grew rapidly when Ronald Reagan was in office (especially during the years when James Watt, a critic of environmentalism, was secretary of the interior) but declined in membership after Reagan retired and particularly after the pro-environment Clinton-Gore administration assumed power. (Much the same thing happened to Greenpeace and the Audubon Society.) The National Rifle Association experienced its most rapid growth as the prospects of the passage of federal gun legislation increased. John Mark Hansen has published evidence that the membership of such groups as the American Farm Bureau Federation, the League of Women Voters, and the National Association of Home Builders will be positively affected by the degree of perceived threat in the group's environment.[5]

To the extent political organizations rely on threat appeals, their leadership will have a stake in magnifying the threat (whatever the reality) and conducting legislative campaigns that demonize opponents (however great the need for allies). This means that such groups will over time appeal chiefly to their most deeply aroused members and be governed by their preferences however large the nominal constituency. The increasing militancy of the National Rifle Association, for example, may reflect its increasing attention to an activist core.

By contrast, organizations that rely on material (or other selective) incentives may empower a staff that is at odds with the rank and file. The AARP offers low-cost insurance, pharmaceuticals, and other benefits to its members, some of whom may be indifferent to the policy positions the staff endorses until (as in the case of health insurance) the staff mistakenly takes a position that some members view as a threat. The National Council of Churches could assume that most Protestants joined their churches for reasons having nothing to do with the political activities of the NCC until those positions were publicized by its critics in ways that seemed to threaten the philosophical beliefs of conservative Protestants.

A crude generalization is this: ideological incentives, especially if threat-oriented, tend to constrain and radicalize the leaders of an association, whereas selective incentives, especially material ones, tend to bestow discretionary authority on such leaders.

The fourth factor is less an explanation of why individuals respond to purposes than of why purposive organizations can exist even without members. No study of member incentives alone can explain the post-1970 explosion of so-called public-interest organizations active in politics. (I say "so-called" because such groups may or may not serve what a reasonable person would call "the public interest." The term, narrowly construed, refers to associations that claim to benefit nonmembers as much as or more than members.) After all, solidary, material, and purposive incentives have always been available. To be sure, recent developments in computer-driven direct-mail solicitation techniques and the skillful exploitation of mass exposure to television have extended the reach and deepened the impact of purposive incentives (especially threat-avoidance ones). Even so, there seem to be more activist groups than one would expect simply knowing of the techniques for exploiting perceived threats.

A large part of the increase in numbers has arisen because of the greater use of sponsors as opposed to members. A sponsor finances all or some large part of an organization; a member merely contributes some tiny fraction of an organization's resources. There have always been sponsors—wealthy men and women who were attracted to a cause—but of late sponsorship has become institutionalized in the form of foundations, government agencies, pro bono work at law firms, and court settlements. It is now relatively easy to start a political organization that has, for all practical purposes, no members at all; it can be supported by foundation grants and government contracts, staffed part-time by lawyers employed by firms that allow them to donate time at no charge (*pro bono publico*, or "for the public good") to worthwhile causes, and earn money by winning lawsuits against corporations and government agencies in which the loser not only pays the fees of the winner but also, at least with respect to corporations, contributes (as part of a negotiated settlement) large sums to the victorious association and its allies. The result is what Jeffrey Berry has called, in his account of the rise of public-interest lobbies, the "advocacy explosion."[6] People may join such groups, often as members of an "advisory board," but their joining costs them nothing except the uses to which the organization will put their names.

Incentive Theory Applied

In the first edition, I discussed political parties, labor unions, business associations, and civil rights organizations. In the intervening two decades, a great deal has happened to all four, more than can be adequately summarized here. A few highlights deserve mention, however.

Parties as organizations have changed somewhat from being local associations that mobilized local electorates to being national entities that direct resources, recruit candidates, and supply expertise. As organizations, the Democratic and Republican parties have become weaker in many cities and counties but stronger in Washington, D.C. The Democratic and Republican National Committees (and the Democratic and Republican congressional campaign committees in the House and Senate) have increasingly used the methods of public-interest lobbying groups to raise money—computerized direct-mail solicitations to obtain many small contributions and face-to-face negotiations with wealthy individuals and groups to raise a few large donations. In short, the parties have become more like institutions and less like membership associations. Because direct-mail solicitations tend to work best with addressees who have an ideological view of politics or perceive a threat to their vital interests, the national party organizations that use direct mail have a stake in appearing to stand for fundamentally different approaches to policy. At the same time, the Democratic and Republican national committees can obtain large donations from affluent groups; under the campaign finance laws as they stood in 1994, any individual can give up to $20,000 a year and a political action committee (PAC) can contribute up to $15,000 a year to a national party committee. These big contributors are typically more interested in advancing their material interests than in furthering some large cause. Thus, national party organizations have come to combine some of the features of a public-interest group with those of a business- or union-related lobby. Local party organizations still exist, of course, and continue to rely on some combination of solidary, material, and purposive incentives, but in some respects they are now overshadowed by the national organizations.

Labor unions have continued to decline in membership and influence, especially in the traditional blue-collar occupations. Only among white-collar unions, notably those employing government workers, have there been significant increases in membership and power. The National Education Association and the American Federation of State, County, and Municipal Employees have become major political forces, not only as lobbyists but as means for recruiting delegates to the national party conventions. These white-collar unions have, in general, been politically more militant than their blue-collar counterparts. In recent years the political action committees associated with both the NEA and the AFSCME have been among the top ten contributors to congressional candidates.

Business associations have always been a prominent feature—numerically, perhaps the most prominent feature—on the interest-group landscape. Their numbers have grown since 1973, though not, proportionally, as much as have those of their rivals devoted to environmental and consumer causes. The biggest change, however, has not been in their numbers but in their political orientation and membership base.[7] Faced with a federal government that, beginning in the late 1960s, adopted a variety of sweeping regulatory initiatives designed to protect consumers, workers, and the environment, business firms were thrown on the defensive and forced to reconsider their tactics and organizational forms.

Organizationally, business began to discount the value of peak associations (such as the National Association of Manufacturers, the Chamber of Commerce, and the Committee for Economic Development) in favor of trade associations and single-firm representation. As government grew in the scope and complexity of its regulatory policies, business found itself deeply divided by industry and even by firms within industries. Only on certain generic issues, such as taxation or labor relations, could peak associations hope to speak for business. This fact was evident when I wrote in 1973, but succeeding years intensified the problem. Accordingly, there was a great increase in the number of firms that had their own representatives in Washington who would work for the interests of their employer; when several firms discovered a common interest, they would often form an ad hoc coalition to press that cause.

Tactically, few firms could any longer afford to content themselves with advancing an antigovernment ideology or to defend themselves with appeals to ideological slogans such as free enterprise or states' rights. Whatever the substantive value of such principles, their political efficacy had been much reduced. The ideological attack on big government that seemed to be the stock-in-trade of peak business associations in the period from 1930 through 1960 was taken over in the 1980s and 1990s by popular movements mobilized by radio talk-show hosts, electronic bulletin boards, and magazines. Business firms had, in their eyes, lost the battle to contain government behind high constitutional walls; now, every aspect of business management and industrial processes was on the political agenda. Most firms decided that the right course of action was to defend pragmatically their own stake in the outcome of the tax and regulatory battles that had now become commonplace. And each firm often concluded that its stake was a bit different from that of another firm in the same industry.

These events greatly magnified the maintenance problems of traditional business associations. They adopted a variety of responses. Some worked hard, using purposive appeals, to recruit as members small businesses that could not afford their own Washington representatives. This was the case, for example, with the Chamber of Commerce. But this created a quandary:

if the Chamber was to retain the support of large firms, it had to adopt a more accommodationist stance reflecting the desire of large corporations to cut the best deal they could with a powerful government. Even doing this was difficult, since these corporations had divergent interests on most issues. But if the Chamber managed to solve this problem it found itself faced with another. Taking a moderate stance often alienated small firms that felt deeply threatened by a host of unprecedented and complex regulations. Big firms could hire experts to cope with such regulations; small firms could not. The Chamber, like the NAM, was buffeted by these cross-pressures during the 1990s. The debate over health care reform in 1993–1994 exemplified the problem. Big firms, thinking such legislation was inevitable, tried to modify its details to suit their own interests; small firms, believing such legislation was ruinous (it required firms to buy health insurance for their employees), sought to block it entirely. Peak associations could not easily straddle such differences nor find a coherent package of incentives that would simultaneously satisfy a variety of firms.

Civil rights organizations had, by the late 1960s, won most of their major legislative victories and had turned their efforts to influencing how these new laws would be interpreted and applied. In the first edition I limited my discussion to those groups representing racial and ethnic (primarily black) interests; today, it is obvious that any complete account would include a discussion of feminist organizations. There are many accounts available of the history of the civil rights and feminist movements.[8] Analytically, perhaps the most important of these is the book by Dennis Chong that attempts to explain how collective action by disadvantaged groups is possible in the absence of any prospect of material benefit.[9] People active in the civil rights movement did not choose to be free riders; in fact, the odds against success were often so high that there was little chance of a policy gain on which one could free ride. Chong uses game theory to analyze the solution to this problem developed by the leaders of this movement. Their tactics included seeking some quick (even if limited) victories in order to buoy rank-and-file spirits, exaggerating the degree of popular support for the movement, creating an atmosphere in which a member's self-esteem would suffer if they failed to do their share, and interpreting their enemies as both wicked and amenable to pressure. Followers had to be convinced that though others were responsible for their oppression, they were capable of overcoming it. All of this required intense face-to-face involvement, a process that was psychologically demanding and difficult to sustain.

We lack, I think, any good account of the postmovement phase of civil rights, the phase, that is, in which small organizations (like the Congress of

Racial Equality and the Student Nonviolent Coordinating Committee) fall away and large, bureaucratic organizations (like the NAACP, the Urban League, and the labor movement) create institutions designed to manage the implementation of new legislation.[10]

External Representation

In the original edition I did not say much about the process of organizational representation in government. This was deliberate. There were then and are now many accounts of lobbying. *My goal was not to explain how interests were represented but how they were defined.* The conventional view of a lobby is that it speaks on behalf of a well-defined "interest" held by a defined group of people. That is often the case, but sometimes—I would say many times—it is not. The examples recounted at the beginning of this preface illustrate the problem. It is hard to think of anyone who has had a greater impact on Washington policy-making since the 1960s than Ralph Nader. But who does Nader represent? In a general sense, many people; in some particular respects, only himself. His influence depended initially on his being perceived as a lonely warrior abused by a large corporation; that initial credibility made the facts and arguments he supplied to journalists and congressional staffers interesting and useful; legislation he endorsed won some major congressional victories and legislators he opposed often beat hasty retreats; as his stature rose, many people (for example, students on college campuses) were willing to contribute to his several causes (on some campuses a portion of student activity fees were automatically sent to Naderite groups unless the students asked that they not be so used). By the time he had become an icon—the embodiment of an apparently selfless advocate of the consumer—he had also acquired a value to economic interests that saw him as an effective spokesman for the advantages they sought to protect. Accordingly, the desire of Nader to help the little fellow fit naturally with the desire of the Association of Trial Lawyers of America to fend off efforts to reform the way courts awarded damages in personal injury lawsuits; that natural convergence of interests led trial lawyers to become an important source of money for some Naderite groups.[11]

Though I did not seek to write a book about lobbying, I said some things about it that flowed from my understanding of how representation was affected by organizational maintenance. Since I first wrote, new forces have appeared on the scene that have changed the representation process and provided new opportunities to examine the relationship between incentives and behavior. Perhaps the most important development has been the creation and proliferation of political action committees. Authorized by campaign finance reform laws passed in the wake of the Watergate scandal in the early 1970s, PACs have proliferated and now supply a large fraction (but still only a minority) of the dollars raised by congressional candidates. Corporations, labor unions, trade and professional associations, and groups of like-minded people may form PACs. In my view, incentive theory can provide an insight into their operation.

There are two levels at which such incentives can operate: the individual who contributes money and the decision-maker who allocates it among candidates. In PACs sponsored by corporations and labor unions, employees and members are solicited by appeals that, though couched in purposive terms ("support democracy," "make your opinions known," "help elect people who will do the right thing"), in fact rely for much of their efficacy on solidary incentives—the desire to go along with the wishes of friends and coworkers and the hope of avoiding blame or reproach. In PACs created by unconnected groups—that is, by people brought together solely by their belief in some goal—the chief incentive is purposive, often conveyed by language that vividly points to real or imagined threats. Because the funds raised by a corporate or union PAC were not, ordinarily, given out of a shared sense of clear purpose, the managers of the PAC will have considerable discretion as to their use. They will be motivated to do two things: avoid giving offense to any contributor and retain the support of elected officials whose actions can help or hurt the firm or the union. Accordingly, such a PAC will often make many small donations to a large and diverse number of candidates (in the case of many corporations, these will range across the entire ideological spectrum). By contrast, the managers of an ideological PAC will be spending money given in response to the cause or threat that they have communicated to their contributors. As a result, the managers will find it possible or even necessary to support challengers and to buy advertising that announces their cause and denounces their opponents.

The effects of the deluge of PAC money are widely assumed to be deleterious; one reads frequent references to "the finest Congress money can buy" and to the power wielded by well-heeled PACs. People persuaded of this view may be surprised to learn that political scientists do not, in general, find any consistent evidence that PAC spending influences the outcome of the legislative battle.[12] This uncertainty is the result of three factors: statistical problems in deciding whether money given to a member induces new action or rewards existing beliefs and in separating out constituency effects from money effects, data problems in discovering how members vote in key committee deliberations, and the political fact that in a universe made up of thousands of competing PACs it is unlikely that any given PAC will have disproportionate influence.

One of the ways by which political organizations have attempted to overcome their fragmented condition is through the formation of coalitions. In 1973 I wrote that coalitions of interest groups were not likely to form. The maintenance needs of each organization worked against any strategy that would allow the distinctive identity of one group to fall under the shadow of another association. Since I wrote, coalitions have arisen far more frequently than I predicted. The Leadership Conference on Civil Rights speaks on behalf of most civil rights organizations on some matters. Business firms have created countless coalitions, such as the long-standing one on Product Liability Reform.[13]

The rise of coalition politics reflects, I think, the great disaggregation and individuation of interest representation. The ease of forming new advocacy groups has filled Washington with associations that have perhaps one or two sponsors, very few members, and small staffs. The disenchantment of business leaders with peak associations and even industry-specific trade associations has given rise to single-firm representation. To overcome the cacophony of ineffective voices rising from the swelling ranks of these small groups, coalitions are an increasingly attractive option. By bringing together several organizations into an ad hoc, temporary alliance around one specific issue, a coalition can pool resources and decide on a common strategy without sacrificing individual group identity and without making any lasting commitments. The coalition lasts only so long as the issue is alive, and no one in the coalition need promise other coalition partners to support them on any other issue.

The typology that I presented in chapter 16 was, I now realize, an effort to predict what kinds of coalitions will form depending on the perceived costs and benefits of some proposed policy. Not long after publishing the book, I refined the typology and gave to each of its four cells a name. When both costs and benefits are widely distributed, we see *majoritarian politics*; when both costs and benefits are narrowly concentrated, we see *interest-group politics*; when costs are distributed but benefits concentrated, we see *client politics*; and when benefits are distributed but costs concentrated, we have the conditions under which *entrepreneurial politics* may emerge.

I have continued to make use of that typology, as have others. What is striking is the decline in pure client politics and the rise of entrepreneurial politics. There are fewer and fewer cases in which some small group (a firm, a union, an industry or occupation) can extract a beneficial policy from government with the tacit consent of an unorganized and unrepresented majority. By contrast, there are more and more cases in which some policy entrepreneur claims, effectively if not reasonably, to be speaking for the majority and succeeds in imposing costs on a well-organized minority.

The reasons for that change have to do with the widespread mobilization of interests involving not only direct but virtual representation. It is hard to imagine a way of classifying people—by age, sex, race, ethnicity, occupation, disability, belief, region, religion, or "lifestyle"—for which there is no organizational counterpart in Washington. In relative terms, the cost of political mobilization has dropped dramatically and the media surveillance of policy-making has increased remarkably. Insider, low-visibility, old-boy politics still exist, but much less than once was the case.[14] Moreover, members of Congress studied old political science texts (perhaps *Political Organizations!*) to learn how narrow interests can defeat broad ones, and then they designed regulatory legislation that would make this more difficult. Interest conflicts were built into legislation, enforced by requirements of public hearings, impact statements, and court reviews, and handed over to high-profile administrators who were given narrow zones of discretionary authority. The result has not been greater service to the public interest, but a greater multiplicity of voices claiming to define the public interest. These voices are uttered by the growing legion of lobbyists.

One of the best recent accounts of who these people are and what they do was based on interviews with more than three hundred government officials and eight hundred lobbyists.[15] I doubt that there has ever been a more comprehensive examination of the subject. Its findings will not satisfy someone intent on discovering a powerful, sinister "They" that dominates Washington politics. Between 1978 and 1982, spanning parts of two presidential administrations (Jimmy Carter and Ronald Reagan), no single category of interest groups was more successful than any other in getting what it wanted. Labor and environmental groups had some success under Carter, but so did business; conservative and business groups won some fights under Reagan but lost a lot of others. The very multiplicity of groups resulting from the explosion of representation in Washington since 1970 meant that the old idea of "iron triangles" (composed of a key congressional committee, a government agency, and a powerful interest group) was no longer accurate. At best one could say that we now have complex issue networks in which many different groups work with and against a variety of committees and agencies in ways that are partially shaped by the ideas debated in the several Washington think tanks. Much of what is called lobbying involves, not exerting influence, but simply gathering information on what an immensely complex and cross-pressured government is doing or may do in the future.

The direction that government takes today—in those cases when one can discern something approximating a direction—increasingly results from either a crisis (such as a war or a recession) or the ideological impetus imparted by our system of nominating and electing presidents and members of Congress. Interest groups scramble to react to the unforeseen or to catch up with an environmentalist Bill Clinton, a tax-cutting Ronald Reagan, or a constitution-amending Newt Gingrich. The result is a political system characterized by immense energy but with little central direction.

Back in the late 1940s, when I was an undergraduate taking my first course in American government, answering an exam question about interest representation was easy: all you had to do was remember seven names—the Chamber of Commerce, the National Association of Manufacturers, the AFL, the CIO, the Farm Bureau Federation, the American Legion, and the American Medical Association. Although none of these has disappeared, today no one would take you seriously if you tried to understand the exercise of influence with reference to seven, or even seventy, groups. Back then, we were told that America had a pluralist system in which almost everybody was represented. It wasn't true. Today it is. So now we say we have gridlock.

Organizations and Policy

How one explains the existence of voluntary political organizations despite the collective action paradox will influence one's judgment about the nature and prospects of democracy. If one believed (as did Mancur Olson in his first book) that few people would join voluntary associations concerned with politics and that these groups would tend to be small in size, then one would predict that rather few demands would be made on government, and those chiefly by economic interests. As a result, the government would underproduce public goods. In the words of Anthony Downs, the government budget would be too small.

But if one believed that creating and sustaining such associations were relatively easy, then (given the right circumstances) there would be many such groups making all sorts of demands. In this case, the government might overproduce certain goods, and so its budget would be too large. By 1982 Olson appeared to adopt the latter position. In his book *The Rise and Decline of Nations*, he suggested that stable societies with unchanged boundaries tend to accumulate special-interest groups—labor unions, trade associations, professional societies, and the like—that will make an ever-increasing number of demands on government.[16] These demands—for subsidies, benefits, tariffs, favorable regulations, and barriers to entry into occupations and industries—will have a harmful effect on a society's rate of economic growth. As the government produces more and more benefits for these groups, it will reduce the efficiency with which its economic market operates, slow the rate at which personal income grows, and produce ever more divisive political conflicts. Olson suggested that his theory helps explain why Japan and Germany grew more rapidly after World War II: the political destruction of these nations by their victorious opponents swept away many of the growth-inhibiting special-interest groups that had existed before the war. Germany and Japan, in effect, could start economic growth afresh, unimpeded by groups making claims for special advantages. By the same token, he proposed that his theory helped explain why some states in the United States, notably those in the South, have grown economically at a faster rate than others, notably those in the Northeast. Its defeat in the Civil War gave the South a "fresh start" that was denied to the victorious North.

The Olson explanation for differences in the growth rates of the American states has been tested by others and found wanting. Virginia Gray and David Lowery did not find that how states differed in their accumulation of interest groups explained how they differed in their rate of economic growth.[17] As states become more advanced, the diversity but not the density of interest groups active in them increases.[18] Whether his theory explains differences among nations has not, so far as I am aware, been tested by others. It is quite possible that there is a connection between interest-group activity and economic growth, but that connection may depend greatly on the nature of the political regime. The United States undoubtedly has more such groups in proportion to its population than does any other large industrial nation, but it also has a political system that is decentralized and fragmented. The multiple pressures exerted in this country on Washington may be, to some extent, self-canceling as members of Congress choose to which group they will pay attention; the efforts of some members to enact their agendas may be confounded by the opposing efforts of other members who are attuned to different groups. By contrast, a nation with but a few peak business and labor associations (for example, Japan) may be strongly influenced by their demands (they have few rivals for power) and find it easy to enact their preferred policies (the government need give less attention to opponents within its legislature). Thus, taken alone the number of groups may explain little about either government policy or government effects on economic growth; the number and diversity of such groups have meaning only in the context of the particular characteristics of government institutions.

Whatever the limitations of Olson's theory, he has undoubtedly highlighted a central problem of modern democracy. How can the representation of interests be reconciled with the requirements of prudent and farsighted action, especially when the relationship between the representative and the underlying interests is often so problematic? I am not one of those who believes that the mere existence of "special-interest groups" is a curse on democracy; as with James Madison, who wrote with great clarity about this problem in 1787, I understand that liberty is to faction as air is to fire. As we wish for liberty and need air, so we must endure faction and cope with fire.

American government proved to be remarkably adaptable in the era in which a few big interests seemed to dominate politics. Without really changing the pattern of representation, we managed at one time to regulate much of business and at another time to deregulate parts of it; we ignored civil rights, then legislated to insure them; we ignored the environment, then strenuously regulated it, and then moderated the regulation somewhat. We have had periods of low taxes and no deficits, low taxes and high deficits, and high taxes and high deficits.

Since roughly 1970 we have entered a new era. Groups once excluded are now included. Pluralism that once was a distant promise is now a baffling reality. And public confidence in government has plummeted. We are all represented by groups, and yet we feel unrepresented. A thousand voices are heard in Washington, but none sounds like our own.

Part of the problem is our inability, so far, to reconcile what we want with what we are willing to pay. We tell the pollsters that we want lower taxes, no deficits, and continued spending on favorite programs, and then we expect our elected officials to put the square pegs of our preferences into the round roles of our resources. But part of the problem is that the groups that represent us do so by perpetually alarming us. To maintain themselves, threats must be evoked—many quite real, but all somewhat exaggerated. Nothing we now get from government must ever be taken away, and the amount we pay government must never be increased. We may feel unrepresented, but in fact we are mobilized as never before by groups that speak for each one of our inconsistent preferences. We do not deliberate, nor do the groups for us; we cope with a large, complex government and the groups its policies have spawned.

NOTES

I wish to thank Professors Virginia Gray and Robert Salisbury for their helpful advice while preparing this Introduction.

1. Mancur Olson, *The Logic of Collective Action* (Cambridge: Harvard University Press, 1965).

2. The late Professor Jack L. Walker levied this criticism at incentive theory in his post-humously published book, *Mobilizing Interest Groups in America* (Ann Arbor: University of Michigan Press, 1991), esp. p. 47.

3. Terry M. Moe, "A Calculus of Group Membership," *American Journal of Political Science*, vol. 24 (1980), 593–632. See also his *The Organization of Interests* (Chicago: University of Chicago Press, 1980).

4. Lawrence S. Rothenberg, *Linking Citizens to Government: Interest Group Politics at Common Cause* (Cambridge: Cambridge University Press, 1992).

5. John Mark Hansen, "The Political Economy of Group Membership," *American Political Science Review*, vol. 79 (March 1985), 79–96.

6. Jeffrey M. Berry, *Lobbying for the People* (Princeton: Princeton University Press, 1977). See also Robert H. Salisbury, *Interests and Institutions* (Pittsburgh: University of Pittsburgh Press, 1992), chap. 2.

7. I review these changes in James Q. Wilson, "The Corporation as a Political Actor," in *The Corporation in Modern Society: A Second Look*, ed. Carl Kaysen, forthcoming. See also David Vogel, *Fluctuating Fortunes: The Political Power of Business in America* (New York: Basic Books, 1989); Graham K. Wilson, *Business and Politics: A Comparative Introduction* (Chatham, N.J.: Chatham House, 1990); and Sar A. Levitan and Martha R. Cooper, *Business Lobbies* (Baltimore: Johns Hopkins University Press, 1984).

8. On the latter, see, for example, Pamela Johnston Conover and Virginia Gray, *Feminism and the New Right* (New York: Praeger, 1983).

9. Dennis Chong, *Collective Action and the Civil Rights Movement* (Chicago: University of Chicago Press, 1991).

10. One critical account, focusing on the work of the Office for Civil Rights, is Jeremy Rabkin, "Office for Civil Rights," in *The Politics of Regulation*, ed. James Q. Wilson (New York: Basic Books, 1980).

11. W. John Moore, "Trial Lawyers on Trial," *National Journal*, December 8, 1990, 2962–2966.

12. For reviews of the conflicting studies, see Gary C. Jacobson, "Parties and PACs in Congressional Elections," in *Congress Reconsidered*, ed. L. C. Dodd and B. Oppenheimer, 4th ed. (Washington, D.C.: CQ Press, 1989); M. Margaret Conway and Joanne Connor Green, "Political Action Committees in the Political Process in the 1990s," in *Interest Group Politics*, ed. A. J. Cigler and B. A. Loomis, 4th ed. (Washington, D.C.: CQ Press, 1995). See also Janet M. Grecke, "PACs and the Congressional Supermarket: The Currency Is Complex," *American Journal of Political Science*, vol. 33 (February 1989), 1–24, and John R. Wright,

"PACs, Contributions, and Roll Calls: An Organizational Perspective," *American Political Science Review*, vol. 79 (June 1985), 400–414.

13. For an account, see Martha Wagner Weinberg, "The Political Education of Bob Malott," *Harvard Business Review* (May/June 1988), 74–81.

14. For a journalistic account of the new breed of interest representation, see Hedrick Smith, *The Power Game* (New York: Random House, 1988).

15. John P. Heinz, Edward O. Laumann, Robert L. Nelson, and Robert H. Salisbury, *The Hollow Core: Private Interests in National Policy Making* (Cambridge: Harvard University Press, 1993).

16. New Haven: Yale University Press, 1982. For a good commentary on this and related matters, see William C. Mitchell and Michael C. Munger, "Economic Models of Interest Groups: An Introductory Survey," *American Journal of Political Science*, vol. 35 (May 1991), 512–546.

17. Virginia Gray and David Lowery, "Interest Group Politics and Economic Growth in the U.S. States," *American Political Science Review*, vol. 82 (March 1988), 109–132.

18. David Lowery and Virginia Gray, "The Density of State Interest Group Systems," *Journal of Politics*, vol. 55 (February 1993), 191–206; Gray and Lowery, "The Diversity of State Interest Group Systems," *Political Research Quarterly*, vol. 46 (March 1993), 81–97

ACKNOWLEDGMENTS

While at the University of Chicago in the mid-1950s, Peter Clark and I became the students of Edward C. Banfield and from him acquired an interest in how formal organizations constrain individual behavior, an interest that has influenced our thinking ever since. In 1961 Clark and I published an article that set forth our preliminary thoughts on the subject; the central ideas of it appear, in modified form, in Chapter 3 of this book. Had Clark not chosen to maintain an organization of his own rather than to study the organizations of others, this book would have been a collaborative effort. Even so, many conversations with him over the years have helped shape the ideas in it, and my debt to him, and above all to my teacher and critic, Edward C. Banfield, is great.

Banfield, Clark, and Dr. Suzanne Weaver read the entire manuscript and made many helpful suggestions that I adopted, as well as many others that, had I the wit and stamina, I would have adopted. Various chapters were scrutinized also by my colleagues at Harvard University and elsewhere who have greater knowledge than I of the particular subjects treated therein: Elizabeth Allison, Samuel H. Beer, Lewis Anthony Dexter, John T. Dunlop, Louis Galambos, J. David Greenstone, Xandra Kayden, Seymour Martin Lipset, Michael Lipsky, Arthur Maass, August Meir, H. Douglas Price, Elliott Rudwick, William Schneider, Frank Sorauf, and Donald Stewart.

The research funds for this study were provided by a grant from the Henry Salvatori Center for the Study of Individual Freedom in the Modern World at Claremont Men's College. The center's first director, Ward Elliott, was both generous and undemanding. A leave of absence from teaching was supported by a Guggenheim Fellowship. Lawrence Brown and Dr. Weaver were valuable research assistants, and Sally Cox and Ellen Munson, invaluable typists. My wife prepared the index with her customary good sense and good cheer.

All of these persons are responsible in various ways for this book, but because literary convention, to say nothing of the requirements of law and the obligations of friendship, necessitates absolving them from a share in this burden, I happily do so.

J. Q. W.

Political Organizations

CHAPTER 1

Organizations and Politics

Some readers will find it strange that in the 1970s a book about American politics should have as its focus the behavior of organizations, especially those organizations that are sometimes called "lobbies" or "pressure groups." Most of the recent writing on politics has been devoted either to studies of voting behavior (or more broadly the "mood of the electorate") or to analyses of public policies and the government agencies that make, or fail to make, them. At one time, of course, pressure groups seemed to be the essence of politics, good or bad according to one's lights, and any "realistic" account of politics would have had to argue that the voters are a disorganized, helpless mass and that government agencies are pawns of private interests. The real decisions were thought to be those made, sometimes surreptitiously, sometimes openly, by powerful business and labor groups and by political machines. From the early 1930s through the 1950s, such organizations were widely thought to play a central political role, and the value of that role—for representative government, for the quality of public policy, for the protection of personal liberties—was hotly debated.

During the 1960s, the focus of popular and scholarly attention shifted. The growing importance of public-opinion polling and of television led some experts to conclude that the mood of the electorate was no longer hard to discern or without consequence for public policy. That mood could not only be known, but could also be manipulated; politicians acquired "images" and policies were hoped to have "voter appeal." The White House began to make extensive use of opinion surveys, and candidates relied increasingly on men who were gifted at creating television films that displayed a political personality in attractive, *cinema verité* techniques. Simultaneously, new issues were emerging that led many concerned citizens to respond in terms of a *movement* rather than an organization. By 1960, the place of the Negro in American society was still the concern of "civil rights organizations," especially the National Association for the Advancement of Colored People (NAACP) and the Urban League, and nuclear disarmament was the province of "peace organizations" (The Committee for a Sane Nuclear Policy, for example). Within a very few years, however, organizations in these areas were only infrequently—and then critically—mentioned, popular attention being reserved for the broader "civil rights movement" and the "peace movement."

Corresponding to these shifts in the practice of politics were changes in theories of politics. Antiorganizational sentiments, always strong among the young, were given vivid expression in the Port Huron Statement, the 1962 manifesto of the newly founded Students for a Democratic Society (SDS) that denounced the "organized political stalemate" of the nation and called instead for a "democracy of individual participation." The Student Nonviolent Coordinating Committee (SNCC) formed in 1960 was resolutely unbureaucratic and antihierarchical. The phrase "New Left" came to mean, in part, a commitment to political change that would be free of the allegedly dehumanizing consequences of large organizations. Even the renewed interest in Marxian analyses of American society led persons to speak often of class interests but rarely of class organizations. The rich and the military were castigated, but as social strata with an influential—and, to their critics, wicked—social consciousness, not as well-defined formal groupings with stated objectives. Indeed, when C. Wright Mills wrote of the "power elite," he explicitly denied that the conventional pressure groups, even those advancing the cause of the industrialists, were of much importance.[1] A New Deal liberal would have been bewildered to find repeated references to a nebulous military-industrial complex but none at all to the National Association of Manufacturers (NAM) or the United States Chamber of Commerce.

One would have supposed that, except for favored government agencies, political organizations were dead or discredited and that politics was wholly a process of the "masses" (among whom were included members of various movements, ethnics, and intellectuals) struggling with "leaders," some of whom were part of a military-industrial complex or an "Eastern establishment." All of these elements dealt with one another through "the media." A political theorist trying to give a systematic account of popular understandings would be pardoned for ignoring such terms as "pluralism" or "interest-group bargaining" or even the two-party system and reaching instead for concepts more suitable for analyzing a conflict of consciousness in a plebiscitarian democracy.

And perhaps there has been a fundamental change, or the beginnings of such a change, in American democracy. No one can doubt the tendency of politicians today to build personal followings independent of party organization, to project an image directly to the voters without the mediating influence of legislative involvement or constituency service, and to defer to the perceptions, if not the judgments, of writers, pollsters, and intellectuals rather than of party leaders or interest-group representatives. One suspects that ideas have always had greater political consequences than imagined by those who would explain political matters by reference to objective social conditions, but recent changes in the structure, technology, and sources of political authority in our society have perhaps given to ideas a force and immediacy that is quite new.

One example may suffice. I think it unlikely that any American political scientist would have predicted in 1960 that before the decade was out one of the most powerful industrial groupings in the nation, producing a product sought and cherished by tens of millions of Americans and including within its ranks the second largest corporation in the world, would almost effortlessly have been made subject to highly restrictive federal regulation as to the kind of product it could produce, and all this without any mass expression of distaste for the product it was already producing. Yet the Highway Safety Act became law over the strenuous objections of General Motors, and Mr. Ralph Nader, the man who was primarily responsible for forcing this legislation, acted with no organization of any kind.

Settling the question of the relative and changing importance of social consciousness, personal followings, mass movements, governmental actions, foreign and domestic imperatives, and organizational processes in determining public policy is not, however, the purpose of this book. At one time it was thought possible to produce *a* theory of American politics in which one element—group activity—was paramount. Arthur F. Bentley, in reaction against the formalistic institutional accounts of government that were conventional at the time, argued in 1908 that "there are no political phenomena except group phenomena"; that indeed society is "nothing other than the complex of groups that compose it." [2] Political action "reflects, represents, the underlying groups," each of which is identical with an "interest." [3] The "great task" is the analysis of these groups, and when these analyses are adequately stated, "everything is stated." Lest anyone misunderstand, Bentley added: "When I say everything, I mean everything." [4]

David B. Truman, writing four decades later, was not prepared to go quite as far as Bentley: "We must acknowledge that we are dealing with a system [the American political system] that is not accounted for by the 'sum' of the organized interest groups in the society." [5] To explain the significance of "such ideals or traditions as constitutionalism, civil liberties, representative responsibility, and the like," one must look beyond organized interests to "potential interest groups" or "tendencies of activity" that are "in the 'becoming' stage of activity." [6] A generally excellent and thoughtful analysis of the role of organized interest groups in politics was marred by an effort to stretch the concept of group to describe what can be seen more simply and directly as preferences, values, and attitudes. And even with respect to formally organized groups, Truman was unable to provide a clear account of why people come together into organizations, of the methods by which their loyalties are retained, and of the consequences of these methods for the political activities of these organizations. Truman was keenly aware that internal cohesion was difficult to sustain, but he felt that it arose out of the fact that an individual generally belongs to several groups and thus experiences conflicting loyalties; [7] to cope with these conflicts and to maintain the necessary cohesion, leaders employ various techniques, among which are propaganda, sanctions, secrecy, and the manipulation of services. [8] Useful as far as it goes, this view does not explain why an individual should develop a loyalty to *any* organization, or the sources of conflict in organizations whose members have no other relevant loyalties (most citizens, after all, belong to no more than one voluntary association), or the circumstances under which leadership techniques will or will not prove effective.

The purpose of this book is not to offer a theory of politics but a theory about—or, more accurately, a perspective on—one important element of politics, namely, the behavior of formal organizations and especially of voluntary formal organizations. Even this objective may seem unimportant to those who think that voluntary associations are either engaged in trivial pursuits or have been supplanted by social movements. But consider the civil rights movement of which so much was heard in the 1960s and so little is heard today; to all appearances, it is dead or dormant. The NAACP and the Urban League, however, are still very much in business, carrying on essentially the same activities as before. The antiorganizational manifesto of the SDS gave way in a few years time to an organizational structure that at the local level was increasingly rigid and authoritarian and at the national level increasingly factionalized and conspiratorial. SNCC resisted organizational regularity so successfully that it no longer exists. In the wake of peace, antipoverty, civil rights, and black nationalist movements can be found a host of small and large formal organizations endeavoring with greater or lesser success to advance objectives, form alliances, raise resources, and select leaders. The 1963 march on Washington was the high-water mark of the civil rights movement, just as the 1969 "Moratorium" was the high-water mark of the peace movement, again *as movements*. If the causes represented by those mass efforts are to continue to be espoused, they will continue through organizational efforts or not at all. Passions can be aroused and for the moment directed; they cannot be sustained. Organization provides continuity and predictability to social processes that would otherwise be episodic and uncertain.

That continuity is in many cases extraordinary. Since its creation in 1910–1911, the NAACP has had but three national executive secretaries and the American Federation of Labor (AFL), since its founding in 1886, has had, except for one brief interlude, only three presidents. Even those organizations whose titular leadership has changed frequently are often run in fact by hired executives who hold office for long periods of time. To some observers, of course, this signifies nothing more than the presence of oligarchy. However that may be, it at least signifies the presence of an enduring social structure that requires explanation even—I should say especially—in an era that tends to remark the unique, the spontaneous, and the changeable.

The political importance of these structures was probably overestimated when scholars first discovered the corporation and the lobbyist, and it was underestimated when they discovered social movements. Whatever any particular organization may accomplish, however, organizations generally are important as sources of rather precisely defined roles—for example, the role of priest, army sergeant, or newspaper editor. If one were interested only in learning all about priests, then individual personality, attitudes, and class background would no doubt be of primary importance in explaining differences in priestly behavior. But if one is interested in understanding the *differences between* the behavior of priests and sergeants, then personality or class would probably have almost no significance or at best a marginal one. What would be of overriding importance is how the Church and the army expect men called priests or sergeants to behave.

This seems so painfully obvious that one is embarrassed to state it. Yet neglecting this consideration is a frequent error in political analysis. Citizens, journalists, and politicians have in common an interest in understanding whatever is immediate, particular, unique, and idiosyncratic. They wish to understand why the president of the United States speaks as he does at a particular press conference or why a senator endorses a particular bill. To understand these individual acts, it is only somewhat helpful to know that presidents or senators are *expected* to do certain things—such expectations, though real enough, leave considerable latitude for particular behavior. And there is one group of politically important persons, the voters, whose behavior cannot be explained by any organizational role at all. Voters engage in occasional, individual, private actions—casting a ballot—and thus to explain voting behavior one must inevitably consider attributes of personality, attitude, and social class.

Between the actions of the president and the mass behavior of the electorate are found the activities of tens of thousands of bureaucrats, civic spokesmen, party officials, labor union leaders, civil rights activists, and trade association lobbyists that constitute much, though not all, of the business of issue agitation and policy-making. Journalists, with their eye on the daily event and the discrete action, often report these activities as if they could be explained in the same terms one employs in explaining voters or presidents: one person, or a unified group of persons, has a "position" or a "demand" that it "presses" on other persons or groups. Thus, if a certain civil rights organization issues a statement, it will be reported as "Negroes demand . . ." or "the NAACP calls for . . ." or "Roy Wilkins, NAACP executive, charges . . ." For purposes of recording daily events, such descriptions are all that is necessary or possible. But for purposes of understanding in a longer time perspective why this organization issues certain kinds of statements and other civil rights groups issue different kinds, it is not very useful to write in terms that suggest that all Negroes agree or even that the NAACP or Mr. Wilkins represents a definable segment of black opinion. They may or may not; what is clear is that a fairly complex social structure—the NAACP—has produced a statement that, whatever else it represents, must at a minimum be responsive to the internal dynamics of that organization, coming to terms somehow with the needs of, and conflicts within, the NAACP.

In brief, organizations are no more than individual citizens, the irreducible atoms of politics. It has long been a commomplace that a democratic government does not simply enact the "will" of "the people" —what people want is rarely very clear, and even when it is, those individual desires rarely add up to a coherent policy. The problem is not solved by substituting groups for individuals, as Arthur F. Bentley did. Obviously, individual interests are not directly aggregated into public policy, but is it any more helpful to argue that group interests determine that policy? The argument is plausible only if two assumptions are made—that individuals will act collectively as groups to advance their interests and that these groups, in dealing with government, have more power than individuals acting alone. Both assumptions seem reasonable, but in fact neither will withstand much scrutiny. In most circumstances, it is no more rational for an individual to join a group to advance his interests than it is for him to try to advance them by dealing with government directly. In both cases there is little probability that his individual activity will affect public policy, unless he is a man of substantial resources and renown. And if a rational person will not join with others to act collectively, on what grounds do organizations claim to represent the interests of a certain segment of the population, and thus for what reason, if any, would public officials defer to such organizations?

The argument of this book is not that organizations by pursuing their objectives or representing their members' interests determine public policy—some do, some do not—but that many persons active in politics and policy-making, in and out of government, are persons speaking for, or acting as part of, formal organizations and that the constraints and requirements imposed by their organizational roles are of great significance in explaining their behavior. To understand their behavior it is necessary to examine the internal processes of organizations to discover how they are formed, why people join them, how leaders and polices are selected, and by what strategies they deal with other organizations, especially government agencies. The central theme of the study is that the behavior of persons who lead or speak for an organization can best be understood in terms of their efforts to maintain and enhance the organization and their position in it.

This is a controversial perspective. It is quite different from, and even opposed to, the more conventional way of examining organizations and their political role—namely, by examining their goals, or interests, and by assessing the extent to which those goals are achieved. To a considerable degree, of course, organizational activity is directed at attaining politically relevant goals, and those goals in fact represent the interests or opinions of the members. A civil rights organization, for example, may desire the enactment of a voting rights bill as part of its program to eliminate racial barriers to political participation, and accordingly its spokesmen and lobbyists will work diligently to influence congressmen to vote in favor of the bill and to strike out undesirable amendments. Other organizations take political positions only as a by-product of activities directed toward quite different ends. A labor union, for example, may or may not take positions (or allow its lobbyist to take positions *for* it) on issues of foreign policy, civil rights, farm subsidies, and urban disorders, yet it would by no means be clear that any of these goals represent the real purposes (if such can be imagined) of the organization. Put another way, political objectives may or may not be stated, and even if stated they may or may not represent a determination that the organization's effort should seriously be directed to their attainment.

Whatever else organizations seek, they seek to survive. To survive, they must somehow convince their members that membership is worthwhile. Under certain circumstances, members can be convinced of the value of membership only if the organization pursues stated political objectives. Understanding those circumstances, and the effect of those circumstances on the manner in which such objectives are pursued, is the central task of anyone interested in how and why organizations become involved in politics. That organizations seek to survive is of course an assumption that may be challenged, and exceptions may be noted; on the whole, however, it seems a plausible assumption that fits most cases. That organizations can best be understood by analyzing their explicitly stated goals, and efforts directed toward those goals, is also an assumption, but to me a less plausible one. At the very least, it prejudges the most interesting question—whether, or under what circumstances, an organization will develop and actively work toward *any* goal other than the satisfaction of the wants of its members.

The differences between the two approaches to the study of organizations are familiar to specialists in the field and have been given their best-known statement in the writings of Amitai Etzioni and Alvin Gouldner.[9] They distinguish between the "goal model" or "rational model" on the one hand and the "natural-system" model of organizational analysis on the other. In the goal, or rational, model, the organization is defined as a collectivity oriented to the attainment of a specific purpose; its ends are given or knowable, and its central internal processes involve "decision-making"; its success or failure is judged by standards of effectiveness and efficiency. Its ideal form is the business firm as classically conceived, an enterprise seeking to maximize profits or to achieve a target rate of return on invested capital. In the natural-system model, the organization is seen as a miniature social system in which goal attainment may be but one of several functions; the maintenance of the system is the preoccupation of its executive, and conflict among members or coalitions of members determines whether and in what way various external objectives will be sought.

There are problems with either approach. The rational model assumes that all organizations have goals beyond member satisfaction, but this may not be the case (try, for example, to state intelligibly the goals of a university); it also assumes that organizational behavior is motivated by a desire to attain its goals, but it is obvious that motives may be quite disparate and unrelated to stated objectives. The natural-system model is subject to all the criticisms leveled at functionalist approaches to social understanding generally—"system maintenance" is at best a tautology, at worst a conservative bias. Saying that organizations seek to survive is not very different from saying that organizations exist, a statement that is of no interest at all and entails the risk of leading one to assume that survival, maintenance, and equilibrium are desirable social states.

Though ingenious efforts, such as those of John Harsanyi, have been made to reconcile into a single theoretical perspective these seemingly competitive views, it appears that they are likely to have little practical effect, for the alternative approaches are responsive to deeply held theoretical and political values among social scientists.[10] The parsimony and economy of the rationalistic model are attractive to some scholars, just as the greater realism of the system model is attractive to others. Furthermore, reliance on the rationalistic model is compatible with a political orientation that considers the relevant variables in human affairs to be objective ones—interests, costs, institutional arrangements—whereas an inclination toward the system model is consistent with a view that the relevant variables are attitudes, values, and expectations. It is important not to overstate such possible relationships between scholarly method and political ethos, but it is equally important not to pretend that intellectual views have neither causes nor consequences.

If organizations could be studied by using procedures characteristic of the natural sciences, the choice among competing theories would be settled by deducing from each predictions that could be confirmed by empirical evidence. Unfortunately, and inevitably, theories about organizations rarely lend themselves to such tests. The behavior of complex social structures are often not amenable to the methods of the natural sciences. A theory, strictly conceived, is a statement in conceptual language of a relationship between two or more variables. To be testable, its concepts must be operational and its postulated relationship observable; furthermore, the act of observing should not alter the relationship. In social science, these conditions are sometimes met. A theory that says that areas inhabited by persons earning over $25,000 a year will in most elections give Republican candidates a majority involves operational concepts (income levels, Republican candidates) and an observable relationship (election results tabulated by areas); finally, inspecting the election does not alter its outcome.

Complex organizations are more difficult to study in this way. The intellectually interesting behaviors are hard to specify operationally (what is a "bureaucratized" or a "militant" voluntary association?) and sometimes hard to observe, and observing them closely (as by participating in them) may change them. Even if these problems are solved, the number of comparable cases, that is, of identical organizations doing identical things, is likely to be small, and thus statistically valid inferences are likely to be few and weak. Because of this problem, much of the scientific inquiry in this field has tended to involve the study of people *in* organizations rather than the study *of* organizations.[11] Indeed, social science generally, recognizing the greater ease of using individuals performing unambiguous acts as the source of data, has produced a view of politics consisting largely of isolated citizens displaying personal attributes and exercising individual choices—a view in which social structure and institutional processes either are hazy background factors or are left out of account entirely.

In recent years, scholars have begun to study organizations as systems of activity, rather than as collections of individuals, and to do so quantitatively and with real as opposed to simulated organizations.[12] Some of these studies are excellent but few are yet of much value to someone wishing to understand the political behavior of associations. Most of these inquiries attempt to explain differences in organizational structure (size, complexity, administrative arrangements, the employment of professional personnel) rather than patterns of external behavior (making demands, negotiating bargains, entering coalitions). To study these latter processes scientifically may be especially difficult inasmuch as they involve a subtle and complex pattern of interaction that resists classification and measurement.

Whatever progress may come in the future, anyone attempting today to give a systematic account of organizational behavior, especially of politically relevant behavior, cannot pretend he is offering a theory in any strict sense. At best, he can offer a theoretical perspective, a way of looking at organizations that directs attention persuasively to a few central processes that seem to explain (though not predict, in any scientific sense) a wide variety of phenomena. Arthur L. Stinchcombe quotes a remark of Philip Selznick that expresses what in nonscientific discourse is meant by "explanation"—one feels one understands something when one can express in a sentence the guts of a phenomenon. Selznick's example was his conclusion that the essential achievement of the Communist party organization was "to turn a voluntary association into an administrative apparatus." [13] Whether the reader agrees that one has explained something—whether he sees in the phenomenon the same guts as the author—depends on how the reader's judgment and experience respond to the author's accounts and distinctions.

The theoretical perspective that will be offered here is that the behavior of persons occupying organizational roles (leader, spokesman, executive, representative) is principally, though not uniquely, determined by the requirements of organizational maintenance and enhancement and that this maintenance, in turn, chiefly involves supplying tangible and intangible incentives to individuals in order that they will become, or remain, members and will perform certain tasks. Though I believe this perspective is useful in understanding the behavior of all organizations, it will be applied here for the most part only to voluntary associations —political parties, trade unions, civic associations, interest groups, and so on. It is with respect to voluntary associations that the effects of incentive systems are most clearly visible, for by definition members cannot be coerced into joining (except, perhaps, in the case of certain labor unions) and most members (professional staff excepted) do not earn their livelihood by their participation.

This perspective requires us to begin the analysis with a consideration of why people contribute to organizations and the consequences for group purposes, leadership styles, and membership experiences of the means employed to recruit and hold members and other contributors. This is the opposite of the conventional procedure whereby one begins with organizations already in being and then proceeds directly to an analysis of their stated purposes or the interests they presumably represent. The approach taken here avoids, I hope, the error of assuming either that every social interest has one or more organizations representing it (the pluralist fallacy) or that every organization represents the underlying objective interests or social condition of its members (the Marxian fallacy).

The value of organizational incentives and the conduct of people in organizations are in part determined by the characteristics of the persons recruited and their position in the social order. We usually summarize and differentiate these characteristics by describing them as aspects of social class, though by so doing we tend to imply that the characteristics are wholly the result of environmental factors and thus we understate the significance of inherited differences in intelligence, energy, or physiognomy. In Chapter 4 some of the consequences of social structure for organizational behavior are discussed.

This relationship is of the utmost importance in any understanding of politics, but, like many important issues and objects, we often pay attention to it without thinking about it. To a Marxist, social structure is everything and class interests are decisive. But nowhere in the writings of Marx do we find any serious account of how a class interest is expressed in organizational, that is, political, terms. Contemporary activists who have seen in the turmoil of the 1960s the sign of growing class consciousness have in general been at a loss to discover an organizational strategy that would turn this new consciousness, if it exists, into concerted political action. This failure to create important new structures may help to explain why so much of the politics of the 1960s was described in terms of "mood" and "movements" and why the leaders of these movements behaved so differently from those who led ongoing organizations. And those organizations that have been formed have often been created around noneconomic issues: racial distance, social esteem, public amenity, or political power. Max Weber understood this fully: the emergence of an association or even of spontaneous social action out of a common class situation is not to be taken for granted but is something to be explained.[14]

Some pluralists are also insufficiently attentive to the relationship between social structure and organizational action. They assume that, given equal stakes, all social strata are equally able to mobilize themselves for political action or that organizations with similar goals will behave in similar ways whatever their social composition. Or when confronted with manifest differences in the rate of organization at different social levels, some observers explain the low participation at one end of the social scale in terms of the apathy or alienation of the members of that group without pausing to consider whether indifference to organizational activity is a rational rather than a pathological attitude.

The distribution of authority in society also affects the number and kind of organizations that will form by affecting the value and accessibility of the rewards of political activity. This relationship is taken up in Chapter 5.

In Part II, these theoretical perspectives—concerning organizational incentives and social and political structure—are applied impressionistically to a number of political organizations: parties, labor unions, business associations, and civil rights organizations. In most cases, these are treated historically, partly because organizational maintenance is a continuous process that cannot be understood by merely glimpsing an organization at a single instant and partly because of my conviction that the formative experiences of an organization are of crucial importance in understanding its subsequent structure, program, and appeal.

Part III deals with the internal processes of organizations—their formation, adaptation, authority structure, leadership pattern, and degree of membership participation—whereas their behavior toward their environment, and especially toward other organizations in that environment, is the subject of Part IV. In Part V, the political activities of organizations aimed at influencing government policy are considered.

NOTES

1. C. Wright Mills, *The Power Elite* (New York: Oxford University Press, 1956), pp. 247, 265–266.
2. Arthur F. Bentley, *The Process of Government* (Evanston, Ill.: The Principia Press, 1908), p. 222.
3. Ibid., pp. 210, 211.
4. Ibid., p. 208. Bentley's use of the term "group" should not be taken to mean what others later meant by organizations or lobbies. He was less the father of "group politics" than of transactional psychology.
5. David B. Truman, *The Governmental Process* (New York: Alfred A. Knopf, 1951), p. 51.
6. Ibid., pp. 35, 51. Truman takes the phrase "tendencies of activity" directly from Bentley, p. 185.
7. Truman, *The Governmental Process*, pp. 155–158.
8. Ibid., chap. 7.
9. Amitai Etzioni, "Two Approaches to Organizational Analysis: A Critique and a

Suggestion," *Administrative Science Quarterly*, V (September 1960), 257–278; Alvin W. Gouldner, "Organizational Analysis," in *Sociology Today*, ed. Robert K. Merton, Leonard Broom, and Leonard S. Cottrell, Jr. (New York: Basic Books, 1959), pp. 494 ff. The Etzioni and Gouldner views differ in certain details, but their general argument is the same.

10. John C. Harsanyi, "Rational-Choice Models of Political Behavior vs. Functionalist and Conformist Theories," *World Politics*, XXI (July 1969), 513–538.

11. Amitai Etzioni, ed., *A Sociological Reader on Complex Organizations*, 2d ed. (New York: Holt, Rinehart & Winston, 1969), p. 495.

12. A good collection of these studies is Wolf V. Heydebrand, ed., *Comparative Organizations: The Results of Empirical Research* (Englewood Cliffs, N.J.: Prentice-Hall, 1973).

13. Arthur L. Stinchcombe, *Constructing Social Theories* (New York: Harcourt, Brace & World, 1968), p. v. The study in question is Philip Selznick, *The Organizational Weapon* (New York: Free Press, 1960).

14. Max Weber, *Economy and Society*, ed. Guenther Roth and Claus Wittich (New York: Bedminster Press, 1968), vol. II, p. 929. (First published in 1922.)

PART

I

A Theoretical
Perspective

CHAPTER 2

Rationality and Self-Interest

If one were asked why people join organizations—and one is not likely to be asked, because the answer seems self-evident—he would probably reply, with Tocqueville, that they join in order better to pursue a common object.[1] Indeed, Tocqueville defined a political association as the "public assent which a number of individuals give to certain doctrines and in the engagement which they contract to promote in a certain manner the spread of those doctrines."[2] For various reasons—chiefly, the existence of social equality—Americans seem more likely than other peoples to form associations, but, no matter who formed them, Tocqueville argued, the motives for the creation of organizations are identical, or nearly so, with the stated purposes of those organizations. This means that because groups of men who have common interests can always be found, associations are inevitable; it further means that with the division of labor and the specialization of interest in society, the number of associations will constantly increase.

Everyday experience seems consistent with this explanation and its implications. The existence of associations would be worth explaining only if we could conceive of a time in which they did not exist, but at least in Western industrialized societies we cannot do so. When we join an organization, we like to think that we do so because we agree with, and wish to further, its objectives, and we assume that others act out of similar motives. There seems little doubt that as our society has grown more complex and more populous, more organizations have come into being. As David B. Truman writes: "The proliferation of associations is inescapable."[3]

Yet what seems self-evident becomes most problematical, if not mystifying, when one considers the theory of human nature implied by this explanation. Various economists, most recently Mancur Olson, have pointed out that unless certain special conditions are met, rational, self-interested individuals will not join organizations in order to achieve their common or group interests.[4] Indeed, a rational man, *even if not self-interested*, will not join an organization that does not meet certain conditions in order to achieve any larger purpose.[5] In any large organization seeking some general objective (lowering tariffs, obtaining the passage of a civil rights bill, conserving a wildlife sanctuary), the potential contribution of any single member will not significantly affect the organization's chances of attaining its objective; furthermore, should the objective be attained, the nonmember will receive the benefits equally with the member. The five dollars in dues sent in by the average citizen or his attendance at a meeting or even the letter he writes to a senator (one among thousands the official may receive on the subject) cannot affect more than trivially the probability that Congress will pass a particular bill. And if the bill passes anyway, the average citizen will reap the benefits whether or not he has joined the organization. Thus, if there is any cost at all to membership, and there almost surely will be, it would not be rational for the average citizen to join this group. Even if the citizen were altruistic in the extreme, it would be irrational of him to bestow his philanthropy (the five dollars in dues) where it can have no perceptible effect.

There are certain conditions that do make it rational for a citizen to join an organization. If the association is small or the potential member is a powerful or celebrated person, the individual's contribution may be significant: a small contribution to a small group or a large contribution to a large one may materially affect the strength of the organization.[6] If an organization can employ coercion (for example, by denying an employee the right to work in a factory unless he joins a union), it would obviously be rational for a person to join even though his membership cannot make a difference to the organization's chances of success in lobbying Congress. Or if a person is offered some special inducement in exchange for joining—if, for example, by joining he becomes eligible for low-cost insurance or if the benefits of the group's legislative efforts can somehow be limited to organization members—then he may want very much to become a member.

Precisely the same considerations explain the circumstances under which another form of political participation, voting, will be rational.

Unless the constituency is very small or the citizen is given a personal inducement to vote (by being paid by a precinct captain, for example), no rational citizen would cast a ballot because he knows that the chance that his single vote will have any effect at all on the outcome is equal to the probability that his vote will make or break a tie, and that probability is absurdly small.

The general proposition is one that has been familiar to economists for a long time but has only lately been applied to politics—namely, that only under special, and sometimes rare, circumstances can the goal of an act serve as the motive for action directed at its attainment. For example, each farmer in a highly competitive market knows that it is in the interest of all to restrict production so as to raise the price that can be charged the consumer, but each farmer also knows that his individual restriction on production will not affect the price at all and thus he, by practicing such restriction, will only lower his own income. Therefore, even a group of public-spirited and selfless farmers will, unless some form of coercion can be applied against all, produce to the maximum.

There are ample illustrations from organizational behavior that are consistent with this theory. Trade unions vigorously seek the closed, or union, shop so that employees who would not otherwise join can be coerced into joining as a condition of continued employment.[7] Political clubs often offer low-cost charter air fares to Europe in order to attract and hold members who otherwise would not find arduous political work rewarding to themselves or efficacious for the candidate.[8] Professional societies often seek to restrict a license to practice a profession to those who are members or they may offer positive inducements—low-cost insurance or "free" subscriptions to their journals. Even voters appear sensitive, within limits, to the existence of selective inducements. A higher proportion of blacks vote in those wards of Chicago that are heavily canvassed by precinct captains offering friendship, favors (and, occasionally, money) than vote in certain districts of New York where fewer such incentives are offered.[9]

The economic view, if correct, has important implications for political theory. Pluralists can no longer be confident that organizations will spontaneously emerge to represent any aroused or socially important interest; even more crucial, certain interest classes will be systematically under-represented owing to their inability to supply either the coercion or the individual inducements sufficient to produce large-scale organization. Those large organizations that do establish themselves will be preoccupied, to a substantial degree, with the operation of those coercive powers—as with certain labor unions and professional societies—or the management of those business enterprises—such as the insurance and cooperative buying functions of national farm organizations—necessary to the maintenance of the membership rolls, all at the cost of failing, in some degree, to represent the true interests of the members.

Although the economic theory obviously explains some things, as stated thus far it explains too much. Unions exist before they attain the power to require employees to join, and in some places they never acquire that power. Farm organizations would no doubt lose members if they no longer offered low-rate insurance, but it is hard to imagine that they would cease to exist entirely. County medical associations would be less powerful if they could not regulate the access of physicians to hospitals, but they would continue to function in some form, just as the American Economic Association operates on a rather large scale even though it cannot grant or deny men the right to call themselves economists or to teach that subject in universities. And in view of the fact that citizens vote by the tens of millions, one ought to be cautious, at the very least, about describing this behavior as mass irrationality.[10]

One rejoinder to this is that the theory is meant to apply, not to all organizations, but only to those that are "economic" associations, by which one means those that are "*expected* to further the interests of their members." [11] More particularly, the theory is meant to "account for the main economic pressure-group organizations." [12] In various asides, however, Olson suggests that "the logic of the theory can be extended to cover communal, religious, and philanthropic organizations"; however, though "the generality of the theory is clear," it is "less helpful in some cases than in others." [13] These other organizations, such as veterans' or church groups, attract members because of the nonmaterial incentives they provide, such as the opportunity to have fun or to seek religious salvation. In addition to monetary incentives, he notes, there are also "erotic incentives, psychological incentives, moral incentives, and so on." [14] A person might contribute to a charitable organization, not from some mistaken notion that his donation would perceptibly enrich the resources of the group, but because he obtained from the act of giving a "feeling of personal moral worth." [15] But a citizen might well join an *economic* organization, not because he wanted any material benefits for himself, but because to join gave him an opportunity to rub elbows with famous people or even instilled in him a "feeling of personal moral worth." Even though coercive sanctions and selective incentives may explain the reasons why some doctors join a county medical society, they cannot explain why all or even most join; many doctors may join medical societies for the same reasons that certain teachers join the American Association of University Professors (AAUP), an "economic" organization lacking either coercion or incentives.

Of course, doctors would not join a truly voluntary medical society any more than professors would join the AAUP *if* doctors and professors were primarily motivated by considerations of self-interest, narrowly conceived. Self-interest is a consideration in almost all human judgments and a decisive one in some, but it is not clear whether Olson means for us to assume that it is always decisive for his would-be members of organizations. Early in his analysis, he uses the term self-interest frequently, as when he argues that "if the members of a large group rationally seek to maximize their personal welfare" they will not do so collectively without coercion or "unless some separate incentive, distinct from the achievement of the common or group interest, is offered to the members of the group individually." [16] Later in his analysis, however, he says that his view of the behavior of the large group holds true "whether behavior is selfish or unselfish, so long as it is strictly speaking 'rational.'" [17]

By "rational" behavior he means behavior that is directed toward objectives, whether selfish or unselfish, by means that are efficient and effective for achieving those objectives.[18] By "efficient and effective" he appears to mean actions that will make a "perceptible" contribution to the attainment of the organization's objectives or to the "burden or benefit" of any other individual in the organization.[19] But surely a man can act rationally with respect to his own objectives, for example, by adopting means that are "efficient and effective" for improving his "feeling of personal moral worth," while not acting rationally with respect to organizational objectives by making no perceptible contribution to the attainment of those objectives. The rationality of action, therefore, depends very much on whether we view a person from the perspective of his own goals or of those of the organization.

What is at issue, not only here but also in thinking about behavior generally, is the usefulness of economic models of social action. Economists recognize the weakness of assuming that organizations emerge spontaneously because of either the herding instinct of man or the structural differentiation of society. By applying an economic model based on a certain conception of rational behavior, they succeed in making us regard as problematical something we always took for granted. Olson shows that it makes little sense to join an organization above a certain size *if* one's sole motive is to increase perceptibly the organization's chances of achieving its goals. Because some rational persons join organizations despite their inability to make a perceptible effect, Olson introduces the concept of the rationally *self-interested* man who will join if he will receive individual inducements, either positive (money benefits) or negative (personal sanctions). But there is still behavior to be accounted for, namely, that of persons who join despite their inability to affect goal achievement and without expectation of material benefit or fear of penalty. The model is useful in making us see a problem but only of limited value in helping us solve it.

The difficulty derives from the special character of economic models of behavior. Economics rests on the assumption that persons and firms will rationally seek to maximize their utility. In principle, utility refers to anything a person values—not only money, but honor, power, fame, or compassion. In fact, economics almost never deals with any of these other values; it treats instead of one value, money. There are two reasons for this.[20] The first is that money is a common measuring rod by which a large number of other values, but not *all* other values, can be compared. All the relevant parameters of economic choice—costs, prices, interest rates, rents, production functions, sales, wages—can be stated in common terms (dollars). There may be some parameters that cannot be stated in money terms, but for purposes of economic explanation—that is, explanation of market and production behavior—they are not likely to be very important in the aggregate. The second reason for the money measure is that it permits one to make a highly simplified, but not unrealistic, motivational assumption—namely, men prefer more money to less, other things, such as effort, being equal. It is not an unrealistic assumption, because it says nothing about the myriad purposes, selfless as well as selfish, for which men might wish money. They may hoard all they earn or spend all they earn or give all they earn to the needy. Economics is not the study of self-interested behavior, but of rational, money-seeking behavior. And it is a theoretically useful assumption, because only one thing (or one kind of utility) is being sought by all persons involved, and thus one can derive unique predictions as to their behavior. If everyone seeks more, rather than less, money, holding effort constant, one can make assertions about their consuming more of something as its price falls and less as it rises or about their borrowing more as interest rates go down and less as they go up. If instead of a single motive, economic actors were assumed to have several different or mixed motives, very few unique, that is, precise and testable, predictions could be made. What could we say, for example, about the consequences of a change in the interest rates if we assumed that most persons were motivated either by a desire to maximize their income or by a desire to avoid the shame of going into debt or by both in some combination?

Olson, like most economists, recognizes that people often act out of nonmonetary motives but claims that, at least in principle, an "economic" theory can cover such cases as well as those in which money is being sought. After all, persons may seek "more" or "less" status, power, or moral satisfaction as the "price" of these things rises or falls. In practice, Olson admits that where motives are nonmonetary, economic theory is not very helpful (as with social clubs) or entirely useless (as with philanthropic or ideological associations).[21] By limiting the cases he discusses chiefly to economic organizations, he seeks to put the case for his theory on the strongest grounds. To a degree, he succeeds, but only to a degree. Not all or perhaps most members of an economic organization join for economic (i.e., money-seeking) reasons and for many who do join the cost of membership in dues will exceed any material gain they receive. While a "selective incentive" could in principle be almost anything, in fact, in almost all his examples, Olson takes this term to mean money incentives. As will be discussed in Chapters 7 and 8, it is far from clear that, even in organizations purportedly serving their members' economic interests, direct money incentives are central, and of course in noneconomic associations they never are.

Economic thinking has of late become fashionable in the social sciences, and it is useful to the extent that it prompts us to search for rational explanations for what heretofore had seemed instinctual, paradoxical, neurotic, habitual, or conventional behavior. Where motives are mixed and the common measuring rod of money is lacking, however, it is unlikely that economic predictions will have more than metaphorical or ambiguous meanings. The efforts of Anthony Downs to predict the behavior of bureaucrats by means of an economic model in which there is no money standard and in which motivational assumptions vary with different individuals are illustrative of the problem: the predictions that result are hard to make operational, tests are difficult to conceive, and if tests were used it is hard to imagine what we could have learned, for behavior produced by one kind of motive could as easily be produced by another or by some combination of the two depending on institutional circumstances.[22]

It would seem that a fresh start is necessary. And in that new attempt, much difficulty will be avoided if one states clearly at the outset that though the question of why people join organizations, and the corollary question of the consequences for organizational behavior of the incentives offered to induce membership, are central, little in the way of a highly predictive theory is likely to emerge from an effort to think through these questions. People join associations for many different reasons—some for status, some for money, some for power, some from a sense of guilt, some because they have been asked by a friend to whom they do not wish to say no.[23] Though a common money measure might be assigned to some of these values (as by asking persons, for example, how much they would have to be paid to forego the pleasures of office on the Council of Foreign Relations or to assume the burdens of joining a club composed of crashing bores), the effort to do so would be largely conjectural, for few such trade-offs are registered in a market of voluntary transactions. And without a money measure, it is not clear that much at all could be said about trade-offs. It is hard to imagine how we could discover how many units of status a person would forego to obtain a unit of power or even what a unit of status is and whether it is the same from person to person or for one person in different contexts. Finally, even if the motives, and trade-offs among motives, of a number of persons could be learned by laboratory experiment or by depth interviewing, the predictions we could make about behavior would hold only for those persons (not persons generally) and then only for such persons so long as their motivational structure remained unchanged.

In this book we assume that people join associations for a variety of reasons and that they are more or less rational about action taken on behalf of these reasons. Thus, they will not for long remain in an organization that offers them the very opposite of what they want (there are few Black Panthers to be found in the NAACP). When organizations are created, the organizational entrepreneur works hard to discover what incentive, or combination of incentives, will attract members, and he takes some risks in betting on his hunches. Once an organization has been launched and has acquired a fairly stable character or ethos, it will prove attractive to some persons and not to others on the basis of their impression of its "dominant character." Though members may join from a variety of motives, there will be a tendency for potential members to respond to the dominant reward, or rewards, of membership. This dominant reward—we shall call it the primary incentive—may be the organization's stated purposes, its exclusive nature, its fun and conviviality, its social prestige, or whatever. Some members will value this incentive more highly than others, and thus the organization will rather quickly become divided into an active or dedicated minority and a more passive majority. For some members, supplementary incentives will become important—the chance to hold office in an organization that is essentially attractive because of its ideology or status.

Those responsible for maintaining the organization will be powerfully constrained in their actions by the need to conserve and enhance the supply of incentives by which the membership is held in place. This constraint, which we shall argue is the chief constraint on organizational leaders, sets the boundaries around what is permissible and impermissible political activity. In some organizations the boundaries will be quite broad, and members will be indifferent to what policy, if any, the organization takes on political issues. In others the boundaries will be quite narrow, and the organization's spokesman will be strictly enjoined to take, or not to take, quite precise positions. Alliances or cooperative ventures with other organizations will depend heavily on whether the alliance enhances or threatens the apparent value of an organization's incentive system.

In such a conception of organizations, stated purposes—especially those that refer to serving the interests of others or to conferring public goods on members and nonmembers alike—may or may not be an important element in the incentive system. Thus it may or may not make any difference that a person by joining must convince himself, if he is rational, that his contribution will make a perceptible difference in goal attainment. Some organizations—social clubs, for example—may have stated purposes that are incidental to the real purpose, which is to have fun. Others may have stated purposes that are central to their nature and activity. Even here, however, it is not clear that a man must believe his contribution to be consequential before he joins. Two persons may share the identical ideology or moral conviction and yet may take different action. One will act on his beliefs by joining an organization that professes those views, even though his joining makes no difference, because a failure to join produces in him a sense of guilt. The other person may decide not to join because his actions are of no consequence, and thus there is no reason for him to feel guilty. In cases such as this, organizations will devote considerable effort to trying to awaken or maintain the sense of guilt in others by, for example, issuing constant appeals and by making public one's refusal to act on those appeals, in which case, of course, the sentiment that is awakened is not guilt but shame.[24]

27

Because this is a study of organizations, not of individuals, in the chapters to come attention will be focused on the organization from the perspective of those in charge of maintaining it (they will be called the executives) rather than from the point of view of would-be members. In this sense, as in many others, our account will be incomplete. We shall describe (ideally, explain) how organizations behave toward persons wanting certain kinds of material and nonmaterial benefactions; we shall not explain, except to offer some passing observations, how it is that certain persons respond to one incentive rather than to another.

NOTES

1. Alexis de Tocqueville, *Democracy in America,* ed. Phillips Bradley (New York: Alfred A. Knopf, 1951), vol. II, p. 106.

2. Ibid., vol. I, p. 192.

3. David B. Truman, *The Governmental Process* (New York: Alfred A. Knopf, 1951), p. 57.

4. Mancur Olson, Jr., *The Logic of Collective Action* (Cambridge, Mass.: Harvard University Press, 1965), p. 2.

5. Ibid., pp. 64–65.

6. Tocqueville was aware of aspects of the "Olson problem," though he offered no explicit solution: "The same social condition [equality] that renders associations so necessary to democratic nations renders their formation more difficult among those nations than among all others. When several members of an aristocracy agree to combine, they easily succeed in doing so; as each of them brings great strength to the partnership, the number of its members may be very limited. . . . The same opportunities do not occur among democratic nations, where the associated members must always be very numerous for their associations to have any power." Tocqueville, *Democracy in America,* vol. II, pp. 107–108. And, he might have added, the more numerous the necessary number of members, the less inducement there is for any single member to join, because his contribution will be trivial.

7. Olson, *The Logic of Collective Action,* pp. 66 ff.

8. James Q. Wilson, *The Amateur Democrat: Club Politics in Three Cities* (Chicago: University of Chicago Press, 1962), pp. 165–168.

9. James Q. Wilson, *Negro Politics* (New York: Free Press, 1960), pp. 44–45.

10. For example, three locals of the Communications Workers of America (CWA) in Indiana enrolled between 62 and 99 percent of their total potential membership and yet had no union security agreement and thus no formal basis for worker coercion. One of the locals provided no selective benefits at all, another provided some social benefits (a few parties each year), and the third provided discount drug purchases and one party. Though there was some relationship between the existence of selective benefits and membership involvement (the smallest involvement was found in the local with no benefits), selective inducements were not crucial to membership. The local with no benefits enrolled almost two-thirds of its potential membership,

and only a trivial minority (less than 4 percent) of the members of the three locals said they joined because of benefits or would leave if they were withdrawn. H. C. Roberts, Jr., "Private Benefits and the Cohesion of Voluntary Associations: A Field Test of the Theory of Collective Action" (Ph.D. diss., Department of Political Science, Ohio State University, 1971), pp. 32–33, 107–108, 112–113, 143.

11. Olson, *The Logic of Collective Action*, p. 6 (italics in the original).
12. Ibid., p. 159.
13. Ibid., p. 6, n. 6; p. 159.
14. Ibid., p. 61, n. 17.
15. Ibid., p. 160, n. 91.
16. Ibid., p. 2.
17. Ibid., p. 64.
18. Ibid., p. 65.
19. Ibid., p. 45.
20. In this discussion I am indebted to Edward C. Banfield, "Are Homo Economicus and Homo Politicus Kin?" mimeographed (Department of Government, Harvard University, November 1963). See also Joseph Schumpeter, *History of Economic Analysis* (New York: Oxford University Press, 1954), p. 429.
21. Olson, *The Logic of Collective Action*, pp. 159–160.
22. Anthony Downs, *Inside Bureaucracy* (Boston: Little, Brown, 1967). His earlier effort to apply economic analysis to politics—*An Economic Theory of Democracy* (New York: Harper, 1957)—relied more narrowly on utility-maximizing assumptions of a traditional sort.
23. Arthur F. Bentley realized that a concern with motives weakened, perhaps fatally, the predictive powers of economics and similar approaches. He took as data only what could be observed (not "soul states") and conceded that his interest in politics was derived from his interest in economic life. As for motives: "They may be as complex as you will. And the more you deal with them the more complex they become. And with them you go into the labyrinth, not into the light." Bentley, *The Process of Government* (Evanston, Ill.: The Principia Press, 1908), pp. 180, 210.
24. The efforts of the Chinese Communist party to create and maintain an ideological commitment among members by "thought reform" and intensive small-group pressures are an extreme form of this process. See Franz Schurmann, *Ideology and Organization in Communist China* (Berkeley: University of California Press, 1966), chap. 1, esp. pp. 45–53.

CHAPTER 3

Organizational Maintenance and Incentives

Organizations tend to persist. That is the most important thing to know about them. Baldly stated, it is an obvious and seemingly trivial observation. In this chapter, and in much of what follows in this book, I shall suggest that organizational persistence implies many things that are neither obvious nor trivial, especially for an organization's political behavior. Owing to differences in their historical origin, the social and political structure in which they are imbedded, and the motives and values of their present and potential members, organizations adopt different strategies and face different constraints in meeting their maintenance and enhancement needs. These strategies and constraints, in turn, significantly influence the way in which they define and pursue political objectives.[1]

Chester I. Barnard was the first to call attention to the importance of organizational maintenance.[2] By "maintenance" he did not mean mere survival, though it is clear that few organizations seek oblivion even when they have accomplished their task or found their goal unattainable. Maintenance includes not only survival, but also securing essential contributions of effort and resources from members, managing an effective system of communications, and helping formulate purposes: in short, producing and sustaining cooperative effort. The person or persons responsible for maintenance thus defined will be called the organizational executive.[3]

Cooperative effort, and thus maintenance broadly defined, is threatened by any number of forces which we might describe generally as "strain." They include the withdrawal of valued members, a decrease in the supply of available incentives, serious conflict over purposes, the challenge of a rival organization, excessive demands on the time and energy of key personnel, and a loss of morale or of a sense of corporate identity. None of these may be a direct threat to survival, but all are forms of strain to which the executive responds. It will be a principal theme of this study that executives seek chiefly to minimize organizational strain. This is not to say that they act always to avoid conflict; some organizations, such as an emergent trade union or black nationalist group, may actively seek conflict with others. In the long term, however, all organizations seek some form of accommodation with their environment, because the costs of sustaining indefinitely a combat-oriented organization are generally too high to be borne by the members. Executives work to reduce strain internal to the organization, by which is meant generally that they seek to avoid or escape situations in which there is a serious discrepancy between the tasks to be performed and the incentives available to induce that performance.

These incentives may be tangible or intangible and include any valued benefit, service, or opportunity in exchange for which an individual is willing to contribute time, effort, or resources to an organization. Persuasion will be treated here as a kind of incentive: motivating a person, by exhortation or example, to share the goals of the organization and instilling in him a sense of duty or a feeling of guilt that impels him to work toward those goals.[4]

Though incentives are important in all kinds of organizations (Barnard, a successful business executive, was especially interested in their role in the firm), we will here be concerned primarily with their use in formal voluntary associations. By "association" is meant what Barnard meant by organization; by "formal" is meant that class of associations with a clearly definable membership (thus excluding loose social movements) and a consciously adopted name (thus excluding many short-lived or casual associations and kinship networks); by "voluntary" is meant associations whose members are generally not full-time employees and do not earn their livelihood as a result of their membership (thus excluding business firms and government agencies). [5] These definitions are obviously not free of ambiguity. A political machine, for example, provides a livelihood (patronage jobs) for many of its members, but here it will be treated not as a firm but as a special kind of political party, one relying chiefly on money incentives. A trade union may require membership as a condition of continuing employment in the industry, but here it will be treated as a voluntary association on the grounds that it, like the political machine, is not an organization directly employing its members to operate an economic enterprise. Formal voluntary associations as commonly understood—civic groups, civil rights organizations, unions, parties, trade associations, and the like— are our subject, and that understanding, rather than a precise definition, will for present purposes suffice.

The kinds and value of incentives supplied to the members of an association, the conflicts between those who compete for a particular inducement, and the differences in behavior among those who seek dissimilar incentives within an organization will importantly affect the character of any organization but will be a principal influence on the character of a voluntary association. By "character" I mean not only goals and tactics but more generally what some have called the "organizational climate" [6] or the "distinctive competence" [7] of the association.

For organizations to maintain themselves as systems of cooperative activity, they must find and distribute incentives so as to induce various contributors (members, donors, supporters) to perform certain acts. The value of these incentives will depend on their relative abundance, on the demand of members for them, and on how burdensome are the tasks that must be performed. Simplifying what is in fact a complex set of relationships, we shall assume that the *availability* of these incentives will be influenced by the political structure (discussed in Chapter 5) and the *demand* for different incentives will be influenced by the social structure (discussed in Chapter 4). To anticipate: the opportunities for altering public policies and for capturing resources for private use will depend on the degree of political centralization in the regime, and the number and variety of associational opportunities will depend on the proportion of the population that is upper class (somehow defined).

Associations will also differ in the *tasks* that members must perform, ranging from making annual donations to serving as a part-time officer, and to carrying out certain highly routinized and repetitive chores such as answering the mail. Organizations managing comparable tasks will differ in how they motivate members to perform them and members responding to the same incentives will differ in their behavior depending on the tasks to be done. For example, all political parties canvass voters from door to door. A "machine" will hire persons to do this with money, a "reform" party will recruit them by its endorsement of various issues and candidates. To explain an individual's behavior, it is often enough to know that he or she is doing the routine, precisely defined work of canvassing. To explain the organization's behavior, however, it is important to know that one association seeks to sustain its members by getting patronage jobs from the city while the other sustains them by debating and taking positions on issues.[8]

In this chapter we shall ignore differences in the availability of and demand for incentives and differences in the tasks to be performed and look merely at the consequences, other things being equal, of using one kind of incentive rather than another. In doing so, we shall assume that individual motives are not easily made commensurable and thus that one must examine the substance of those motives and the results, in organizational terms, of appealing to one motive rather than another.

A substantive theory of motives and incentives is awkward, for it requires one to classify motives knowing that no single classification can possibly be adequate: either it will be too general to treat of the small but important differences between similar but not identical motives (between, for example, a professor who values popularity among students and one who values popularity among professional colleagues), or it will be too specific to deal with differences among broad categories of motives (among, for example, a professor who values money income, one who values political power, and one who values scholarly recognition). Furthermore, there has been little useful research on the consequences for associational behavior of any particular motive or incentive, however classified. But we must begin somewhere. The reader should simply understand that the classification that follows is suggested only because, at the level of generality employed in this book, it seems useful. Finally, we shall make no assumptions about what incentives serve a person's "self-interest," or even what self-interest means.[9] Four general kinds of incentives can be distinguished:

Material incentives. These are tangible rewards: money, or things and services readily priced in monetary terms. They include wages and salaries, fringe benefits, reductions in taxes, changes in tariff levels, improvements in property values, discounts on various commodities and services, and personal services and gifts for which one would otherwise have to pay (and for which one *could* pay in a market).

Specific solidary incentives. These are intangible rewards arising out of the act of associating that can be given to, or withheld from, specific individuals. Indeed, their value usually depends on the fact that some persons *are* excluded from their enjoyment. They include offices, honors, and deference. Some of these intangible rewards can on occasion be purchased, as in buying an office or honor from a corrupt regime, but they are not ordinarily exchanged on a regular market and they typically have little resale value; for all practical purposes they can be regarded as nonmaterial. Because these specific solidary rewards within an organization must be scarce if they are to be valued (even in fraternal organizations where virtually everyone has an office, the offices are nonetheless ranked in a prestige hierarchy), they can rarely, if ever, be used as the sole, or even the primary, inducement for organizational maintenance. Typically they are supplementary incentives used in all organizations, and their distribution is frequently a source of organizational conflict.

Collective solidary incentives. These are intangible rewards created by the act of associating that must be enjoyed by a group if they are to be enjoyed by anyone. They have some of the characteristics of what economists call a "public good" in that particular individuals within the organization cannot feasibly be excluded from their benefit. They involve the fun and conviviality of coming together, the sense of group membership or exclusiveness, and such collective status or esteem as the group as a whole may enjoy. To a limited degree, individuals within a given organization may be precluded from enjoying some collective solidary rewards available to others, as when cliques or friendship networks form, but in no case can such rewards be made specific to a single individual—if the group is to have social distinction or fun, more than one person must have it.

Purposive incentives. These are intangible rewards that derive from the sense of satisfaction of having contributed to the attainment of a worthwhile cause. They depend crucially on the stated objectives of the organization and are general in that any member of such a group can derive some satisfaction from group efforts even if he himself contributed nothing but his name. The concept of organizational purpose or goal used here is different from the one conventionally employed. In one sense, all organizations have a goal, and indeed most scholars define an organization as a goal-seeking collectivity.[10] What they mean by "purpose" is rarely clear. All human behavior is in one sense goal oriented unless it is random or compulsive. "Purpose" in this sense is another word for "activity," that is, a description of what the organization does. A shoe factory has the goal of making shoes, but for few members is this meaningful: for the stockholders, the goal is to receive profit; for the chief officers, it may be to acquire status, power, and wealth.[11] The Committee Against Legalized Murder, by contrast, seeks a goal in the sense meant here—it strives to bring into being a more or less clearly defined state of affairs that will chiefly benefit nonmembers (it is not the committee members who seek to avoid being hanged); if the members also benefit, they will benefit indirectly and intangibly.

Purposive incentives derive from demands for the enactment of a certain law, the adoption of certain practices, or the alteration of certain institutions for the benefit of a larger public; examples include protests against corruption or injustice, a desire for conservation and beautification of the environment, a call for revolution or patriotism, and the like.

These four kinds of incentives differ in two important respects. First, they vary in the precision with which they can be used to constrain or direct individual behavior. Material incentives are the most specific and divisible, and, though they rarely can be used to produce the exact action desired (individuals differ both in their scruples and in the marginal value they assign to the dollar), they are considerably more precise in their effect than intangible rewards, especially those solidary and purposive ones that cannot be given to, or withheld from, single individuals. Second, they vary in the extent to which they implicate the stated purposes, if any, of the organization. Persons motivated chiefly by money incentives will display greater indifference to purposes than persons motivated by purposive incentives; the latter group will often care passionately about goals. Persons motivated by specific solidary rewards —the status of office—will care about goals to the extent that retaining office requires one to work toward them. Those motivated by collective solidary rewards will care about purposes only if their pursuit threatens the conviviality of meetings or the social distinction of membership.

In the remainder of this chapter, we shall suggest how these two differences in the effect of various incentives shape the character of those organizations that rely primarily or exclusively on one or the other inducement. Though examples will be drawn from existing organizations, it should be understood that we are here dealing with ideal types— organizations that (unrealistically) depend entirely on a single, distinctive incentive. In reality, most organizations employ combinations of incentives; even a business firm, as Barnard emphasized, tries to develop other inducements—pleasant working conditions and a sense that the firm is producing socially desirable products—as supplements to money wages. Furthermore, incentives may vary with the motives of individual members. Some persons may be attracted to a revolutionary organization to seek personal identity or even sexual partners, whereas others may join a group agitating to lower their own taxes out of a passionate commitment to the theory of free enterprise. We shall discuss the influence of simple incentive systems in ideal-typical organizations partly because this helps make clearer the nature of the theoretical perspective but partly also because some organizations do in fact rely primarily, if not exclusively, on a single incentive for most members. In later chapters the perspective here developed will be applied to more complex (and thus more realistic) cases.

Material Incentives

The ideal-typical organization relying on material incentives is an association that either distributes tangible benefits that are directly under its control or regulates access to these benefits. A business firm is the closest example; trade unions with closed- or union-shop agreements and political machines are others. In these cases, the material inducement is either exclusive or individual. An *exclusive* benefit is one to which all organization members, but only organization members, are equally entitled. The use of tennis courts or a swimming pool in a private club, the availability of low-cost insurance or charter air fares, and buying privileges at a consumers' cooperative are instances of material incentives that are exclusively reserved to members but are equally accessible to all members. An *individual* benefit is one that varies in value and is given to specific individuals, usually as compensation for contributions to the organization. Wages and salaries are the obvious examples, but more important in voluntary associations are patronage jobs and contracts dispensed by a political machine or club and a union's differential willingness to activate grievance procedures for "deserving" or "undeserving" members. In principle, of course, almost any exclusive benefit can be made individual simply by limiting access to it to those members who have earned it on the basis of some measure of performance. In fact this is rarely done, because it appears to violate important norms of equity and fair play. Or to say the same thing in other words, organizations dispensing exclusive material benefits usually are expected also to cater to the desire of members for certain solidary rewards—comradeship, conviviality, and equality in deference—that work against distinctions based on achievement, especially when the measures of achievement are likely to be equivocal or ambiguous.

As a result, exclusive material benefits are useful for attracting and holding members, but not for motivating present members to take on additional burdens or to perform particular tasks; individual material incentives, on the other hand, are designed precisely to secure, not new members, but specific contributions of time and effort. A political club of unpaid amateurs may enlarge its membership by sponsoring charter air trips to Europe for members, but by this strategy it rarely inspires individual members to work harder at getting out the vote.[12] A professional political machine, by contrast, may spend little on attracting members—indeed, a nonmember will probably find it rather difficult to join—but it will attempt to allocate patronage jobs and other favors in a way that rewards those who get out the largest vote, or the largest straight-ticket vote. Members join, not to get an exclusive benefit, but to have a chance at winning a much more valuable individual benefit.[13]

The chief consequence of the use of material incentives is that the organization and its executive pay relatively little attention to stated purposes or even to the substantive goals implied by their activities. To a purely utilitarian organization, public policy is of minor significance; all that matters is the dollar value of the ongoing activity. Because a conspicuous display of self-interest in public life is often thought illegitimate or socially distasteful, materially induced organizations with high public visibility will undertake ritualistic expressions of lofty purpose, largely for external consumption but partially to help members feel that larger purposes are served by their private interests. A downtown businessmen's association, for example, will describe its "purpose" as "revitalizing the city" or "ending blight," when in fact such language is often a cover for a clearly understood desire to improve the businessmen's own property values, stabilize retail markets, or reduce taxes. In addition, some of the businessmen may believe, possibly rightly, that a greater volume of trade in their department stores will be good for the city as a whole. If the organization in fact relies primarily on material benefits, then its stated, extraorganizational purposes are of little importance as an inducement, and hence such purposes, if they are stated at all, can be easily changed. A political machine will have little interest in public policy but considerable interest in finding a candidate for the top of the ticket who will increase the chances of winning the election and at the same time be responsive to the rank and file's desire for a share in the proceeds of winning.

The extent to which member opinions constrain executive performance with respect to the benefit-producing activities of the organization varies with the marginal value of the benefit. Large organizations offering members modestly valued exclusive incentives will probably enjoy the greatest freedom of choice with respect to their activities and, if they wish to espouse them, their purposes. For example, a man who joins the American Farm Bureau Federation (AFBF) solely in order to get cheaper insurance or to take advantage of the AFBF's other business services is likely to be indifferent to the position the AFBF takes on farm price supports and probably only somewhat interested in whether his insurance discount is 20 or 25 percent. Executives in organizations of any size offering members highly valued individual benefits will experience few constraints with respect to stated purposes but sharp ones with respect to the maintenance of the value of the benefits. Political machines are often regarded as monolithic structures with autocratic leadership, but in fact changes do occur based largely on successful challenges to leaders who have failed to "produce" on jobs.

Intermediate between organizations offering exclusive benefits of low marginal value and those offering individual benefits of high value are organizations offering members the *prospect* of shared benefits that, if received, will be quite valuable. A property-owners' association seeking lower taxes or a trade association demanding higher tariffs or a business group desirous of seeing an urban renewal program launched in its area will be composed of persons with differing estimates of the probability of winning the benefit and with differing values they would assign to the benefit if won. Members of such groups, especially if small, are likely to exert heavy pressure on the executive—some will charge him with being insufficiently vigorous ("wearing kid gloves"), while others will accuse him of being too blunt ("taking a meat-axe approach"). Those members who assign a high utility value to the expected benefit will be quite active; others, giving it a low value, will be freeloaders. These are the "economic groups" with which Olson is chiefly concerned, and much of his analysis is directly applicable. Olson notes that organizations of this sort tend to be fairly small, because when the organization grows beyond a certain modest number of members a prospective member, unless he is especially powerful or wealthy, will view his potential contribution as quite small, even trivial. If he is rational and is concerned only with the potential benefit, he will not join unless he is coerced or is offered a supplementary individual benefit.

And in fact, as E. E. Schattschneider has noted in a different context, most business trade associations are quite small in size. Of the 421 such associations in the metal products industry, 153 have a membership of less than twenty. In the lumber, furniture, and paper industries, about one-third have a membership under twenty.[14] This is the result of the highly specialized nature of the interests involved—there are few firms in many of these industries, and very few especially large ones, and hence it is in the interest of the member firms to come together in an organization because the contribution of each to the group's success is significant and perceptible in other members. If one combines the virtues of smallness with the sometimes high stakes involved, it is easy to see why each potential member firm of such an association would believe that his support may significantly affect the probability of winning the benefit and thus that his contribution increases its expected utility.[15] By contrast, less than 1 percent of all consumers have joined the National Consumers' League, another group attempting to provide material benefits, both because the size of the possible benefit is quite small (a few pennies off on some grocery items, for example) and because the chance that any one of millions of consumers could increase the likelihood of getting the benefit is slight.[16]

Within a materially induced association relying on individual benefits or formed to attract shared benefits, the chief source of conflict will be over the distribution of incentives. In labor unions, for example, the perceived homogeneity of the rank and file behind a wage demand will usually conceal important conflicts over the incidence of those benefits among different classes of workers—lower-paid workers will favor a cents-per-hour increase, but higher-paid ones will be more likely to favor a percentage increase; both groups will be keenly sensitive to reducing (as lower-paid workers would like) or increasing (as higher-paid ones would like) wage differentials.[17]

Solidary Incentives

For the most part, organizations relying on solidary incentives must depend primarily on those whose effect is collective (sociability and prestige) rather than specific (status and power).[18] Specific solidary incentives, to be of value, must have limited distribution and thus cannot be given to all organization members. There is one form of solidary incentive, however, that is both specific in effect and widely, if not universally, employed in civic associations—namely, the maintenance of the goodwill of a specific other person. This incentive is especially important when membership entails few other rewards (the activity is neither fun nor prestigious) but some significant burdens (a member must perform onerous duties).

All solidary incentives have in common the fact that they depend for their value on how the recipient appears in the eyes of others. The differences among the kinds of solidary rewards result from whether the relevant others are fellow members (as with sociability and camaraderie) or an audience of nonmembers (as with social prestige) and whether the relevant others are a group (as with individual status and officeholding) or a single individual (as with personal friendship). Thus, solidary rewards as a whole differ from material ones in that their effect, and indeed their existence, depends on the maintenance of valued social relationships (money benefits, but not social ones, may be received and enjoyed anonymously and even in isolation and where public they are as valuable when received from an enemy or a faceless benefactor as when received from an acquaintance). As a consequence, the organizational effect of solidary incentives can never be as precise as the effect of material ones because more than one person is necessarily affected by any change in their value or distribution. For example, a political club composed of persons attracted by the chance to play pinochle with fellow Irishmen, or Italians, or whatever, is one in which the political leader's capacity to get individuals to work hard at canvassing voters or to penalize slackers is severely constrained—any effort to give orders to one man has consequences for others who do not wish to see the pinochle game broken up or who feel obliged to "stick together" with a comrade who complains of being unjustly harassed. Similarly, the executive of an exclusive social club cannot increase the prestige of the club for one member without increasing it for everybody.

Even though solidary incentives are less flexible than material ones in that their incidence and value are hard to regulate with any precision, they are often more attractive than material ones in that they are immediately available. A member need not be willing to defer gratification or gamble that his investment of effort will be worth the expected utility of the benefits he may receive as he must do in those cases (such as newly formed unions or political machines) where the money is available only if the effort is successful. As a consequence, organizations intending to develop material incentive systems usually rely heavily at the outset on solidary ones, or even, as we shall see, on purposive ones. A union lacking exclusive bargaining rights or a closed-shop agreement will not only be small, it will often emphasize the virtues of personal contact that smallness affords by appealing to the prospective members' desire to maintain the esteem of fellow workers, to their sense of ethnic or religious solidarity, or to their fear of ostracism.[19] By the same token, an organization with purposive incentives that conspicuously fails to achieve its purpose may emphasize its members' mutual interdependence and need for solidarity against a hostile or critical world. Thus, a particular religious sect whose apocalyptic predictions of the end of the world were unambiguously disproved experienced, not immediate collapse, but closer interpersonal relationships and greater efforts at proselyting.[20]

The immediate availability and relatively diffuse effect of solidary incentives determine in great part the extent to which contributions of effort beyond mere membership can be obtained through their use. To the extent that they have a collective effect, they can be given or withheld but cannot be modified as to value, except within narrow limits. And once given, they can be withdrawn only with difficulty. There are a few organizations that, because of their exceptionally high status in the eyes of prospective members, can threaten the exclusion of members for failure to perform certain tasks. The Junior League, an organization of upper-class women, requires new members to engage in many hours of civic work and other tasks on penalty of expulsion. The ladies' committee or ladies' auxiliary of certain high-status civic organizations, such as fine arts museums and hospitals, sometimes have tasks—raising certain sums of money or providing volunteer work in the institution's gift shop —that must be performed each year by members if they are to remain in good standing.[21] Only when the incentives available from the organization are highly valued and when few alternative sources of such rewards are available can the withdrawal of collective solidary benefits, such as social prestige, be threatened. And sometimes in such groups, and often in organizations devoted to sociability, such as fraternal associations and lodges, the threat is confined to a probationary period after which a member has, in effect, tenure.

The executive of such organizations will endeavor to increase, or at least maintain, the value of collective solidary rewards. In a fraternal organization, this may mean nothing more than arranging successful social events and finding ways to pay for a clubhouse; in an association conferring social status, it will mean in addition ensuring that no one who will cause the group to suffer a loss of status is accepted as a member and, if possible, actively seeking new members who can enhance that status.

A striking characteristic of such organizations is that so large a proportion of them profess to have important civic or public purposes. A lodge such as the Elks or the Moose will raise money for a children's hospital, a black sorority will buy a life membership in the NAACP, and a businessmen's luncheon club such as Rotary or Kiwanis will provide scholarships to deserving students or help run a Little League baseball program. This need to cloak the quest for status or the search for conviviality with larger purposes and more serious intent may be a peculiarly American phenomenon. Just as a voluntary organization based on money incentives will avoid appearing to act solely to further the material self-interest of its members, so a group seeking solidary benefits will try to avoid creating the impression that status and conviviality are ends in themselves—or even that they are important. This is especially true among organizations that do not stand at the peak of the community's deference hierarchy. Persons wishing to advance in status must prove themselves worthy of such advancement. Although business or governmental success is the chief avenue for status promotion, persons denied these routes—or persons wishing to accelerate their progress in the conventional route—will find that a record of having done good works in lesser organizations is valuable. This may explain why clubs of the very highest status, the most exclusive men's clubs—the Somerset, the Racquet, the Brook—make no pretense of being anything but what they are. Having become a member, a man need no longer prove himself to anyone.

But there is another explanation, not inconsistent with the desire to appear "serious." There are countless opportunities for conviviality and dozens of ways of defining one's social status. If one wishes to have fun in a lodge, one can choose among the Elks, the Moose, the Odd Fellows, the Veterans of Foreign Wars, the American Legion, and many others; if one wishes to become more closely associated with other small businessmen, one can select among the Lions, Rotary, Optimists, Kiwanis, and so on. Such organizations need to differentiate themselves one from the other as well as to reassure a prospective member that joining would not label him a frivolous person. Service activities and worthwhile causes are ways of providing distinctive identities to otherwise indistinguishable groups. And sometimes the use of purposes does indeed change the character of the organization by giving it a different feel or style and attracting to it a rather more specialized segment of the population. Martin S. Weinberg has shown, for example, that people join nudist camps primarily to meet people and enjoy low-cost mountain resorts and not because of a commitment to the presumed therapeutic benefits of sunshine or the ideology of nudism. Obviously, however, the nature of the "cause" is such that only a certain segment of the population will find the nudist creed sufficiently interesting or tolerable to make the social and material benefits of membership worthwhile.[22]

The purposes espoused must be of a special nature and of course they must not be taken too seriously; otherwise, they would get in the way of the fun. Above all, the purposes must to the group be noncontroversial, because solidary benefits can be devalued by any activity that either divides the membership or lessens the group's status in the community. The purposes selected, therefore, tend to be related to some *cause* (the distribution of benefactions to deserving persons) rather than to some *issue* (the conflict of ends). "Politics" must be avoided assiduously. Having a worthwhile cause to serve not only dignifies the fun of belonging to a solidary association, but also can even enhance the value of those solidary benefits by providing the group with an opportunity to obtain favorable publicity and with a reason for holding banquets at which speeches are made and awards conferred, all of which heightens the members' sense of collective importance and rewards individuals for exceptional service.

Middle-class solidary associations must carry out service activities through their own efforts; upper-class ones can hire professionals to stage an "April in Paris" ball or to run a theatrical benefit. But whether in the form of effort or money, these member contributions must somehow be elicited, and this generally requires the use of more selective incentives. Of course, a very exclusive social club may have such high dues that all the money necessary is raised by the desire of members to retain their affiliation, but most organizations—even upper-status ones —must make special efforts to get the additional resources necessary to make possible doing good while having fun.[23] And there is a large class of civic associations and fund-raising organizations in the health, welfare, cultural, and educational fields that can offer no collective solidary rewards at all—they confer relatively little status and being a member is not especially fun for any but a handful of persons who like going to committee meetings or who are seeking such individual status as office can confer. In a typical upper-middle-class suburb, for example, there will be Parent-Teachers' Associations (PTA), civic groups to improve the schools or beautify the streets, historical societies, and fund-raising organizations for everything from supporting the Community Chest to curing diseases known only to specialists. To some degree, persons active in these organizations, as well as the more active members of the largely social organizations, may be so out of a personal commitment to the cause being served. To this extent, they are responding to a purposive incentive and not solidary ones; consideration of this behavior will be taken up later in this chapter. But for most persons in most organizations of this type, some form of specific solidary incentive must be found to induce the necessary effort.

There are essentially two specific solidary incentives found in these organizations—individual status and the obligations of friendship. Solidary associations tend to multiply offices: lodges and fraternal organizations bestow a bewildering array of titles, and civic associations usually have fairly large boards of directors. This is partly because the work of the organization can be done only if it is parcelled out to a large number of people, but partly also because the opportunity for office is a source of specific solidary rewards that will call forth contributions of effort and money beyond mere membership.[24] The value of office as a reward is enhanced to the extent that service in one office can lead to promotion, not only to higher office in the same organization, but to offices in more distinguished or important organizations. In suburban or small-town politics, and to some degree in big-city politics as well, aspiring politicians follow a career line in civic work, beginning with duties in a neighborhood property owners' association and a veteran's organization, and progressing up through the PTA and the Lions Club, and thence on to heading a part of the local Red Cross or Community Chest drive, and finally culminating in election to the board of education or the city council.

For the rank-and-file membership of such groups, however, office may not be important, especially in those fund-raising efforts that involve essentially ad hoc organizational work. Here the claims of friendship operate. David Sills, in his study of volunteers in the March of Dimes, found that most workers were recruited by friends—friends to whom, one suspects, the new member "didn't feel he could say 'no.'" [25] Almost all friendship networks involve exchange relationships; one will do a favor for somebody on the unspoken understanding that a debt is thereby created that can be called due by a future request for equivalent service. It is the civic equivalent of the informal social bookkeeping system of every hostess—who "owes" us for dinner and whom do we "owe"? The norm of reciprocity is deeply ingrained in most of us and no doubt bears an important relationship to our natural sense of justice.[26] The strength of the norm varies with the burdens of the duties asked and the importance of the person asking. An acquaintance can obtain a minor favor with no thought of any reciprocal obligation; a celebrated person of great status can ask a large favor of an ordinary person with little fear that the lesser person will ask him to reciprocate. But going to a fund-raising dinner or knocking on doors for the Muscular Dystrophy drive or on behalf of a political candidate, when done as a result of a request of a friend, creates in both parties a sense that the friend is now vulnerable to similar requests. Were this norm not to operate, the civic and political life of many communities would come to a virtual standstill. Even in ongoing organizations, a desire to please fellow members is important. In a study of various local branches of the League of Women Voters reported by Rensis Likert, it was shown that the effectiveness of the leagues (as judged by national league officials) was directly related to the degree to which local members felt pressure from fellow members, but inversely related to the extent they felt such pressure from League officers.[27]

The basic source of conflict in solidary associations will involve status, especially the distribution of recognition and the admission of new members. Such conflicts can be fully as bitter as those over money in utilitarian organizations, for status discrepancies—treating persons other than as their self-conception requires—arouse some of the more basic emotions. And conflict in a utilitarian organization can be sometimes solved by side payments—a man not promoted to vice president can still be given a raise in salary. Few such side payments can be made in solidary associations, and thus personal slights may develop into organizational conflicts.

Purposive Incentives

Strictly speaking, a purposive incentive does not, unlike a solidary one, depend for its effect on how the recipient appears in the eyes of others. A person acting because of his belief in a larger purpose, or in order to avoid a sense of guilt for not having so acted, should be willing to act anonymously, or at least independently of the opinions of others. And in fact such actions do occur, as when individuals send anonymous contributions to a worthy cause or when a person out of political or religious conviction acts in a manner that exposes him to universal opprobrium. As a practical matter, however, acting on behalf of purposes in an organizational context is usually done with at least some regard for the opinions of others—partly because participation in an organization (other than merely responding to appeals for funds) implies cooperative activity and partly because most people who have strong beliefs wish to be known for those convictions and to receive the esteem of those who think likewise. In the concrete case, then, purposive motives are usually found in association with solidary ones. The primacy of the former over the latter is revealed, however, by the willingness of members to antagonize friends or create organizational tension over issues of principle.

A purposive organization is one that works explicitly for the benefit of some larger public or the society as a whole and not one that works chiefly for the benefit of members, except insofar as members derive a sense of fulfilled commitment or enhanced personal worth from the effort. Three kinds of purposes, and thus three kinds of organizations relying on purpose as an incentive, can be distinguished: goal-oriented, ideological, and redemptive.

Goals are images of desirable future states of affairs and in this sense are identical to purposes; here, however, the term will be used to refer only to such images as are confined to a particular aspect of society or a particular set of problems. *Goal-oriented* organizations in this sense include those that have a single, specific purpose (such as the Anti-Saloon League or a local Welfare Rights Organization or the Committee Against Legalized Murder) or a set of purposes with respect to a particular segment or aspect of society (such as the Salvation Army, the Womens' Christian Temperance Union, and associations for the prevention of cruelty to children or to animals).

Ideology, as it will be used here, refers to a systematic set of assumptions, theories, and values that offer an interpretation of, and program for, man in all aspects of his life or for society as a whole. An *ideological organization* is one that espouses such a systematic critique and program; the goals it favors are seen by it as having an important interrelationship and being derived from fundamental assertions about the nature of man and society. Because of the comprehensive quality of their outlook, ideological organizations tend to be either theological or political, though it is possible to conceive of one that said nothing about either God or politics. And having a comprehensive view, ideological organizations hold out the promise, in some degree, of benefits to members—personal salvation or a better life in a new society. For purposes of analysis, however, we shall consider them to be types of purposive organizations if their principal focus is on the reconstruction of society in general or the redemption of men generally. Following Bryan Wilson's analysis of religious sects, we are here concerned with conversionist movements, which seek to alter radically the lives of others, rather than with adventist or gnostic movements, which seek to perfect, redeem, or specially enlighten the lives of their own members.[28] Politically oriented ideological organizations include the American Communist party, the Progressive Labor party, certain factions of the Students for a Democratic Society (SDS), and the John Birch Society.

A third kind of purposive political organization, one that is recognizable concretely but difficult to define analytically, seeks not only to change society and its institutions, but also to change its members by requiring them to exemplify in their own lives the new order. The way in which goals are sought is as important as their substance. Moral and political enthusiasm are to be made evident in the routine activities of the members and in all organizational meetings, just as spirituality and grace are daily to be made evident in the lives of members of pietistic religious sects.[29] This preoccupation with showing by one's own conduct a model for a new social order makes members impatient with, or only casually interested in, the detailed working out of an ideology or even thinking ahead in specific terms about long-range objectives. Such organizations will be called *redemptive*. The Student Nonviolent Coordinating Committee (SNCC) before 1965, the faction of the Industrial Workers of the World that was opposed to the Marxist wing of that group, and certain elements (those stressing brotherhood over the ownership of the means of production) of the American Socialist party are examples of redemptive organizations.[30]

By their nature, organizations relying on either ideology or redemption to hold and motivate members tend to attract persons prepared to make deep and lasting commitments to the cause, if not to the particular organization. The incentives available have great value to members, unlike in many goal-oriented organizations where a limited and specific objective exercises a limited and specific appeal.[31] Because of this, ideological and redemptive organizations display little flexibility about their objectives or, if the objectives are changed, the transformation exacts a heavy price in associational conflict and personal tensions, often resulting in factionalism and sometimes in fissure.

The differences between ideological and redemptive political organizations are similar to those Ernst Troeltsch discerned between churches and sects as forms of religious association.[32] Ideological organizations, like churches, seek to explicate a doctrine; the test of membership is acceptance of the doctrine; authority within the organization is vested in those most adept at doctrinal formulations or most "correct" by doctrinal standards; and considerable tactical flexibility in pursuit of ultimate objectives is allowed. The organization can expand in membership to the extent that prospective members are willing to agree to the doctrine or, in the case of the church, to the creed, but as it expands a distinction develops between those at the center who are doctrinally sophisticated (the inner leadership, the politburo, the priesthood) and those in the rank and file who are to be educated and led. Gabriel Almond, in his study of the American Communist party, distinguished between "esoteric" and "exoteric" members, the former having "true" knowledge (in a church, the ordained) and the latter having "partial" knowledge (the communicants).[33] There is no incompatibility between ideology and bureaucracy, because bureaucracy is an instrument to achieve the ends stated in the ideology. Large ideological organizations are often not only hierarchical but bureaucratic and develop a code of conduct or a canon law.[34]

A redemptive organization, like a religious sect, does not explicate a doctrine, but instead stresses the importance of an authentic personal commitment. The test of membership is not accepting a credo, but manifesting appropriate personal qualities—commitment, courage, and sacrifice. Unless there is a leader endowed with charismatic qualities—and by "charisma" is meant not popularity, but literally the "gift of grace"— few if any distinctions among members emerge. It is a fellowship as much as an organization, made up of an elect claiming a special enlightenment. A redemptive organization or religious sect typically remains small, because few can qualify for membership and the organizational implications of greater size (recruitment efforts, centralization of authority, routinization of tasks and duties, the development of a bureaucratic staff) are rejected. Very little flexibility about tactics will be displayed, because how one acts is as important as, perhaps even more important than, the ends toward which the action is directed. A person might join the Communist party as long as he were judged doctrinally sound; a person could join SNCC, after it had become sectlike, only if he passed a trial (for example, had been jailed or had engaged in a dangerous organizing campaign), and later the additional qualification of being black was imposed. Obviously in a redemptive organization, the collective solidary rewards of camaraderie, shared risks, and intense fellowship are likely to become almost as important as the purposes themselves, whereas in an ideological or churchlike organization the selective solidary rewards of office, power, and status become important supplementary inducements.[35]

The executive function of sustaining the organization is especially difficult in purposive associations. Only rarely do ideological organizations attain their ends; progress toward them often requires tactical alliances that may offend the sense of ideological purity of some members; and even if power is attained, the realities of governance usually lead to important modifications in, or postponements of, doctrine. To sustain membership contributions, large ideological organizations must often rely on small group pressures on members, and thus must revert to a federated or cell-type structure. Redemptive organizations never attain their larger ends. Though a society may occasionally be captured by an ideological organization, it is never transformed by a redemptive one. Hence, redemptive groups are forced to choose among collapse, inward-looking sectarianism, or acts of rage and despair. Anarchists are not necessarily terrorists, but the failure of a moral vision can lead some visionaries to conclude that mankind and its institutions are corrupt beyond redemption and must be destroyed. It is interesting in this regard that the violent Weathermen faction of the SDS did not emerge out of the highly ideological Worker-Student Alliance (or PLP) caucus but out of the moralistic, nonideological wing. An ideological organization, by contrast, cannot explain failure by the view that society is beyond fundamental change, for to do so would be to discredit the assumptions of the ideology. Redemptive groups tend, thus, to be short-lived, except for those that elect to become isolated communes. The latter in effect abandon a conversionist role and find instead a way to survive as an adventist or gnostic sect. SNCC lasted no more than six or seven years, and the political function it once served as the militant edge of the black consciousness movement was taken over by the Black Panther party, an ideological and strongly hierarchical organization imbued with a Marxist perspective.

A more detailed analysis of purposive organizations than is possible here would distinguish carefully between the public association and the secret, or conspiratorial, one. The former is especially prone to divisiveness, argumentation, and factionalism. The latter, which faces more keenly the problem of sheer survival, must recruit members more selectively and suppress factionalism more strenuously; failure to do so would breach the conspiracy and render the members liable to arrest or attack. The underground Communist parties and the Irish Republican Army must, unlike above-ground parties, stress mutual aid in the face of a real or imagined foe. Such groups, formed to seek some large purpose and always animated to a degree by that sense of mission, tend over time to substitute solidarity for purpose as the dominant incentive. Brought together by common goals, the members are in time held together by common fears. Dissent becomes treachery, and thus differences over goals are suppressed in favor of similarities as to destiny, with the pleasures of comradeship being reinforced by the threat of execution or exposure. As a result, such organizations often lose any sense of goals, or of the rational adaptation of means to those ends, and instead engage repetitively in acts that express a common life style and a common fate, for example, violence or espionage.

A goal-oriented organization, especially one which typically plays a segmental rather than consummate role in the lives of its members, must work hard to survive, but, if it is willing to be staff led, that is, willing to pay people to do the main work of the organization, it can survive. Many goal-oriented organizations endure by ceasing in some sense to be organizations, and thus, systems of cooperative activity, at all. They become instead a single man or small group with an office and letterhead and are supported by voluntary contributions or the proceeds of various service activities, for example, subscriptions to newsletters or journals. The National Committee for a More Effective Congress, though it raised large sums of money to finance the campaigns of favored congressional candidates, was never more in organizational reality than a tiny executive board.[36] Other goal-oriented organizations develop supplementary incentive systems, as when political reform clubs in New York or Los Angeles have lecture programs and social events for their members. Organizations formed to combat certain diseases often hire professional fund raisers who are paid by receiving part, sometimes a very large part, of the proceeds of the fund drive, a method analogous to that once employed by governments that collected taxes by allowing tax collectors to keep everything they could get from the peasantry above the sum required by the king.

Given the difficulties in relying wholly or primarily on purposive incentives, it is striking that organizations ever do. But such inducements have the virtues of their defects. Above all, a commitment to purposes is available to groups lacking money resources, political power, or social prestige. Sectlike organizations almost always arise out of the ranks of the powerless, and so do ideological organizations to a substantial degree. But as Troeltsch pointed out, ideological or churchlike organizations tend rather quickly to acquire other resources by an emphasis on fund raising and political influence, whereas sects remain in the domain of the powerless. Furthermore, men can be induced to perform in the name of duty or a cause acts they could not be hired to do, though this value of purposes is frequently exaggerated. Shils and Janowitz, in explaining the cohesion of the *Wehrmacht* in the face of staggering military reversals during World War II, note that the Nazi ideology played little part in maintaining the fighting readiness of the average soldier—the solidary rewards of small-group life were much more important—though it did play some role among the officer corps.[37] A commitment to purposes also permits an organization to avoid the charge of being self-seeking, though it may expose it to the charge of being extremist or radical. Finally, some groups may believe that a reliance on purposes will influence the values and attitudes of nonmembers and thus extend the impact of the association beyond the perhaps insignificant progress it is making toward the realization of those purposes.

This discussion of incentives is meant to suggest the ways in which attention to their nature may help one understand organizational dynamics. It is not meant—and on this one must be emphatic—to suggest a taxonomy by which all or even most organizations can be classified. Though there are many organizations that exemplify in nearly pure form the attributes of the ideal-typical utilitarian, solidary, or purposive association or their subtypes, as many or more other organizations do not. This is partly because organizations in reality often rely on more than one inducement, partly because the appeal of certain incentives varies over time and among different population groupings, and partly because an organization may consist of a coalition of smaller formal or informal organizations, each having a different incentive mix (the differences between the active lay officers and the dues-paying membership of a voluntary association is only one example).

Furthermore, the incentives available to organizations represent only one element in any explanation of the larger patterns of organizational behavior. Equally important are the demand for those incentives among prospective members and the opportunities afforded by the political structure of the society for effective organizational activity, two subjects that will be discussed in Chapters 4 and 5.

NOTES

1. This chapter is a revised and elaborated version of a perspective first presented in Peter B. Clark and James Q. Wilson, "Incentive Systems: A Theory of Organiza-

tions," *Administrative Science Quarterly*, VI (September 1961), 219–266. The reader will note the parallels between this analysis of incentives and Amitai Etzioni's discussion of "compliance" in his *Comparative Analysis of Complex Organizations* (New York: Free Press, 1961). His description of coercive, utilitarian, and normative organizations partially overlaps my classification of incentives. Rather than attempt a systematic comparison of the two views at each appropriate point (and there are many), the reader is here simply alerted to the parallels. My view is that when dealing with voluntary associations, the concept of inducement is more fruitful than that of compliance chiefly because the relationship between member and executive is not generally seen by either one as a "subordinated actor" behaving "in accordance with a directive supported by another actor's power." Etzioni, p. 3.

2. Chester I. Barnard, *The Functions of the Executive* (Cambridge, Mass.: Harvard University Press, 1938), pp. 73, 217.

3. Ibid., p. 215.

4. Ibid., chap. 11, esp. pp. 139–153. In his treatment of religious organizations, Barnard himself does not really distinguish between incentives and persuasion; indeed, at one point (p. 152) he refers to "the persuasion of religious incentives."

5. These definitions are similar to those employed in David Horton Smith, "Types of Voluntary Action: A Definitional Essay" (Paper presented to the American Sociological Association, 1970).

6. George Litwin and Renato Taquiri, eds., *Organizational Climate* (Boston: Harvard Business School, 1969).

7. Philip Selznick, *Leadership in Administration* (Evanston, Ill.: Row, Peterson, 1957).

8. A study of a political campaign organization found that many of the persons most attracted to it because of the cause it served were assigned the most routinized tasks (e.g., canvassing), while those attracted to it by the desire for power were given the most complex and important tasks (e.g., deciding on issues). Xandra Kayden, "The Political Campaign as an Organization," *Public Policy* (forthcoming).

9. The generally unexamined status of the concept of self-interest in analyses of politics raises problems, beyond those sketched in Chapter 2, for theorists of organizations. Even if the term is defined so as not to constitute a tautology (that is, so self-interest does not refer to anything a person *acts* as if he wants), there remains the difficult question raised by Marxists of the relationship between "true" (or "objective") interest and "felt" (or "subjective") interest. Such matters are beyond the scope of this book and hence the word "self-interest" will not be used henceforth except, on occasion, to refer strictly to money income or economic privilege. See the interesting discussion in Isaac Balbus, "The Concept of Interest in Pluralist and Marxist Analysis," *Politics and Society* (February 1971), pp. 151–174.

10. Note, for example, Talcott Parsons, "Suggestions for a Sociological Approach to the Theory of Organizations," *Administrative Science Quarterly*, I (June 1956), 63–85; Peter M. Blau and W. Richard Scott, *Formal Organizations* (San Francisco: Chandler, 1962), p. 5; W. Richard Scott, "Theory of Organizations," in *Handbook of Modern Sociology*, ed. Robert E. L. Faris (Chicago: Rand McNally, 1964), p. 487; Amitai Etzioni, *Modern Organizations* (Englewood Cliffs, N.J.: Prentice-Hall, 1964), p. 3.

11. Herbert A. Simon, almost alone, has tried to give a careful statement of the meaning of "organizational goal" in a way that would reconcile an inducements-contributions perspective with the rationalistic, goal-seeking perspective. He notes correctly that in any problem solving situation there are usually a number of constraints to be satisfied and that although we may single out one and call it a goal (or objective function or criterion function), in principle any constraint could be called the

goal, and vice versa. He suggests that organizational goal can best be used to refer to that set of constraints that define the organizational roles at the highest hierarchical level—in short, that the goals are what the bosses are expected to say they are. This leaves us, I think, where we began—namely, that it is less a matter of definition than of empirical inquiry to discover the kinds of organizations (or the circumstances in any organization) in which what the bosses are expected to say about goals is an important constraint on membership activity. See Simon, "On the Concept of Organizational Goal," *Administrative Science Quarterly*, IX (June 1964), 1–22, reprinted in Amitai Etzioni, *A Sociological Reader on Complex Organizations* (New York: Holt, Rinehart & Winston, 1969), pp. 158–174.

12. James Q. Wilson, *The Amateur Democrat: Club Politics in Three Cities* (Chicago: University of Chicago Press, 1962), chap. 6.

13. James Q. Wilson, "The Economy of Patronage," *Journal of Political Economy*, LXIX (August 1961), 369–380.

14. E. E. Schattschneider, *The Semisovereign People* (New York: Holt, Rinehart & Winston, 1960), p. 32.

15. Mancur Olson, Jr., *The Logic of Collective Action* (Cambridge: Mass.: Harvard University Press, 1965), pp. 144–148.

16. Schattschneider, *The Semisovereign People*, pp. 35–36; Olson, *The Logic of Collective Action*, p. 142. A study of a sample of Wisconsin members of various farm organizations suggests that attendance at meetings is significantly greater among persons who believe that the benefits they receive are contingent on participation. Most farmers named low-cost insurance as the chief benefit of membership, and almost all recognized that it was not necessary to go to meetings to get this; thus, apparently, few who were interested in this particular benefit participated. Those valuing the social or educational benefits of membership did attend. W. Keith Warner and William D. Heffernan, "The Benefit-Participation Contingency in Voluntary Farm Organizations," *Rural Sociology*, XXXII (June 1967), 139–153.

17. Leonard R. Sayles and George Strauss, *The Local Union*, rev. ed. (New York: Harcourt, Brace & World, 1967), chap. 3.

18. The use of the term "solidary" here should not be confused with that found in Max Weber, *The Theory of Social and Economic Organization*, trans. A. M. Henderson and Talcott Parsons (New York: Free Press, 1957), pp. 136–143. Weber refers to two kinds of "solidary social relationships"—pure, self-serving associations (*Zweckverein*) and absolute or ideological associations (*Gesinnungsverein*). I would call the former utilitarian, and the latter purposive, associations.

19. Joel Seidman, Jack London, and Bernard Karsh, "Why Workers Join Unions," *Annals of the American Academy*, CCLXXIV (March 1951), 75–84.

20. Leon Festinger, Henry W. Riecken, and Stanley Schachter, *When Prophecy Fails* (New York: Harper Torchbooks, 1964), pp. 226–229.

21. For an analysis of welfare associations among upper-class Chicago women, see Joan Moore, "Stability and Instability in the Metropolitan Upper Class" (Ph.D. diss., University of Chicago, 1959). Upper-class men are chronicled in E. Digby Baltzell, *Philadelphia Gentlemen* (New York: Free Press, 1958).

22. Martin S. Weinberg, "The Nudist Camp: Way of Life and Social Structure," *Human Organization*, XXVI (Fall 1967), 91–99.

23. If the status of the organization is high enough, of course, one can charge very high dues for merely being listed as a member. The American Academy of Arts and Sciences and similarly prestigious scholarly societies obtain twenty dollars a year or more in dues from persons who never attend meetings or obtain any benefits other than knowing that each year their name will be printed in the directory of members.

24. Economists are beginning to subject status to the kind of analysis formerly

reserved for money. One important example is John C. Harsanyi, "A Bargaining Model for Social Status in Informal Groups and Formal Organization," *Behavioral Science*, XI (September 1966), 357–369. Harsanyi, like many economists, finds it hard to believe that anyone can value status (that is, deference) for its own sake and therefore offers explanations of status-seeking that treat it as an instrumental value useful in attaining other things.

Certain Communist nations, notably China and Cuba, have tried to use specific solidary rewards (which they sometimes call, inaccurately, "moral incentives") as a principal substitute for money wage differentials to induce effort from workers. For large numbers of persons to be willing to work arduously to obtain honors and titles or to avoid opprobrium, it is necessary to engage in massive ideological mobilization (the "cultural revolution") or to evoke massive threats to societal life ("war communism," "capitalist encirclement"). See Robert M. Bernardo, *The Theory of Moral Incentives in Cuba* (University, Ala.: University of Alabama Press, 1971), esp. pp. 26–27, 48–49, 54, 57, 61–62, 124–128, and Ezra F. Vogel, "Voluntarism and Social Control," in *Soviet and Chinese Communism*, ed. Donald W. Treadgold (Seattle: University of Washington Press, 1967), pp. 168–184.

25. David L. Sills, *The Volunteers* (New York: Free Press, 1957), pp. 102, 109–115. Sills notes that over half of all March of Dimes workers were recruited by personal friends, and that the most common basis for the enlistment was an implied "exchange for services rendered."

26. The two major works developing the theory of exchange in social relations are George C. Homans, *Social Behavior: Its Elementary Forms* (New York: Harcourt, Brace & World, 1961), and Peter M. Blau, *Exchange and Power in Social Life* (New York: John Wiley, 1964). Homans deals with the norm of justice as it governs social exchange in chapter 12. See also Alvin W. Gouldner, "The Norm of Reciprocity," *American Sociological Review*, XXV (April 1960), 161–178.

27. Rensis Likert, *New Patterns of Management* (New York: McGraw-Hill, 1961), chap. 10.

28. Bryan R. Wilson, "An Analysis of Sect Development," *American Sociological Review*, XXIV (February 1959), 3–15.

29. Many of the characteristics of a redemptive organization as I describe them are similar to those said by Weber to be typical of a social structure based on charismatic authority: household communism, a rejection of rules and formal adjudication, direct democracy, a commitment to changing society by changing human nature, and a rejection of alliances with political parties. I argue that these attributes may be present in certain organizations even without a charismatic leader. See Max Weber, *Economy and Society*, ed. Guenther Roth and Claus Wittich (New York: Bedminster Press, 1968), vol. III, pp. 1114–1120, 1204–1208. Other important accounts of sects are Norman Cohn, *The Pursuit of the Millennium*, rev. ed. (New York: Oxford University Press, 1970), and Ronald A. Knox, *Enthusiasm* (Oxford: Clarendon Press, 1950).

30. Emily S. Stoper, "The Student Nonviolent Coordinating Committee: The Growth of Radicalism in a Civil Rights Organization" (Ph.D. diss., Department of Government, Harvard University, June 1968), esp. pp. 164–165; Patrick Renshaw, *The Wobblies* (Garden City, N.Y.: Doubleday, 1967); Martin Diamond, "Socialism and the Decline of the American Socialist Party "(Ph.D. diss., Department of Political Science, University of Chicago, 1956); Daniel Bell, *Marxian Socialism in the United States* (Princeton, N.J.: Princeton University Press, 1952, 1967), chap. 7.

31. Goal-oriented organizations can and do have enthusiasts as members, of course. All that is being asserted here is that there is an empirical tendency for ideology and redemption to have higher salience for the average member than specific goals.

32. Ernst Troeltsch, *The Social Teachings of the Christian Churches* (New York: Harper Torchbooks, 1960), vol. I, pp. 331–343. The original German edition was first published in 1911.

33. Gabriel A. Almond, *The Appeals of Communism* (Princeton, N.J.: Princeton University Press, 1954), pp. 5–6, 68–76.

34. Robert Michels, *Political Parties,* trans. Eden and Cedar Paul (New York: Free Press, 1958). An interesting example of an ideological organization that resisted with partial success the emergence of bureaucratic authority is the American Baptist Church as described in Paul M. Harrison, *Authority and Power in the Free Church Tradition* (Princeton, N.J.: Princeton University Press, 1959), esp. chap. 11.

35. Kenneth Keniston observed in his study of young antiwar activists that a strong sense of purpose held by a few amidst an indifferent or hostile majority creates intense feelings of solidarity and separateness; this partial substitution of solidary incentives for purposive ones he calls "encapsulation." Keniston, *Young Radicals* (New York: Harcourt, Brace & World, 1968), pp. 150–160.

36. Harry M. Scoble, *Ideology and Electoral Action* (San Francisco: Chandler, 1967), chap. 3.

37. Edward A. Shils and Morris Janowitz, "Cohesion and Disintegration in the *Wehrmacht* in World War II," *Public Opinion Quarterly,* XXII (Summer 1948), 280–315, and Roger W. Little, "Buddy Relations and Combat Performance," in *The New Military,* ed. Morris Janowitz (New York: Russell Sage Foundation, 1964), pp. 195–223.

CHAPTER 4

Social Structure and Organizations

Organizations do not recruit and motivate members from a homogeneous population of equally interested, or uninterested, prospects; rather, they offer inducements to persons who differ importantly in the extent to which they are aware of, or responsive to, these rewards and thus in the manner in which they behave after they have entered the organization.

The most obvious and best-documented example of this is the finding that the higher a person's social class, as defined by income, education, or occupation, the more likely he is to join a voluntary association.[1] Social stratification powerfully affects the kinds of persons who can be mobilized and thus the kinds of voluntary associations that will exist. Furthermore, there are good reasons for believing that participation is a family characteristic—persons from families where the parents are joiners tend disproportionately to become joiners themselves.[2] It would be easy to draw from these studies the conclusion that voluntary associations tend to represent the interests of the well-to-do and that this tendency is carried forward from one generation to the next.

But it is by no means clear what the interests of the well-to-do are, nor is it at all obvious why the upper classes should form more associations than the lower classes. The Marxist answer to the first question is clear, to the second, ambiguous. The interests of the bourgeoisie involve the maintenance of their control over the means of production and the management of those crises and contradictions that periodically, and with growing intensity, afflict the capitalist order. Bourgeois associations, in this view, exist to defeat the efforts of workers to organize, to set prices and otherwise reduce competition in the face of chronic overcapacity, and to ensure that government adopts regulatory measures that protect and enlarge the holdings of the capitalist class. Of course, the bourgeoisie frequently create religious, civic, or aesthetic associations, but these to a Marxist are but expressions of class interest. Engels argued that the Protestant Reformation and Calvinism were simply part of the bourgeois struggle against feudalism,[3] and presumably present-day religious groups are but ways of maintaining bourgeois authority in the derivative realm of the spiritual.

Though it may be true that much of modern history can be viewed as a period in which the socially dominant interests are those of the bourgeoisie, such a view obscures the equally crucial fact that most of the politically relevant conflict has occurred within the middle classes and not between that class and some other. Nationalist and religious struggles have generally been led by rival middle-class figures. Workers' movements have existed in Europe and America, but they have either had middle-class leadership or have depended crucially for success on the development of a schism within the governing elements of the middle class. Student and intellectual protest against governmental policies is only the most conspicuous example of such a schism.

Even assuming that associations serve bourgeois interests, it is hard to understand why the bourgeoisie should join them. As economic men *par excellence*, the upper classes would surely recognize the irrationality of joining a business association that would cost something and, if successful, would benefit them whether or not they participated. It is the bourgeoisie who have supposedly "pitilessly torn asunder" all social ties and left remaining "no other nexus between man than naked self-interest, than callous 'cash payment.'"[4] It seems particularly strange that some of these associations should seek to influence the government, inasmuch as "the executive of the modern state is but a committee for managing the common affairs of the whole bourgeoisie."[5] If the government requires outside direction, then its subordination to class interests would seem to be neither secure nor automatic; and if this outside direction requires concerted action, then incentives for eliciting that action must be found and manipulated. Unless we assume, as certain passages in Marx and Engels imply, that class activity spontaneously follows class interest or that (despite its implications for the doctrine of historical materialism) politics and ideology have some independent force in human affairs, an explanation for the emergence of large bourgeois voluntary associations remains obscure.[6]

Even more difficult to understand is why working-class associations should form. Because the workers are both more numerous and more disadvantaged than the bourgeoisie, they lack to an exceptional degree, at least in Marxian theory, both the resources and the prospects that would make large-scale organization attractive. The individual worker had at the outset both more to lose and less to gain by associational effort than his middle-class counterpart; only a very distant time horizon and an exceptional willingness to defer present pleasures for future benefits would be sufficient to induce participation. Marx and Engels almost never dealt with this problem, preferring instead to speak, rather in the manner of Hegel, of the working-class movement growing "instinctively" out of the conditions of production,[7] or of socialist action being a "reflex" of the contradictions of capitalism,[8] or of "improved means of communication" assisting the proletariat to "feel" its strength and allow organization to "rise up." [9]

The absence of a satisfactory psychology of social classes is a problem not only for Marxists, but for social scientists generally. The link between organizational activity and subjective state is far from clear. Discovering that the better-off join more associations than the not-so-well-off merely states the problem, it does not solve it. Most important, the reasons a person of high or low status joins an association may well influence profoundly the nature of his participation and thus the character of the organization. As T. H. Marshall wrote, the word, "class" is often "little more than a middle term in the chain that links position to opinion." [10]

Participation in voluntary associations may be influenced by the attributes of persons, by the opportunities or barriers created by the political environment, or by both. In the next chapter the structure of political opportunity will be considered; in this chapter, the focus will be on individual characteristics.

There are at least three characteristics, each roughly corresponding to an alternative definition of social class, that might account for differential participation. The first is *economic:* some persons have more of those resources, chiefly money and personal control over time schedules, that enable them to join more associations than are joined by those lacking such resources. Social class in this view is defined by the possession of wealth and its material concomitants. The second attribute is *social position:* some persons are more likely than others to join either because they enjoy special esteem or because they are members of a distinctive, self-conscious subculture that forms a natural basis for associational life.[11] The celebrity and the man of distinction are courted by associations desirous of maintaining or enhancing the organization's prestige. Social class here means position in a deference hierarchy. But the hierarchy may not be uniform across the society; particular ethnic, geographical, political, or religious subcultures will have their own internal status rankings and a sense of collective identity (for example, Polish veterans, radical sociologists, suburban softball players) and these factors may be sufficient to provide a basis for organization independent of their position in the larger society. Individuals with neither status nor a sense of belonging to a larger whole will be unorganized. The third attribute is *psychological:* upper-class persons are those who are most likely to display those attitudes and personality traits that facilitate not only associational membership but competence in a wide range of human endeavors. These include ego-strength,[12] a sense of personal and political competence,[13] achievement motivation,[14] a distant time horizon,[15] and a strong sense of duty.[16] Taken together, these traits produce for each class a distinctive life style. It is also possible, as Reddy and Smith have pointed out, that such personal capacities as intelligence and energey may importantly influence associational memberships, but curiously these factors seem to have been ignored in the scientific literature.[17]

These explanations for the influence of social class, variously defined, on associational life are not mutually exclusive. It is likely that persons with bigger incomes also receive more deference and have a strong sense of personal competence and a keen desire for achievement; at the same time, it is also possible that one of these factors exercises a predominant or decisive influence in their associational or political lives. Little research has been done to assess the relative importance of these factors. We can, however, speculate on the organizational consequences of each factor taken separately and then compare our speculations with what we know of associations that recruit from different parts of the social structure.

Assume that persons differ primarily in their economic resources—that is, that class as defined by wealth is the chief source of social differentiation. If an association offers material incentives in exchange for contributions of money and time to a lower-class person with little wealth, he will be recruited only if the inducement clearly exceeds in value the necessary contributions; because a lower-class person has little money, the marginal value to him of a dollar spent on dues will be high and thus he will part with the dollar only if he is almost certain to get more than a dollar, or its equivalent in services, in return. To an upper-class person who has considerable wealth, the marginal value of the dollar dues will be low, even trivial, and thus cost will rarely be a factor in whether he joins or not. On the other hand, the nominal material benefits offered by most associations using such incentives will also have a slight value for an upper-class person; thus, his memberships in such organizations may be few or many, but they will tend to be random. It matters little to him which ones he joins—perhaps he will join the first few that ask him—unless the benefit is likely to be quite large, in which case he will certainly join. If the association offers instead solidary or purposive inducements, then the lower-class person will join only if the cost is very low, ideally zero, whereas the upper-class person will join, if he is so inclined, with relatively small regard for cost.

If it is a difference in wealth alone that influences membership, then perhaps upper-class persons "consume" more association memberships for the same reason that they consume more magazines, television sets, and automobiles—they can afford them. To a considerable extent, this is the case. A 1962 survey showed that of those earning less than $2,000 a year, 69 percent belonged to no association and only 14 percent belonged to two or more, whereas of those earning over $7,500 a year, only 45 percent belonged to no association and 35 percent belonged to two or more.[18] For only one kind of association, churches, do lower-income persons join more frequently than upper-income ones,[19] and this might be explained by the fact that churches, unlike other associations, depend on voluntary contributions rather than fixed dues for their support; thus, a person can belong to a church and pay nothing if he wishes.[20] Various laboratory studies have shown that working-class children are more likely to respond, when given a task, to a material reward than to a symbolic or abstract one. Middle-class children, by contrast, are likely to be influenced equally by both kinds of incentives.[21]

But there are some facts that cannot be so easily explained by economic considerations. Though a single dollar is worth little to an upper-income person, it is worth something; why should he spend it at all on associational dues unless he expects something more in return? And among lower-income persons, there are some striking variations in affiliations. A 1966 sample of Boston residents showed that among those earning under $6,000 a year and having less than a high school education, 40 percent of the Negroes but only 23 percent of the Jews and 10 percent of the Italians belonged to two or more associations.[22] Other studies have also shown that, holding income constant, Negroes are often more likely than whites to be joiners.[23] Finally, among all the measures of socioeconomic status used in certain studies, levels of schooling often turn out to be better predictors of participation than levels of income.[24] The ability to afford an associational membership is clearly important, but it is not decisive: ethnic and educational factors, and perhaps many others of which we are unaware, influence participation in important ways.

Assume now that social position rather than, or in addition to, mere income is the operative element in explaining differential rates of association. The solidary, rather than material, incentives an organization offers then become crucial. Upper-status persons will, owing to their existing prestige, be more sought after as members than lower-status ones. Because one's social position is, at least initially, determined by that of one's parents, upper-status persons will be from the outset afforded more opportunities for memberships that confirm their status and maintain the camaraderie and status of the organizations themselves. In choosing among such groups, the upper-status person will naturally pick those that enhance his status; at a minimum, he will avoid those that might jeopardize or reduce it. He may of course also join organizations offering material or purposive incentives, but he will ordinarily take care to avoid those that threaten his status; accordingly, he will shun materially induced associations that appear "grubby" and avoid purposively induced ones that are deeply controversial. Lower-status persons, by contrast, have far fewer opportunities in society; their presence in many associations is not valued except at times when it serves some symbolic purpose; and persons of the very lowest status often come from disorganized or unstable families that provide little encouragement for associational life.

To the extent that a person has a low status because he or she constitutes a separate caste, as has been the case with Negroes, he may join a range of status-ranked associations that replicate in miniature those of the larger society. Even in the absence of rigid caste boundaries, common ethnicity will provide a basis for associations for persons who receive little deference from society as a whole. Indeed, the general tendency of low-status persons is to find alternative bases for self-respect and the maintenance of social distance between themselves and those still lower in the status hierarchy; among the associational devices used to achieve these ends are ethnic associations, veterans' groups, and fraternal lodges. If a person ranks low in status by the standards of the whole society or has found a basis for status independent of the deference hierarchy of that society, then he is freed of many of the constraints that operate on higher-status persons. Should he join a utilitarian or purposive organization that he finds especially attractive, he is less likely than a high-status person to feel he must avoid conflict or embarrassment. If he has little status to lose, or if his status is secure by the standards of a separate caste, the costs attached to "uncivil" or "immoderate" political behavior in the larger society are minimized.

Assume finally that it is the subjective state of the person that defines his class position and explains his associational affiliations. An upper-class person, one who feels personally efficacious and optimistic, and who has a distant time horizon and a strong achievement motivation, will evaluate material incentives quite differently from a lower-class person who has the opposite traits. He will take the long view, and thus be more likely to respond to a chance of obtaining in the distant future a large benefit; he will also be more likely to identify with an abstract entity, for example, the community, that has goals that can be furthered only organizationally. The lower-class person, defined subjectively, will be uninterested in abstract entities and will respond only to incentives immediately available from an ongoing organization. In considering whether to become part of a solidary association, the upper-class person will take for granted the sincerity and civility of its members, especially if they are like him; the lower-class person, by contrast, will be suspicious and distrustful of other members, even if they are like him. A person of lower status will be more likely to be part of informal and unstable street-corner groups than of formal, ongoing associations, and the characteristic style of such groups will be expressive and assertive, preoccupied with questions of manhood and honor. And a purposive organization will hold little appeal for a lower-class person unless it can induce an immediate sense of rapture or effect a personality transformation in him, as is the case on an episodic basis with various Pentecostal sects and on a more lasting basis with such groups as the Jehovah's Witnesses or the Black Muslims. An upper-class person, by contrast, is more responsive to symbolic rewards and will choose purposive associations on the basis of personal convictions and his sense of duty, which is likely to be strong, rather than on the basis of his experiencing a conversion. A select minority of upper-class (in psychological terms) persons

—those with the strongest sense of duty and civic morality, the longest time horizon, and the most confident feelings of personal efficacy—will constitute a much larger fraction of the membership of purposive organizations than their proportion in the society as a whole, especially at the time during young adulthood when the familial and job costs of such actions are minimal.[25]

Defining class in subjective terms has at least one empirical advantage: it directs attention toward those factors that help explain not only *why* people join organizations, but *which* organizations they join. A study of the members of several peace associations revealed, as one would expect, that the overwhelming majority were college educated and thus on objective grounds middle or upper-middle class. But controlling for education and social status, members differed from nonmembers in their orientations toward the world: the members were much more likely than nonmembers to have strong feelings of personal efficacy—that is, they believed that a person could control his own destiny and could deal effectively with elite groups—and to believe that human nature was not fixed or beyond socially induced improvement. Furthermore, the more radical the peace organization, the more likely its members were to believe in the perfectibility of human nature, to feel alienated from the values of society as a whole, and to consider themselves personally efficacious. The members of the more radical organizations were not in educational levels very different from the members of the more conventional ones, but subjectively they were quite different.

At the same time, the members of these peace groups did not join these associations spontaneously or because, after searching, they had found the organization that fit each of their psychological states. Rather, in most cases, the members were recruited into these associations because of a prior connection with one or more members. The potential members became actual members because they were part of an existing social network linking them to organization members. These social networks had formed along lines of age, occupation, and community status. Hence, "class" defined in status terms tends to reinforce, by means of social networks, the impact of class defined in psychological terms. This and other studies confirm the importance of the mediating role of social networks for associations of all kinds. Membership in voluntary associations can be most economically explained by the principle that "likes attract likes" as, through the exercise of the norm of reciprocity or because of appeals to duty, members of specific peer groups invite one another to become members of various associations.[26]

It is not possible to more than speculate on how the attributes of members affect their participation in, and thus the behavior of, voluntary associations. Until more is learned, the best that can be done is to examine the inner workings of associations that have managed to recruit particular segments of society to discover the relationship that exists between appeals and actions. Organizations that have enrolled lower-class persons, somehow defined, are especially interesting in this regard, in part because the lower class so rarely participates at all and in part because of the contemporary interest in finding ways of mobilizing such persons for various purposes. Here "lower class" will be defined in a way as will satisfy no one, but our definition will at least bring together elements of all three principles of social stratification—the economic, social, and psychological. A lower-class person is one with a low income, an unstable family, and an episodic employment pattern. In credit terms, he is a bad risk. Whether these characteristics are situationally determined by the person's objective conditions or are culturally, or even genetically, implanted in his subjective state need not concern us for the moment. An organization of lower-class persons is one that consciously coordinates the activities of a significant number of such persons. We exclude organizations that are little more than an organizer, a news conference, and a letterhead bearing a catchy acronym.

Based on the analysis presented earlier in this chapter, we would expect that a lower-class organization would, as compared to one composed of middle- or upper-class persons, either require incentives that are immediately and directly available and of high value to the recipients or achieve a personality transformation so that the members, though lower class on recruitment, soon become middle class, at least expressively if not economically; we could expect further that such an organization would be located in familiar surroundings in order to minimize the uneasiness of its members with regard to new experiences. It is also probable that the organization will be started by entrepreneurs who are not themselves lower class, because the creation of such an association requires a willingness to defer satisfactions and please others; and finally the organizational "style" will likely be such as to minimize the number of alliances it has with other associations or with government agencies.

Perhaps the largest organization of persons who are indisputably lower income, who come from or live in unstable families, and who have spotty employment records is the National Welfare Rights Organization (NWRO), or more accurately its constituent chapters.[27] The NWRO headquarters in Washington consists of a small staff formerly headed by a college professor with a thoroughly middle-class background, but the state and local WROs enroll many thousand (in 1970, an estimated 22,000) mothers living on welfare allowances provided under the program for Aid to Families of Dependent Children (AFDC). These welfare mothers meet frequently and carry out demonstrations and hold conventions.

The Massachusetts Welfare Rights Organization (MWRO) is an example of an especially successful local affiliate. Begun in 1968 by a paid organizer sent to Boston from national headquarters, it had by 1970 enrolled approximately 4,000 welfare mothers in its many local chapters and had conducted a number of successful demonstrations at local welfare offices. These demonstrations were chiefly aimed at securing special needs grants for AFDC recipients—that is, at obtaining funds available at the discretion of local welfare officials to cover the cost of items such as furniture, winter or Easter clothing, and holiday food orders for which an individual had a special need above and beyond what she could purchase with her basic monthly grant. The local welfare rights groups that conducted these demonstrations were composed of women, black and white, recruited by full-time organizers who followed a mobilization strategy carefully designed to appeal to persons with low incomes, little or no organizational experience, and considerable suspicion of outsiders. The essence of this strategy, as described by Lawrence Bailis, was to persuade a potential member in a face-to-face conversation at her doorstep that she would receive a direct material benefit within a very short time after coming to her first meeting, but *only* if she came to the meeting.

To identify the potential members and to make the organization's appeal convincing, the organizer draws up a list of AFDC recipients in the neighborhood—sometimes by getting such a list (normally kept confidential) from a friendly welfare worker or a local antipoverty agency, sometimes by setting up a table at the supermarket where women cashed their welfare checks and then asking the women waiting in line whether they knew all their rights under the welfare law. The organizer, together with an already recruited welfare mother, then goes door to door, calling on the prospects. Each potential member is first shown a list of items, such as furniture, to which she is entitled and is asked whether she has everything on the list; when, as is invariably the case, she replies she does not, the list is taken back and the woman is then told that by coming to a meeting she can learn how to get the missing items quickly. The list, by the way, contains things that welfare officials have approved as special grants in the past. The meeting is held in the morning at a nearby church and opens with a minister offering an invocation; the locale, the clergymen, and all other aspects of the meeting are designed to ease any fears the new recruit may have about unfamiliar surroundings or radical influences. At the meeting, the women are asked to fill out a form requesting the desired furniture or other items and are told that they will then go immediately, on foot or by waiting buses, to the local welfare office to introduce themselves and hand in the forms. Words such as "demonstration" or "confrontation" are carefully avoided in order to minimize the perceived costs of the action. A dues payment of one dollar is collected from each member, temporary officers are elected, and the group sets off for the welfare office. Throughout, the professional organizers are fully in control. No vote is taken as to whether to go to the welfare office; that is taken for granted from the start.

At the office, the group demands to see the supervisor, hands in its forms, and begins firing questions at him. The presence of so many people, many accompanied by restless children, in a room that is frequently small creates a noisy and tense atmosphere, especially if the supervisor is unsure of himself or unprepared for the meeting. Suggestions that the agency's response be deferred or that a small delegation meet with the supervisor are rejected by the women. They point out that the items requested have been given to some persons; why not to them? And why not now? Almost invariably, the supervisor accedes to some or all of the demands and either issues vouchers on the spot or agrees to a specific date in the near future when they will be sent out. The group then departs.

Throughout the encounter, the organization experiences the benefits of collective action—as a group, they get to see the supervisor when none could probably see him as individuals; each mother gets to state, or shout, her complaints; the officials appear to be on the defensive; the members witness the capitulation and get their grants on the spot or soon after.

These immediate material incentives are not the only inducements available to the organization, but they are the decisive ones. Some members join to overcome loneliness or a sense of isolation. Other members, especially those who later become officers, enjoy the status and opportunities conferred by leadership. These persons, it should be noted, tend to have traits quite different from those of the rank and file. Bailis found that the leaders, as compared to the followers, had more schooling (three-fourths of the former were high school graduates) and were more likely to have belonged to other voluntary associations, to be registered voters, and to have held steady jobs in the past. In short, the welfare mothers who were more responsive to the solidary, or even purposive, incentives of the MWRO were more likely to have working-class or middle-class, rather than lower-class, attributes.

The consequences of the incentive system and membership characteristics of the MWRO were predictable: quick, early successes were hard to duplicate, members who got their benefits or had their complaints adjusted tended to drop out of the organization, and the availability of inducements was vulnerable to government action (in 1970, the state abolished the special needs grants and replaced them with a lump sum payment). Furthermore, the rewards of the young, white, middle-class organizers were quite different from those of the welfare mothers; unlike the mothers, the leaders wanted to organize a mass movement with broad political and reform objectives rather than merely run a money-getting, furniture-collecting service. But mobilizing welfare mothers in large numbers around large and general issues such as income maintenance, ending the Vietnam war, or improving public housing proved difficult if not impossible, and as a result some organizers became disenchanted.

With the ending of the special needs grants, MWRO could still perform some services for its members. It succeeded in pressuring certain department stores to extend credit to those welfare mothers represented by MWRO (*not*, it should be noted, to welfare mothers generally), and it was able to counsel members in the handling of individual grievances against the welfare office and to assist members in staying abreast of changes in welfare rules. But generally these programs were not as effective as getting special money grants, and by 1971 the organization was in decline accompanied by considerable internal dissension.

Not all materially induced organizations involving significant numbers of lower-class members need deliver cash benefits. Some may exist by successfully defeating a threat to the interests of members. If a threat is, or can be made to appear, sufficiently real and large, people generally are more likely to concert their efforts, and lower-class persons are no exception. This has been the strategy followed in San Francisco by the Western Addition Community Organization (WACO) that organized a number of persons, including lower-class residents of the area, to oppose an urban renewal project in the neighborhood. Some victories were scored, including the waging of a successful lawsuit. Once the threat of renewal had passed, however, maintaining WACO became more difficult. Though the area had any number of problems, such as inadequate police and public school services, few of them involved the clear personal threat represented by urban renewal and thus did not provide a satisfactory basis for the continual involvement of the lowest social stratum.[28]

Recent experience with the Community Action Program (CAP) of the federal war on poverty suggests that persons in low-income areas, including some from the lowest stratum, can be organized around a non-protest strategy to deal with neighborhood problems. Ralph M. Kramer argues, on the basis of his survey of five CAPs in the San Francisco Bay area, that under the right circumstances, residents of low-income neighborhoods, "including a very small proportion of low-income persons, demonstrated their ability to serve in policy-making, advisory, program planning, review, administrative, and budgeting roles." [29] No doubt some such involvement on a limited scale by genuinely lower-class persons is possible. But Kramer also observes that the CAPs were "controlled by some of the more upwardly mobile and assertive members of ethnic minorities" as a result of a "creaming process" whereby "previously affiliated individuals with strong ethnic identification prevailed in a pseudodemocratic system with very low accountability to an amorphous electorate." [30] Finally, other studies have shown that many low-income participants in neighborhood CAPs have been paid for their involvement (a fee for attending meetings, plus carfare) and that when this payment stops their participation declines sharply.[31]

Some observers have criticized such efforts as CAP on the grounds that it has not attracted the truly poor in large numbers or that it has been dominated by the not so poor. Whatever the other merits or faults of CAP, this second criticism seems hardly to be warranted—after all, any organization will inevitably be officered by those with the taste and talent for leadership. One purpose of having a new organizational intervention in poor areas is to provide an opportunity for the superficially lower-class person to distinguish himself from the truly lower-class one, and the organizations with not-so-poor leaders may be able better to represent the poor than organizations with truly poor (in a monetary sense) leaders. In an earlier era, the political machine served much the same function.

Organizations can attract lower-class members with nonmaterial inducements as well as with material ones, but whether they can attract large numbers and for causes external to the members' lives is unclear.

Perhaps the most important of these associations are churches and sects, typically fundamentalist or spiritualist ones with lower-class congregations.

St. Clair Drake and Horace R. Cayton vividly described these churches and their appeal to lower-income blacks living in the "Bronzeville" section of Chicago in the 1930s.[32] The central group activity involved active audience enjoyment of, and participation in, preaching, during which the minister generally concentrated on the sinfulness of the world, especially of the lower-class world from which his congregation was drawn, and retold the chief biblical stories with dramatic flair and a call for personal redemption through repentance and faith. Such churches, perhaps like churches generally, attract primarily female members to whom the preaching is a vindication of, and source of support for, their struggle to maintain a family in the face of the awesome challenges of unemployment, crime, alcoholism, and infidelity. Ministers in the Baptist and Methodist churches in "Bronzeville" castigate sin, but recognize its inevitability, and aim only, in the words of one preacher, at "snatching a few brands from the burning." The holiness and spiritualist sects, by contrast, brook no compromise with evil or worldliness and demand a complete personality transformation of the faithful, who by accepting the "gift of the Holy Spirit" will be able to live a "clean" life. Services in such churches tend to emphasize shouting, frenzied speaking, and movements reflecting the agonizing raptures of the devout.

Among whites, especially in the rural South, Pentecostalism is also more likely to be found among lower-class persons rather than among those who are somewhat better off. Obviously, not all persons from "deprived or disorganized home conditions"[33] become Pentecostals, but those who are in that sect tend to have lower-class backgrounds, unlike those belonging to the fundamentalist, but nonenthusiastic, Southern Baptist churches.[34] Psychological tests suggest that members of holiness sects, compared to persons in conventional fundamentalist churches, obtain from the intense emotionalism of their religious experience the feeling that a valuable and satisfying personality transformation is underway.[35] And the music, singing, body movements, and shouting of a holiness church also provide an immediate gratification, part spiritual, part sensual, as well as an opportunity to ridicule the exclusive and stuck-up aspects of the higher-status churches.[36]

The transports of a Pentecostal service are momentary; the transformation they work in the lives of their members outside the confines of the church is hard to assess. Other voluntary associations have sought to achieve this transformation and thus to recruit a sizable lower-class constituency by other, less frenzied, means. Among blacks, the most important examples have been the various nationalist and separatist movements, of which the Nation of Islam, or the Black Muslims, is only the most recent example. Father Divine's Peace Movement, the Universal Negro Improvement Association of Marcus Garvey, and the Nation of Islam, along with other less well known groups, had in common an effort to assert and defend a self-conception and destiny for blacks that was independent of their status in white society. Some sought this by denying the relevance of race or color, others by reaffirming the importance of the African origins and present African ties of blacks, and still others by elaborating a religious perspective that linked blacks to a theological tradition—for example, that of the Muslims—superior to that of white Christianity.[37]

It is not clear to what extent black nationalist groups have successfully recruited and transformed the personalities of lower-class members and to what extent they have provided simply a new sense of identity and mission for upwardly mobile persons with relatively stable working-class or lower-middle-class backgrounds. The best study of black nationalism, that by E. U. Essien-Udom, is not explicit on this. The official policy of the Nation of Islam according to its leader, Elijah Muhammad, is to uplift the "Negro in the mud"—the lower-class blacks of the urban North. And indeed, many of Elijah Muhammad's followers have little formal education, are recent migrants from the rural South, and have been part of the world of alcoholism, petty crime, narcotics, and predatory sexuality.[38] Perhaps the best-known Black Muslim, Malcolm X, was brought into the movement while serving a jail sentence and after having been a criminal and a drug user. For such persons, the transformation they experience in the movement is striking: they become expressively, if not economically, middle class, and are conspicuous for their self-control, abstemiousness, sense of property, politeness to women, and willingness to work hard. On the other hand, most individuals who described to Essien-Udom their reasons for joining the nation were people who had relatively conventional working-class backgrounds —many of the women had already managed to avoid the casual sexual contacts of street life, and the men had worked rather steadily at various jobs and had managed to educate themselves. Even some of those reporting having led a "fast life" were scarcely derelicts or thieves. Essien-Udom concludes that it is misleading to think of Black Muslims as having come predominantly from among the antisocial elements—some have, but for others the Nation of Islam offers an escape from a personal or familial crisis, a solution to the problem of being black in a white society, and a means of moral reaffirmation.[39] In this sense, the Nation of Islam supplies by its lower-middle-class style what the Pentecostal sects supply by their lower-class one: a sense of worth, lasting in the former case, fleeting in the latter. Max Weber has noted the importance of salvation religions and movements for disprivileged groups:

. . . the sense of honor of disprivileged classes rests on some guaranteed promise for the future which implies the assignment of some function, mission, or vocation to them. What they cannot claim to *be*, they replace by the worth of what they will one day *become*, . . . by their sense of what they *signify* and achieve in the world as seen from the point of view of providence.[40]

Associations may exist among lower-class persons without transforming them provided they offer a means whereby the focal concerns of the lower classes may be more easily and immediately achieved. As Walter B. Miller and others have indicated, these concerns include, at least for males, the assertion of manhood and the maintenance of peer-group respect, demonstrated ability to achieve sexual conquests and to defeat personal rivals, and a carefully honed suspicion of others, especially of those thought to be hustling or putting something over on an individual.[41] These concerns are served by a group that confers respect and (within its small compass) status on the individual, that cooperates with him in occasional, and often quite spontaneous, fights or thefts, and that provides a setting for social and sexual pleasures. Typically, such a group is an informal gang or clique, never troubling to formalize its identity or regularize its meetings. From time to time, however, and for reasons that are not entirely clear, this process of formalization does occur and a voluntary association of sorts emerges out of a street-corner society. Such associations sometimes adopt exotic and assertive names and may wear jackets or other insignia of membership. These groups often come and go with the passing of a street-corner generation or because of conflicts with the police. Frequently in the past, and to a lesser extent today, such groups played a political role, as with those New York City gangs, such as the Hudson Dusters, or Chicago gangs, such as Reagen's Colts, that were allied with local political machines and practiced vote frauds in exchange for protection and perhaps money.[42]

In recent years some of these gangs have had the process of formalization aided by outside forces seeking to use such groups as ways of dealing with social problems; the support given to the Blackstone Rangers in Chicago by various antipoverty agencies is the best-known case. And to some extent, such associations, among them the Young Lords in New York, have added to their solidary incentives an expressed interest in political issues and have begun to use the anti-Establishment, self-determination rhetoric of middle-class radicals, thereby adding a sense of larger purpose to what is essentially a fraternal association. It is far from clear how seriously such views are taken by members; though it is conceivable that they constitute the intrusion of a loose ideology into a lower-class milieu, it is equally likely that such opinions represent merely a new way of expressing the conventional and aggressive rejection of the values of a larger society that is typical of those who live in it without being part of it.[43]

Though solidary associations, such as street-corner gangs, and a few associations with a partially purposive appeal, such as nationalist and religious organizations, may from time to time attract significant numbers of lower-class persons, it is unlikely that large and enduring organizations among the lower class will exist without the use of selective, individual incentives. Because of the economic, social, and psychological position of the lower-class person, he is likely to be the archetype of Mancur Olson's rational man—unwilling to concert his action with that of others, except in very small groups, unless he is directly and immediately rewarded by such action. Economically, he cannot afford to defer his gratifications, psychologically, he may be unable to do so, and socially, he is uncomfortable with unfamiliar surroundings and unfamiliar with comfortable ones.

A leader of a militant group of the very poor put it this way: "Your street cat wants action—you can explain it to him later. Education doesn't precipitate action, not in street people—it's the reverse." [44] Representatives of the North City Area Wide Council of Philadelphia, an outspoken neighborhood group created under the Model Cities program in a poor neighborhood, reflected on their experiences:

Lesson Number Five: You can't organize a community without "deliverables." By this we mean that community people are daily struggling with basic bread and butter survival issues for themselves and their families. Attempts to organize them around their mutual problems for their mutual gain are doomed unless they can see tangible results of their efforts. The Model Cities planning process, which required great personal sacrifices in hopes of uncertain payoffs 12 months later, was a poor vehicle for building and maintaining a representative community coalition.[45]

If this analysis is correct, then lower-class persons can be induced to join voluntary associations by any incentive provided only that the benefits of that incentive are immediate, substantial, and personal. If money, it must be forthcoming promptly or threatened directly; if solidarity, it must provide opportunities for vivid and uninhibited expression of core life-style values; if a sense of purpose, it must involve personal and intense, not anonymous or vicarious, experience. Because the salience of the incentives must be great, the action induced may be unconventional and unconstrained; the lower-class person, in Joseph Schumpeter's words, is disposed toward an "abstract pugnacity" that values the fight as much as the victory, and the victory as much as the program.[46]

The unanswered question is whether it is possible to organize large numbers of lower-class persons to work toward larger objectives without either immediate material rewards or extreme or personality-transforming nonmaterial ones. Perhaps the most famous contemporary effort to bring very low-income, episodically employed persons into a more or less conventional organizational mold is the effort by Cesar Chavez to form a union out of migratory agricultural workers in California. The obstacles to such unionization were formidable—a largely indigent and illiterate work force, seasonally employed under conditions of a labor surplus and thus with little if any effective economic power, confronting a history of consistent failure on the part of all previous organizers and laboring under the added burden of racial and ethnic discrimination. Furthermore, agricultural workers were excluded from the benefits of the National Labor Relations Act, which protects the right to organize and to bargain collectively.

Despite these burdens, Chavez succeeded in creating and maintaining the United Farm Workers Organizing Committee (UFWOC) and in compelling a number of growers to sign contracts with it that provided for wage increases and other benefits. The size and durability of the UFWOC are hard to estimate, but there is as yet no reason for discounting the union as a trivial or ephemeral effort.

To some extent, Chavez simplified his organizational task by electing to begin with the best-paid, least-transient farm laborers, the grape workers of Delano, where work is available almost all year round.[47] Furthermore, he was able to capitalize on the common Mexican ancestry and language of the workers and on the talents available to him from several middle-class white volunteers. Nevertheless, the survival of the UFWOC was an extraordinary achievement, especially because economic successes were slow in coming in the face of determined grower resistance. The key to understanding the success is apparently Chavez himself, an exceptional personality who built his association by great diligence in establishing personal relationships with each recruit—helping them with their problems, meeting with them continuously, never taking anything for himself, and refusing almost all offers of outside financial aid. (Some antipoverty agencies, by contrast, have been rent by internal conflict over the control of federal funds.) The success of the farm strikes, however, had much less to do with the UFWOC and much more to do with the response of middle-class urban liberals to the grape boycott.[48] Chavez became a personal friend to his followers and a symbol to his admirers; the solidarity of the former kept the union in being, the purposeful behavior of the latter enabled it to succeed. In no previous case of attempted farm-worker unionization was the association in effect an extended personal following and in almost no previous case did the personality of its leader capture a substantial segment of the popular imagination.

There is very little about the history of the UFWOC that suggests it represents a strategy that can be made general, just as there is little reason to believe that the isolated successes of combative neighborhood associations, such as WACO in San Francisco, are likely to become widespread. The organizational resources of UFWOC are too idiosyncratic and special, and the opportunities for effective opposition of WACO too limited, to be the basis for a mobilization of lower-class persons equivalent to the extensive mobilization of middle-class ones.

We have not considered, however, whether fundamental changes in the self-conceptions of lower-class persons or in the structure of political opportunities that confront them may make obsolete the foregoing analysis. Some would argue that the development of a revolutionary consciousness along class or racial lines is possible, and efforts to develop such slogans as "black power" may be seen as attempts to foster a new mood that will engender a sense of self-respect and political competence that in turn will facilitate organization. Though it is always possible that a major crisis will produce the "objective revolutionary situation" long sought but rarely found by Marxian radicals, what is more likely is that efforts to stimulate group consciousness will have a strong effect on the few but only marginal effect on the many. The Black Panthers, currently the best-known group emphasizing militant solidarity among a deprived stratum, is composed disproportionately of persons with college experience and middle-class backgrounds; though it and its slogans may have a general impact, that has thus far been of a marginal and conventional sort. Those radicalized by it have in the main been upper-middle-class white youth to whom it is attractive and lower-middle-class whites to whom it is repellent. As for the likely effect of changes in political structure, it is to that subject that we now turn.

NOTES

1. Morris Axelrod, "Urban Structure and Social Participation," *American Sociological Review*, XXI (February 1956), 13–18; Murray Hausknecht, *The Joiners* (New York: Bedminster Press, 1962); Herbert H. Hyman and Charles R. Wright, "Trends in Voluntary Association Memberships of American Adults," *American Sociological Review*, XXXVI (April 1971), 191–206.

2. Raymond Payne, "Relative Interest of Fathers and Mothers in Their Children's Participation in Formal Organizations" (paper presented to the American Sociological Association, 1955); Robert W. Hodge and Donald J. Treiman, "Social Participation and Social Status," *American Sociological Review*, XXXIII (October 1968), 722–740.

3. Friedrich Engels, "On Historical Materialism," in *Marx and Engels: Basic Writings on Politics and Philosophy*, ed. Lewis S. Feuer (Garden City, N.Y.: Anchor Books, 1959), pp. 55–58.

4. Karl Marx and Friedrich Engels, *Manifesto of the Communist Party*, in Feuer, *Marx and Engels*, p. 9.

5. Ibid.

6. Engels was not entirely consistent on this. Compare the relentlessly "materialist" tone of his *Ludwig Feuerbach and the End of Classical German Philosophy* with some of the "idealist" views of his last letters. See Feuer, *Marx and Engels*, pp. 396–398.

7. Karl Marx, *Capital* (New York: Modern Library, 1906) chap. 10, sec. 7.

8. Friedrich Engels, *Socialism: Utopian and Scientific*, in Feuer, *Marx and Engels*, p. 91.

9. Marx and Engels, *Manifesto*, in Feuer, *Marx and Engels*, p. 16. Lenin, of course, despaired of any spontaneous mobilization of the masses, especially for political action; at best, he felt, they might engage in bread-and-butter trade unionism. Only a disciplined cadre of trained revolutionaries, drawn from intellectual and professional ranks, would be capable of waging a broad political struggle. Lenin was not at all troubled by the theoretical price he had to pay for his practical concerns —namely, the explicit admission that, contrary to Marx, class consciousness, if it emerges at all, will not lead spontaneously to class action. V. I. Lenin, "What Is to Be Done?" in *Essential Works of Lenin*, ed. Henry M. Christian (New York: Bantam Books, 1966), pp. 81–86.

10. T. H. Marshall, *Class, Citizenship and Social Development* (Garden City, N.Y.: Anchor Books, 1965), p. 142.

11. Derek L. Phillips, "Social Class, Social Participation, and Happiness," *Sociological Quarterly*, X (Winter 1969), 3–21, esp. 13–17.

12. Hausknecht, *The Joiners*, pp. 71–82; David Horton Smith, "Voluntary Activ-

ity in Eight Massachusetts Towns" (manuscript, Department of Sociology, Boston College, 1970); John W. C. Johnstone and Ramon J. Rivera, *Volunteers for Learning* (Chicago: Aldine, 1965); Richard D. Reddy and David Horton Smith, "Personality and Capacities as Determinants of Individual Voluntary Participation" (paper presented to the American Sociological Association, 1970).

13. Gabriel A. Almond and Sidney Verba, *The Civic Culture* (Princeton, N.J.: Princeton University Press, 1963), pp. 307–310; Arthur Neal and Melvin Seeman, "Organization and Powerlessness," *American Sociological Review*, XIX (April 1964), 216–226; Wendell Bell, "Anomie, Social Isolation, and the Class Structure," *Sociometry*, XX (June 1957), 105–115.

14. Smith, "Voluntary Activity."

15. Edward C. Banfield, *The Unheavenly City* (Boston: Little, Brown, 1970), pp. 46–64; Stanley Greenberg, "People, Violence, and Power" (Ph.D. diss., Department of Government, Harvard University, 1972).

16. Lester W. Milbrath, *Political Participation* (Chicago: Rand McNally, 1965), pp. 61–64.

17. Reddy and Smith, "Personality and Capacities," p. 35.

18. Hyman and Wright, "Voluntary Association Memberships," pp. 197–199.

19. Hausknecht, *The Joiners*, pp. 71–82.

20. Hodge and Treiman, "Social Participation and Social Status," p. 728.

21. Leonard Berkowitz, "Social Motivation," *The Handbook of Social Psychology*, 2nd ed., ed. Gardner Lindzey and Elliot Aronson (Reading, Mass.: Addison-Wesley, 1969), vol. III, p. 76, and studies cited therein.

22. James Q. Wilson and Edward C. Banfield, unpublished survey data, Department of Government, Harvard University.

23. Nicholas Babchuck and Ralph V. Thompson, "The Voluntary Associations of Negroes," *American Sociological Review*, XXVII (October 1962), 647–654; Anthony M. Orum, "A Reappraisal of the Social and Political Participation of Negroes," *American Journal of Sociology*, LXXII (July 1966), 32–46; Everett F. Cataldo et al., "The Urban Poor and Community Action in Buffalo" (paper presented to the Midwest Political Science Association, 1968).

24. Almond and Verba, *The Civic Culture*, pp. 304–305, esp. n. 3 and p. 379; Alex Inkeles, "Participant Citizenship in Six Developing Countries," *American Political Science Review*, LXIII (December 1969), 1132–1133.

25. Seymour Martin Lipset, "Youth and Politics," in *Contemporary Social Problems*, 3rd ed., ed. Robert K. Merton and Robert Nisbet (New York: Harcourt Brace Jovanovich, 1971), pp. 781–787.

26. Charles D. Bolton, "Alienation and Action: A Study of Peace-Group Members," *American Journal of Sociology*, LXXVIII (November 1972), 537–561; David L. Sills, *The Volunteers* (New York: Free Press, 1957), p. 111; Nicholas Babchuck and Alan Booth, "Voluntary Association Membership: A Longitudinal Analysis," *American Sociological Review*, XXXIV (February 1969), 42.

27. Lawrence N. Bailis, "Bread or Justice: Grassroots Organizing in the Welfare Rights Movement" (Ph.D. diss., Department of Government, Harvard University, 1972).

28. Ann V. Bastian, "The Politics of Participation" (senior honor's thesis, Department of Government, Harvard University, 1970). It is sometimes claimed that The Woodlawn Organization (TWO) in Chicago is an important example of how the presumably lower-class residents of an impoverished black neighborhood can concert their efforts for various community benefits. TWO has indeed been a notably successful and militant organization, but it is not an association of poor individuals, or indeed of individuals at all. As the account of one of its founders makes clear, TWO

is a coalition of other civic organizations in the area, with each member organization entitled to send delegates to TWO in return for the payment of $150 a year in dues. The elected leadership, from its inception, was composed chiefly of various local Protestant ministers, and the initial organizing work was done with the aid of over $100,000 in church and foundation grants and a staff from the Industrial Areas Foundation headed by Saul Alinsky. See Arthur M. Brazier, *Black Self-Determination* (Grand Rapids, Mich.: W. B. Eerdmans Co., 1969), pp. 24–28, 33–36. For a critique of TWO, see Frank Riessman, "The Myth of Saul Alinsky," *Dissent* (July–August 1967), pp. 469–478.

29. Ralph M. Kramer, *Participation of the Poor* (Englewood Cliffs, N.J.: Prentice-Hall, 1969), p. 267.

30. Ibid., pp. 258–262.

31. Henry Foley, "The Incentives of the Inner City Development Project" (unpublished paper, Department of Government, Harvard University, 1970).

32. St. Clair Drake and Horace R. Cayton, *Black Metropolis* (New York: Harcourt, Brace, 1945), pp. 611–657.

33. William W. Wood, *Culture and Personality Aspects of the Pentecostal Holiness Religion* (The Hague: Mouton, 1965), p. 66.

34. Ibid., p. 37; Liston Pope, *Millhands and Preachers* (New Haven, Conn.: Yale University Press, 1942), chap. 6; John Kenneth Morland, *Millways of Kent* (Chapel Hill: University of North Carolina Press, 1958), p. 226.

35. Wood, *Pentecostal Holiness Religion*, chap. 6.

36. Pope, *Millhands and Preachers*, pp. 134–135.

37. E. U. Essien-Udom, *Black Nationalism* (Chicago: University of Chicago Press, 1962), pp. 31–62.

38. Ibid., pp. 182–184.

39. Ibid., chap. 4, esp. pp. 85, 100, 106.

40. Max Weber, *Economy and Society*, ed. Guenther Roth and Claus Wittich (New York: Bedminster Press, 1968), vol. II, p. 491. For the upper strata, Weber argues, religion offers not future salvation but the legitimizing of their own life pattern on earth.

41. Walter B. Miller, "Implications of Urban Lower-Class Culture for Social Work," *Social Service Review*, XXXIII (September 1959), and Miller, "Lower Class Culture as a Generating Milieu of Gang Delinquency," *Journal of Social Issues*, XIV (1958); Gerald D. Shuttles, *The Social Order of the Slum* (Chicago: University of Chicago Press, 1968), pp. 103–104, 124–130.

42. Shuttles, *The Social Order of the Slum*, pp. 107–112; Frederick Thrasher, *The Gang* (Chicago: University of Chicago Press, 1926).

43. See Brazier, *Black Self-Determination*, chaps. 7, 8, and 9, for an interesting though one-sided account of the Blackstone Rangers.

44. Quoted in Peter Matthiessen, *Sal Si Puedes* (New York: Delta Books, 1969), p. 309.

45. Sherry R. Arnstein, "Maximum Feasible Manipulation," *Public Administration Review*, XXXII (September 1972), 389. Italics in the original.

46. Joseph Schumpeter, *Capitalism, Socialism, and Democracy*, 3rd ed. (New York: Harper Torchbooks, 1950), p. 340.

47. Matthiessen, *Sal Si Puedes*, p. 54.

48. John Gregory Dunne, "To Die Standing: Cesar Chavez and the Chicanos," *Atlantic* (June 1971), pp. 39–45.

CHAPTER 5

Political Structure and Organizations

If the social structure powerfully influences the extent to which persons can be mobilized by voluntary associations, then political structure helps determine the kinds of associations that will exist. Economically advanced nations, in which the proportion of persons in the lowest stratum (whether defined psychologically, economically, or socially) is the smallest, will have the largest proportion of persons in voluntary organizations. For example, Gabriel Almond and Sidney Verba found that 57 percent of all Americans, but only 25 percent of all Mexicans, belong to some voluntary association.[1] But not all of these organizations are relevant to politics nor are those which are relevant equally successful in pressing their causes before governmental authorities. Indeed, with respect to many kinds of organizations, Americans are no more likely to belong—and in some cases, less likely to belong—than citizens of other countries. Fourteen percent of a sample of American adults belong to a labor union, but this is less than among Englishmen (22 percent) and Germans (15 percent) and not much more than among Mexicans (11 percent). Nine percent of the Italians and 6 percent of the Mexicans said that they belonged to a charitable organization, compared to only 3 percent of the Americans.[2]

There are two kinds of associations to which Americans, compared to citizens of other countries that have been studied, are more likely to belong—church-related organizations and civic-political ones. The importance of church organizations is probably the result of the religious stratification of American society—Protestants, Catholics, and Jews have each created a distinct social structure [3]—and the decentralized, congregational tradition of most American Protestant sects; the significance of the latter is in great part the result of the decentralized structure of American government.

Eleven percent of Americans, but only 3 percent of Englishmen and Germans, mentioned belonging to a civic or political association.[4] And when asked what they would do to protest an unjust local regulation, 56 percent of the Americans interviewed said they would try to organize their neighbors and friends for collective action directed at the government, but only 34 percent of the Englishmen and 13 percent of the Germans gave the same response.[5] Arnold M. Rose has suggested that voluntary associations, especially those directed at political ends, are relatively uncommon in France,[6] and though his argument has been modified by other students of France, it has not been refuted.[7] Tocqueville expressed it this way: "Whenever at the head of some new undertaking you see the government in France, or a man of rank in England, in the United States you will be sure to find an association." [8]

In the United States, the separation of powers among the various branches of the government, combined with the dispersion of those powers among various levels of government, offers manifold opportunities for politically active voluntary associations to intervene and in turn makes officeholders at every level attentive to, though rarely bound by, the views of such associations. If local governments had little or no discretionary authority, if candidates for office received the nomination solely at the pleasure of a centrally led political party and were elected solely on the basis of their appeal to the voter as a party rather than to voters as individuals, and if once in office the politicians discovered that the chief source of power was the executive head of the government, there would be few opportunities to act for voluntary associations interested in government issues. Local associations to protest or demand the building of a highway, to register or block the registration of Negro voters in a particular country, or to obtain or prevent the construction of a housing project would have no incentive to come into being if the decisions they sought to influence were not made at the local level but at the national one.

Some organizations would still form because they could represent the nationwide interests of their members before national agencies. But only certain kinds of interests are national in scope and thus only certain kinds of interests are likely to form national associations. Businessmen will in principle be concerned about tax, tariff, and regulatory policies, though, as we shall see in Chapter 8, only a fraction of all businessmen will unite even over these matters; union members will be concerned about nationally imposed minimum wage rates and nationally determined collective bargaining procedures; veterans will be interested in the size of their benefit checks from the relevant national agency. But many purely local issues and even national ones that have different consequences for different localities will not provide the stimulus for the formation of an association, except perhaps a short-lived one that confines itself to symbolic agitation aimed at a national audience rather than to practical bargaining directed at local officials.

And even national organizations are likely to be relatively weak if power with respect to the organization's objectives is lodged in one or a few hands in the government. Though associations will form if there is a chance of influencing the key official with respect to the policies he controls, more associations will form and will be more vigorous if there are many officials involved in decision-making, each with his legally or constitutionally protected sphere of authority. Increasing the chances of making a difference in policy is likely to increase the number and vigor of associations seeking to make that difference.

Indeed, a national association confronting a centralized national government is likely to play its largest role, not with respect to decisions whether or not to adopt a major policy, but with respect to the administration of those policies that have already been adopted. A bureaucracy provides the many points of access and the details over which to bargain that a legislature in a centrally led government cannot.

This view of the relationship between political structure and voluntary association activity is borne out by—indeed, it was largely suggested by—a comparison of the British and American experiences. In the United States, there are at least three major farm organizations, the largest of which is a federation of state and county associations; at least three separate veterans' organizations; and a host of business associations. Professional societies, such as the American Medical Association and the American Bar Association, exist at the national level, but the average member is primarily affiliated with the many city or county units that direct their attentions principally to the policies of local governmental agencies and institutions. In the United Kingdom, by contrast, there exists a single farm organization (the National Farmers' Union), a single veterans' organization (the British Legion), a dominant business association (the Federation of British Industries), and professional societies, such as the British Medical Association, that are almost entirely national in their orientation.[9]

Some have argued that the monolithic, centralized, noncompetitive structure of British political associations derives from the same social conditions that have produced a centralized, executive-led government —the relative homogeneity of the British people and their agreement on major issues. Samuel H. Beer and others have argued persuasively that such homogeneity is exaggerated—workers, businessmen, professionals, and ethnic groups are often internally as divided and externally as rivalrous as their American counterparts.[10] Whatever may have produced the essential features of the British government, it is the resultant political structure, and not general attitudes of consensus and deference, that is chiefly responsible for the structure of politically active voluntary associations.

This is best shown by examining the changes that have occurred in these associations since their formation. After World War I, there were a variety of veterans' organizations in Britain, distinguished one from the other by their members' rank, service, and extent of war injuries—just as American veterans' groups are today. But the government ministry charged with administering the Pension Act, desirous of dealing with one organization rather than many, was able to stimulate the merger of the competing groups into the British Legion.[11] Before the British government decided it was necessary to regulate and increase food production, the National Farmers' Union (NFU) was a small group trying, not very successfully, to lobby Parliament on behalf of farmers. Wartime necessities led to a vast increase in the scope of activity of the Ministry of Agriculture, and this turn led to a rapid growth in the size and influence of the NFU.[12] The British Medical Association, though publicly often quarreling with the Ministry of Health, privately and routinely has an informal partnership with the Ministry for the purpose of interpreting and carrying out the policies of the agency that oversees the complex, state-supported and state-controlled health services.[13] Mobilization during World War I led to the formation of employers' associations, and in 1965 the three peak associations—the Federation of British Industries, the National Union of Manufacturers, and the British Employers' Confederation—merged into a single "super-peak" association. And even after that degree of consolidation had been obtained, a Royal

Commission criticized the association for not having a sufficiently strong central authority.

British local government is relatively free of the agitation of civic associations so characteristic of American city politics. A study of planning and housing decisions in London revealed little participation by neighborhood civic associations even though the matters at stake were of considerable moment. One reason for the absence of that participation is that administrators, not councils, tend to make the important decisions, and that often it is not the local authority, but the corresponding national ministry, that sets the decisive policies.[14] Another study of London county government revealed little activity on the part of those groups—business associations in particular—that are to be found in any American city. The reason was partly that the national government, rather than that of the county, made the crucial decisions and partly that such decisions as the London County Council could make were taken on the basis of a party vote along lines set down by the party leadership.[15]

There are no doubt other factors that contribute to the very different pattern of British, as opposed to American, associational activity. The British have for so long accepted the view that the government *governs* rather than *represents* citizens that decisions made by planners or other civil servants are simply accepted without a struggle. The British Cabinet and the party leaders are the source of policy decisions as opposed to mere proposals; if the citizen dislikes the decisions, he may vote against the party in the next election, or he may write a letter to the newspapers, but he will not ordinarily press his objections through group action. Such theories may be valuable partial explanations, but they hardly seem conclusive. When a political structure is altered so as to provide a reward for organized action, organized action is forthcoming whatever may be the ethos of the citizenry. (General views may explain the maintenance of a particular structure, but they rarely explain particular acts taken by a minority within that structure.) The doctors, the veterans, and the farmers have not, out of any exaggerated sense of deference, shown themselves reluctant to carve out a large role for themselves in running the health scheme, the veterans' pension plan, or the agricultural controls program.

When private associations acquire a privileged position vis-à-vis a government agency, they can often increase their membership dramatically. By being the sole authoritative interpreter of agency decisions and the favored avenue by which citizens aggrieved by these decisions can seek redress, these associations acquire a quasi-public status and a valuable resource for organizational maintenance. As Sapolsky observes:

These [government] agencies seek to order their environment by offering to a single organization, often of their own creation, the exclusive right to act as a client representative in policy planning and administration. This license provides the designated organizations with extremely persuasive incentives [to potential members].[16]

The result is that some of the monopolistic voluntary associations in Great Britain have recruited a much larger proportion of their potential members than have their more competitive counterparts in the United States. The NFU enrolls 75 to 80 percent of all British farmers; the Federation of British Industries is supported by 85 percent of all firms employing ten or more workers. By contrast, only about one-third of all American farmers belong to one of the three major farm organizations, and only a small fraction of all firms belong to either the United States Chamber of Commerce or the National Association of Manufacturers.[17]

The greater decentralization and dispersion of political authority in the United States help explain the greater variety of politically active American voluntary associations. However, this fragmentation of government is not uniform throughout the country, nor unchanging over time, and thus there are important variations in the extent to which political structure impedes or encourages organizational activity, just as there are variations in the extent to which the social structure helps or hinders organizational entrepreneurs. Indeed, it is possible that in certain cases a limited-access political structure and a disadvantaged social position may combine to exclude some potential groups from ever becoming effective organizations at all.

One constraining structural influence in America is the existence of a mechanism whereby the formally separate and competitive bits of constitutional authority are informally but effectively brought together under a single pattern of leadership. The urban political machine is, of course, the best-known example of this. Cities or counties with such organizations monopolize many political resources, limit drastically the points of access to government, and concentrate power in the hands of a single leader or a small group of leaders at the top. In Chicago, for example, unions for city employees are generally weak or nonexistent because the party machine does not tolerate an alternative claim on employee loyalties; neighborhood organizations that are both independent and effective are rare except in well-to-do areas because the not-so-well-off residents find it more profitable to take their problems to the party's local representative; and ethnic associations are typically either nonpolitical or, if political, a dependent part of the party organization. Organizations challenging the machine arise, but only when they are in secure command of political resources not under the control of the dominant party.

By contrast, in cities in which no strong party or other extralegal structure of influence has managed to concert the acts of the many independent officials, a wide variety of independent and competitive voluntary associations in the political sphere arise. In Los Angeles, where political parties are weak or virtually nonexistent, unions for city employees have become large and powerful. In New York, civil rights and neighborhood associations, as well as unions, have become an important feature of local politics in part because candidates for elective office in a city with highly factionalized parties are led to cultivate all segments of opinion in the hope that the electoral gains from those attracted by such cultivation will outweigh the electoral losses from those repelled by it.[18] This is made easier in New York because of peculiar legal arrangements that permit the existence of four major political parties—Democrats, Republicans, Liberals, and Conservatives—rather than just two; hence, the center-seeking tendencies of politicians concerned with defeating a single opponent are reduced in favor of the enthusiast-seeking tendencies of politicians who believe they can win if their active minority remains intact.

J. David Greenstone and Paul E. Peterson have compared various efforts to create new political organizations among the poor in America's four largest cities—Chicago, Los Angeles, New York, and Philadelphia. Under the Economic Opportunity Act of 1964 (the "war on poverty") an attempt was made, using federal funds, to create in the poorer neighborhoods of cities "community action programs" that would "assist the poor in developing autonomous and self-managed organizations which are competent to exert political influence on behalf of their own self-interest."[19] Though the mayors of the four cities welcomed any economic aid the federal government was prepared to allot to the poor in their communities, they unanimously opposed any move that would do so by way of community political organizations that were independent of city government. In Chicago, a politically centralized city, the mayor was able to obtain the most economic aid per poor person from the government while successfully keeping the control of the local poverty program out of the hands of representatives of poor neighborhoods. In New

York, a city with weak parties and a mayor who believed it was good politics to improve his standing among poor black voters themselves and, equally important, among those voters who were concerned about blacks, the per capita economic aid received was much lower, but the level of representation from poor neighborhoods in the management of the program was the highest. In Philadelphia and Los Angeles, per capita aid and neighborhood representation tended to fall between these extremes.[20]

Though variations in local political structure may affect the kinds of *groups* and *areas* achieving organized influence within the government, it is less clear that these variations affect the kinds of *people* achieving such influence. In New York City, where half the votes in the poverty council were allotted to representatives of poor areas, those representing these areas were chosen by neighborhood conventions attended chiefly by representatives of community organizations and churches, many of whom were no doubt middle class.[21] Indeed, efforts to select neighborhood representatives by direct elections, as in Philadelphia, produced a rather ineffectual pattern of local control over the poverty program. Only a tiny fraction (about 3 percent) of the eligible voters participated, and those elected tended to be lower-income "friends and neighbors." In office, the representatives soon lost interest in antipoverty policies and increasingly focused their attention on employee hiring. Within a year, the elected council members relinquished their authority over the director of the neighborhood service center in exchange for the right to be hired by him to work in the center. Paul E. Peterson, in summarizing his analysis of these programs, observes that an elective process in poor neighborhoods produces formal but not substantive representation of the poor, with the elected representatives concerning themselves with particularistic interests and divisible, material benefits, whereas a nonelective process of organizational representation produces substantive but not formal representation and an interest on the part of the representatives in general policies and programs rather than with particular benefits.[22]

If Peterson's analysis is correct, then changes in the political structure of a community may be a necessary condition, but not a sufficient one, for the effective organization of certain social groups. Lower-class persons are not likely to form large organizations or play a policy-oriented role in public affairs whatever the political structure; on the other hand, groups of persons, themselves not lower class, who claim to speak *for* the lower classes may emerge and organize rapidly when the structure of political opportunities is altered. This pattern of virtual or substantive representation is neither unique nor necessarily suspect—almost all citizens, whatever their class, are represented in democratic legislatures by persons unlike them in income, schooling, and occupation.[23]

The effectiveness, as opposed to the representatives, of those new organizations created by the injection of federal funds and expectations into city political systems seems to depend in part on how broadly the new organizations define their tasks. In an analysis of community action agencies in 100 American cities, James J. Vanecko and Bruce Jacobs find that those agencies most strongly committed to mobilizing and organizing in poor neighborhoods have a greater impact on key urban institutions—the schools, welfare agencies, and private employers—than do those agencies that emphasize instead the provision of services.[24] The analysis is complex and the conclusions are subject to a number of qualifications, but it appears that the new antipoverty agencies are more likely to affect the behavior of local sources of jobs, welfare assistance, and schooling if the agencies are committed to a community organization strategy. One might suppose that this is evidence of the capacity of the very poor to change the conditions that affect their lives if they are given an opportunity by the political system. That capacity may or may not exist, but the experience of the community action agencies thus far does not confirm it. The Vanecko-Jacobs analysis also showed that there was no significant relationship between the participation of poor persons in the community action agencies and the commitment of those agencies to an effective organization strategy.[25] It is possible that there occurs in these 100 cities the same process that Peterson found in New York and Philadelphia—when the very poor are involved in such agencies, they become more interested in services than in mobilization, and though this interest may lead to their acquiring greater benefits from various institutions, it does not lead to the adoption of any strategy that will make important changes in the policies of those institutions.

The evidence is not clear, however, and much depends on how one defines the "very poor," the "poor," "workers," and "middle class," and so forth. A study of political leaders in black ghettos found that they had modest incomes, but incomes that were still about one-third greater than the incomes of the general ghetto population ($7,610 as opposed to $5,700 per year) and that they had somewhat more schooling than the average ghetto resident, though only 10 percent were college graduates.[26]

In short, the results of altering the structure of political opportunities are ambiguous. There can be little doubt that injecting into a community new political resources free of control by existing government officials will lead to the creation of new organizations pressing new demands. Those committed to pressing the hardest tend to obtain the most changes from existing institutions. But whether those mobilized by these resources and engaged in expressing those demands are a new group of previously inactive citizens, or persons already playing leadership roles in other associations who now converge around new and more abundant resources, or some combination of both, is not clear. Furthermore, we have only fragmentary evidence as to the consequences of participation by these different groups. The very poorest, especially those elected because they are friends and neighbors, may, because of their class characteristics, seek certain objectives but not others—jobs and services rather than institutional changes—or may seek a variety of objectives by unconventional means, for example, engaging in highly expressive and combative behavior. Or the new leadership may well be solidly working class and middle class in origin, but may be led, by the nature of their constituencies and the power relationships between them and city agencies, to abandon the constraints that usually inhibit the political style of the middle classes; they may become instead secretive, suspicious, and aggressive both because they feel that this is what is expected of them by those for whom they presume to speak and because they have been frustrated by previous governmental interventions in neighborhoods, interventions that have promised much but delivered little.

The impact of political structure on associational activity is not limited to groups representing the black or the poor. The kind and level of activity of upper-middle-class business and civic associations varies with the opportunities afforded them by city governments and their leaders. Edward Banfield's study of Chicago politics in the late 1950s found that the major issues confronting that city were not raised, nor their disposition importantly affected, by the civic associations such as the Metropolitan Housing and Planning Council, the Association of Commerce and Industry, the Civic Federation, or the Welfare Council.[27] In great part this was because, as Banfield notes, such groups are likely to be divided or otherwise immobilized by controversial issues. But it is also possible that the extreme centralization of political influence in the city and the county meant that very few groups could decisively affect the outcome of any issue, and only a few organizations, chiefly large institutions with material needs, were taken seriously as sources of issues. In other kinds of cities, associations may play a larger role.

Martin Shefter's comparison of civic association activity in Boston and New York suggests that this may indeed be the case. Civic associations in New York City have enjoyed good relations with municipal agencies, especially during the administration of Mayor Robert Wagner. Shefter gives examples of policies proposed by the associations that were adopted by the agencies with little argument.[28] Theodore Lowi shows that several such organizations have also played an important role in selecting important city commissioners.[29] Business associations, on the other hand, have had less influence. After Mayor Wagner appointed a committee of bankers and others to advise on financial problems, he ignored much of their advice. In Boston, by contrast, civic groups have played a relatively small role and business groups a somewhat larger one. One important reason for the difference is to be found in the contrasting positions of the mayors and the bureaucracies over which they exercise control. Mayor Wagner was sympathetic to the aims of the civic associations, skeptical of business groups, and desirous of adopting policies that represented a consensus between his administrators and their civic association counterparts in such fields as housing, health, and education. Furthermore, mayoral elections in New York are closely fought and attract the attention and participation of newspapers, citizen's organizations, political reformers, and the like. To be in good standing with such groups is a valuable political resource, and to maintain that good standing many mayors have sought and taken their advice. Furthermore, until recently, the mayor of New York did not have strong legal powers enabling him to act with minimum consent from others.

In Boston, newspaper opinion counts for little, citizens' groups play a small part in elections, and neither parties nor party reformers are especially active. And the mayor of Boston has great formal powers over almost all aspects of city government; if he chooses, he can ignore many sources of opposition. Throughout most of the 1960s, the mayor of Boston felt confident that he did not need the support of the civic groups, and they in turn thought his executive agencies were badly staffed and poorly managed. As a result, civic associations in Boston are relatively few in number and ineffective in activity. (At least at the city level. Boston associations are more likely to carry their programs to the state legislature, often over the opposition of city hall.) Business groups, on the other hand, have enjoyed good access to Boston mayors because of a common interest in stabilizing the property tax rate and restoring "business confidence" in the city, and these groups have often supported his proposals before the legislature.

Individual personalities alter this relationship from time to time, but rarely for long. A progressive mayor of Boston, such as Kevin White, may for a while seek to ally himself with civic rather than business groups, but inevitably that tendency will be checked by the overwhelming political issue of the tax rate. Whatever he may privately wish, in time the mayor will come to take a "tax-opposing" rather than "service-demanding" pose, and thus civic associations—which tend to demand services rather than oppose taxes—will count for less in the local political process. In New York, the mayor has typically been a "service-demander" and thus has been the natural ally of the civic associations. From time to time he may worry about the tax rate, and occasionally a mayor may be elected who makes that his chief concern, but over the long term, New York politics do not reward politicians who advocate doing less rather than more or who otherwise offend the liberal sensibilities of the active parts of the electorate.

Comparable differences among cities are also evident in the conduct of teachers' associations. Alan Rosenthal found in New York City a pattern of militant teacher unionism aimed, at least in part, at increasing organized teacher influence in school administration and policy-making. In Boston, by contrast, he discovered a pattern of "accommodation politics" in which the teachers' union was less likely to advocate striking and appeared more interested in obtaining money benefits for its members than in acquiring institutional power for its leaders. Both patterns of organizational activity, Rosenthal maintains, reflect differences in the opportunities afforded by the prevailing political structure.[30]

In sum, the greater the decentralization and dispersion of political power, the greater the incentive for the formation of many voluntary associations; this appears to be the case as between nations, as among cities within a single nation, and, over time, within a single city as political resources are redistributed by outside forces. Furthermore, the constituencies to which elective officials feel they must appeal influence the access to them that different kinds of associations will enjoy, or, to say the same thing in different words, the rewards a politician seeks affect the opportunities an association will have. The extent to which altering either the structure of politics or the rewards of politicians will result in the organization of previously unorganized groups is problematic: some will be newly mobilized, others will simply shift the locus of their ongoing activities from an area of scarce resources—money, publicity, access—to one of more plentiful resources.[31] Whether a governmentally stimulated organization, such as a community action agency or a model cities board, can outlast the governmental support and become either a regular part of a city's decision-making system or an independent voluntary association is not yet known. In particular, whether changes in political access can overcome the impediments to organizational formation created by class characteristics remains to be seen. It is likely that increasing the opportunities and rewards for organizational action will prove to be means whereby what appears to be class-induced apathy will, for some persons, disappear and will be replaced by a high level of activism. It is also likely that for others, no structural change whatever will alter, except momentarily and on the basis of immediate benefits, the disinclination to participate.

NOTES

1. Gabriel A. Almond and Sidney Verba, *The Civic Culture* (Princeton, N.J.: Princeton University Press, 1963), p. 302. See also David Horton Smith, "Modernization and the Emergence of Volunteer Organizations" (paper, Department of Sociology, Boston College, 1970). Some of the differences in membership among the nations studied by Almond and Verba are due to the much greater level of participation of women in the United States when compared with the other nations. Almond and Verba, p. 303.

2. Almond and Verba, *The Civic Culture*, p. 302.

3. Edward O. Laumann, "The Social Structure of Religious and Ethnoreligious Groups in a Metropolitan Community," *American Sociological Review*, XXXIV (April 1969), 182–197. See also the important historical study by H. Richard Niebuhr, *The Social Sources of Denominationalism* (New York: Holt, 1926).

4. Almond and Verba, *The Civic Culture*, p. 302.

5. Ibid., p. 194.

6. Arnold M. Rose, *Theory and Method in the Social Sciences* (Minneapolis: University of Minnesota Press, 1954), pp. 50–115.

7. Orvoell R. Gallagher, "Voluntary Associations in France," *Social Forces*, XXXVI (1957), 153–160.

8. Alexis de Tocqueville, *Democracy in America*, ed. Phillips Bradley (New York: Alfred A. Knopf, 1951), vol. II, p. 106.

9. This analysis follows Harvey M. Sapolsky, "Organizational Competition and Monopoly," *Public Policy*, XVII (Cambridge, Mass.: Kennedy School of Government of Harvard University, 1968), 355–376, and Samuel H. Beer, "Group Representation in Britain and the United States," *Annals of the American Academy*, CCCXIX (September 1958), 131–140.

10. Harry H. Eckstein in *Patterns of Government*, 2d ed., ed. Samuel H. Beer and Adam B. Ulam (New York: Random House, 1962), pp. 170–175.

11. Graham Wootton, *The Politics of Influence* (Cambridge, Mass.: Harvard University Press, 1963).

12. Peter Self and Herbert J. Storing, *The State and the Farmer* (Berkeley: University of California Press, 1963), chap. 2.

13. Harry H. Eckstein, *Pressure Group Politics: The Case of the British Medical Association* (Stanford, Calif.: Stanford University Press, 1960), p. 48.

14. Stephen Lloyd Elkin, "Public Interest Politics: The Control of Development by the London County Council" (Ph.D. diss., Department of Government, Harvard University, 1968), pp. 273–288.

15. Edward C. Banfield, "The Political Implications of Metropolitan Growth," *Daedalus* (Winter 1961), 61–78.

16. Sapolsky, "Organizational Competition and Monopoly," pp. 364–365.

17. Ibid., p. 366.

18. Edward C. Banfield and James Q. Wilson, *City Politics* (Cambridge, Mass.: Harvard University Press, 1963), pp. 214–216; Ralph T. Jones, "City Employee Unions in New York and Chicago" (Ph.D. diss., Department of Government, Harvard University, 1972).

19. Office of Economic Opportunity, *Community Action Workbook* (Washington, D.C.) III, A, 7.

20. J. David Greenstone and Paul E. Peterson, "Reformers, Machines, and the War on Povery," in *City Politics and Public Policy*, ed. James Q. Wilson (New York: John Wiley, 1968), pp. 267–292, esp. 282, 287.

21. Ibid., p. 282.

22. Paul E. Peterson, "Forms of Representation: Participation of the Poor in the Community Action Program," *American Political Science Review*, LXIV (June 1970), 501, 506. A study of the Harlem-East Harlem Model City Policy Committee in New York revealed the same pattern of aggressive involvement of largely middle-class residents, many of whom were quite suspicious of both city agencies and one another's motives and actions. Seymour Z. Mann, "Participation of the Poor and Model Cities in New York City" (paper prepared for the National Academy of Public Administration, 1970), pp. 22–30.

23. The difference between community action and legislative representation is in the pattern of accountability—legislators must face regular elections in which a substantial fraction of the voters participate, whereas many poverty council members do not. Furthermore, the former must vote on both tax and benefit measures, but the latter usually vote only on benefits.

24. James J. Vanecko and Bruce Jacobs, "The Impact of the Community Action Program on Institutional Change" (report issued jointly by the National Opinion Research Center of the University of Chicago and Barss, Reitzel & Associates of Cambridge, Mass., May 1970), p. 86.

25. Ibid., p. 21.

26. Barss, Reitzel & Associates, *Community Action and Institutional Change* (report to the Office of Economic Opportunity, July 1969), p. VIII–15.

27. Edward C. Banfield, *Political Influence* (New York: Free Press, 1961), pp. 269–270, 274–275, 297–301.

28. Martin Allen Shefter, "City Hall and State House: State Legislative Involvement in the Politics of New York City and Boston" (Ph.D. diss., Department of Government, Harvard University, 1970), chap. 8.

29. Theodore Lowi, *At the Pleasure of the Mayor* (New York: Free Press, 1964).

30. Alan Rosenthal, *Pedagogues and Power: Teacher Groups in School Politics* (Syracuse, N.Y.: Syracuse University Press, 1969), chaps. 4, 5.

31. An analysis of data from five nations suggests that under certain circumstances participation in organizations may be increased independently of increases in economic development and that this greater organizational involvement will lead to a higher level of political participation generally without any change in the social status of the member. See Norman H. Nie, G. Bingham Powell, and Kenneth Prewitt, "Social Structure and Political Participation: Developmental Relationships, II" *American Political Science Review*, LXIII (September 1969), 808–832, esp. 825–827.

PART

II

The Perspective
Applied

CHAPTER 6

Political Parties

The political party, at least in the United States, is a conspicuous exception to the general tendency for society to become increasingly organized, rationalized, and bureaucratized. Parties, as organizations, have become, if anything, weaker rather than stronger; present party organizations have shown little sign of becoming bureaucratized; and the loyalties of voters to party labels have neither increased in intensity nor been rationalized along ideological lines. The political machine, once a conspicuous feature of urban and country life, is now found in relatively few places; party leadership is on the whole a part-time avocation of volunteers who can lay claim to special resources of time, money, favor, or popularity, rather than the full-time occupation of appointed functionaries; the proportion of voters who vote a straight ticket has declined sharply since 1948.

Parties are more important as labels than as organizations. Their chief effect on election outcomes is as an organizing principle to enable voters to identify with various candidates. Sometimes the right to use that label can be won by a candidate who participates in no organizational processes at all—as when a person wins a primary election by campaigning as an individual rather than as an organizational representative. But party organizations do exist (because they are mostly local entities, no one knows how many there are) and they perform a variety of functions, ranging from candidate endorsement through fund raising to systematic electoral canvassing. By "party organization," I mean a group of persons who consciously coordinate their activities so as to influence the choice of candidates for elective office. A "party member" is a person who involves himself in these coordinated activities, who not only votes for the party candidate, but also attends the meetings of, or undertakes to perform tasks on behalf of, a party organization.

The reason for the organizational structure of American parties is to be found in the distribution of those political resources that can be converted into incentives to induce individuals to act in an organizational capacity. In this country, parties seek resources—office and influence—that are chiefly available locally rather than nationally. As a result, parties have been highly decentralized. Furthermore, the value of some of the resources available to parties has been declining relative to the value of equivalent resources available through extraparty channels. Patronage jobs and material favors are increasingly less attractive when compared with nonpolitical opportunities for employment and business, at least for the rank and file. Social solidarity is an incentive available from a host of nonparty clubs and voluntary associations, and often more cheaply; that is, in nonpolitical clubs, the member is asked to do less in return for the opportunity for camaraderie. And the value of solidarity is often debased in a political organization because it must strive to be inclusive, whereas a social club strives to be exclusive: political organizations seek to attract rich and poor, white and black, both sexes and all races; social clubs seek to find a principle of homogeneity that will limit membership to one kind of person. Furthermore, controversy is often the enemy of solidarity, and a party organization by its nature involves its members in controversy; a nonparty solidarity association shuns conflict. Finally, "politics," in the opinion of many, provides less status than "civic work," even though the latter may be in some sense as political as the former. The more society becomes middle class, the more it is likely to draw a distinction, and an invidious one, between "doing good" and "playing politics."

This leaves purpose, principle, and ideology as a major source of incentives for party organizations. When a candidate can find a cause or issue salient to the lives of many followers, he can often mobilize considerable activity. It is possible that purpose and principle have increased in importance as political incentives with the increased level of schooling of the citizenry and the heightened impact of the media on public affairs. But purpose and principle are also episodic in their salience and divisive in their impact. One thing is clear—many party organizations, including the 1972 Democratic National Convention, have altered their structure and procedures to make them more accessible to persons who wish to enter them out of a sense of mission or ideology.

The inability of parties to become nationally led, centrally funded, bureaucratically staffed organizations is not a recent phenomenon. During the Gilded Age when the Republican party controlled the federal government and most state governments, no elaborate, continuous, or powerful institutions for national party cooperation were created. Robert D. Marcus has shown how, even with the political skills of Mark Hanna and the considerable wealth of the new industrial elite, the Republican party remained a decentralized coalition of local entrepreneurs and part-time politicians. "Almost every newly active group in 1888 further diffused power, creating new centers of administration and increasing uncertainty as to who was in charge. . . ."[1] And the reforms of party organization that came quickly after the Hanna period—nonpartisanship, the direct primary—further reduced the possibility of strong state or national organizations.

A decentralized party structure will, among other things, use a variety of appeals to enlist members. And for each kind of incentive, there is a corresponding organizational style and pattern of internal control, though perhaps not a characteristic strategy.

The Machine

A political machine is a party organization relying chiefly on the attraction of material rewards.[2] These rewards include patronage jobs—appointive positions in government awarded wholly or partly on the basis of party service; preferments, such as contracts to provide, and opportunities to receive, government goods and services, allocated wholly or partly on the basis of party service; economic opportunities in the form of enhanced business and professional opportunities deriving from political contacts though not directly from government business; and, finally, exemptions, such as freedom from the strict enforcement of laws governing the collection of taxes, the suppression of vice, or the regulation of commerce. Such rewards may go to persons not active in the party organization—voters, influential citizens, newspapers—as well as to members, and not all members may receive such rewards. But in a machine, most members either receive these rewards or hope to receive them.

The machine is a form of political organization characteristic of a certain social milieu and political structure. James C. Scott has suggested that the machine is likely to emerge when traditional patterns of loyalty and deference are weakened during periods of rapid change in the composition of the population (as from massive in-migration) and in socio-economic organization (as from industrialization), especially when these changes occur in a political structure in which formal authority is fragmented.[3] A governing coalition can be created out of disparate groups of voters who have no settled loyalties, face acute problems of economic survival and social acculturation, and thus are receptive to particularistic material inducements. Leaders who can successfully assemble such coalitions obtain large rewards: the perquisites of office and the opportunity to "sell" an electoral majority to higher-ranking state or national political leaders or to groups seeking locally franchised economic benefits, such as utility or traction monopolies. The opportunities for machine organization decline as new loyalties to larger collectivities are gradually formed (to social classes, to the city as a whole, or to the race), as acculturation is accomplished, as economic opportunities widen, and as the supply of governmentally controlled incentives that can be awarded on a particularistic, rather than categorical, basis dwindles.

No one knows the extent to which material rewards for party service are available. In 1957, James Reichley counted 46,761 state jobs in Pennsylvania that were not under civil service and presumably available to party members and others; one can only guess how many preferments, economic opportunities, and exemptions were also at the disposal of the party in power.[4] In 1961, a survey showed that in each of two Manhattan congressional districts there were between 80 and 120 patronage jobs available, whereas in districts of about the same size in Chicago, the total was probably between 350 and 450.[5] Another survey found that the Democratic governor of New York in 1955 could personally allocate 1,765 nonjudicial patronage jobs, three-fourths of which awarded on the recommendation of, or after clearance with, local Democratic party leaders.[6] In California, by contrast, there were few paying jobs to which appointment could be made on political grounds. Former-governor Edmund Brown estimated in 1959 that he could make no more than 600 political (as opposed to civil service) appointments. His actual appointments during one particular year showed that he conferred 346 posts on residents of the largest county, Los Angeles, the great majority of which were purely honorific.[7] In Detroit in 1956, one-third of the twelve district chairmen in both parties, but only 10 percent of the several hundred precinct leaders, held government jobs, and some of these may not have been awarded on a purely patronage basis.[8]

As is often remarked, the importance of patronage has been decreasing in American politics, partly because the inroads of civil service have decreased the supply and partly because the more common, low-paying governmental jobs have lost their attractiveness to a largely middle-class society. Many jobs, nominally patronage in nature, in fact are given to people who have done no party work at all. Frank Sorauf interviewed 123 (almost all) of the highway workers in a rural Pennsylvania county in the 1950s, a period of Republican domination, and found that fewer than half had ever performed any party services either before or after their appointment except to contribute financially to the party coffers; indeed, fewer than half stated they had ever voted the straight Republican ticket. Their supervisors, by contrast, perhaps because of the greater value of these jobs, had almost all campaigned actively for their party.[9] Tammany Hall once dispensed a vast supply of patronage jobs; by the early 1960s, however, it could provide no more than twenty positions for the members of even the largest clubs. One club, responsible for fifty-three election districts populated by 20,000 registered Democrats, had jobs for only four of its district captains.[10]

To the extent a party member is motivated by material rewards, he will be indifferent to, or at least not make his party work contingent on, the policy positions of either the party or its candidates. To the extent these material rewards are of sufficiently high value, accounting for a larger rather than a smaller portion of the recipient's income, they will make the member vulnerable to discipline from party leaders and sensitive to the challenge of others seeking to displace him from the job. The best empirical study of how patronage-rewarded party workers behave is that of Phillips Cutright, in which he compared the precinct committeemen (or captains) of "Partisan City" (apparently Gary, Indiana) with those of "Nonpartisan County." [11] In both places the precinct committeeman is elected every two years by the voters of his party living in that precinct, with vacancies filled by higher party authorities. In Partisan City, however, one-third of the 206 committeemen also held patronage jobs, whereas in Nonpartisan County only 3 percent of the 229 committeemen did. Furthermore, patronage jobs were available in Partisan City for other persons—an average of six jobs per precinct—and thus the committeeman had others to whom he could turn for assistance in performing his electoral duties. Most of the Partisan City committeemen who did not have patronage jobs received or expected other kinds of material rewards—preferments, business advantage, and exemptions.

The committeemen in Partisan City were by almost every measure more fully and frequently in contact with the voters and with other party leaders and worked harder at getting out the vote than did their counterparts in Nonpartisan County. Though the committeemen in both areas were equally likely to belong to the various community-serving organizations, the Partisan City committeemen were more likely than those in Nonpartisan County to have daily contact with precinct residents, to receive requests for aid and to render that aid, to canvass door to door at election time, and to take a preelection poll of their precincts. To a degree, of course, these differences were due to the structure of government more than to the rewards of the party member—if a committeeman in Nonpartisan County can do no favor for the voter owing to the way public services are administered, then obviously few voters will ask him for a favor. But the structure of government cannot explain, for example, why 63 percent of the Partisan City committeemen, but only 15 percent of those in Nonpartisan County, got in contact with ten or more neighbors every day.

Because of the rewards of party work, the Partisan City committeemen are frequently challenged in elections. Almost two-thirds of the Democratic committeemen had to face a rival in the preceding election, compared to only one-fourth of those in Nonpartisan County.

The relative indifference of patronage-induced party members to the policy implications of electoral contests has been frequently noted. In Chicago, for example, the Negro machine of former Congressman William L. Dawson worked hard to bring out a straight-ticket vote for the Democratic party even in contests when the Republican opposition offered a black candidate against a white candidate endorsed by the Democrats. The black alderman elected with machine support voted in the city council with the white majority even on issues, such as open occupancy in housing, generally supported by issue-conscious black spokesmen.

This does not mean that considerations of policy are entirely absent from materially induced party organizations. One policy in particular is of great importance—namely, whether or not the candidate is prepared to take care of his supporters if elected. And publicly, policy is much discussed. Meetings of precinct workers holding patronage jobs are often devoted, at campaign time, to fiery speeches denouncing the record and policies of the opposition on all the important issues of the day. Partly this is ammunition being passed out to workers so that they in turn can use it on voters, most of whom receive nothing of material value directly from the party and whose questions and concerns need to be dealt with.

Partly also it is a way of reassuring the workers that, though paid to work, they are also serving a larger cause and not only their own self-interest. It is little different from the sales manager who assures his salesmen that though they are working on commission, they are also selling a worthwhile and socially desirable product. And finally, some workers have mixed motives; the job alone is not sufficient to keep them interested in politics.

Even more important, political machines in most cities have sought to appeal to a constituency broader than merely that responsive to direct material rewards or to the friendship of precinct captains. Not only Mayor Richard J. Daley in Chicago, but before him the leaders of the Pendergast machine in Kansas City, the Cox machine in Cincinnati, and the Crump machine in Memphis all attempted in various ways—usually by sponsoring civic improvements—to win middle- and upper-middle-class votes.[12] The difference, of course, is that only votes, not active membership in the party, were sought from these citizens, and thus the issues used to appeal to them did not alter the internal incentive system of the party itself.

The Purposive Party

Purpose is rarely the sole motivating force in a party organization. A party by definition is an officeseeking grouping, and even the purest devotees of principle would usually prefer to see their principles put into practice, and that requires power. But it has been the dominant incentive in certain parties, especially certain socialist and Marxist organizations, and it is an important incentive, though not the sole one, in certain contemporary political clubs, both liberal and conservative.

The distinction made in the preceding chapter between ideology and purpose should be repeated here: an ideological party, such as the Socialist Workers' party or the Socialist Labor party, has an inner life and relationship to power different from a party in which principle and purpose, but not a systematic world view, are important motivations. Ideological parties have been distinguished, at least in American politics, by their intense inner factionalism arising in large part over efforts to define and keep pure ideological doctrine. The purposive or amateur political club, on the other hand, is composed of persons concerned about the goals of public policy and the views of candidates, but usually within the more conventional framework of American political discourse. They are not radical in that they neither systematically question the fundamental premises of American political institutions nor conceive of far-reaching alternatives to it. In the Democratic party, for example, a purposive political party tends to display an ad hoc liberalism that expresses alarm at problems but believes that the existing major parties can activate the government to solve these problems if they take the correct position on the issues and hold their candidates accountable to those stands.[13]

An ideological party need not, of course, be a Marxian one, but in American history most parties professing a systematic world view and a radical critique of existing institutions have in fact been Marxian. Their commitment to a class interpretation of politics and to the goal of public or proletarian ownership of the means of production, as well as to the other tenets of scientific socialism has meant that current party doctrine was rarely a response to the current issues in American politics. As Daniel Bell has phrased it, the American Socialist party was "in the world, but not of it"—it proposed specific reforms of society, but it did not come to grips with the practical alternatives then open to government.[14] By its standards, of course, such alternatives—and even the word "practical"—were irrelevancies, and dangerous ones at that, because they narrowed political vision by drawing attention toward symptoms and away from causes. "What but meaningless phrases are 'imperialism,' 'expansion,' 'free silver,' 'gold standard,' etc., to the wage worker?" asked Eugene V. Debs in 1900. Bryan and McKinley may be interested in these "issues," Debs continued, "but they do not concern the working class." [15] The Socialist Labor party of Daniel De Leon refused to adopt a policy platform, issuing instead a general statement of principles. Even the more broadly based Social Democratic party, while it called in 1898 for various immediate changes, such as public works, shorter work hours, and workmen's insurance, took no positions on some of the liveliest issues of the day, including the farm question, the money question, tariffs, immigration, the Spanish-American War and imperialism generally, and the problem of the Negro.[16]

Distant from power and preoccupied with finding a correct statement of their ideology, the Marxist parties were and, insofar as they remain, continue to be racked with internal quarrels, factionalism, and hostility toward those parties seemingly closest to them in doctrine. With their eyes on the millennium, the members are confident of the ultimate goals, but they find no sure way of inferring from these final ends immediate objectives or even ways of testing positions on current issues. The American Socialist party, throughout its history, "has never, *even for a single year*, been without some issue which threatened to split the party and which forced it to spend much of its time on the problem of reconciliation or rupture." [17]

Because of the ideological rivalries and the widespread suspicion that some socialists would attempt to use the party to gain personal power and preferment rather than to advance the long-term interests of the workers, most Marxian parties, especially the Socialists, were highly decentralized. Individual state and local units were almost entirely autonomous. Referenda were held on almost all major policy questions. Bureaucratization was so feared that the national secretaries were closely checked; six different men held the post in the American Socialist party between 1901 and 1919.[18]

We have no careful study of the process by which members of the various Marxist parties were induced to join, and thus it is difficult to speak confidently about the incentive systems employed. For many dues payers, ideology alone must have sufficed, for there were few other rewards. The opportunity to wield governmental power was available to some, as when local Socialist candidates captured city offices. In 1912, over 1,000 Socialists held elective office, including 56 mayors and over 300 city councilmen or aldermen.[19] But many of these men were soon repudiated by the party itself, for to hold office almost surely meant that compromises had been made in socialist doctrine and alliances made with socialist enemies. That same year, Eugene V. Debs, as the Socialist candidate for president, polled 6 percent of the popular vote, the highest proportion ever attained by the party; at the same time, however, the dues-paying membership declined sharply, largely because of the expulsion of the left wing for various doctrinal sins.

The most successful local Socialist parties were those that developed supplementary incentives in addition to ideological appeal. The Non-Partisan League in North Dakota, organized by Arthur C. Townley in 1915, was led by socialists but its appeal was rural and populist. Above all, its organizing strategy was businesslike: farmers in each county were designated as organizers and given a large commission for each member they enrolled. The recruiters called upon their neighbors, delivered a carefully rehearsed sales talk, asked them to sign a pledge to support league candidates in primary elections and to back the league plan calling for, among other things, state ownership of the flour mills and terminal elevators, and collected what for the time was a large dues payment—initially $2.50 a year, but increased as success grew to $9 a year. The organizers were paid $4 for each cash membership obtained; $3.50 if it was paid for by a postdated check. In return the farmer got a subscription to the league newspaper. Retaining the thousands of farmers thus enrolled required quick proof of the value of the league, and it was forthcoming. Within a year it captured the Republican party's nomination for governor and other state offices by entering its own candidates in the primary; they won easily in the general election, giving the league control of the lower house of the legislature as well as the governorship. The coming of the agricultural depression in 1920 undercut the financial basis of the party, however. In its eight years of existence, the league had accumulated $2 million worth of postdated checks from farmers, all written to be paid when the October harvest was in. When crop prices fell, the checks were never paid, the organizers lost their commissions, and the league lost its financing. Though its organizational vitality was weakened, its value as a political label remained strong, and league candidates won office in North Dakota well into the 1930s. Throughout it all, the Socialist party predictably attacked the league on the grounds that its members were not fully schooled in socialist principles and that its leaders were "opportunists." [20]

A somewhat different incentive system was employed by socialist organizers in the Oklahoma Territory. The homesteaders there were organized by combining the principles of religious revivalism with the attractions of county fairs. Week-long encampments would draw thousands of families who would come to live in tents to make and renew acquaintances around the campfires and cookstoves. The expenses of the encampment were often defrayed with funds raised from the local bankers and merchants for whom an encampment, even a socialist one, was good business. Parades, singing, and fervid oratory combined to enlist farmers in the Socialist party, and the mutual reinforcement derived from the group setting intensified emotions, provided a sense of personal efficacy, and held members true to the cause after the encampment broke up. The intense solidary incentives of Oklahoma rural socialism converted impoverished farmers into party members proportionately as numerous as the Non-Partisan League membership of North Dakota. The party at its height cast one-third of the total vote in the state. But out of the encampments also grew, perhaps inevitably, a different kind of organization as well, the violence-prone Green Corn Rebellion, which arose in the sharecropper areas of eastern Oklahoma. It is but a step from an encampment to a secret order, a fact discovered by the Ku Klux Klan as well as by populists.[21]

The urban Socialist parties also were to a degree based, especially by the end of World War I, on solidary incentives. In 1912, only 13 percent of the party's 118,000 members belonged to the foreign-language federations; by 1918 the proportion was 30 percent and by 1919 it was 53 percent, the bulk of it from Russia and other East European countries.[22] In 1923, the American Communist party published one English-language weekly, but *nine* foreign-language *dailies*.[23] Only one of its thirteen constituent federations was English speaking. The Marxist parties, as the tide of immigration rose, were places where new arrivals could find companions, a familiar dialect, news about the homeland, and the latest European views on socialism. These collective solidary rewards made recruitment easier, but they also served to keep the Marxist parties divided along national lines, to limit their capacity to address themselves persuasively to an American constituency, and to base party recruitment on a wasting asset. In time, the American-born sons and daughters of the immigrants would find the party dominated by persons who literally as well as figuratively did not speak their language.

One of the most important problems in understanding the Marxist parties as organizations is to explain why one of them—the American Communist party—became significantly different: a highly centralized, tightly disciplined, internationally controlled group with a covert underground and considerable tactical flexibility. In 1920, the Communist International set down rules for the affiliation with it of other Marxist parties, and the application of the American Socialist party was rejected as failing to conform to these rules, especially those that required deference to the Moscow leadership and expulsion of "reformist" elements.[24] By 1925 the group officially recognized as the American Communist party was firmly under Comintern control, its membership lists regularly purged and its officers frequently changed at the behest of Stalin.

One explanation is that those who became Communists were of a particular psychological type with a strong desire to be dominated by a larger cause and in turn to manipulate others.[25] Here our attention, however, is not on the extent to which various individuals prefer certain organizational arrangements, but on the organizational strategy designed to tap those preferences. Philip Selznick has given an account of the Bolshevik organizational strategy that emphasizes the building of a vanguard rather than a mass party in which members are insulated from other organizational loyalties, and disputes over doctrine are discouraged; this "combat party," in turn, is oriented to the unceasing struggle for power in all arenas of the larger society. Though members are recruited from among the ideologically committed, the dominant incentive in the Bolshevik party vanguard is the struggle for power by cadres and not the pleasures to be derived from doctrinal refinement or endless discussion meetings. Its central problem is that "it wins members on ideological grounds and yet wishes to use them for the technical . . . work of power aggrandizement." [26] It solves this problem by emphasizing, at least for the inner circle, indoctrination and training in the most intense forms, touching all aspects of the member's life and sometimes absorbing virtually all his time. The cell structure facilitates this by permitting small-group reinforcement of higher-level directives. Perhaps in no voluntary association has the problem of organizational maintenance been faced so squarely or made so explicitly a part of the group's purpose.

The distinctive organizational contributions of Stalinism were to ban all factions within the party, to organize members on the basis of small cells, and to make ideology subservient to organizational maintenance and the acquisition of political power.[27] Members who sought to perpetuate the factional warfare of other Marxist parties or to operate outside the scope of their own cells were simply expelled. Leadership was vested in those loyal to Moscow, not those popular among the rank and file. Ideological correctness was no longer the standard by which to test the value of action; successful action was the standard by which to test, within the broad confines of Marxism, ideology. Not all or even most members could accept these organizational requirements, and thus there was a heavy turnover in membership.[28]

The amateur political clubs that are part of the regular Democratic and Republican parties are a different matter, even though some of their members joined after earlier experiences with the Socialist or other Marxist parties. By "amateur" is meant a person who finds an enterprise —here, politics—intrinsically rewarding because it expresses a commitment to a larger purpose. Though an amateur is not indifferent to considerations of partisan and personal advantage or unmoved by the sheer fun of the game or the opportunities to meet people and wield influence, he is distinctive in that he takes the content of public policy and the outcomes of government seriously. That policy ought to be set deliberately, he believes, and not as the by-product of political action undertaken for different reasons; the ends of government ought to serve as the motives for working toward those ends.[29] The political ideologue is thus a special case of the political amateur; the ideologue has an elaborate, systematic, and comprehensive political world view that entails a fundamental critique of institutions not in accord with it, whereas the amateur insists only that politics ought to be motivated by a desire to attain some desirable ends though not necessarily a logically interrelated or radical set of them.

Because establishing the proper relationship between means and ends is vital to the amateur, he is concerned with devising mechanisms to ensure not only that the right ends are selected, but also that they are selected for the right reasons and that effort toward them on the part of political leaders is continuous and sincere. Accordingly, political amateurs in this country, and perhaps generally, are vitally interested in mechanisms to ensure the intraparty accountability of officeholders and party leaders. They are concerned with repealing the iron law of oligarchy as described by Michels, and for his reasons: unless party leaders are responsive to the party rank and file, they will be corrupted by the rewards of office and compromised by their participation in the government.[30] They are aware, as Schlesinger has observed, that as a party comes close to power, it tends to be dominated by the officeseekers; once in power, it will tend to be controlled by its officeholders.[31] Maurice Duverger noted this process in European mass parties: unlike the traditional "caucus of notables" party that has virtually no bureaucracy, the mass parties, such as the German Social Democrats, tend to proliferate a large paid staff and as they win legislative seats to acquire members with dual loyalties (to the parliament as well as to the party).[32]

The concern for policy implies a concern for mechanisms, such as intraparty democracy, to ensure that the correct policy is followed. In addition, a chance to participate in making decisions is in itself an important incentive for the members of amateur clubs. Fascist and Bolshevik mass parties, of course, reject internal democracy in favor of either the "leadership principle" or "democratic centralism," by which is meant "centralism." These parties are unlike truly ideological or amateur groupings in that they are strongly power oriented: the prospects for winning power and the social solidarity to be found within the ranks of the would-be powerful are probably more important as incentives than doctrinal refinement or immediate policies.

John W. Soule and James W. Clarke, in a study of delegates to the 1968 Democratic National Convention, found that political amateurs, that is, those with a strong desire for programmatic, internally democratic, uncompromising parties, were not strikingly different from party professionals on matters of public policy, a fact that suggests that a purposive attitude toward party involvement can be characteristic of either liberals or conservatives. In contrast, a study of amateur and professional party groups in Columbus, Ohio, suggests that the content of a member's political views is more important than merely his amateur role in explaining why he remains in a particular kind of political club: the amateurs were more liberal, the professionals more conservative.[33]

In a study of party activists in the heavily amateur Democratic and Republican parties in Los Angeles in 1956, Dwaine Marvick and Charles Nixon found that almost two-thirds of the Democratic activists thought themselves more liberal, and nearly half of the Republican activists saw themselves as more conservative, than their nonactivist friends. In each case, however, the activists said their political views were about the same as those of their fellow workers. Perhaps "a distinct factor leading people to become active workers is their desire to find a group with whom they are in ideological accord, thus relieving the tension they feel with their daily associates."[34]

The club basis of amateur politics, like the branch and cell basis of Marxist politics, is essential to organizational maintenance. Some persons, of course, will join as individuals, contributing money by mail and receiving campaign instructions by phone or letter. But for many, the contact with like-minded persons in local meetings is essential if they are to be mobilized for even routine tasks. And of course the meetings provide occasions to supplement purpose with other incentives, such as sociability, contact with celebrities, and various games and amusements.

The organizations created by both amateur and ideologue suffer from comparable maintenance problems. Though many may join an amateur club or a socialist party branch, only a small fraction are likely to value the rewards of affiliation so strongly, or to seek the more personal benefits of office and influence sufficiently, that they will be very active in the organization. Thus, low turnout and high turnover are problems in both kinds of political parties.[35] In addition, ideological parties and amateur clubs are alike in their reluctance to vest discretionary authority in their leaders; while this increases the accountability of the leaders to the followers, it decreases their capacity to make timely and flexible appeals to the general electorate or to negotiate useful alliances with other groups. Those leaders who succeed in winning office often are not able to reconcile their competing obligations to electorate and to party and thus are either defeated by the former or repudiated by the latter. Partially offsetting these problems is the fact that, to the extent there exists a segment of the electorate disenchanted with the conventional political candidates, the zeal, honesty, and commitment to principle of the purposive politician exercises a strong appeal.

There is conflicting evidence as to whether the most active purposive politician is also ideologically the most committed or extreme. On the one hand, persons rising in influence in an amateur club or a Marxist party are likely to be those who have a talent for getting people to work together, who must grapple with, and thus appreciate, the difficulties of maintaining the organization and managing relations with other political groupings, and who are personally attracted by the selective rewards of office and status. Perhaps for these reasons, Marvick and Nixon found that the more prominent Democratic party workers in Los Angeles had policy views which they felt were about the same as those of other workers, whereas the rank-and-file members felt they were more liberal than their fellows. "It would appear that volunteers with relatively moderate views were able to gain power in the Democratic party organization." [36]

By contrast, Samuel H. Barnes reports in his study of a local branch of the Italian Socialist party in the province of Arezzo that the proportion of "militants" (defined as those who attended the most party meetings and did the most party work) giving ideological responses to political questions was larger by a factor of two or three than the proportion of nominal or marginal members giving such responses. The nominal members, by contrast, were much more likely to discuss politics in terms of personalities.[37]

These findings may be reconciled and made part of a larger theory of organizational life if those who belong are divided into members, militants, and officers. The *member* is induced to join by the persuasion of a friend, by a concern for a particular issue, or out of a weak sense of duty. He only occasionally attends meetings, primarily those addressed by celebrities or at which major issues are fought out. It is difficult to motivate him to work. He sees politics in terms of "good guys" versus "bad guys" and interprets events in terms of a general political position, not in the light of a coherent or elaborate political philosophy.

The *militant* is powerfully attracted to the cause, joins out of ideological, or at least strong, convictions, and attends meetings frequently. He works at party tasks and also speaks out, sometimes at great length, at party gatherings. He has considerable knowledge of politics, follows events closely, has a strong sense of personal efficacy, and insists that the party do what is right and not what is expedient. He may antagonize other militants who disagree with him or who see him as a rival for influence within the party. Some will become officers, but typically as board members or in other posts where their views will be represented but where essential executive tasks need not be performed.

The *officer* is an active participant in the organization, but he is more concerned that work of the organization gets done than that a single point of view prevails. He has been selectively recruited from among those known to be committed to the party and is one with whom others find it easy to get along. He is in touch with nonparty groups and must take their pressures into account in making his decisions. He discusses organizational work in nonideological terms, lamenting more the apathy than the naiveté of the average member.

Barnes notes of the Italian Socialist party that the party secretaries, unlike the militants, have a "pragmatic, nonideological approach to politics." [38] They take the longer view, knowing from personal experience that the revolution may be farther in the future than the militants suppose. The principal constraints on the activity of the officer are the views and challenges of the militants. It is to this group that the officer must answer (except in centralized Bolshevik parties), and it is from this group that potential rivals will emerge. The rank-and-file members are the resource over which a muted competition proceeds. If a militant can find a dramatic issue or an apparent error on which to capitalize, he might be able to mobilize enough members to either depose or powerfully constrain the officer. By the same token, if a militant makes a premature or imprudent challenge to an officer, the latter can appeal successfully to the members for a reaffirmation of their support.

Solidary Parties

Though the machine, the ideological party, and the amateur club dominate scholarly accounts of the organization of local parties, the commonest organizational form is in fact none of these. Though we have no survey on this score, it is likely that the majority of persons who are active members of local party organizations seek neither material benefits nor the achievement of large ends, but merely find politics—or at least coming together in groups to work at politics—intrinsically enjoyable. Collective solidary incentives are important to some extent in all political organizations, including the machine and the Communist cell, but they are the dominant incentive in many, if not most, local parties.

In a study of 118 members of Democratic ward and township organizations in St. Louis County, Robert H. Salisbury found that almost no one mentioned issues as the reason for joining; most cited instead their desire, at least initially, to help a particular candidate they knew. About three-fifths gave the influence of friends and family as the cause of their participation.[39] In Detroit, Samuel J. Eldersveld found that about 75 percent of the Democratic precinct leaders and about 55 percent of the Republican ones mentioned social contacts, political fun, and the pleasure of being on the inside as the chief attractions of party work. Only 3 percent of the Democrats, but 17 percent of the Republicans, mentioned issues. Furthermore, of those who began their party work with various impersonal motivations, such as a commitment to a candidate, most who remained as precinct leaders experienced a change toward more personal incentives of a largely nonmaterial sort.[40]

The political party is likely to be a valued source of camaraderie and friendship for groups that are not part of other solidary networks of equal or greater value. The member of a reform or liberal Democratic club is likely to be a young college graduate involved in a professional career who has many other organizational affiliations; politics, for him, may supplement his opportunities for sociability, but it is not likely to be the only or the primary opportunity.[41] The purposes of the club must be appealing if the club is to induce him to add it to his list of associations. By contrast, the person who joins a party because it is a small group of neighbors and provides a chance to work and gossip together often has few other associational contacts. Salisbury found in St. Louis that the average ward organization member is likely to be older, Catholic, poorly educated, and a long-time resident of both the neighborhood and the county; almost half were female. For them, politics is the chief associational activity, for over half were not active in any other organization.[42]

In Detroit, the typical precinct leader was Catholic, a blue-collar worker earning under $10,000 a year and with no more than a high school education, and a long-term resident of the area. Very few received any patronage in return for their work. Those workers chiefly interested in social contacts were concentrated among the low income, the blacks, and the elderly; those few who were interested in ideology were concentrated among the college educated; those who were disillusioned with political activity and were likely to abandon party work were concentrated among the higher income groups.[43]

The chief organizational consequence of collective solidary incentives is that to benefit from them one must be in a group setting. Some political work, such as addressing envelopes or discussing strategy, can be done in such a setting, but other political tasks, such as canvassing a precinct, cannot. Not surprisingly, predominately solidary party organizations are good at the former jobs but poor at the latter. Salisbury found that 87 percent of the St. Louis ward organization members attended meetings regularly—much higher than the proportion who attend purposive club meetings—but that over one-fourth performed no electioneering tasks.[44] The Detroit precinct leaders were not much more active—of the three political jobs of registering, canvassing, and bringing voters to the polls, only 17 percent of the leaders did all three, and only 38 percent did even two in the 1956 election.[45] It is possible that even this level of activity is better than that found in purposive clubs; members of solidary groups are more likely to be locals with strong neighborhood ties, and thus are more likely to derive some satisfactions from seeing old friends in the course of canvassing for votes. The political reformers are often newcomers to the area or perhaps live outside the area altogether.

Similarly, rewards that depend on group contact are not well suited to the purposes of personal discipline. A worker not doing his share of the canvassing cannot be fired from a job; he has no party job. Similarly, he cannot easily be fired from the club, because expelling him would arouse the enmity of his friends in the organization and would be taken as a sign of disloyalty on the part of the leader toward an old ally. Many of the Tammany clubs in Manhattan whose candidates were defeated by reformers had, except for a few members, long since ceased to be machines; they were solidary associations of old cronies who now lacked the motivation to take on the purposive amateurs in a serious political fight.[46]

The active members of solidary party organizations are likely to be those who derive additional satisfactions from politics beyond sociability. In Detroit, for example, only one-fourth of the members of the executive board of the Democratic party mentioned solidary benefits as a reason for their participation; one-half mentioned issues, ideology, or other moral satisfactions and one-fourth cited the opportunities for material gain.[47] It is, of course, hard to know how much confidence to place in such answers; people do not always state, and may not even know, their true motives. After all, the higher officials in the party had accepted these jobs, and may well have worked hard to get them; the specific solidary rewards of status and power are likely to have played some part in these decisions. Stated another way, the satisfactions derived from playing the game of politics will be greater for those who play in the more important positions, where information is more abundant, contacts with higher-level politicians more frequent, and decisions of greater consequence are made.

Whatever the precise contours of their motives, those occupying the leading positions in party activity must face the problem of reassuring the rank and file that their motives and ambitions are not incompatible with the best interests of the group. This may on occasion be a delicate matter, because, as the Detroit study makes clear, the more active, higher-ranking party officials will tend to be those with the strongest commitment to the party, whereas the less active, lower-ranking ones will be those most disillusioned about political work and party life. Disillusionment about an organization is often expressed as cynicism concerning its leaders.

There are a variety of methods by which ambition and group affiliation can be reconciled. One is to appear reluctant to accept higher office, requiring others to talk one into it; another is to develop a personal following in the group by bestowing attention, favors, and flattery on colleagues; a third is to reveal extrapersonal reasons for seeking higher office, such as the need to defeat a visible enemy or to serve a larger cause; a fourth is to be so popular that neither envy nor malice can find expression.

Which strategy is adopted will depend partly on the kinds of constraints and suspicions a leader faces. In an ideological party or an amateur club, the realities of leadership are likely, as was stated earlier, to temper and render more pragmatic the views of those in leadership positions. Such persons are thus exposed to the charge of the militants that they have sold out or are compromising. Militants are ready to charge, as a former president of the California Democratic club movement ruefully put it, that the "volunteer type quickly acquires the habits of the professional without acquiring his means of livelihood." [48] Leaders in such clubs must constantly reaffirm their commitment to the principles of reform, liberalism, conservatism, or whatever. In a solidary party organization, the leaders are likely to be men and women who take politics and political issues *more* seriously than their followers. They will rarely be ideologues, but they obviously see politics as something more than an opportunity to meet friends and exchange gossip. Their problem will be to energize the rank and file and to do so in a way that does not weaken the solidary attractions of club life. As a result, they are, paradoxically, likely to be criticized for injecting "politics" into a political organization.

The differences in constraints felt by leaders in these two kinds of party organizations are similar to the differences Ernst Troeltsch found in the priesthood in sects and churches. In a sect, the communicants are more devoted than the priests and indeed resist the notion of a priesthood at all, believing instead in the priesthood of all believers. In a church, the priests are more militant than the communicants and must continuously strive to arouse them by sermons and sacraments.[49]

The differing incentive systems in solidary party organizations as opposed to purposive ones as well as the differing relationships between leaders and workers in each kind of party are probably responsible for the distinctive patterns of conflict in each kind. Few parties, and indeed few large organizations of any kind, are monolithic structures free of disagreement and faction. Indeed, parties, being voluntary associations, are especially likely to be a coalition of subgroups that operate in uneasy alliance with one another. Eldersveld's study of the Detroit Democratic and Republican parties stressed the number of factions in each party, and of course factionalism has been rife in the ideological and amateur organizations.

In a solidary party, however, the basis of cleavage into factions is likely to be along lines of group identity and ethnic, areal, and economic interest, whereas in purposive parties the cleavage will be expressed in terms of ideological differences. As one Detroit party leader put it:

In our district we have a Polish section, a Negro section, a Jewish section, and any number of smaller groups. I have to be a jack of all trades. My job is to get as many people in these groups happy as I can and see that they get the votes out.[50]

In the reform clubs of New York, on the other hand, cleavages were rarely described in ethnic or economic terms; indeed, the reform club members tended to be similar in their personal characteristics. Rather, the cleavages were between the regular and the insurgent clubs, between the West Side militants and the East Side moderates, between the compromisers and the purists, and between those concerned with principle and those with power.

The stronger the collective solidary benefits stemming from membership in a local party unit, the greater the likelihood of conflict among units. These benefits will be most valued in a situation of social and cultural homogeneity—that is to say, group bonds will be the strongest when the members are alike one another in age, class, schooling, ethnicity, and religion, and weakest when the members are different in these respects. And obviously in a heterogeneous city, the more alike the members of one party unit are, the more they will be unlike the members of other units.[51] Thus, no one should assume that because solidary incentives arise out of the pleasure of association that the larger associations thereby created are always pleasurable or harmonious. And when one adds to the conflicts between different solidary groups the tensions created by the presence of purposively oriented and money-oriented members, it is evident that the executive task of maintaining a solidary party is not much easier than that of maintaining any other kind.

Trends and Consequences

The value of material incentives to political parties has declined, and, as a consequence, the value of solidary and purposive ones has increased. There are fewer jobs and contracts that can be awarded on purely political grounds and fewer people for whom at least low-paying jobs are attractive. This has led, as frequently noted, to the decline of machines and the rise of party organizations relying, at least for the rank and file, on nonmaterial rewards. In many of these organizations, the candidate himself and his chief campaign aides still are attracted to politics as a vocation: if successful, they will win paying jobs, while their followers must be content with either the fun of the game, the sense of victory, or devotion to the cause.

Among these forms are not only reform or amateur clubs but candidate organizations—that is, groups mobilized by, and personally loyal to, a single candidate or to a small group of closely allied candidates. These personal followings are similar to many amateur clubs with two important differences—they have an intermittent, rather than continuous, existence, and the distribution of authority, at least at the highest level, is not an issue. Because these followings come into being only at campaign time, they do not face the same problem of organizational maintenance as do institutional clubs; because they are led by the candidate himself, struggle for office is replaced by struggle for access to the candidate's ear and favor.

The chief consequences of these trends have been a change in the process of candidate selection and in the nature of electoral appeals. Party organizations composed of persons motivated by material rewards have a strong interest in winning an election, for only then will their rewards be secured. Provided there are competitive parties, candidates, at least at the top of the ticket, will be selected and electoral appeals fashioned so as to attract votes from the largest possible number of citizens. When the organization consists of members motivated by purposive rewards, the candidate selected must be one that can attract their enthusiasm, even if he cannot attract voter support, and the appeals issued must be consistent with their preferences, even if voters find them repugnant. Personal followings occupy an intermediate position. Unlike the machine-style organization, the support of the followers cannot easily be transferred to a candidate other than one to whom they have given their loyalty; unlike amateur clubs, the followers will not be as inclined to insist on doctrinal orthodoxy.

NOTES

1. Robert D. Marcus, *Grand Old Party: Political Structure in the Gilded Age, 1880–1896* (New York: Oxford University Press, 1971), pp. 138, 252.

2. Edward C. Banfield and James Q. Wilson, *City Politics* (Cambridge, Mass.: Harvard University Press, 1963), chap. 9.

3. James C. Scott, "Corruption, Machine Politics, and Political Change," *American Political Science Review*, LXIII (December 1969), 1142–1158.

4. James Reichley, *The Art of Government: Reform and Organization Politics in Philadelphia* (New York: Fund for the Republic, 1959), pp. 24n., 102n.

5. James Q. Wilson, "The Economy of Patronage," *Journal of Political Economy*, LXIX (August 1961), 372.

6. Daniel Patrick Moynihan and James Q. Wilson, "Patronage in New York State, 1955–1959," *American Political Science Review*, LVIII (June 1964), 289.

7. James Q. Wilson, *The Amateur Democrat: Club Politics in Three Cities* (Chicago: University of Chicago Press, 1962), p. 203.

8. Samuel J. Eldersveld, *Political Parties: A Behavioral Analysis* (Chicago: Rand McNally, 1964), p. 275.

9. Frank J. Sorauf, "State Patronage in a Rural County," *American Political Science Review*, L (December 1956), 1048–1050.

10. Wilson, *The Amateur Democrat*, p. 205.

11. Phillips Cutright, "Activities of Precinct Committeemen in Partisan and Non-partisan Communities," *Western Political Quarterly*, XVII (March 1964), 93–107.

12. Edward C. Banfield, *Political Influence* (New York: Free Press, 1961), pp. 245–248; Zane Miller, *Boss Cox's Cincinnati* (New York: Oxford University Press, 1968); Lyle Dorsett, *The Pendergast Machine* (New York: Oxford University Press, 1967).

13. Wilson, *The Amateur Democrat*, pp. 156–163.

14. Daniel Bell, *Marxian Socialism in the United States* (Princeton, N.J.: Princeton University Press, 1952, 1967), p. x.

15. Quoted in ibid., p. 8.

16. Ibid., pp. 53–54.

17. Ibid., pp. 9–10. See also Karl Mannheim, *Ideology and Utopia* (New York: Harcourt Brace Harvest Book, n.d.), pp. 239–247.

18. Bell, *Marxian Socialism*, pp. 81–82.

19. Ibid., p. 71.

20. Robert L. Morlan, *Political Prairie Fire: The Nonpartisan League, 1915–1922* (Minneapolis: University of Minnesota Press, 1955), pp. 22–46, 87–91, 346–355.

21. A good firsthand account of the encampments, enlivened by a sense of humor rare in socialist memoirs, is Oscar Ameringer, *If You Don't Weaken* (New York: Holt, 1940), pp. 263–267, 347–355.

22. Bell, *Marxian Socialism*, p. 79.

23. Irving Howe and Lewis Coser, *The American Communist Party* (Boston: Beacon Press, 1957), pp. 27–28, 42–43, 103; Theodore Draper, *The Roots of American Communism* (New York: Viking Press, 1957), pp. 188–193. Draper estimates that East European language groups accounted for 75 percent of the Communist party membership in 1919; only 10 percent of the members were English speaking.

24. Bell, *Marxian Socialism*, p. 114; Howe and Coser, *The American Communist Party*, pp. 82–85; Philip Selznick, *The Organizational Weapon* (New York: Free Press, 1960), pp. 61–62.

25. Gabriel Almond, *The Appeals of Communism* (Princeton, N.J.: Princeton University Press, 1954).

26. Selznick, *The Organizational Weapon*, chap. 1, esp. p. 24.

27. One estimate of American Communist party membership during the 1930s and 1940s suggests that the turnover was as high as 90 percent per year. On the basis of interviews with 300 former Communists, Ernst and Koth concluded that the "peak age" for joining was between eighteen and twenty-three but that a majority had left the party by the time they were twenty-three. Morris Ernst and David Koth, *Report on the American Communist* (New York: Henry Holt, 1952), pp. 2–4. See also Seymour Martin Lipset and Everett Carll Ladd, Jr., "College Generations—From the 1930's to the 1960's," *The Public Interest* (Fall 1971), p. 105.

28. Howe and Coser, *The American Communist Party*, pp. 530–536, 542–548.

29. Wilson, *The Amateur Democrat*, pp. 2–13.

30. Robert Michels, *Political Parties*, trans. Eden and Cedar Paul (New York: Free Press, 1958).

31. Joseph A. Schlesinger, "Political Party Organization," in *Handbook of Organizations*, ed. James G. March (Chicago: Rand McNally, 1965), p. 767.

32. Maurice Duverger, *Political Parties* (New York: John Wiley, 1959), pp. 154, 182–190.

33. John W. Soule and James W. Clarke, "Amateurs and Professionals: A Study of Delegates to the 1968 Democratic National Convention," *American Political Science Review*, LXIV (September 1970), 894–895; C. Richard Hofstetter, "Organizational Activists: The Bases of Participation in Amateur and Professional Groups" (paper delivered to the American Political Science Association, 1972).

34. Dwaine Marvick and Charles R. Nixon, "Recruitment Contrasts in Rival Campaign Groups," in *Political Decision-Makers*, ed. Dwaine Marvick (New York: Free Press, 1961), pp. 212–213. In a national study, David Nexon found that Republican activists tended to have much more conservative views than Republican voters and that this difference could not be explained by demographic factors, that is, by the fact that Republican activists had higher incomes or more education than Republicans generally. The Republican party, Nexon concluded, recruited proportionately more amateur activists than the Democratic party did. This was, of course, prior to

117

the McGovern candidacy in 1972. Nexon, "Asymmetry in the Political System," *American Political Science Review*, LXV (September 1971), 716–730. See also Herbert McClosky et al., "Issue Conflict and Consensus Among Party Leaders and Followers," *American Political Science Review*, LIV (June 1960), 406–427.

35. Wilson, *The Amateur Democrat*, pp. 226–232; Howe and Coser, *The American Communist Party*, pp. 224–226.

36. Marvick and Nixon, "Recruitment Contrasts," pp. 213–214.

37. Samuel H. Barnes, "Party Democracy and the Logic of Collective Action," in *Approaches to the Study of Party Organization*, ed. William J. Crotty (Boston: Allyn and Bacon, 1968), p. 123.

38. Ibid., p. 131.

39. Robert H. Salisbury, "The Urban Party Organization Member," *Public Opinion Quarterly*, XXIX (Winter 1965–1966), 550–564.

40. Eldersveld, *Political Parties*, pp. 278, 287.

41. Wilson, *The Amateur Democrat*, pp. 13–16.

42. Salisbury, "The Urban Party," p. 557.

43. Eldersveld, *Political Parties*, pp. 296–297.

44. Salisbury, "The Urban Party," pp. 557, 559.

45. Eldersveld, *Political Parties*, p. 350.

46. Wilson, *The Amateur Democrat*, pp. 312–316.

47. Eldersveld, *Political Parties*, p. 278.

48. Wilson, *The Amateur Democrat*, p. 171.

49. Ernst Troeltsch, *The Social Teachings of the Christian Churches* (New York: Harper Torchbooks, 1960), vol. I, pp. 338–340. The original German edition was published in 1911.

50. Eldersveld, *Political Parties*, p. 76.

51. Ibid., pp. 89–97, analyzes the subcultural variation in local party identification.

CHAPTER 7

Labor Unions

Because a labor union is an organization that seeks to enroll most or all of the workers in a plant or industry and to become their permanent representative, it faces in extreme form the general problem of developing an incentive system adequate to its maintenance. A political party, by contrast, need be no more than a small caucus that can control the use of a party label and attract voters to a particular candidate; it is under no necessity to make all or most voters members of the party in any meaningful sense. And a civic association, though it no doubt would like to attract as members many more citizens than it does, can survive and pursue its objectives with the support of only those few in the community who are responsive to its nonmaterial incentives. If a labor union could survive merely by enrolling those few workers who were willing to join out of a sense of duty or a feeling of comradeship, it would be little different from other voluntary associations with similar inducements. But for a union to supply material benefits, in the form of negotiated wage increases or adjusted grievances, to any of its actual members, it is necessary that it first obtain votes and dues payments from most or all of its prospective members. It is as if the NAACP, before it could file suit on behalf of a single Negro, had first to obtain the consent of 51 percent of all Negroes.

To maintain a union organization that has been established as the bargaining agent of the workers in a plant or industry, union leaders in the United States rely chiefly on a device not ordinarily available to other voluntary associations—a union security agreement. This is a legal or contractual stipulation requiring that a worker in a plant pay union dues if he wishes to remain a worker.[1] Such an agreement, creating what is called a union shop, is obviously a form of coercion, though a form that the vast majority of workers willingly accept, and thus to this extent a trade union is not strictly a voluntary association at all. From the very earliest efforts at organizing, unions have sought such security agreements. John R. Commons, in reflecting on the vast body of information that went into his four-volume history of labor in the United States, observed that if they had to choose, union organizers would invariably prefer getting a union shop to getting better wages and hours.[2] A careful review of the history of the union, or closed shop, concluded that "practically every trade union prior to the civil war was in favor of excluding non-members from employment." [3] This was also the conclusion of employers, for they directed their most concerted antiunion efforts not at combatting wage demands, but at fighting the union shop. Between 1829 and 1842, eight unions were prosecuted for conspiracy because of their attempts to limit access to the workplace to union members.[4] Massive antiunion drives were launched in 1900–1908 and again, following World War I, in 1920–1922 under the name "The American Plan." The chief target was the union-shop agreement.[5] A major legislative victory for organized labor was the Wagner Act of 1935, which made the union shop legal under federal law, so that contracts providing for the dismissal of employees who refused to join the union could no longer be challenged in court.[6]

Mancur Olson argues that "by far the most important single factor" enabling unions to grow beyond a small group of like-minded men "was that membership in these unions, and support of the strikes they called, was to a great degree compulsory." [7] Only in this way could workers who would benefit from whatever gains the unions achieved by way of better wages and hours be induced to contribute to the cost of obtaining those benefits. The union-shop contract is the method by which that compulsion, essential to the survival of most large unions, is secured.

But obviously unions must first exist before they can bargain for a union-shop agreement, and therefore they must somehow solve their short-term maintenance problems out of their own resources before they can compel the employer to assure the long-term maintenance of the union through contractual terms. Clearly, incentives other than legal compulsion are necessary at some stage in the life of every union, and for some unions that do not obtain exclusive bargaining rights and union-shop agreements these other incentives continue to be of decisive importance.

There are unions that exist, and some that have managed to thrive, without benefit of a union-shop agreement—the Patrolmen's Benevolent Association (PBA) among police officers, for example, or the United Federation of Teachers (UFT). There are even unions without exclusive bargaining rights. Admittedly they are the exception—about 75 percent of all unionized workers are covered by some type of union security agreement—but they are important ones.[8]

Furthermore, trade unions in many European countries exist on a large scale without either union security agreements or sole bargaining rights. In England, for example, only 16 percent of all workers and only 39 percent of unionized workers are employed under union-shop or closed-shop agreements.[9] No comparable survey of such agreements on the Continent is available, but a survey of the legal status of union security provisions in eight countries found that there the issue has not been that central to labor-management disputes or political agitation.[10] In the Netherlands, membership in the Dutch Federation of Trade Unions is entirely voluntary.[11]

The incentive systems of many European unions explain both why compulsory membership is not necessary and why many such unions oppose it. These unions rely in part on religious (Catholic or anti-Catholic) and ideological (Communist, Socialist, anti-Marxist) appeals to mobilize members. Given the religious and political differences that define, and even make possible, voluntary union membership, it would clearly be contrary to the interests of many unions to permit any given union to have exclusive bargaining rights or a union shop. The union winning a majority of the votes would, under the compulsory system, be able to destroy its rivals in an industry or plant, and thus could impose a religious or ideological tendency on the minority workers.

The incentive system employed by unions in their formative stages explains much of their subsequent style and history, especially the degree and kind of factionalism within them and their political activities. That unions display great diversity in such matters, despite the common interest which they exist to represent, is beyond dispute. For the first thirty or forty years of its history, the American Federation of Labor (AFL) and most of its affiliated unions opposed, in the name of voluntarism, certain forms of government intervention in labor-management affairs or indeed in the economy generally, even when the proposed legislation was aimed at improving the welfare of workers (as with minimum-wage or maximum-hour laws or unemployment insurance).[12] By contrast, the Congress of Industrial Organizations (CIO) and most of its affiliated unions favored from their inception sweeping legislative programs on behalf of workers. Today, a few unions, such as the United Auto Workers (UAW), the United Steelworkers (USW), and various garment unions, work actively toward broad legislative goals, whereas others, such as those in the postal service and the building trades, focus on specific union-related political objectives almost to the exclusion of larger issues.[13] At the local level, certain unions, such as the Building Service Employees (BSEIU), work closely with political parties, but others, such as the UFT, have bitterly fought them.

Some of these differences can be explained by the characteristics of the workers and the industrial structure of which they are part. Craft unions have generally recruited the more skilled, better-paid workers whereas industrial unions have organized lower-skill and lower-income employees. Some unions have large numbers of blacks and other minorities; others are virtually all white. But not all political differences can be accounted for in this way. There are many blacks in the postal and building service employee's unions, but neither of these has displayed the same general interest in civil rights laws as has the UAW. Both the Amalgamated Meat Cutters and the Packinghouse Workers serve the meatpacking industry and enroll similar members, but the former (once in the AFL) has been less aggressive in national politics than the latter (once in the CIO).[14] Miners have been organized at one time or another into unions of almost every conceivable political hue: the United Mine Workers (UMW), led by conservative John L. Lewis; the Western Federation of Miners (WFM), frequently under Socialist leadership and in 1905 one of the organizing parties of the Industrial Workers of the World (IWW), and the National Miners' Union (NMU), dominated by Communists.

A complete account of these and other features of trade unionism, especially one that explained the differences between American and European varieties, would draw importantly on an analysis of the distinctive ethos of the American worker, the characteristics of the economy, and the structure of government. For now, we shall take the distinctive attitudes of American workers and the structure of industry and government as given and ask how, or by what alternative means, unions in their formative stages adapt to these conditions so as to create a viable organization. The incentive system of the union, to put the matter technically, will be regarded as the intervening variable between what is attitudinally or structurally given and what the organization in fact does. If this were a comparative study of unions in many countries, these given factors might well be the most important ones for explanatory purposes. But within one country, the incentive system assumes major importance, because it is the only aspect of the situation subject to direct organizational control—the union leader may wish that his members were more, or less, class conscious or that the government was more, or less, centralized, but he can do little about such matters.

There are several kinds of incentives that a union in its formative stages or one lacking a union-shop agreement can employ to attract and hold members. Perhaps the most important is the sense of purposeful solidarity directed against a common enemy that every union organizer desires to achieve. Rousing men to act in concert toward economic ends is not done merely by making an oratorical appeal to an audience of workers. It requires the incessant cultivation of men in face-to-face and small-group contacts so that the beliefs of one are reinforced by the convictions of all. This mobilization is made easier when the men who are its objects are not divided by important differences in location, skill, income, religion, or ethnicity—when, in short, they are sufficiently alike to value one another's esteem and thus to follow one another's expectations. It is this factor, rather than some general predisposition to favor the more advantaged workers engaged in small-shop crafts, that accounts for the fact that so many of the early examples of successful unionization were characterized by the organization of workers practicing a single skill in small shops for roughly the same wage. As late as 1932, the AFL was composed of 26,352 locals claiming about 2.5 million members, or less than 100 members per local.[15]

The possibility of forming a bond of purposeful solidarity was enhanced when, in addition to similarities in skill, the workers were alike ethnically and isolated geographically or occupationally. Cigar makers were frequently German Jews who worked together around a table while someone read to them from political or philosophical tracts. Typographers often work at night and sleep by day and were thus thrown into one another's company for such social life as they might enjoy.[16] Miners, both those in the western copper mines organized into the International Union of Mine, Mill, and Smelter Workers and those in the Pennsylvania anthracite coal fields organized by the UMW, engage in hazardous work and live in small communities composed almost entirely of other miners. On the other hand, isolation and common ethnicity, though they make the development of a viable incentive system easier, did not ensure it. For example, lumberjacks as late as the 1930s had proved themselves utterly resistant to AFL organizing efforts.[17]

An additional incentive to members was material—not the prospect of future wage gains, but the promise of death, unemployment, old-age, or disability benefits. As Olson notes, the first viable large union in Great Britain was the Amalgamated Society of Engineers, established in 1851, and it offered a wide range of benefits covering many forms of personal distress.[18] In 1931, only 15 of the 105 national unions in the AFL did not offer some benefits and of these, 3 were organizations of government employees covered by public retirement and insurance programs. The most common material incentive was the death benefit, usually $100 to $500, paid out of the dues collected from members. Forty-six unions also had sick-pay benefits, thirty had unemployment benefits, and so on. In 1931, AFL unions paid their members over $23 million in benefits, or an average of nearly ten dollars per member; considering that the average dues assessment was between twelve and eighteen dollars a year, the members were getting back on the average a substantial fraction of what they were paying in.[19] Indeed, in some unions so generous were the payments and so lacking in a grasp of insurance principles were the officers that when the membership rolls fell in a recession, there was not enough money in the treasury to cover the union's obligations.

Today, of course, a few unions, such as Teamster's Local 688 in St. Louis and Local 3 of the International Brotherhood of Electrical Workers in New York City, offer a vast and expensive array of educational programs, scholarships, medical and dental care, and resort facilities for their members. These may or may not make the union more attractive to potential members, but they differ from the earlier benefit programs of small unions in that only a very large local—and thus one with firm union security guarantees—can afford to sponsor such costly programs.[20]

The consequences for political action of the incentive system employed by the early craft unions are not hard to imagine. The small craft-based principle of organization, made necessary by, among other things, the kinds of appeals useful in mobilizing workers, led to the development of a pattern of many small locals, each with a modest jurisdiction. Just as such locals were preoccupied economically with local work conditions, so they were concerned politically with licensing regulations and local court and police behavior. National legislative issues were of only secondary concern, and often of no concern at all. Furthermore, treating the AFL unions as part of a single political coalition was extremely difficult inasmuch as there was no way to prevent various locals from making their own alliances with whatever party was in power locally.

The doctrine of "voluntarism" enunciated by Samuel Gompers reflected not only his distrust of government intervention in labor-management affairs (a distrust he thought well supported by the record of police, army, and court efforts to break strikes) but also his canny understanding of the nature of the incentive system that fledgling unions struggling for security had at their disposal. Gompers spoke often of the need to protect on principle the "freedom of the workers to strike and struggle for their own emancipation through their own efforts." [21] But an AFL vice president, John P. Frey, suggested that the struggle for union recognition and better wages was itself an important incentive for the maintenance of local organizations, an incentive whose value might be threatened if the government by legislative action provided higher pay and shorter hours:

If you feed lions cooked meat, they are not going to roar. If you want the lions to roar you will have to hold raw meat under their noses and then they will roar. The only way to get wage-earners interested in the trade-union movement and to make it a driving force is to convince them that . . . it is only through the . . . fighting strength of economic organization that you are going to get higher wages and shorter hours.[22]

Should the AFL under Gompers have wished to pursue a national legislative strategy, it would not have had the organizational resources with which to act. The staff of the national AFL for many years consisted only of Gompers and the Federation secretary, who were paid, in 1898, $1,800 and $1,000, respectively.[23] The AFL was built on the principle of individual union autonomy, Gomper's leadership was personal more than bureaucratic, and almost all the money that national headquarters had went to hire field organizers to help form new unions.[24]

The political and legislative activities that were undertaken by the AFL in its early years were responsive to its organizational needs rather than expressive of any broad social philosophy. Perhaps the most important political objective was to obtain passage of an anti-injunction bill so that strikes and organizing drives could not be broken by court action. A small step in this direction was taken in 1914 with the passage of the Clayton Act that exempted trade unions from the antitrust laws and a larger one in 1932 with the passage of the Norris-LaGuardia Act, which outlawed "yellow-dog contracts" (ones in which workers agree not to join a union) and made organizing efforts and strikes immune from injunctive attack.[25]

Simultaneously, the local unions comprising the AFL sought to control the supply of labor and the rules governing access to the skilled trades. "The major part of a union's work," wrote Lorwin, "is to extend the area of its control over jobs and to exercise control over the supply of labor so as to be able to find jobs for all its members." [26] In many AFL unions, strict apprenticeship regulations were important means for developing that control, and thus local political action to obtain state laws or city ordinances giving legal status to these regulations was often undertaken.

Nationally, the objective of reducing the labor supply so as to ensure jobs for those already at work was sought through the AFL's efforts to restrict immigration into the United States. Because a large portion of all union members were themselves immigrants, this was in some ways a difficult position for the organization to take; by the same token, no action more clearly demonstrates the importance of organizational imperatives over political philosophy. In 1897, the AFL convention voted for the first time in favor of restriction, and that position was repeated and strengthened in 1906, 1912, 1918, and indeed, well into the 1920s.[27]

The exclusion of Negroes from AFL locals to a substantial degree reflected antiblack attitudes prevalent among white, especially southern, workers. But even if racial prejudice had played no part in their views, AFL leaders in all likelihood would have followed substantially the same course of action. The black workers were typically the lowest paid, the least skilled, and those with the highest unemployment rate. Their entry in large numbers into the skilled-labor market would have depressed wage levels and, what to the AFL was worse, would have provided a pool of workers upon which employers could draw in order to replace those on strike. The black worker was an especially visible representative of what the unions term "scabs." Furthermore, bringing black workers into white locals, at least during their formative years, would have been to introduce an element of social heterogeneity that would have reduced the solidary incentives of union membership. Finally, the admission of any new workers into an organized craft, whether they be white or black, would have increased the supply of workers without increasing the supply of jobs and weakened the capacity of certain craft locals to restrict access to new jobs to a few carefully selected apprentices, often drawn from among the sons of present journeymen. Accordingly, while the AFL nationally expressed a pro forma commitment to racial equality, after 1901 international unions were accepted for affiliation even though they constitutionally barred nonwhite workers from membership; encouragement was given to the formation of all-Negro locals as a way of meeting their organizational interests. Little serious organizing activity went on among blacks, however. Black workers, especially those who came north after World War I and during World War II, increasingly sought employment in the mass production industries.[28]

The exclusion policy that was easy to follow when the supply of workers was large relative to the number of jobs became harder to sustain when a tight labor market developed. Employers during World War II greatly increased their hiring of blacks in order to fill vacancies, and these employees then automatically entered the union under the terms of the union security agreement. At the same time, leaders of certain all-black unions, such as A. Philip Randolph of the Brotherhood of Sleeping Car Porters, rose to prominence in the AFL and eventually gained seats on the executive council. As a result of these pressures, coupled with civil rights laws, the number of unions expressly barring Negroes from membership fell from twenty-seven in 1930 to fourteen in 1943 to none in 1964.[29] Such exclusionary policies as remained were enforced informally and by acts of omission rather than commission.

The early organizational experiences of the CIO were quite different. When men with a variety of skills, pay levels, and ethnic antecedents are to be organized, and organized in large numbers, it is difficult to rely either on material or on solidary incentives. In a large, diverse industrial work force with a high employee-turnover rate, attempting to create a union organization along the lines of a fraternal association providing small-group camaraderie or an insurance society offering death and unemployment benefits would have been futile. Diversity is the enemy of solidarity, and unstable employment levels would have quickly bankrupted any insurance scheme. Furthermore, in industries where large numbers of unskilled or semiskilled workers were employed, it would be exceptionally difficult for a union to gain control of the hiring process—the union could not claim it had skills to teach by apprenticeship programs, and the employer would be manifestly under the economic necessity of laying off large numbers of workers when business was poor and hiring large numbers when it was good. Finally, in many industrial firms, the manufacturing process was not organized around the shop unit; it was instead organized around the assembly line. The shop unit—for example, of clothing workers or of machinists—was a setting in which informal social organization could become quite strong, and thus was one in which union organization could find a social base; furthermore, in the shop, work and production levels could be set informally by the social structure developed there. An assembly line or any other continuous-flow process, by contrast, discouraged social inter-action and hence informal social organization, and production levels were set more by the rate at which the line moved than by any informal agreement among workers.

In these industrial settings, a very different organizing strategy would be necessary, one that could unite men despite the social and economic barriers that separated them and one that in addition could motivate them to direct action despite the large numbers involved and the contin-gent nature of the gains expected. By and large, only purposive incen-tives, powerfully articulated and made highly salient to the workers, would suffice. The would-be union members had to be aroused by emo-tionally charged and comprehensive appeals to their lot as a dispos-sessed class. The employer would not, as with craft organizing drives, be charged merely with particular grievances, but with systematic exploita-tion. The plight of the individual workers would have to be set into the larger context of group or class subjugation.

The industrial unions that appeared before the emergence of the CIO and its successful organizing drives of the 1930s tended to rely on class-oriented purposive appeals. The Western Federation of Miners (WFM), created in 1895, embraced the full range of skills in the copper mines and smelters and soon found itself locked in bitter and often bloody struggles with employers at Leadville, Coeur d'Alene, and Cripple Creek, battles that in the end the union lost. Remnants of the WFM, to-gether with other industrial unions, met in Chicago in 1905 to form the Industrial Workers of the World (IWW). Instead of the AFL slogan of a "fair day's wage for a fair day's work," the IWW called for "abolition of the wage system." [30] Socialist and anarchist thought deeply influenced IWW language and action, and of the 150 strikes led by it, many were intense, violent struggles. The charismatic style of William "Big Bill" Haywood was a vital element in achieving IWW leadership of local strike activities, but this mercurial leadership and its ideological ap-peals, combined with the itinerant and often unemployed character of much of the membership, meant that the IWW was never able to estab-lish a stable organization structure. Indeed, organization and collective agreements were anathema to many of the more militant Wobblies (IWW members), and their rejection of a wage-bargaining strategy meant that the union had great difficulty in establishing its position in any particu-lar industrial setting.

Other efforts to form industrial unions in low-skill industries also failed, broken by management counterattacks, from the Homestead strike of 1892 until well into the 1920s. The AFL offered little support to these efforts and, with respect to such industrial unions as did form, often granted affiliation only on condition that they reorganize along craft lines. To the AFL leadership, maintaining existing craft unions meant giving them the right to raid emerging industrial locals in order to enlist workers on the basis of skills.[31] After a prolonged controvery, the Committee for Industrial Organization (soon to become the Congress of Industrial Organizations, CIO) was expelled from the AFL in 1938 and took with it many of those AFL unions that had already developed an industrial form, particularly the UMW, the Amalgamated Clothing Workers, and the International Ladies' Garment Workers' Union (ILGWU).

Over the next few years, the CIO made impressive gains in organizing industrial workers, especially those in the steel, auto, and rubber industries. To explain this success, neither the CIO's newly won freedom from AFL restrictions nor its ability to impose closed-shop or union-shop agreements on employers will suffice. Few of the major industrial unions obtained during the early years of their existence a tight union security agreement with the employers because they did not have the bargaining power for so large an objective. A small craft union, enrolling all or virtually all the skilled workers available in an area can demand and get a closed shop; a large industrial union representing low-skill workers in an industry with rapid turnover in employment is in a weak position to obtain such a rule. Mancur Olson implies that coercive membership regulations are the "essence of unionism" and "the source of the union's membership." [32] And there can be little doubt that such organizational security has been the aim of industrial unions, as well as of all other kinds. But Olson is wrong if he means to suggest that no mass membership industrial union can survive for a significant period of time without such security agreements. There were no union-shop agreements in the contracts between the USW and United States Steel until 1956, and none in the contracts between the UAW and General Motors until 1950; only in the contract between the UAW and Ford, first signed in 1941, four years after the creation of the UAW, was the union shop and the automatic dues check-off accepted by management.[33] For several years, the steelworkers had to be content with the right to represent their own members only, not even being able to insist on the right to act as the exclusive bargaining agent for all employees.[34] As late as 1946 a Bureau of Labor Statistics survey showed that only about one-half of all unionized workers were covered by either closed-shop or union-shop agreements. By 1954, that proportion had risen to 65 percent.[35]

How, then, were the large industrial unions created? There were at least two alternative strategies, each leading to different formative experiences and thus each leading to different political styles. The steelworkers were organized, at least in the dominant United States Steel Corporation, by a process of centralized negotiation following a period of recruiting efforts by a large number of paid organizers.[36] The Steel Workers Organizing Committee (SWOC) was created, and dominated, by John L. Lewis and Philip Murray, both key leaders of the UMW. It was financed, between 1936 and 1942, not by dues collected from rank-and-file members, but by grants and loans from the UMW and the CIO totalling over $1.6 million. More than 150 full-time organizers and other staff workers were assigned the task of recruiting union members who would be charged no initiation fee and only one dollar a month in dues. All that was asked of the workers, apart from the modest dues, was that they vote for the SWOC in a representation election. Existing company unions were infiltrated and their leadership was captured on behalf of the SWOC. Complaints were filed before the National Labor Relations Board against company unions that would not cooperate, alleging unlawful company domination. Then, dramatically, the chairman of the board of United States Steel announced that he had agreed with Lewis to recognize the SWOC as the bargaining agent for its members, provided there would be no union shop or other form of membership coercion. There was no strike; indeed, at the time the SWOC was recognized, there was no single steelworkers' union in existence—what was later to become the USW emerged out of SWOC, itself ostensibly a coalition of existing small unions in the steel industry, but in fact the organizing arm of the CIO leadership. Though the SWOC underwent a bitter struggle with the "Little Steel" companies after their success with United States Steel, it never lost its character as a centrally led enterprise that succeeded by selling key management personnel as well as many steelworkers, though a minority of those employed in the industry, on the virtues of industrial unionism.

The UAW was born out of a quite different experience. There was no cadre of experienced or well-known outside organizers, and no large campaign fund. The money and the staff had to be supplied by rank-and-file union members. Nor were there any business executives willing to avoid conflict by recognizing the union; at General Motors and Ford, lengthy and sometimes violent sit-down strikes occurred.[37] The grassroots nature of UAW activity, the resistance of the employers, and the dramatic nature of the confrontations, all made auto organizing attractive to persons whose own political and ideological convictions were of a character and a strength sufficient to induce them to play key roles as unpaid activists. Many skilled radical leaders gravitated to Flint and Detroit in 1936–1938 and much of the subsequent history of the UAW can be understood only as part of a continuing struggle to either confirm or eliminate radical influence in the union. For the great majority of workers who joined the UAW, the incentive probably had less to do with the prospect for higher wages—average hourly earnings in the industry were as high or higher than earnings in other industries—and more with a desire to redress grievances and eliminate what they took to be the capricious or unjust impact of layoffs and speedups. Indeed, the initial demands of the UAW leadership made no mention of a wage increase at all. In short, the concerns of the average worker in the auto industry seemed to be of a character that not only made group action important in order to obtain collective bargaining but also made individual membership desirable in order that one's own grievances might receive a hearing and an adjustment. To some extent, the prospects for a grievance procedure provided an individual incentive (obviously, the union was not likely to process grievances on behalf of nonmembers) that supplemented the general sense of collective combat against an unyielding employer. The UAW settlement with General Motors in 1937 gave the union the right to bargain for its members, but not for nonmembers, and created a grievance system.

Between 1935 and 1945 there was great growth in union membership, and initially at least most of this growth took place among the industrial unions. Not all of these followed either the USW's or the UAW's strategies—some, such as the ILGWU, though industrial in the sense of representing all skills, were organized around the small shop—but all of them were able to take advantage of certain factors that made that growth possible even in the absence of written union security agreements.[38] Chief among these was the posture of the national government, which, first with Section 7-A of the National Industrial Recovery Act of 1933 and then with the Wagner Act of 1935, recognized the right of unions to organize, provided for election machinery to determine the bargaining agent, and required the employer to bargain with a duly recognized union. In addition, the Wagner Act made the closed shop legal (it was later made illegal by the Taft-Hartley Act of 1947) but not mandatory. Little of this was new; earlier enactments had contained many of the same provisions, at least with respect to certain industries. What was new was that labor organizers sensed, beginning in 1935 and certainly after Roosevelt's resounding electoral victory in 1936, that the national government was on their side. John L. Lewis, in rebuilding the

UMW from the low estate into which it had fallen by the early 1930s, plastered the mines with the slogan "The President Wants You to Join." [39] And management and the workers also recognized this government support for unions; the political legitimacy of large-scale unionization not only emboldened the organizers and disheartened their opponents, it magnified the incentives to each prospective member—he could see himself as part of a mass movement supported by his government and directed at a broad range of economic problems. Furthermore, rising levels of employment after 1935, and especially after the beginning of the war in 1941, made it easy for the unions to add new members and difficult or unrewarding for management to resist.

The war brought not only a tight labor market and thus new union members, it brought also various federal agencies—such as the Defense Mediation Board and the War Labor Board—that sought to minimize industrial strife by finding formulae that would adjust union-management differences. One such difference was over union security. The formula applied was the "maintenance-of-membership" rule—instead of granting the union shop to the unions or denying it on behalf of the employers, the federal boards ruled that all workers who were at that time (1942) members of a union would be required to remain members for the duration of the contract.[40]

Whether an industrial union was organized by elite appeals (as was the USW) or by mass action (as was the UAW) had a profound effect on the subsequent history of the association. The UAW has long had a tradition of internal factionalism; by 1954 it had changed its chief officers four times, and in 1963 one-third of all local officers were defeated in union elections. There have been frequent disputes over the social and political objectives and tactics of the UAW, but the general thrust of all factions has been to commit the union nationally to a strong position on legislative matters—indeed, it has partly been by outbidding rivals on the question of political militance that officers have been able to maintain their positions. Local unions within the UAW retain considerable autonomy, and wildcat strikes or refusals to accept nationally negotiated settlements are not uncommon. By contrast, until David MacDonald was defeated by I. W. Abel for the USW presidency on an issue of effectiveness rather than ideology, there were scarcely any serious challenges to the national leadership and certainly none while Philip Murray was alive. The USW has always been highly centralized; locals rarely dispute national decisions, and policies on political issues have not been deeply controversial.[41]

It seems plausible that the decisive difference between the USW and the UAW is less in the structure of the organizations than in the kinds of appeals it was necessary to make to their early members and thus in the nature of the contribution expected of them. This is born out by the history of the unions in the meat industry. The Amalgamated Meat Cutters and Butcher Workmen (AMCBW), though an AFL union, was from its inception in 1897 committed to industrial unionism.[42] It made relatively little progress in organizing meat packers or butchers; a strike it called in 1921 was defeated by the employers, with a resultant sharp drop in union membership and unpleasant memories of the cost of industrial warfare. In 1927, however, the head of the AMCBW testified before a congressional committee in opposition to legislation that would have broken up food chain stores. So impressed were the heads of the major food chains with this display of voluntarism that, beginning with A&P, the major chains chose to cement the alliance by recognizing the union without a struggle. Progress was also made in signing agreements with meat packers by exerting nonstrike pressures, chiefly by means of the organized boycott of certain meat products by union members in their capacity as consumers. The boycott scarcely burdened the union members, because they could shift their purchases to competing brands of the same product, but it could well harm the sales of the manufacturer.

The rival union, first called the Packinghouse Workers Organizing Committee (PWOC) and later the Packinghouse Workers Union, pursued a more militant organizing strategy and found itself frequently locked in bitter strikes with management. In 1933 a CIO local forcibly occupied a meatpacking plant; in 1937 PWOC conducted a sit-down strike in Kansas City and in 1938 another in Sioux City, this one resulting in violence and mass arrests. Throughout its turbulent early history, the PWOC was characterized by intense factionalism that continued well into the 1940s, much of it centering on the rival demands of radicals, followers of John L. Lewis, and noncommunist, pro-Roosevelt leaders.

The differences in political style between the USW and the UAW, or between the Amalgamated Meat Cutters and the Packinghouse Workers, are important but should not obscure the general impact that industrial unionism, and in particular the emergence of the CIO, had on union political activity. The UMW contributed half a million dollars to Roosevelt's 1936 campaign fund, and a group of unions organized Labor's Nonpartisan League to support Roosevelt Democrats. By 1943 the CIO had created the Political Action Committee (PAC) to institutionalize its concern for mobilizing not only union votes, but the votes of Democrats generally, and to bring pressure to bear on Congress that would further labor's legislative interests. These interests were broadly defined to include not only measures designed to protect and advance the organizational needs of unions but also those that would redistribute economic resources in favor of workers. The early UAW activists, still in the grip of the passions and sense of solidarity fostered by their participation in the sit-down strikes, almost immediately after winning a contract began to turn their attention to ways of altering the distribution of political power at the local level—partly to ensure against the use of police against strikers and partly to advance union interests by electing prolabor local officials. Even in 1937, shop stewards were organized by wards in such cities as Lansing and Flint.[43]

Indeed, for a while it seemed as if industrial unionism would produce a lasting and organized radical impulse in American politics. Walsh, an early prolabor historian of the CIO, expressed the hope in 1937 that to those conventional items in labor's platform (social security, wages-and-hours legislation, support for the Wagner Act) would be added a demand for public ownership of various basic industries, but neither Labor's Nonpartisan League nor the PAC took up the socialist view.[44] In time, and surely no later than 1950, the CIO had become, not an alternative to the Democratic party, but an adjunct to it, concentrating on helping candidates get elected within the two-party system and supporting liberal Democratic measures, at least on domestic issues, in Congress. The AFL, finally abandoning its position of voluntarism on social questions, began to become actively involved in politics, first by giving informal and personal help to Democratic candidates in elections from 1928 to 1944, then by forming Labor's League for Political Education, which worked in 1948 for Democratic candidates (without, however, formally endorsing Harry S. Truman), and finally in 1952 by officially endorsing the Democratic presidential candidate, Adlai Stevenson. Furthermore, the AFL became more interested in national legislative issues, supporting the Wagner Act in 1935, the Full Employment Act of 1946, and various minimum-wage and welfare measures. The AFL, in short, was becoming more activist and more "liberal" at the same time the CIO was becoming less radical and more conventional. Indeed, by the early 1950s, various commentators on American politics were deploring the "crisis" in American unionism represented by the decline of organizational militancy and political radicalism.[45]

A full account of the forces that activated the AFL's political interest and moderated the CIO's political radicalism would require careful attention to the central importance of the political perceptions and attitudes of the American worker and the structure of American politics. As to the former, the CIO enthusiasms generated by the sit-down strike and industrial warfare proved short-lived, just as the AFL preoccupation with local affairs proved myopic. And as for the latter, the decentralized structure of politics and government made it difficult and unrewarding to organize a mass, programmatic party for the capture of national power. These factors, though important, are mediated in their impact on union members and officers by the effects of organizational form and the rewards of union and partisan activism.

The emergence of a national economy and mass-production, mass-market industries, the growth of central government regulation of that economy, the need to deal with a few large employers, and the weaker economic bargaining position of many low-skilled workers as opposed to a few high-skilled ones gave the CIO unions an inevitable interest in national affairs, just as the fragmented and localistic nature of the construction and printing industry, combined with the existence of many small employers heavily dependent on skilled labor, had given many AFL unions an inevitable interest in local affairs. As AFL and CIO unions became more alike in their political interests, the organizational structure originally shaped by industrial conditions and recruitment needs continued to constrain the nature of the political activity of the union leaders.

An industrial union was, of necessity, centrally led; as Georg Simmel remarked, organizations tend to acquire the form of their organizational opponents. Funds within such a union go, in substantial measure, to the national office in order to supply the needs of a staff originally recruited to assist in organizing drives but which, as these drives are completed, is maintained for other purposes—education and welfare programs and, of course, political action. At contract time, a large national union staff is needed to cope with equivalent expertise on the side of management; between contract negotiations, a large staff of "international representatives" is required to supervise the enforcement and interpretation of the contract among the various locals. The principal paid officials of such unions as the UAW and USW, thus, are hired, funded, and directed by national or international headquarters, and among them will inevitably be found staff specialists in legislation, voting, and the like. An AFL craft union, by contrast, vests most authority in the local, and the chief hired officer—the business agent—is a local official concerned with managing relations between local members and local employers.

The existence of a large national staff has meant that a concern for legislative and political matters quickly became institutionalized within the ÇIO unions, but such concerns were for long erratically spontaneous in the less-bureaucratic AFL. After the merger of the AFL and CIO in 1955, some of these differences, at least nationally, disappeared. The AFL-CIO legislative department, located in Washington, D.C., lobbies Congress actively not only on behalf of union-related measures, such as proposals concerning prevailing wage rates in federal construction projects, but increasingly on behalf of broad welfare and civil rights measures, many of which have little direct bearing on the lives of most union members and some of which may even be opposed by substantial numbers of unionists.[46] In the mid-1960s, for example, a survey of white members of a large industrial union showed that 69 percent of the paid international staff thought that national progress in desegregating schools, housing, and jobs, was too slow, but only 21 percent of the rank-and-file members had that view; as a matter of fact, 30 percent of the rank and file felt that desegregation was moving too fast.[47]

One consequence of the growth and institutionalization of union security agreements is that much of the political activity of unions can be directed toward ends that large numbers of union members either do not share or actively oppose. These political activities, once powerfully constrained by their incentive effect on members (localistic and job oriented in the case of craft unionists, national and issue oriented in the case of industrial unionists), now reflect, in all probability, more the interests of professional staff members and key union leaders and their active rivals. Insofar as politics has an incentive effect, it is more for the union activists than for the rank and file.

The same is probably true in some measure of the Committee on Political Education (COPE), the political action arm of the merged AFL-CIO. With a national staff of twenty and a large political fund, it became a leading force in the alliance that existed until the 1972 presidential campaign between organized labor and the liberal wing of the Democratic party. Aided by similar units at the state and sometimes the local level, COPE has to a degree routinized and bureaucratized union political activity and thus to an important degree has reduced the variation in that activity that once resulted from the differences among individual union leaders and their supporters over the value they attached to particular candidacies and causes.[48] The convictions and interests of COPE staff members and their associated volunteers have become more determinative of union political activities than the views of those unionists primarily concerned with organizational maintenance and the advancement of economic interests.

Though the bureaucratization of the political function has reduced differences formerly maintained by the differing philosophies of various unions, it has hardly eliminated them. Greenstone reports as late as 1969 that there can still be detected differences in political emphasis between AFL-CIO staff members with an AFL as opposed to a CIO background.[49]

Organized labor remains essentially a decentralized structure, and COPE is no exception to this pattern. In making endorsements, state and local labor federations are free to choose any candidates they wish, though national COPE officials may try to persuade them to follow one course rather than another. And individual unions remain free to make or not make endorsements without regard for what the state or local federation may do. Nor are individual unions under any obligation to contribute financially to COPE; though fund-raising quotas have been established for each member union, they are entirely voluntary.[50] As a result, union political activity runs the entire gamut from support of an independent political party (as with the backing of the Liberal party in New York by various garment and hatters' unions) to support of whatever political party is locally dominant with little regard for its stand on particular issues (as with the backing given by certain craft unions to the Democratic party machine in Chicago).

Because of labor's increased interest in national political issues, the dominant form of permanent political organization has come to be the congressional district COPE. The strength, stature, and activity of these district units, however, varies greatly as Greenstone has shown.[51] At one extreme, a single powerful union, the UAW, operates a permanent COPE organization in each of the congressional districts of Detroit. At the other extreme, many cities have no standing union political organization at all, and experience labor activism only on an ad hoc basis in particular campaigns.

In Wayne County (Detroit), the six congressional district COPE units operate as a standing political caucus within the Democratic party. The choice of Democratic candidates to run in these areas is powerfully affected by the views of the COPE leaders. Furthermore, under the stimulation of full-time, paid COPE coordinators, union members are induced to run for posts as precinct delegates to the regular Democratic party. So successful has this been that Samuel J. Eldersveld found that over three-fourths of all Democratic party district leaders in the city were union members, mostly from the UAW.[52] The status incentives that induce union members to run for precinct office are not, however, sufficient to lead most of them to perform the routine and uncelebrated tasks of party organization and voter canvassing. To attract persons for these tasks, the UAW has had at its disposal other kinds of rewards. Money is one: the district coordinators are paid for full-time work in this capacity and in 1962 union members who performed campaign tasks were given from twenty to twenty-five dollars a day.[53] Though having such centrally controlled financial resources has given the UAW an advantage in political activity over other kinds of unions, it has not enabled it to produce serious and permanent precinct organization. The money paid a union member for canvassing is not an addition to his income but a replacement for money he loses by not reporting for work at the auto plant during election time. (By contrast, a party machine consists of persons whose regular job it is to work the precincts and for whom failure to canvass means a net loss of pay.) To mobilize large numbers of activists for these tasks, the UAW has had to draw on its capacity to provide purposive incentives, and for a time that was not difficult—the militancy and ideological interests of the formative years of the UAW carried over for a time into local political activity. The need to fight antiunion candidates was an important appeal to workers who still remembered how antiunion officeholders had once deployed the police. But as those memories faded and a new generation of union members came to the fore, the appeal of purposive incentives declined. An effort to restore the members' ideological commitment by starting a "Great Decisions" study program failed to catch on in all but one district.[54] Furthermore, though union members maintained a strong allegiance to the Democratic party and would support liberal candidates and issues at the state and national levels, they came increasingly to see local politics as a domain in which their own interests as homeowners, parents, and neighbors were involved. In Detroit's nonpartisan local elections, it became easy for unionists to express this aspect of their political attitudes by voting for relatively conservative local candidates. Occasionally, a candidate capable of arousing a strong sense of purpose and mission among the union activists, if not among the rank and file, will emerge, and then COPE district coordinators can enlist large numbers of volunteer workers. Such was the case, for example, when a liberal university professor ran for the city council. As the president of one UAW local said: "In twenty-five years I don't think I've ever seen the UAW secondary leaders have greater personal enthusiasm for a candidate." [55] In short, the infrastructure of labor politics in Detroit, maintained with material incentives, requires for its full activation the kind of purposive inducements that are to be found in an amateur political club.

The local politics of the USW displays a somewhat different style owing in part to the differing motivations of its members and in part to the contrasting history of its structure. In Chicago the USW is the largest CIO union. Though the dominance of the Democratic party machine in Chicago would temper the enthusiasm and reduce the scope of any union political activist, even allowing for this the USW there displays a political style quite different from that of the UAW in the same city. The greater importance, in the history of the union, of strong leadership as opposed to mass participation has meant that the USW has played its political role more by deciding, at the highest levels, which candidates to endorse and to fund than by attempting to induce a broadly based political activism among the rank and file. Lengthy debates over issues at union meetings have been discouraged, no "Great Decisions" course has been organized, and precinct work by the USW has often been carried on in cooperation with, rather than in opposition to, regular Democratic precinct captains.[56]

Craft and small-shop unions, such as those of painters, carpenters, machinists, and sheet metal workers, have tended to play the least active role in COPE or in similar enterprises. Where, as in Chicago, the political party is strong, they are likely to be entirely subordinate to that party's leadership, as has been the case with the Building Service Employees Union.[57] Where the party is weak, as in Los Angeles, these craft unions rarely, except under exceptional leadership, have the will or the capacity for inducing any sizable number of members to play active political roles. The machinists', painters', and carpenters' unions there have not generally been affiliated with COPE, and if they have been involved in campaigns at all, it has been by conducting voter registration drives among their members. These unions are decentralized, the business agents of the locals have small staffs (if any) that they can assign to politics, and the members have not historically seen the role of their union as including participation in broader movements. Even if the national or city leaders of such a craft union should decide that strong precinct work is of vital importance, they would have few if any incentives with which to induce the heads of the local unions or their members to engage in such work.[58]

NOTES

1. Derek C. Bok and John T. Dunlop, *Labor and the American Community* (New York: Simon & Schuster, 1970), p. 98.

2. John R. Commons, "Introduction," in *History of Labor in the United States, 1896–1932*, by Don D. Lescohier and Elizabeth Brandeis (New York: Macmillan, 1935), vol. III, p. xxiv.

3. Jerome L. Toner, *The Closed Shop* (Washington: American Council on Public Affairs, 1942), p. 60.

4. John R. Commons et al., *History of Labour in the United States* (New York: Macmillan, 1918), vol. I, p. 405.

5. Selig Perlman and Philip Taft, *History of Labor in the United States, 1896–1932* (New York: Macmillan, 1935), vol. IV, pp. 129–149, 489–514.

6. In 1947, the Taft-Hartley Act outlawed the closed shop and modified the union shop by permitting it to be made illegal by state law. By the mid-1960s, such laws had been passed in nineteen states.

7. Mancur Olson, *The Logic of Collective Action* (Cambridge, Mass.: Harvard University Press, 1965), p. 68.

8. Rose Theodore, "Union Security Provisions in Major Union Contracts, 1948–1959," *Monthly Labor Review*, LXXXII, 2 (December 1959), 1348–1356. Olson (*The Logic of Collective Action*, p. 75) erroneously states that 95 percent of all unionized workers are covered by various kinds of security schemes. This would be true only if one included sole bargaining rights as a kind of union security, which is not necessarily the case. The Theodore figures may have an unknown bias, because they are derived from a survey of agreements covering 1,000 or more workers.

9. W. E. J. McCarthy, *The Closed Shop in Britain* (Berkeley and Los Angeles: University of California Press, 1964), pp. 28, 78, 161–175.

10. Harry Brickman, "Freedom of Association in Eight European Countries," *Monthly Labor Review*, LXXXVI, 2 (September 1963), 1020–1025.

11. Mark van de Vall, *Labor Organizations* (Cambridge: Cambridge University Press, 1970), pp. 83–84, 92.

12. J. David Greenstone, *Labor in American Politics* (New York: Alfred A. Knopf, 1969), pp. 25–26; Lewis Lorwin, *The American Federation of Labor* (Washington, D.C.: Brookings Institution, 1933), pp. 408–411; Marc Karson, *American Labor Unions and Politics, 1900–1918* (Carbondale: Southern Illinois University Press, 1958), pp. 128–135.

13. Bok and Dunlop, *Labor and the American Community*, p. 395.

14. Greenstone, *Labor in American Politics*, p. 69.

15. Lorwin, *The American Federation of Labor*, p. 301.

16. Seymour Martin Lipset, Martin Trow, and James Coleman, *Union Democracy* (New York: Free Press, 1956), pp. 135–140.

17. Lorwin, *The American Federation of Labor*, p. 497.

18. Olson, *The Logic of Collective Action*, p. 72.

19. Lorwin, *The American Federation of Labor*, pp. 316–318.

20. Bok and Dunlop, *Labor and the American Community*, pp. 375, 383.

21. Gompers, quoted in Bok and Dunlop, p. 389.

22. Frey, quoted in Bok and Dunlop, pp. 389–390. It is not clear from the historical record how great a threat to union organizing drives general wages-and-hours

laws would have been. There was opposition to Gompers' views within the AFL, notably from William Green, who was to become Gompers' successor. See Greenstone, *Labor in American Politics*, p. 26, and Philip Taft, *The AFL in the Time of Gompers* (New York: Harper & Row, 1957), p. 148. The value of voluntarism for organizational maintenance is analyzed in Michael Rogin, "Voluntarism: The Political Functions of an Apolitical Doctrine," *Industrial and Labor Relations Review*, XV (July 1962).

23. Lorwin, *The American Federation of Labor*, p. 50.

24. Ibid., p. 60.

25. Karson, *American Labor Unions*, chaps. 2–4; Lorwin, *The American Federation of Labor*, pp. 271–277, 397–402.

26. Lorwin, *The American Federation of Labor*, p. 313.

27. Ibid., pp. 53, 402–403; Karson, *American Labor Unions*, pp. 71, 81, 115, 136.

28. Lorwin, *The American Federation of Labor*, p. 72; Karson, *American Labor Unions*, pp. 138–140.

29. Bok and Dunlop, *Labor and the American Community*, pp. 120–121.

30. Lorwin, *The American Federation of Labor*, p. 86.

31. J. Raymond Walsh, *C.I.O.: Industrial Unionism in Action* (New York: Norton, 1937), pp. 30–34.

32. Olson, *The Logic of Collective Action*, pp. 71, 75.

33. Theodore, "Union Security Agreements," p. 1350; Walter Galenson, *The CIO Challenge to the AFL* (Cambridge, Mass.: Harvard University Press, 1960), p. 183. The USW had before 1956 a "maintenance of membership" clause by which workers who were union members had to remain members until the termination of the existing contract, but no worker could be required to join the union and an escape period was provided during which time union members were free to resign from the organization. See Theodore, pp. 1351–1352.

34. Galenson, *The CIO Challenge to the AFL*, pp. 113, 115.

35. Sumner H. Slichter, James J. Healey, and E. Robert Livernash, *The Impact of Collective Bargaining on Management* (Washington, D.C.: Brookings Institution, 1960), pp. 28, 33.

36. The account here of the steel organizing drive follows Galenson, *The CIO Challenge to the AFL*, chap. 2, and Philip Taft, *The Structure and Government of Labor Unions* (Cambridge, Mass.: Harvard University Press, 1954), chap. 6.

37. The account here of the auto organizing drive follows Galenson, *The CIO Challenge to the AFL*, chap. 3, and Taft, *Structure and Government*, chap. 6.

38. Doris E. Pullman and L. Reed Tripp, "Collective Bargaining Developments," in *Labor and the New Deal*, ed. Milton Deber and Edwin Young (Madison: University of Wisconsin Press, 1957), p. 338.

39. Walsh, *C.I.O.*, p. 29.

40. Bryce M. Steward and Walter J. Couper, *Maintenance of Union Membership* (New York: Industrial Relations Counselors, Inc., 1943), p. 8.

41. Taft, *Structure and Government*, p. 213.

42. The account here follows Galenson, *The CIO Challenge to the AFL*, chap. 10.

43. Walsh, *C.I.O.*, pp. 135–136.

44. Ibid., p. 258.

45. See, for example, Paul Jacobs, *The State of the Unions* (New York: Atheneum, 1963).

46. Greenstone, *Labor in American Politics*, pp. 336–343.

47. Bok and Dunlop, *Labor and the American Community*, p. 134.

48. Ibid., pp. 192–193. The most active members of unions are typically those with the greatest interest in union involvement in politics and larger issues. See Ar-

nold S. Tannenbaum and Robert L. Kahn, *Participation in Union Locals* (Evanston, Ill.: Row, Peterson, 1958), pp. 122–123.

49. Greenstone, *Labor in American Politics*, pp. 334–335.

50. Bok and Dunlop, *Labor and the American Community*, pp. 193, 393–394.

51. Greenstone, *Labor in American Politics*, chap. 6.

52. Samuel J. Eldersveld, *Political Parties: A Behavioral Analysis* (Chicago: Rand McNally, 1964), p. 156.

53. Greenstone, *Labor in American Politics*, p. 180.

54. Ibid., pp. 187–188.

55. Quoted in Greenstone, *Labor in American Politics*, p. 119.

56. Ibid., pp. 103, 199–205.

57. Ibid., pp. 93–94.

58. Ibid., p. 209.

CHAPTER 8

Business Associations

Business associations, as E. E. Schattschneider has observed, dominate almost any listing of organizations active in seeking to influence public policy.[1] Whether these lists are representative of the actual universe of politically active associations is another matter, and whether one can make any reasonable inferences about the influence of business groups from their prevalence is still another. An equally interesting—and perhaps equally misleading—list would be a tally of all the major pieces of federal legislation enacted in the last thirty or so years. Such a list would almost certainly show that only a minority of the new programs, policies, and regulations of the Congress have been designed to increase the freedom of action of businessmen, enlarge their incomes, or make more secure their property holdings; most have had, on the contrary, the opposite intention (whether the opposite effect is hard to say)—business firms have been subjected to, on the whole, rising levels of taxation, increased regulatory supervision, and stronger injunctions against unfair labor practices.

Indeed, a historian might well argue that business values most thoroughly dominated government during the three decades after the Civil War when business associations were fewest in number. Before the 1890s, there were relatively few well-organized associations of business firms and almost none that were national in scope.[2] Perhaps because government was seen as irrelevant to business concerns, perhaps because there appeared to be a natural, or at least spontaneous, harmony of interests between business and government, perhaps because the individual firm acting alone could obtain all that it wanted from a state or national legislature, efforts to bring together similar firms into permanent associations for the purpose of advancing in the public arena the interests of those firms were not conspicuous until almost the turn of the century. There then appeared what Kenneth E. Boulding has called the "organizational revolution"—the extraordinary proliferation of national associations of all kinds in every field of endeavor.[3] Clarence E. Bonnett, in his history of employers' trade associations, refers to the "boom" in such organizations that reached a peak in the 1890s.[4]

The fact that business associations have been formed more rapidly and in greater numbers in some periods rather than in others should in itself be good reason for doubting the easy assumption that any economic interest naturally or inevitably expresses itself in organized political action. This is not to say that business firms are indifferent to their economic interests, but only that the value of organized efforts to pursue those interests must be demonstrated—a persuasive appeal must be made that will induce firms to concert their actions for political, or at least common, ends, and the association thus created will acquire maintenance needs of its own that are not inevitably the same as the direct economic interests of the member firms.

On the other hand, business firms have certain advantages over workers in forming associations. Workers have in the past had to overcome the resistance of firms in order to organize; the reverse has not been true. The average firm has a larger net income than the average worker; hence, the cost of associational membership for firms has been much lower in relation to income. Finally, in any given industry, there are far fewer firms than workers; thus, the number of wills to be concerted is fewer in the case of firms, and, accordingly, the affiliation of any single firm with an association is more likely either to make a measurable difference in the association's resources or to have a demonstration effect on other firms, or both, and thus the firm sees its affiliation as rational.

These reasons probably account not only for the large number of business (or "trade") associations but also for the fact that most are small in size. As the Temporary National Economic Commission (TNEC) found and as both Schattschneider and Mancur Olson stress, the median membership of a trade organization in a typical industry is from twenty-five to fifty firms.[5] It is not necessary, or at least no one has shown that it is necessary, to assume that the United States is dominated by business values or that wealth is associated with high social status and disproportionate political power in order to explain why there are so many small trade associations: it is enough to know the situational factors of property ownership, large disposable incomes relative to the size of associational dues, and the few number of potential member firms in many industries.

But though these situational factors explain a great deal, they do not explain everything worth knowing about business politics. They do not explain why trade associations were relatively few in number and only weakly organized at certain periods, whereas at later times they were numerous beyond count and professionally staffed. More importantly, they do not explain how certain industries characterized by large numbers of very small enterprises (retail druggists, for example) are organized—the income of the corner druggist is not much larger, and may well be smaller, than that of a skilled worker, and the affiliation of any given druggist with an association will produce neither a measurable increase in association resources nor a significant demonstration effect on other druggists. Despite these constraints, the National Association of Retail Druggists had, in 1965, 37,000 members accounting for 76 percent of all the retail firms in the business.[6] Indeed, of the sixty-five trade associations with more than 500 members surveyed by the TNEC in 1938, 9 percent had enrolled as members more than three-fourths of the firms in their industries and 25 percent had enrolled more than one-half.[7] Nor are all trade associations dominated financially by a few large member firms: among the 242 associations (as of 1938) with 51 to 250 members, over two-thirds received less than 20 percent of their funds, and over five-sixths got less than 40 percent, from their four largest members.[8]

Finally, the situational advantages of small size do not explain the creation of national business organizations—the National Association of Manufacturers, the United States Chamber of Commerce, and the Committee for Economic Development. The problem of generating incentives sufficient to produce and maintain organizations of either numerous small enterprises or of highly diverse enterprises with quite different economic interests is not easily solved, and the solutions that are available impart special characteristics to the way in which the economic interests of members are, or are not, represented politically.

These larger peak associations are better understood in light of the prior development of the smaller single-interest trade associations. The growth of the latter after the Civil War is sometimes explained by reference to changes in the structure of industry itself—the emergence of national markets and nationwide firms, the advent of mass production, the rise of the large impersonal corporation, and the development of a more sophisticated technology.[9] But it is not clear why the growth of large, complex corporate structures serving a national market would in itself stimulate the growth of trade associations; indeed, to the extent that such firms as Standard Oil or United States Steel engaged in horizontal and vertical integration or otherwise achieved a dominant market position, they would have *less* need of a trade association—whatever political or bargaining problems they had, they could handle by acting alone or in informal agreement with one or two other corporate giants. Though examples of formal associations with but two or three members are not unknown, the value of association is precisely that it purports to make possible actions that could not be successfully undertaken by one or two firms acting alone.

A review of available, but by no means exhaustive or representative, accounts of early trade associations suggests that it was in those industries characterized by fragmentation, competition, and localism that trade organizations principally emerged. Associations formed disproportionately, it appears, in those industries that were unable to achieve control over their resources and markets by growth or merger. Of course, if the producers in such industry were very numerous, creating an association became difficult, though not impossible; the thousands of one-man candy stores were so hard to organize it was scarcely in anyone's interest to try, except perhaps on a local basis. There may have been in the early years an optimal size of an industry for associational purposes, one with neither too few firms to make organization unnecessary nor too many to make it impossible.[10] The literature about late-nineteenth-century associations is replete with examples of industries with a manageable number of firms, a high level of competition, and a regional location that created enough proximity to ensure frequent face-to-face contacts: dark tobacco growers, northern and southern cotton spinners, wool manufacturers, stove foundries, garment manufacturers, machine shops, and coal mine operators.

But why should industry that is suitable for organization become organized? One possibility is that members all see the opportunities available to them if they combine—new laws can be obtained that will favor their products, politicians can be elected who will sympathize with their problems, and prices can be set and production controlled so as to enrich all. Some trade associations did emerge out of a common recognition of the gains that will accrue to combined efforts. The Typothetae of New York was formed in 1862 in part to achieve greater price stabilization among printers, and the New England Cotton Manufacturers' Association was created in 1865 to enable mill agents and superintendents to exchange information on technological developments while they enjoyed pleasant dinners together.[11] Neither engaged in political activity during their early years. The National Association of Wool Manufacturers began in 1864, chiefly to get higher tariffs on imported wool materials to compensate domestic manufacturers for the high tariffs they had to pay on imported raw wool.[12] These early organizations typically had low dues, no staff, and little continuity of leadership, and relied heavily on the solidary attractions of social events to keep the group together. All suffered from the problem of the "free rider." Their substantive accomplishments were not large—the cotton manufacturers never attempted much, the Typothetae discovered it could not control prices in so highly fragmented an industry, and the wool manufacturers, though they obtained tariff increases, collapsed as an organization because ·of internal conflict over whether the new tariffs helped one firm more than others.

Louis Galambos, in his excellent study of trade associations in the cotton textile industry, aptly characterizes this period between 1860 and the 1890s as one of "dinner-club associations." They were locally based, relied on solidary incentives either primarily or as an important supplement to the prospect of material benefit, lacked any clearly expressed business ideology, had no professional staff, and had little success at improving the profitability of the member firms. Galambos finds this pattern evident not only in textiles, but in iron and steel, petroleum, and lumber as well.[13]

Even the politically active associations had a clublike atmosphere and style. The Arkwright Club was formed in Boston in 1880 because of fears raised among mill owners about the implications of a recently passed state law restricting the working hours of women. Being limited to the directing officers of the mills, it became a prestigious association; being prestigious, it could afford to be selective. Unlike other such associations, it was able to raise large sums by assessing member firms according to payroll size. With these resources, the Club engaged in episodic lobbying. Its efforts, however, were amateur, though perhaps no less effective for that, and were carried on by individual members rather than by any paid staff. Twelve years elapsed before it hired a permanent secretary, and even then the rank and file did most of the occasional work.[14]

The rise around the turn of the century of strong, well-staffed trade associations that deeply involved the interests of member firms seems to be associated, not with the recognition of opportunities for extending business influence, but with the dawning awareness of serious threats to existing business practices and profits. These threats were three in number: the enactment of state and federal regulatory laws, the rise of organized labor, and the existence in certain industries of a profit squeeze created by chronic overcapacity, rising fixed costs, falling demand, or all three.[15] Existing trade associations were able to extend their membership and new associations were able to form, not because firms believed that good conditions could be made better through collective action, but because they realized that difficult conditions might become worse without it. Among firms as among individuals, a threat—especially one that can be personified by an "enemy"—is a more powerful incentive for organization than an opportunity.

The cotton textile industry illustrates this process. By the turn of the century, northern textile manufacturers had entered into a depression that was to last for several decades as southern competition undercut northern prices at a time when northern mill capacity was at a peak and foreign markets were dominated by English and Asian producers. Though World War I restored profits temporarily, the postwar period produced a further deterioration. At the same time, organized labor was becoming more militant. Though craft unions had existed for some time in northern mills, the union movement generally was growing rapidly—AFL unions increased their membership more than fourfold between 1897 and 1904 [16]—and the United Textile Workers, formed in 1901, led a series of strikes in the South that, though invariably won by management, aroused the fears of the employers at the same time as they increased the frustrations of the workers. Politically, the northern mill owners were confronted with the passage in a number of states of factory laws limiting the use of child labor, reducing the working day for women, granting workmen's compensation, and establishing minimum wages.[17] Though some businessmen supported what became known as the Progressive movement, others organized to combat it, not only for ideological reasons or out of a concern for business practices generally, but because such laws, being enacted by certain states and not others, were placing them at a competitive disadvantage.[18] Northern mill owners had to pay the costs associated with factory legislation from which most southern operators were exempt. Finally, the textile manufacturers, unlike meat packers or oil producers, were unable to create industrial giants through mergers that would reduce or eliminate price competition. Such efforts were made in the North, but they invariably foundered on the rock of southern competition.

The organizational response to these forces was dramatic. In 1906 the New England Cotton Manufacturers' Association changed its name to the National Association of Cotton Manufacturers (NACM), and by 1916 it had a substantial income based on company assessments, a professional staff, and a full agenda of political and economic action. The Arkwright Club at the same time was creating specialized committees and bureaus—the New England Cotton Freight Claim Bureau, the Cotton Bureau, a Cotton Classification Committee, and a Board of Appeal—to handle new problems. The Southern Cotton Spinners' Association was renamed the American Cotton Manufacturers' Association (ACMA) in 1903, and by 1916 it too had a staff, a large budget, and numerous committees. In 1913, the mutually suspicious, if not downright hostile, northern and southern groups formed a National Council of American Cotton Manufacturers in an attempt to iron out some of their differences and to explore efforts at price stabilization.[19] Similarly, the Typothetae became a national organization to meet the challenge of the International Typographical Union.[20]

These groups were on the whole more successful in dealing with external political problems than with internal economic ones. The textile manufacturers, for example, organized a campaign that ensured that their interests were well looked after in the 1921 revisions of the tariff laws.[21] The southern-based ACMA was able to prevent southern legislatures from passing equivalents of the northern factory laws, though in New England the northern textile groups were regularly defeated before the legislatures of Massachusetts and Connecticut. Southern mills continued to defeat labor organizing drives. But efforts to avoid price competition by association activities were not very successful. Though it was in the interest of the industry as a whole to have a uniformly high price level, it was to the advantage of each individual firm to undercut that level, and the association had no sanctions with which to ensure that collective benefits would override individual rationality.[22] It increasingly became clear that a voluntary association was no substitute for a centrally controlled hierarchical organization. The NACM could not accomplish for textiles what Standard Oil could achieve in petroleum.

Virtually every industry, certainly every competitive one, seems to have experienced the same proliferation and bureaucratization of associations during this period. Organization creates the need for further organization; as Galambos puts it: "There was a kind of bureaucratic acceleration principle at work." [23] A labor organization was seen as a threat by businessmen, who in turn organized; that association aroused the fears of rival businessmen, who in turn associated; the existence of such groups gave further impetus to the drive to establish state and federal regulatory bodies intended to prevent price discrimination and rate fixing; the need to deal with such agencies further stimulated the creation of new associations, and so forth.

Perhaps the largest number of new or reorganized business associations arose in conjunction with the "open-shop" movement aimed, as mentioned in the last chapter, at preventing closed, or union, shops. As an outgrowth of the activities of the Knights of Labor in 1885–1886 and of the Haymarket Riot of 1886, semisecret "Law and Order Leagues" were formed in a number of cities, especially those served by the railroads controlled by Jay Gould. The Leagues combined ideology, interest, and fraternity in about equal proportions, drawing members who feared union power as well as those who enjoyed the passwords, secret handgrips, and recognition signs utilized by the group.[24] More typical and more enduring, however, were organizations created by firms in particular industries to deal with union challenges of a specific and immediate nature. Characteristic of these was the Stove Founders' National Defense Association created in 1886. If, in the event of a labor dispute, a member firm accepted the Association decision, he would be supported by all members in fighting the strike; if he refused, he was left to his own devices. The support consisted of a pledge by other stove makers that they would, during a strike, take the struck employer's patterns and make his stoves for him. The system worked imperfectly, for often the supporting firms would themselves be struck in retaliation and the struck firm sometimes did not welcome the idea of business rivals handling its patterns; as a result, by 1892 the Association was bargaining with the unions instead of opposing them.[25]

The experience of the Stove Founders' Association showed that merely a recognition of joint interests, even when reinforced by a willingness to help a struck firm to fill its orders, was not enough—any individual firm always had an incentive to settle the strike and get back into production while its competitors were still closed down. Filling a struck firm's orders was well and good, but it raised the possibility that those doing the filling would succeed in permanently diverting the trade to themselves or in stealing a technology advance. The National Metal Trades Association dealt with this problem by devising a system of sanctions to impose on members. The Association adopted a policy of non-recognition of, and no concessions to, the International Association of Machinists. The employers' group then proceeded to infiltrate the union with labor spies, to recruit strikebreakers, and to collect a strike fund. Any member firm that bargained with a union or refused to accept the Association's authority was expelled, and thus lost access to the strike fund and the scab workers.[26]

Another strategy for maintaining a common position was to use a union agreement to coerce members and to secure a competitive advantage over nonmember firms. The Central Competitive Coal Operators' Association, beginning about 1898, formed an alliance with the United Mine Workers (UMW) by the terms of which the mine operators in the central fields (chiefly Indiana, Ohio, and Pennsylvania) would grant a contract and a wage increase to the miners on the understanding that the UMW would, by strikes and other means, force up the wage rates in the low-cost mines of Kentucky and West Virginia.[27] The UMW for many years was unable to bring the West Virginia operators into line, and lengthy disputes ensued between central operators and the union over who was to blame for the failure to eliminate price competition. Within the central fields, however, the prospect of a strike was often enough to ensure that members of the operators' association would stay in line.

The abortive effort of the National Recovery Administration (NRA) in the early 1930s to end the depression by authorizing trade associations to develop codes of fair trade (in short, price-fixing agreements) that would then have legal force gave a substantial stimulus to the formation of such groups. Legal authority would underwrite what once had depended on informal understandings, thereby solving the problem of how to maintain cooperative effort. Nearly one-fourth of the associations in existence in 1938 were formed between 1933 and 1935.[28] When the Supreme Court nullified the National Industrial Recovery Act in 1935, over 500 trade associations disbanded, and others relapsed into their previous pattern of guarded and only partially successful efforts to persuade one another to avoid seizing competitive advantages.[29] The fact that the creation of the NRA caused an increase in associational activity and its demise a decrease is evidence that suggests the difficulty of maintaining purely voluntary agreements.[30]

Business associations have on the whole been most successful when they have been able to reach their objectives through obtaining favorable legislation and least successful when they have had to rely on voluntary agreements. Though methods are available to maintain trade policies—expulsion from the association, predatory price cutting, boycotts, public disparagement, and the withdrawal of credit—these are unattractive not only because they are likely to attract the attention of federal prosecutors concerned with enforcing the antitrust statutes, but because they often create within the association an atmosphere of bitterness and distrust. Legal coercion is much to be preferred. The "fair trade" laws are a case in point. The National Association of Retail Druggists (NARD), formed in 1898, began almost immediately to force firms in the drug business to observe uniform retail prices. Retail druggists pledged themselves to boycott wholesalers or manufacturers that sold to retailers who cut prices. These agreements were held to be unlawful under the Sherman Act. Various attempts to reinstate these agreements were perpetually frustrated by a combination of government action and price competition from cut-rate drug stores. NARD then shifted to a legislative strategy. Between 1933 and 1940, it obtained the passage of retail price maintenance laws in forty-four states; in 1937 alone, twenty-eight states passed such acts. It also played a key role in securing passage by Congress of the Robinson-Patman Act.[31]

Though trade associations often were created in response to a commercial or governmental threat, and though many have at one time or another sought to nullify that threat by various efforts at reducing competition or obtaining new legislation, most trade associations today, to judge from the scanty literature about them, exist primarily to provide services to member firms for which the latter are willing to pay. These range from services with a direct monetary value, such as the arrangements for long-distance ordering of flowers provided by the Florists' Transworld Delivery Association, to the more common provision of information about government actions, technical developments, and commercial practices. All of these functions could in fact be supplied, probably at less cost, by a profit-making enterprise that gathered and disseminated the information for subscribers. What seems to make the associational format almost universal, however, is the widely felt need among members that they "be represented" in dealings with government —obviously a function that a profit-making firm selling trade information could not perform, or at least could not perform with a claim to legitimacy and authority. In the TNEC survey of trade association executives in 1938 [32] and again in the Chamber of Commerce survey of association members in 1966,[33] "governmental relations" were invariably cited as the most important associational activity. In the 1966 survey, 41 percent of the sample association members mentioned this function, almost twice as many as those who cited informational services.

If creating and maintaining a business association in a single industry is difficult, launching a general, or "umbrella" business association is doubly so. Any organization that seeks to speak politically for all, or any substantial part, of businessmen will confront the fact that the particular interests of various firms are often in conflict. Though businessmen as a class may be presumed to have certain general interests in common, they are highly general indeed ("maintaining the private enterprise system," "avoiding high taxes") and can easily lead to inconsistent policy positions—for example, do we maintain private enterprise by eliminating regulatory control over the railroads or by bringing all other forms of transportation under equivalent control? Occasionally, an issue is presented on which the class interests of at least big businessmen may coincide (maintaining the special tax treatment of capital gains, for example), but more often the concrete political choice is between alternatives that require more divisive trade-offs (should the corporate income tax be reduced and the lost revenue be made up by eliminating the oil depletion allowance?). Furthermore, there are millions of businessmen, and thus the "free rider" problem exists—no single businessman has an incentive to contribute to the attainment of what all will receive if the organized political efforts are successful.

It appears that the same forces that led to the growth of specific trade associations led to the formation of many of the earliest general business associations; namely, threats posed by external agencies, notably the government. The Illinois Manufacturers' Association (IMA) was founded in 1893 in response to the passage by the Illinois legislature of a bill limiting the workday for women and children to eight hours. The IMA hired an attorney who persuaded the courts to declare the law unconstitutional. The same strategy was followed four years later when the IMA sought judicial repeal of a state fire law; though the association lost the court case, the legislature eventually rescinded the law. The membership of the association fluctuated with the immediacy of the threat, declining whenever the politicians failed to come up with a new regulatory measure aimed at business. Recognizing this, the IMA hired a permanent executive whose slogan was, "always have an issue." Though the issues he found were somewhat disparate, ranging from support for the Spanish-American War to antiunion drives, they were effective in attracting members and in getting the IMA accepted in state government as a force to be dealt with.[34]

The Pennsylvania Manufacturers' Association (PMA) was also founded because of business fears and grew most rapidly when events intensified those concerns. Created in 1908 by Joseph Grundy, the PMA was a response to the decline in the state's economic growth and the passage of unwelcome social legislation. Most of its efforts, however, did not deal with stimulating growth, which would have required complex, sustained action that would have conferred benefits, if any, quite unevenly, but with fighting factory laws, a simpler task involving the mobilization of businessmen against specific threats. It operated a legislative bureau in the state capital and urged the formation of local associations that would influence the election of state legislators. The PMA membership contained disproportionate numbers of small, family-owned textile mills—in short, those firms most vulnerable to small increases in production costs—and failed to include most of the state's very large enterprises, such as the oil companies and the interests of the Mellon family. It supplemented its political appeals to members with a successful fire and workmen's compensation program.[35]

It is the National Association of Manufacturers (NAM), however, that best illustrates the threat-oriented nature of general business associations during this period, for it was founded as an organization to further the expansion of business opportunities and then eight years later shifted dramatically to a militantly antiunion posture. Just as dramatic was the increase in membership and funds that accompanied this substitution of threats for opportunities in the NAM's statement of goals.

When first organized in 1895, the NAM hoped to speak for manufacturers who wished to extend foreign trade, improve the consular service, build the Nicaragua canal, enlarge the merchant marine, obtain uniform freight classifications, and the like. It specifically disavowed any interest in labor relations, believing such matters were best left to specific trade associations.[36] Apparently there were about 1,000 industrialists willing to join an organization with such goals, but not many more, for by 1900 membership had declined by 17 and by 1902 it had declined still further.[37] The NAM seemed destined to fade away when, at its 1902 convention, a new element succeeded in capturing the presidency and the secretaryship with men pledged to convert the NAM to an antiunion vehicle in the open-shop movement.[38] The following year the open-shop group consolidated its hold on the organization, defeating an effort of foreign-trade enthusiasts to stage a comeback. The militant leadership, all owners of small- to medium-sized manufacturing plants in the Midwest, ran the NAM under tight reins and created for it a leading position in the open-shop struggle. "When the common enemy was discovered," Gable writes, "the NAM experienced new life." [39] In 1903 membership rose by almost 1,000; by 1907 it had tripled and the association's income had increased fivefold. Simultaneously, attendance at the annual conventions dwindled.[40]

Though the members of the NAM obviously must have believed that the open shop would help their businesses, it was not business advantage simply that led to their joining the organization. After all, an association of nearly 4,000 members would not benefit from the addition of any given new member, whereas a prospective member would benefit from the open shop whether or not he joined. Furthermore, there were many other organizational vehicles through which one could participate in the labor problem, ranging from specialized groups with specific benefits, such as the National Metal Trades Association, to organizations seeking to moderate industrial strife and reach an accord with the unions, such as the National Civic Federation. What was distinctive about the NAM is that it offered an ideological opposition to all forms of intrusion, whether from government, labor, or the trusts, in the free enterprise system of the small capitalist. The NAM not only attacked unions, it attacked Wall Street, the American Bankers' Association, the Merchant Marine League, and the National Civic Federation; it in turn was attacked on the editorial page of the *Wall Street Journal*, and its leadership was rejected by the National Metal Trades Association.[41] By 1913, the lobbying activities of the NAM were the subject of a congressional investigation.[42]

The importance of purposive incentives in such organizations as the NAM, the IMA, and the PMA is suggested by their behavior when they found themselves with substantially reduced influence over government policies. The state bills opposed by the IMA and the PMA were all eventually passed; of thirty-eight major legislative proposals enacted by Congress between 1933 and 1941, the NAM opposed—unsuccessfully—all but seven.[43] To be sure, these associations were often able to delay this legislation and, when its passage was inevitable, were sometimes able to soften it, but there is little evidence of any decline in membership support or leadership vigor when their access to government was reduced or their legislative power curtailed.

Quite the contrary. During the economic prosperity and political laissez faire of the 1920s, the NAM faced a crisis, for national normalcy was an organizational disaster.[44] The appeal of the NAM was much reduced by the absence of a threat, and membership fell sharply from 5,350 in

1922 to less than 1,500 by 1933. The advent of the New Deal led to the revitalization of the association, with membership growing to 3,000 by 1936 and to 8,000 by 1941.[45] The administration of President Roosevelt, the resurgent labor unions, and the passage of the Wagner Act gave a new edge to NAM militancy; though it could not stem the tide of government intervention during the 1940s, the NAM helped in securing the passage of the Taft-Hartley Act in 1947 during the Republican-controlled Eightieth Congress. With that law on the books, NAM membership and enthusiasm began to decline again.[46]

Because it relies on purposive incentives, the NAM enrolls as members only a small minority (variously estimated at 6 to 8 percent) of all manufacturing establishments in the nation.[47] On the other hand, those firms that do belong are among the largest in the country and account for most manufacturing, and these larger firms have in recent years occupied a disproportionate share of the offices and committee seats in the association.[48] What this proves is not clear: larger firms may feel they have more at stake, or may be more sensitive to the ideological issues involved, or may simply have the money and executive time that permits extensive participation.

The disproportionate participation of officers of large firms on the committees of the NAM and the fact that large firms pay a disproportionate share of the NAM's budget (in 1971, about 8 percent of the corporate members paid about one-half the membership fees) are sometimes taken as evidence that the NAM is not really a large, national association at all, but is, as Olson puts it, "based on a *single* small group of very large businesses," [49] which, because of its size, is relatively easy to organize. Thus, the NAM is neither remarkable nor representative. This is too simple a view of the matter. The 8 percent of corporate members that pay half the dues (about $3 million annually) total roughly 1,000 firms—hardly a small group. And the 12,000 members who supply the other half of the association's dues income pay an average of $250 each, scarcely a rational action if what they get in return for this money is merely the opportunity to serve as window dressing for corporate giants. Furthermore, though General Electric may pay thirty times as much in dues as the Mini Widget Company, it has the same number of votes— one.

The NAM exists, not because it is small or oligarchical, but because it has discovered that out of the several hundred thousand manufacturing enterprises in the United States, it can attract as members between 13,000 and 15,000 by purposive appeals aimed at the ideological belief of certain firms in the importance of a militant defense of the "free competitive enterprise system." [50] To the very largest corporations, the cost of NAM membership, even at the highest dues quota of $65,000 a year, is trivial; they constitute, therefore, a stable core of the membership relatively immune to fluctuations in the business cycle or the tides of politics. For the smaller firms, the dues even at the lowest rate of $200 per year, are not trivial, great efforts must be made by association salesmen to recruit and hold them, and the turnover is high, especially when business profits are pinched or perceived political threats are few. One staff member estimated to an interviewer that about 40 percent of those who join on a trial one-year basis fail to renew their membership, with more renewals when the Democrats are in the White House and utter antibusiness remarks. It would be interesting to know the characteristics of those small firms that elect to remain in the NAM, but because the association's membership list is secret such a study is impossible. What is clear is that the heads of some small corporations occupy key committee chairmanships, less to give a "small business" image to the NAM than because, as one staff member put it, "these guys are gung ho on the principles involved and willing to work."

In recent years, the NAM has sought to change both its image and its practice. Beginning with the appointment in 1962 of a full-time, highly paid president, the NAM has sought to develop private and governmental alternatives to programs it once simply opposed. At that time the NAM was suffering from one of its periodic slumps in memberships and dues, despite the efforts of 126 field representatives working around the country to recruit new members. The cost of obtaining a new member sometimes exceeded the dues it paid.[51] The NAM policy positions moved slightly more toward the center, better relationships with some government officials were established, and several firms that had once quit in disagreement rejoined.[52] George Romney, then Governor of Michigan, told the NAM's 71st Annual Congress that if he were still head of the American Motors Corporation he would now reverse his decision in 1954 to pull AMC out of the association. (The firm did not take his advice.) Whether the new NAM stance will permit it to solve its maintenance needs or improve its governmental effectiveness remains to be seen. When an ideological organization shifts its political stance, it always leaves itself vulnerable to a challenge from its more ardent supporters who can claim that it has deserted its principles.

The United States Chamber of Commerce solved the problem of creating a broadly based, general-interest business association by a quite different strategy. By 1912, when the Chamber was formed, it was clear to the organizers that certain incentives were ineffectual, too costly, or self-defeating. If one merely announced the formation of a national organization that everyone could join, few would—the early experiences of the NAM and the almost-defunct National Board of Trade proved that. The latter purported to be an organization of all business associations, but very few groups attended its annual conventions, with the result that the Board was easily captured by a succession of special interest groups wishing to apply the Board's name to its own policies.[53] Being unable to lobby for all business interests, it soon failed to lobby for any. A militant, highly political, ideological organization was possible, but the NAM example showed that such a group could not draw together a wide range of associations. And if a few major trade associations sought to federate for their own advantage, other business groups would become suspicious of their dominance and stay aloof. Finally, if the creation of the organization was associated with any particular policy, it would alienate those businessmen opposed to that program.

The impetus for the new organization came from a few local Chambers of Commerce, especially those in Boston and Chicago; the incentive they offered was that of a single association to which all other associations could belong that would service the local groups from a Washington office; the legitimacy and the status of the new organization was ensured by having President William Howard Taft attend the inaugural meeting in Washington. The underlying motives to which the Chamber appealed derived from a sense of insecurity among businessmen about the seemingly antibusiness policies of President Theodore Roosevelt and the enforcement of the Sherman Acts.[54] But the appeal was cautiously stated in order to avoid either indifference or divisiveness. The first officers of the Chamber announced that the new organization would play no role in partisan politics, would moderate business opposition to labor unions, and would resist being captured by the needs of particular business interests.[55]

These bland assurances successfully avoided divisiveness, but they seemed to court indifference. Elbert Gary of United States Steel let it be known at the time that he did not think the Chamber would amount to anything, and the New York and Philadelphia Chambers of Commerce adopted a wait-and-see attitude toward the national organization.[56] At first money was slow to come in.

As it turned out, the blandness was an asset, for it permitted the Chamber to avoid the suspicions and jurisdictional fears of other associations while its field staff was signing them to membership. The Chamber was sold to prospective members on a door-to-door basis. The first field agent received $200 a month for canvassing on the condition that he obtain no fewer than forty members per month; for each membership beyond forty, he received 20 percent of the fee.[57] By 1915, the field staff consisted of a manager and eleven field secretaries.

By 1971, the Chamber had enrolled nearly 40,000 business or professional members—individuals, firms, and corporations—and over 3,500 organization members—local chambers of commerce and various trade associations. The scope of its appeal varies among membership categories. It has enrolled virtually all of the local, state and regional chambers of commerce, but only about 10 percent of all the trade associations in the country (but almost all the important ones) and less than 6 percent of all the business enterprises (though the vast majority of the largest ones). Only the delegates of the organizational members can vote in Chamber affairs.

The fact that the Chamber is in part a federation of other organizations helps solve its maintenance problems, which in part are simply delegated to the constituent organizations, most of which are relatively small, local associations that provide members with business and social contacts, a chance to "boost" the community, and an opportunity to work on local economic problems. Olson, however, overstates this element of the Chamber, writing that it is "only" a federation of which the "principal" members are other organizations.[58] This is not the case. Business and professional members outnumber organizational ones by better than ten to one and are, and always have been, the chief source of the Chamber's money. In 1971, the affiliated organizations paid less than half a million dollars in dues while the business and professional members paid nearly $8 million. Nor, as Olson has alleged, does the bulk of these corporate contributions come from a few "very large businesses." [59] In 1966, the average business or professional member paid about $180 in dues; half the total dues income (over $3 million) came from firms and individuals subscribing less than $500. To be sure, 146 firms paid over $3,000 a year for a total of nearly $1.2 million, but, though important, these large payments were only 20 percent of business dues.[60]

The maintenance of the Chamber, in short, is only in small part the result of being a federation of local chambers. These organizations, plus the largest contributors for whom Chamber dues (the top payment is $60,000 a year) are a trivial part of the cost of doing business, constitute a core to which the organization then makes strenuous efforts to add smaller firms and trade associations. Fifty salesmen work in the membership department to find and hold these recruits. Losses each year are a large fraction of new additions, but the net is usually favorable, resulting in a growth of business and professional membership from 26,292 in 1960 to 39,869 in 1971.[61]

The new members, in exchange for the payment of (typically) $100, receive a subscription to *Nation's Business* and various newsletters and a chance to participate in formulating Chamber policy by serving, by appointment, on one of nearly forty committees and advisory panels and by responding to various Chamber opinion polls.

The appeal of the Chamber to prospective business members is essentially the same as that of the NAM—the "duty" of firms to support the activities of an organization that seeks to defend "the American philosophy of enterprise favoring limited government and the motivation of production by incentives within the framework of a free competitive market economy." [62] But unlike the NAM, at least until recently, the Chamber pursued this objective in a relatively low-key fashion, and thus its general goal was, for those who accepted it, less of an incentive than the more militant posture of the NAM. But if the purposive benefits were less, so were the costs—in 1971 the average NAM member paid about $400 a year, the average Chamber member, about $190.

The policy-making procedure within the Chamber is designed to ensure substantial member involvement and the avoidance of issues that might divide the group. Any member may propose a policy, but the Chamber's board will reject without further consideration one that is not "national in character, timely in importance and general in application." [63] In concrete terms, this means avoiding taking positions on particular tariffs, prices, rates, regulatory policies, import quotas, or any other matter that affects firms differentially or that sets one segment of industry against another. Intrabusiness controversy is anathema. A proposed policy is reviewed by various committees and panels; if it is a new or different one, it is usually submitted to a referendum in which each affiliated organization may vote.

In this process, most issues become formulated in general terms, with modifying phrases to accommodate virtually any interest or contingency, and accordingly the referenda produce lopsided majorities for the committee-framed proposal. And because almost no one objects to these proposals and because many are of interest only to certain kinds of businesses, many affiliated associations do not trouble to vote.[64]

The views expressed in the Chamber's 154-page policy book are sometimes quite specific, but only when such a position commends itself to virtually every member or when it will make at least one member better off without making any worse off. An example of the former is the desire to reduce the maximum personal income tax rate below 50 percent; an example of the latter is the Chamber's opposition to the extension of the Mineral Leasing Act of 1920 to metalliferous metals. The typical policy, however, is either quite general—monetary policy, for example, should be "flexible" and combined with "sound fiscal policy" —or occupies simultaneously two sides of an issue—the electoral college, for example, should be reformed *either* by having a direct election of the President *or* by having electoral votes cast by congressional districts.[65] In recent years, NAM policy statements have come more to resemble Chamber ones as the NAM seeks to strike a new, less militant posture. One might suppose that a large manufacturing corporation might someday wonder whether it is worth contributing to both the Chamber and the NAM, but the prospect of it making such a choice is probably reduced by the fact that among its executives will be found men who have served or are serving in important and status-conferring offices in both associations and who will come to the defense of whichever association is in jeopardy.

The creation and maintenance of an association such as the Chamber, which seeks to represent all business in general and no business in particular, has been a considerable accomplishment. Only a few other organizations have been able to enroll as many firms as the Chamber. Some of these, such as the National Association of Retail Druggists (NARD) and the National Association of Retail Grocers (NARG) followed the conventional pattern of trade associations—a group of firms offering a similar product or service is mobilized by a threat to their economic well-being, in this case, that resulting from the price-cutting practices of chain stores, cut-rate outlets, and the like, and seeks by internal controls and friendly legislation to end the threat and make secure the affected industry. By 1939, NARG had enrolled 40,000 grocers and NARD 28,000 druggists. It is not entirely clear how these associations attract so many members in such a fragmented, geographically dispersed business, or why NARD has managed to enlist over half of its potential members, whereas NARG has enrolled only a tenth. Apparently drugstores are on the average larger than independent grocery stores and vary less in size, and druggists, compared to grocers, are more likely to think of themselves as professionals with special training and a special duty to support "the profession." [66]

Other organizations, however, have sought to give political representation to *all* small businesses, regardless of the particular economic activities. These include the National Federation of Independent Businessmen (NFIB), the National Small Businessmen's Association (NSBMA), the Conference of American Small Business Organizations (CASBO), and others. Each of these organizations began as an expression of the entrepreneurial activity of a single man, the founder or his successor, and to a large extent they remain so. Almost all were formed in the aftermath of a 1938 Small Business Conference sponsored by the United States Department of Commerce at the suggestion of President Franklin Roosevelt. He had apparently hoped to get small business allies for his policies to offset the opposition of larger corporations. Those invited, a haphazard selection of various small businessmen, lost no time in disappointing him. Finding little of substance on which they could agree except a dislike for the New Deal, they devoted their energies to a denunciation of it. Despite this lack of common objectives, several of those involved saw an opportunity for organizational development. Competing organizers struggled to establish a group that could claim to speak for small businessmen and that would have privileged access to the Department of Commerce, an agency that by then wanted nothing to do with small businessmen. Both the NSBMA and the NFIB developed a sales force of 35 to 200 agents who were assigned regions to work on a commission basis. The salesmen received 50 percent of the first year's dues for every new membership obtained. Because they were canvassing among businessmen with highly divergent interests, the appeals tended to be purposive rather than material. Prospects were told that the NSBMA (or whatever) was engaged in "stopping socialistic trends" and that by means of a referendum the member could add his voice and vote to the effort. The NSBMA stresses restoring an unregulated, free-enterprise economy; the NFIB emphasizes "fair competition" by means of regulations designed to protect small businesses from big ones.[67] The former finds the enemy chiefly in government, the latter principally in "bigness" and monopolies. Both organizations apparently experience a substantial turnover in membership; Zeigler estimates that in the case of the NFIB it is 90 percent per year.[68] Many businessmen can be attracted once to a militant, ideological cause, but few will renew their membership after the initial enthusiasm passes and the absence of progress—either toward the reversal of harmful social trends or the provision of concrete benefits to members—is noted. But some members will remain and still others are awaiting initial recruitment. To sustain the interest of those who rejoin and to attract the interest of those who might join for the first time, it is essential for the organization to maintain a combative, ideological posture. Unlike the NAM or Chamber, however, small business organizations suffer from the crucial disadvantage of not being able to count on the continuing membership of a few very large firms that provide out of big dues payments a stable core budget.

Nationwide small business organizations that ignore these organizational imperatives have trouble surviving. The National Association of Independent Businessmen, formed in 1952, sought to articulate a moderate policy: it accepted government intervention in the economy and the permanence of large corporations, but demanded more generous benefits, such as government loans, for small firms. Whatever the merits of this view, they were clearly not sufficient to sustain the organization. By 1961 it had become dormant, with perhaps 100 members.[69]

A national business association can exist and can take positions that are designed neither to satisfy a diverse constituency by their generality nor to attract a militant minority by their ideology, but to do so it must either find a different incentive system (by changing, for example, into a social or status-conferring organization) or become selective in its membership. The Committee for Economic Development (CED) has done both.[70] Formed in 1942 at the instigation of a few businessmen, notably Paul Hoffman and William Benton, who were concerned about the possibility of a postwar depression and the need for industrial planning to avoid it, the CED was guided from the outset by a hand-picked board of top business executives who shared this view. The initial board members were personally selected and recruited by Secretary of Commerce Jesse Jones, himself a well-known and wealthy businessman, from a list of suggestions offered by Hoffman, who became its first chairman and brought in a fellow executive of the Studebaker Corporation to organize local chapters around the country. A research group of academic experts was assembled under the direction of another business leader. During the war, the national CED and its thousands of local affiliates devoted their energies to compiling information about expected levels of postwar production and employment and to encouraging industrialists to plan for reconversion.

This data gathering was not controversial, though some criticized the CED for diverting attention from the war effort, and led, by happy accident, to the CED's correct prediction, contrary to much labor and governmental opinion, that there would *not* be massive postwar unemployment.[71] The roster of distinguished men on its board, the data-gathering service and industrial planning effort it had inspired, and the startling accuracy of its economic forecast gave the CED enormous prestige. With the end of the war, however, it faced a crisis—it had earlier promised the NAM and the Chamber of Commerce that it would go out of existence after the war emergency and would in no way attempt to compete with them as a general spokesman for business. Reluctantly, it voted to disband its Field Division—that is, its local affiliates and the national organization servicing them.[72] It decided to keep its Research Division, however, and to continue to make economic studies in association with academic experts.

Many of these studies on tax, labor, fiscal, and tariff policy proved highly controversial among businessmen and got the CED labeled as "liberal" compared to the NAM. Some financial supporters and board members quit in protest. On a number of occasions, the CED lost substantial sums of money because of its criticism of right-to-work laws and its position on various tariff and credit issues, but it was able to survive and prosper because it did not seek a mass base in the business community. The 200-man board of trustees of the CED *is* the CED, and businessmen are co-opted for service on it after having been carefully screened to ensure that they represent the right combination of business status and intellectual agreement with CED objectives and methods. No one can "join" the CED; he must be invited, and some businessmen have waged campaigns, not always successfully, to get invited. Members who are not active are dropped at the end of their three-year term. The funds to support the research staff are solicited from firms (about 3,000 contribute a total of $1.5 million) and from foundations. The staff in turn prepares papers for discussion with board members and various advisory committees. These papers rarely serve specific business interests; neither are they always harmlessly bland.

Taking controversial positions is possible because the CED does not seek a large membership and does not claim to perform a representational function; at the same time, its prestige and selectivity make it attractive to those businessmen who share its views. It is, in short, a prestigious club for "business liberals."

This review of the organizational strategies and political postures of various business associations suggests that, though the economic interests of members are important, the organizations have a wide variety of appeals with which to attract those members and thus display a considerable variety in how they define and advance such interests.

The clearest congruence between member interest and organizational activity can be found among the small and medium-sized trade associations that seek to cope with the threats to business advantage posed by union activity, market competition, and government regulation. Such groups may from time to time indulge in inflammatory or ideological rhetoric, but their daily preoccupation is with the details of costs, prices, freight rates, wage scales, import duties, and tax policies. Their chief organizational problem is to find a way of securing member compliance without arousing government prosecution. If there are not a very large number of firms in the industry, the trade association can often recruit the great majority into its ranks by a combination of the opportunities for getting acquainted, exchanging market and technological information, keeping an eye on the competition, and avoiding the charge of being an outsider or being selfish. Such associations are not unlike the smaller craft unions in their objectives, seeking to reduce the degree of competition for jobs or markets while maintaining a satisfactory price or wage. Unlike the craft unions, however, the trade associations cannot as easily enforce compliant behavior on their members—the unions can bargain to set a common wage rate but the firms cannot lawfully agree to set a common price. Thus the association must develop a variety of methods, involving chiefly persuasion—and occasionally, when the government is not looking, collusion and coercion—to reduce or eliminate price competition. When the opportunity is presented—as with the NRA or the Robinson-Patman Act—for trade associations to obtain legal sanction for establishing minimum price schedules and penalizing price cutting, they are quick to seize it. Without such legal tools, however, most associations appear to have had only limited success in reducing competition, and the success is least in those industries where the competition is the greatest. Furthermore, attempting to browbeat recalcitrant members into conforming to "fair trade" practices is a task that is neither easy nor pleasant, and few trade association executives would relish it even if the government might tolerate it. All trade association statements of purpose place strong emphasis on "government relations" partly to get the government to do their work for them and partly to provide the staff with a role that minimizes conflict with members.

Where the potential member firms in an industry are very numerous, the opportunities for voluntarily concerting their wills are correspondingly less. Organizations do exist in industries with many small firms, such as retail sales, but the incentive appeal must be different. The need for a common enemy becomes proportionately greater and the demand for legislative remedies proportionately stronger.

It seems likely, though there is no direct evidence of this, that small firms calculate the costs and benefits of joining a trade association differently from very large ones. To the small firm, costs are significant and thus the material or purposive benefits of joining must also be significant. To the large firm, costs are trivial and benefits need not be substantial; indeed, many large firms probably support a variety of associations for little reason other than the feeling that they have a duty to do so, supplemented by the solidary benefits of office and prestige that such associations confer on many of their senior executives. To put it somewhat differently, small businessmen ordinarily act more like "economic men" than larger ones, though a small fraction (but in absolute numbers, a sizable group) of small businessmen feel so strongly about matters of principle and ideology that they are willing to join even large organizations without receiving individual benefits.

A large national business organization, therefore, appeals differently to firms of different characteristics. The very large firms are the easiest to recruit despite the large dues they must pay, and these constitute a more or less stable core of members, and a more or less stable source of a minimum budget, that can be used as a base from which to recruit the smaller firms by more purposive appeals. Small business organizations, lacking such large members, must rely almost exclusively on either purposive or individual material incentives. If this hypothesis is correct, then large organizations with many large firms as members will be *less* preoccupied with either ideology or selective material inducements than large organizations without many large firm members. This is only conjecture, but the examples studied are consistent with it. The NAM was at its most militant when it was dominated by relatively small businessmen; though big firms came to play a larger role in it while it still struck a militant posture, in time it may have been the existence of such large members that enabled it to shift its strategy to one of bargaining.

To the extent that they rely on a combative posture or an ideological appeal, broadly based business associations have tended to centralize policy-making powers: though the NAM's board of directors dominates the organization, selects the president, and nominates members to fill its ranks, the various small business organizations have been virtually one-man shows. The members of these organizations are called upon to supply funds, but rarely to meet and deliberate over policies. The executives of such organizations have both more and less freedom of political action than those of more participatory organizations: more in the sense that policies need not be compromised to fit a wide range of diverse interests, less in that the ideologically motivated inner circle will not often countenance any softening of language to make policies more palatable to those in government or elsewhere whose actions and approval are being solicited.

Because of the relationship between political position and membership incentives, business organizations probably have less freedom with respect to setting a political course than do national labor organizations. The Chamber of Commerce must often state its views in the most general language so as to avoid offending any segment of membership opinion; the NAM in the past has had to frame its opinions so as to maintain the enthusiasm of the ideologically sensitive active minority. Those who have sought to have the Chamber take sharper positions or to have the NAM take more politic ones have generally failed. The NAM resigned from the Chamber in 1922, in part because it disliked the latter's unwillingness to denounce Democrats and all forms of government interference in the economy; by the same token, certain firms quit the NAM in opposition to associational belligerence. When such organizations are internally divided, as they were over tariff policy in the early 1960s, they will either issue weak statements, as in the case of the Chamber, or remain silent, as did the NAM.[73] Labor union members, by contrast, do not join their organizations because of the positions they take on national issues and probably would not be inclined (and, if in a union shop, would not be free) to resign should they disagree.[74] For unions, legislative positions have little value either as an incentive or as a disincentive for members, though they may have a considerable value as incentives for active staff members. Like the more bureaucratized segments of the national AFL-CIO, national business associations have staffs that develop an interest in a wide range of policies of little direct connection to business interests, partly out of a desire that the organization seem balanced and well-rounded in its views and partly to satisfy their own concerns. Unlike the national labor staffs, however, the bureaucracy of business associations probably has less freedom of action to campaign vigorously for positions that are not entirely consistent with the broad, though often vague, general consensus of businessmen.

NOTES

1. E. E. Schattschneider, *The Semisovereign People* (New York: Holt, Rinehart & Winston, 1960), pp. 30–32.

2. Temporary National Economic Committee (TNEC), *Trade Association Survey,* Monograph No. 18 of *Investigation of Concentration of Economic Power* (Washing-

ton, D.C.: Government Printing Office, 1941), p. 12. The TNEC survey of over 1,300 trade associations in 1938 revealed only 2 that had been in existence before 1860 and 10 that antedated 1870.

3. Kenneth E. Boulding, *The Organizational Revolution* (New York: Harper, 1953).

4. Clarence E. Bonnett, *History of Employers' Associations in the United States* (New York: Vantage Press, 1956), chaps. 10–12. See also TNEC, *Trade Association Survey*, p. 12.

5. Schattschneider, *The Semisovereign People*, p. 32; TNEC, *Trade Association Survey*, p. 360, table 3; Mancur Olson, *The Logic of Collective Action* (Cambridge, Mass.: Harvard University Press, 1965), p. 144.

6. George E. Prochaska and Joseph J. Schramek, "The Drug Industry" in *The Politics of Distributive Trade Associations*, ed. Henry Assael (Hempstead, N.Y.: Hofstra University Yearbook of Business, 1967), p. 29.

7. TNEC, *Trade Association Survey*, p. 361, table 7.

8. Ibid., p. 368, table 18.

9. See Harmon Zeigler, *Interest Groups in American Society* (Englewood Cliffs, N.J.: Prentice-Hall, 1964), pp. 96–97.

10. As of 1938, those trade associations whose members produced over 75 percent of the industry's volume were found disproportionately in the fields of transportation equipment, chemicals, machinery, iron and steel, and finance; many fewer such associations were found in the areas of printing, lumber, petroleum, and construction. TNEC, *Trade Association Survey*, p. 363, table 8. The former industries had a relatively small number of competitors; the latter, a relatively large number.

11. Leona Margaret Powell, *History of the United Typothetae of America* (Chicago: University of Chicago Press, 1926), pp. 5–8; Louis Galambos, *Competition and Cooperation: The Emergence of a National Trade Association* (Baltimore: Johns Hopkins Press, 1966), pp. 19–23.

12. Harry James Brown, "The National Association of Wool Manufacturers, 1864–1897" (Ph.D. diss., Cornell University, 1949).

13. Galambos, *Competition and Cooperation*, p. 35, esp. n. 79.

14. Ibid., pp. 23–30.

15. In his survey of eight major trade associations, Simon N. Whitney concludes that such groups have been formed more often in industries with unsatisfactory, rather than satisfactory, profit levels. Whitney, *Trade Associations and Industrial Control* (New York: Central Book Co., 1934), p. 142.

16. Leo Wolman, *Ebb and Flow in Trade Unionism* (New York: National Bureau of Economic Research, 1936), p. 16.

17. Thomas C. Cochran and William Miller, *The Age of Enterprise*, rev. ed. (New York: Harper Torchbooks, 1961), pp. 276–284.

18. Galambos, *Competition and Cooperation*, pp. 47–48. This is not the place to enter the lively debate as to the role of businessmen in supporting or opposing Progressive reforms. Robert H. Wiebe in *Businessmen and Reform: A Study of the Progressive Movement* (Cambridge, Mass.: Harvard University Press, 1962) finds evidence that some businessmen supported and some opposed these laws. Galambos's detailed study of one industry group (cotton textiles) suggests that these businessmen opposed most such reforms (p. 48, n. 3). Neither he nor Wiebe find evidence to support Gabriel Kolko's thesis that Progressivism was precisely what big businessmen wanted because it made secure their control over the nation's wealth. Kolko, *The Triumph of Conservatism* (New York: Free Press, 1963), p. 280. Kolko attempts to support his thesis by a selective examination of Progressive laws, emphasizing those federal enactments that regulated competition and neglecting those state laws that protected workers.

19. Galambos, *Competition and Cooperation*, pp. 55–60.
20. Powell, *History of the United Typothetae*, pp. 16–21.
21. Galambos, *Competition and Cooperation*, pp. 60–61.
22. Ibid., p. 76.
23. Ibid., p. 53.
24. Bonnett, *Employers' Associations*, pp. 248–256.
25. Ibid., pp. 261–262, 287–288, 350–351.
26. Zeigler, *Interest Groups*, p. 98.
27. Bonnett, *Employers' Associations*, pp. 453–471.
28. TNEC, *Trade Association Survey*, p. 12.
29. Ibid., p. 13.
30. Whitney concluded from his pre-NRA study of eight trade associations that of the seven that attempted to control competition and increase profits, four had little or no success and the three that enjoyed success found it short-lived as their enhanced profits attracted new entrants into the industry or increased foreign competition. The least success was enjoyed by industries with many competitors experiencing unsatisfactory profits. Whitney, *Trade Associations* pp. 142–144. Several trade associations have been prosecuted for attempting to restrain competition, but the record is far from clear as to the extent to which such restraint was successful and, if successful, what effect it had on prices. See the extensive discussion of cases involving manufacturers of hardwood lumber, linseed oil, maple flooring, and cement in I. L. Sharfman, "The Trade Association Movement," *American Economic Review*, XVI (March 1926 Supplement), pp. 203–218, and the discussion that follows (pp. 219–239).
31. Joseph Cornwall Palamountain, Jr., *The Politics of Distribution* (Cambridge, Mass.: Harvard University Press, 1955), pp. 90–106, 235–253.
32. TNEC, *Trade Association Survey*, pp. 21–26, 373–374, tables 25, 26.
33. *Members Appraise Associations* (Washington, D.C.: Association Service Department, Chamber of Commerce of the United States, 1966), p. 5. Government relations was also the function that members felt was being performed best (p. 17).
34. Alfred H. Kelly, "A History of the Illinois Manufacturers' Association" (Ph.D. diss., University of Chicago, 1938).
35. J. Roffe Wike, *The Pennsylvania Manufacturers' Association* (Philadelphia: University of Pennsylvania Press, 1960).
36. Richard W. Gable, "Birth of an Employers' Association," *Business History Review*, XXXIII (Winter 1959), 537.
37. Ibid., p. 545.
38. Wiebe, *Businessmen and Reform*, p. 26.
39. Gable, "Birth of an Employers' Association," p. 545.
40. Wiebe, *Businessmen and Reform*, p. 28; Albert K. Steigerwalt, *The National Association of Manufacturers, 1895–1914* (Ann Arbor: Graduate School of Business Administration, University of Michigan, 1964), pp. 152–153.
41. Wiebe, *Businessmen and Reform*, pp. 30–32; Gable, "Birth of an Employers' Association," p. 542.
42. Steigerwalt, *The National Association of Manufacturers*, pp. 138–147. A Senate committee issued no report on the investigation, but a House committee issued a critical one. After this episode, the direct political activities of the NAM were reduced. See also H. H. Wilson, *Congress: Corruption and Compromise* (New York: Rinehart, 1951), chap. 2.
43. Alfred S. Cleveland, "NAM: Spokesman for Industry?" *Harvard Business Review*, XXVI (May 1948), 357.
44. Zeigler, *Interest Groups*, p. 44.
45. "Renovation in NAM," *Fortune* (July 1948), p. 75.

46. Richard W. Gable, "NAM: Influential Lobby or Kiss of Death?" *Journal of Politics*, XV (May 1953), 260.

47. Ibid., p. 257; Cleveland, "NAM," p. 366.

48. Cleveland, "NAM," pp. 364–365.

49. Olson, *The Logic of Collective Action*, p. 146.

50. National Association of Manufacturers, *Official Policy Positions, 1971*, p. v. A staff member of the NAM told an interviewer that many prospective members are approached with the "opportunity to salve their consciences" because their failure to support the organization's defense of free enterprise was tantamount to getting a "free ride."

51. "NAM Is Playing By a New Set of Rules," *Business Week*, December 17, 1966, p. 116.

52. These firms included Gerber, Kellogg, United Fruit, and Royal Typewriter. Ibid., p. 118.

53. Wiebe, *Businessmen and Reform*, p. 33.

54. Harold Lawrence Childs, *Labor and Capital in National Politics* (Columbus: Ohio State University Press, 1930), p. 8.

55. Wiebe, *Businessmen and Reform*, pp. 37–40.

56. Childs, *Labor and Capital in National Politics*, p. 13, nn. 13, 14.

57. Ibid., p. 25, n. 44.

58. Olson, *The Logic of Collective Action*, p. 146.

59. Ibid.

60. U. S. Chamber of Commerce, "Statement Indicating Number of Business Members and Total Dues as of July 1, Each Year," mimeographed (July 1, 1966).

61. In the same period, the number of organization members declined from 3,678 to 3,560.

62. U. S. Chamber of Commerce, *Policy Declarations, 1970–1971*.

63. U. S. Chamber of Commerce, *By-Laws* (as of January 1968), Article XII, section 1.

64. During the 1920s, the last period for which there is a published analysis, about half the members did not vote. Childs, *Labor and Capital in National Politics*, p. 166.

65. U. S. Chamber of Commerce, *Policy Declarations, 1970–1971*, pp. 26, 61, 64, 118.

66. Palamountain, *The Politics of Distribution*, pp. 83–84, 92–93.

67. Harmon Zeigler, *The Politics of Small Business* (Washington, D.C.: Public Affairs Press, 1961), pp. 16–20, 32–34, 43.

68. Ibid., p. 22.

69. Ibid., p. 63.

70. The early history of the CED is told in Karl Schriftgiesser, *Business Comes of Age* (New York: Harper, 1960). The postwar policy papers of the CED are discussed in Schriftgiesser's later volume, *Business and Public Policy* (Englewood Cliffs, N.J.: Prentice-Hall, 1967).

71. Schriftgiesser, *Business Comes of Age*, pp. 54–59. The CED was right, but for the wrong reasons: its data were shaky, its inferences simplistic, and its assumptions erroneous. But it was right, and that was all that then mattered.

72. The CED first offered its Field Division, more or less intact, to the Chamber of Commerce, but the Chamber's staff, perhaps fearful of the disruption absorbing such an enterprise into an existing organization would entail, declined.

73. Raymond A. Bauer, Ithiel de Sola Pool, and Lewis Anthony Dexter, *American Business and Public Policy* (New York: Atherton Press, 1963), pp. 333–336.

74. Ibid., pp. 337–338.

CHAPTER 9

Civil Rights Organizations

From time to time, important segments of opinion have become preoccupied with the conditions and status of blacks in American society—during the agitation over slavery, in the aftermath of Southern Reconstruction, at the time of the race riots of 1908 and 1919, following any particularly brutal series of lynchings during the 1910s and 1920s, in the depression of the 1930s, after the Detroit riot of 1943, at the time of the school desegregation cases in 1954, and finally between 1960 and 1967 in the midst of a civil rights movement and ghetto insurrections. Though in each of these periods, organizations of every description were formed to advance black interests, only two of national significance and substantial scope have endured. Both were created at about the same time (1909–1911) and each has displayed remarkable continuity in leadership and purpose. The National Association for the Advancement of Colored People (NAACP) and the Urban League have, almost alone among scores of organizational attempts, succeeded in institutionalizing a concern over race relations.

Many other associations have enjoyed a brief existence—the Constitution League, the Niagara Movement, the Equal Opportunity League, the March on Washington Movement, the Student Nonviolent Coordinating Committee (SNCC)—and a few of these exercised, for a limited time, an influence all out of proportion to their small size or their brief life span. Some, such as the Congress of Racial Equality (later CORE), founded in 1942, have endured for several decades in one form or another and from time to time have had substantial resources and an important leadership role, but on the whole their operations have been episodic, their leadership changing, their posture in flux, and their very life dependent on the uncertainties of public mood and national events.

The NAACP, by contrast, has had during the last fifty years only three executives (James Weldon Johnson, Walter White, and Roy Wilkins). Though it has occasionally felt it necessary to modify its tactics to respond to internal criticisms, its fundamental posture and goals have hardly changed at all. And though its financial support and public reputation have been subject to the vicissitudes that afflict most voluntary associations, it has managed to enlarge its professional staff, win an impressive list of legal battles, and retain the support, as measured by public opinion polls if not by money contributions, of the overwhelming majority of black citizens. Similarly, the National Urban League has grown from a small committee created in New York City in 1910 to coordinate the work of various social service agencies to an organization with units in about 100 localities, a national headquarters, a budget of $15 million, and a professional staff of 3,000, and all this despite the fact that it has been dependent on white contributors, and business contributors at that, during a period of growing racial pride and rising demands for self-determination.

Furthermore, these two associations were created, not at a time of broad agreement among blacks as to the proper course of action, but in a period when blacks were deeply divided. Since the 1890s, Booker T. Washington, head of the Tuskegee Institute in Alabama, had urged blacks to adapt to the realities of life in the South by developing their economic skills through vocational education and agricultural enterprise. In the early 1900s, William E. B. Du Bois, who had arisen as the major critic of Washington, was the spokesman for granting full civil rights to blacks and the leader of the college-educated "Talented Tenth" of Negro Americans. In 1905, Du Bois formed the Niagara Movement to serve as the organized opposition to Washington; many of its members later joined the NAACP in 1909–1910. The NAACP was from the first led by opponents of Washington and was the object of Washington's counterattacks. Indeed, a major problem confronting the new association was whether to mute or to intensify the conflict between the pro- and anti-Washington groups. The issue repeatedly came to a head because of Du Bois's insistence that the journal of the NAACP, *The Crisis*, be free to attack publicly those black leaders, especially, but not only, Washington, with whom it disagreed.

The organizational strategy adopted by the NAACP was, in retrospect, an ingenious solution to the problem of organizational survival. It was, first of all, a threat-oriented association. Though the organization's name included the word "advancement," it would have been more accurate to substitute the word "defense." Oswald Garrison Villard described in a letter to Washington the group he wanted to see formed as a "strong central defense committee" and James Weldon Johnson, the NAACP's first black secretary, called it a "watchman on the wall, sounding the alarms that called us to defense."[1] Some of the earliest local branches styled themselves "Vigilance Committees." "The Call," the famous document issued in 1909 by whites with familial and ideological links to the abolitionist tradition, was prompted by the 1908 race riot and lynchings in Springfield, Illinois, Lincoln's home town, and spoke of the revolting brutalities and disfranchisement being directed at Negroes.[2]

Condemning such brutalities was something about which all blacks and many liberal whites could agree. And they supplied the association with an obvious agenda—legal action and publicity directed against specific evils. The general goal of Negro advancement, though important, was scarcely attainable by associational activity, and efforts to agree on what this advancement required were likely to prove divisive. But court challenges to the "white primary" and segregated railroad cars and legal defense provided to blacks accused of crimes in the South, though by no means assured of success, offered at least the reasonable hope of victory in the short term. Furthermore, such actions, as well as the publicity campaigns directed against lynchings, could be centrally led and professionally staffed by a relatively small number of experts. The earlier Niagara Movement, while sharing many of the same general goals of the NAACP, was never able to settle upon a concrete agenda for specific actions or to attract money and influential white support. Though it had the advantage of having for a time Du Bois as its spokesman, it soon disintegrated.[3]

To sustain itself, the NAACP had to induce persons to contribute time and leadership. Initially, these contributions came almost entirely from white Progressives and Socialists such as Mary White Ovington, Oswald Garrison Villard, Moorfield Storey, William English Walling, and Joel Spingarn. They occupied the principal offices in the organization, and Du Bois was appointed Director of Publicity and Research, with special responsibility for editing *The Crisis*. These key supporters acted out of a sense of purpose that sometimes led to bitter struggles over the allocation of offices. But it was futile to expect that a mass following would develop or respond to the continuing financial appeals of a small national committee, however worthwhile its objectives, especially inasmuch as blacks, the natural constituency for such a group, were, on the average, poor.

Accordingly, the NAACP from the first began to encourage the formation of branches in various cities. The name, structure, and general purposes of these units were controlled by the national organization—for example, it encouraged the branches to include some white members[4]—but the specific activities, and especially the incentive systems, of the branches were allowed to vary widely. In parts of the South, an NAACP branch was virtually a semisecret society of those few blacks willing to risk white reprisals; in Boston, the branch leadership was a select gathering of well-to-do whites having a family tradition of abolitionism with whom were associated a few Negro intellectuals; the New York City branch, originally called the Vigilance Committee, was run by a small group of liberal whites and Negroes as an agency for legal redress, as in cases of police brutality, and protest, as in cases of segregation at theaters and amusement parks; in Indianapolis, the branch was an association of women, mostly schoolteachers, for whom the group was probably a combination sorority and professional society; in Washington, D. C., many black government employees joined to protect their federal jobs from the inroads of segregation and to improve their chances for advancement; in Detroit, the first branch was limited to men only; and so on. By World War I, the NAACP drew most of its income from these branches, the great majority of the members of which were black.[5]

In short, the branches employed a great variety of incentives, but from the national office's point of view all were geared to the same end —half of every dollar collected in dues was sent to headquarters in New York. As time went on, many of these branches came to rely heavily on solidary rewards: meetings, especially as units became predominately black, were often social occasions for the emerging Negro middle class. They also were places where aspiring black lawyers could call attention to themselves and their professional practices without actually advertising, and would-be officeholders could begin to gather constituencies for electoral campaigns.[6] All this was possible, however, only so long as the branches were successful in institutionalizing themselves and the national office was able to supply the branches with sufficient benefits, so that their allegiance to its program and their willingness to remit funds were unimpaired.

To a considerable degree, both of these requirements were met by the extraordinary success enjoyed by *The Crisis* under the leadership of Du Bois. In 1917, *The Crisis* had a circulation in excess of 40,000 copies per month even though total NAACP dues-paying membership was still less than 10,000.[7] Well written and outspoken, it became for many blacks the public image of the NAACP. To the NAACP itself, especially to key black as well as white board members, *The Crisis* was the independent and often cantankerous image of Du Bois personally. He was relentlessly and single-mindedly absorbed in advancing black interests, at least as he defined them; the NAACP, on the other hand, sought to represent a broad spectrum of black and liberal white opinion and, to that end, wished to take positions that would unify rather than divide its constituency. Du Bois, in the pages of *The Crisis*, frequently attacked blacks with whom he disagreed and white institutions he disliked. Some white board members may have winced when they read in *The Crisis* that "while the most ordinary Negro" is an instinctive gentleman, "it takes extraordinary training, gift and opportunity to make the average white man anything but an overbearing hog."[8] But what aroused their ire were Du Bois's attacks on other blacks and his insistence that *The Crisis* was editorially independent of the NAACP. Du Bois repeatedly criticized not only the followers of Booker T. Washington, but also Negro ministers ("pretentious ill-trained men . . . dishonest and otherwise immoral" who preach "silly and empty sermons") and the Negro press (much of their output was not "worth reprinting or even reading").[9]

Though surely unintended, the cleavage between board-managed projects and Du Bois-inspired rhetoric proved in the long run to be an important key to success. At the level of general argument and tone, the NAACP projected a powerful sense of purpose; at the level of practical programs, it brought lawsuits, investigated lynchings, and lobbied against bills that threatened black interests. Its sense of purpose helped mobilize support for the association and gave it a dominant position among the many small contenders for race leadership; its practical programs helped it avoid the paralyzing and divisive effort of finding ways to launch a broad, comprehensive program for economic and social, as well as political, advancement.

Furthermore, the legal strategy gave to the national office a specific resource with which to maintain branch loyalty and focus branch efforts. In large part as the result of the efforts of NAACP lawyers, the Supreme Court in 1915 struck down the "grandfather clause" of the Oklahoma Constitution, a clause that exempted from burdensome voter-registration requirements those whose grandfathers had voted, who of course could only be whites.[10] In 1917, NAACP lawyers filed the brief that led the Supreme Court to hold unconstitutional a municipal residential-segregation ordinance in Louisville.[11] And in the 1920s, the NAACP was deeply involved in the long series of white-primary cases that eventually resulted in a clear Supreme Court ruling that blacks could not be barred from participating in primary elections held by political parties to select candidates for office.[12] These successes not only enhanced the standing of the association, but also encouraged local branches to seek assistance from the national office in preparing briefs, obtaining lawyers, and enlisting the official endorsement of the NAACP for their efforts.[13]

This legal work, together with the continuing program to create new branches, find more members, investigate more lynchings, and obtain favorable legislation, was not in the hands of Du Bois, the public image of the NAACP, but in the hands of part-time white officers at first and then, beginning in 1916, in those of a Negro, James Weldon Johnson, who was field secretary from 1916 and executive secretary after 1920. Johnson had been a supporter of Booker T. Washington and while a reporter for the (black) *New York Age* had on occasion been critical of *The Crisis*. Above all, he was, in the opinion of a white former secretary, "a good mixer, . . . a good talker, and would offend no group nor any audience."[14] And he turned out to be a skillful executive.

One measure of his ability was soon evident. The circulation of *The Crisis* reached its peak in 1919 and thereafter declined, falling by more than two-thirds by 1925. But funds obtained from memberships remained constant and even grew somewhat during that same six-year period.[15] Though the depression years were as hard on the NAACP as they were on labor unions and other associations, income from membership never fell below $20,000 a year and by 1939 had risen to nearly $40,000. *The Crisis*, however, had by 1939 a circulation of only slightly more than 10,000, compared to the nearly 100,000 two decades earlier, and was in grievous financial and editorial troubles.[16] In short, the NAACP had successfully institutionalized itself.

From time to time the posture, goals, and organization of the NAACP have come under attack from within and without, but every attack has been weathered without having to make fundamental changes. During the 1930s, many blacks, including Du Bois, called for a shift from a strictly political and legal strategy to an economic one in response to the worsening material conditions of blacks. Du Bois suggested black consumer coöperatives and boycotts. Various young militants, such as Abram Harris, rejected both the separatist implications of Du Bois's position and the legal protest strategy of the NAACP and called instead for measures to develop alliances with the industrial unions and for "working-class solidarity."[17] Such solidarity, of course, required that the NAACP cease attacking unions for their discriminatory practices, or at least that it confine its attack to those unions in which discrimination was most blatant, and ally itself with groups such as the United Mine Workers (UMW), the International Ladies Garment Workers (ILGWU), and later the United Auto Workers (UAW). Harris, a professor at Howard University, was asked to chair a committee on the "future plan and program" of the NAACP as a way of responding to the demands for an economic strategy.

The committee's report called for an emphasis on building an industrial labor movement that would unite blacks and whites, conducting "workers' education" classes, supporting social welfare legislation, organizing cooperatives on an integrated basis, and, of course, continuing, but obviously with less attention, the traditional legal and political action against discrimination. To carry out these programmatic changes, the branches would have to become "permanent centers of economic and political education and agitation," and the national office would have to be reorganized in a way that would lessen the authority of the board and the secretary and enhance that of a new Committee on Economic Activities.[18]

The report was intensively discussed. In the end, most of its language was adopted, but few of its structural changes were made. In this, the NAACP maintained the strategy it had evolved during the Du Bois period: bold statements to build and retain support and moderate action to achieve feasible objectives. Assistant secretary Roy Wilkins, later to become secretary, stated the key objections to the new strategy: Negroes suffering under the burden of being colored could not be expected to shoulder the additional burden of appearing economically radical—it was bad enough to be black without being "Red" as well. And how were these economic objectives to be attained? For one thing, vague appeals to working-class solidarity would not generate much income for the association. As Wilkins put it at the time, it is a "splendid program," but there is "not a single item in it which will catch the emotional fancy of the people to such an extent that thousands of dollars can be raised." [19]

In retrospect, Wilkins was probably correct. The New Deal legislation would have passed whatever posture the NAACP took; bolder legislation calling for changes in the capitalist system had little chance of success; NAACP support could not have aided it and might have hurt both it and the association. The experience of the National Negro Congress (NNC), created by John P. Davis, was illustrative of the problem. Many black dissidents who had been unable to capture the NAACP, such as Harris, Du Bois, E. Franklin Frazier, Ralph Bunche, and A. Philip Randolph, spoke at a conference organized by Davis, and each was critical of the New Deal, Bunche calling for "social planning" and the abolition of private capitalism, and Randolph denouncing the "profit system." [20] The NNC was launched in 1936, in the wake of this conference and on the wave of rhetoric that flowed from it, as an organization of organizations. It scored some quick successes, enlisting the support of various local CIO unions, stimulating various boycotts, and testifying before Congress. But by 1940 it was virtually moribund. Many local black leaders disliked its radical stance; union delegates to its conferences began to dominate the proceedings; it was not able to win any major victories that could serve to institutionalize its role in black politics; and it came to be influenced by the American Communist party. During the period of the Popular Front, the NNC and the Communists together denounced Nazi Germany and fascism; after the Nazi-Soviet Pact of 1939, both organizations called on America to stay out of "the imperialist war" in Europe; after the German invasion of Russia, the NNC reversed itself again and called for American intervention in Europe.[21] Ironically, in an effort to develop its financial base, the NNC in 1938 became involved in the antilynching campaign that its leaders had once criticized the NAACP for giving excessive attention to. Lynching cases were the one sure way to raise money, and Wilkins and Walter White, who by then had become NAACP secretary, were bitterly critical of Davis and the NNC for cutting in on their program and thus dividing their meager potential resources.[22] The NNC was not successful in this effort and was led to depend even more heavily on the unions and (chiefly white) radical groups for funds, and thus its demise as a mass black organization was assured.

A second challenge to the NAACP arose in 1941 with the announcement by A. Philip Randolph, who had recently quit the NNC in disgust, that he would lead a march on Washington, D.C., to end discrimination in national defense work. The March on Washington Movement (MOWM), as it came to be called, had the personal endorsement of the executives of both the NAACP and the Urban League, but neither organization devoted much resources to helping mobilize for such a march, and some leaders in each displayed a good deal of skepticism about whether such an effort was feasible or appropriate. On June 25, 1941,

President Roosevelt issued an executive order on fair employment practices, and thus the march, scheduled for July 1, was called off, much to the disappointment of some younger leaders who had rallied to Randolph's effort. In general, however, the victory was hailed by blacks. But Randolph decided to keep the MOWM in existence, partly as a threat to deter the government from reneging on its commitments, partly because he had created a mass-based organization he was reluctant to disband, and partly to respond to the enthusiasms of activists in the movement. Though the NAACP continued its official endorsement of the MOWM, it was doubtful of its value, opposed to its all-black membership policy, and probably alarmed at the rival influence of Randolph as a public figure.[23] The skepticism at least was well founded: a one-man appeal to a large mass with no clear and dramatic single objective could not sustain an organization such as the MOWM, and soon it was moribund.

The NAACP faced and survived a third and more serious challenge in the 1960s led by so-called "Young Turks" who wanted the association to place a greater emphasis on direct protest action instead of petitioning for legal redress and on community organization in the urban ghettoes. By 1964 their attacks had become sharper: they called for the resignation of executive secretary Roy Wilkins and the replacement of the white president with a black. By 1968 they were prepared to deny the appropriateness of integration as an association goal and called for a "black approach" in lieu of an interracial strategy. After prolonged and often intense struggle, the established leadership of the NAACP defeated the insurgents in various elections at the conventions. At the high point of their influence, the Young Turks had only twelve of the sixty seats on the board of directors. After the 1968 convention, when they received only one-third of the votes, many of the Young Turks resigned from the board.[24]

Since its creation, the NAACP has undergone important changes, but they have been both gradual and consistent with its integrationist and legal-protest posture. In the 1930s, it adopted much of the Harris report on economic matters and began to develop an alliance with various CIO unions, but without abandoning the primacy of political objectives sought by centralized strategies. Over the years, it steadily reduced the number of whites in influential positions so that by the time of the "black power" movement of the 1960s, it could fairly claim that virtually every important policy position was held by a black. And when young members demanded a greater voice in the association, it enlarged its board of directors, provided representation of the Youth Councils on the board, and gave local councils greater autonomy. The centralized, bureaucratized structure of the NAACP, as Rudwick and Meier have explained, made the association relatively stable in goals and tactics.

CORE and SNCC, on the other hand, have displayed the greatest instability. CORE began in 1942 as a small band of white pacifists and middle-class black intellectuals that pioneered the sit-in strategy in various restaurants and amusement parks in the North. In the summer of 1961, CORE brought its methods to the South in the form of "freedom rides" intended to integrate southern transportation facilities, and in 1962 it used the same methods against segregated restaurants along southern highways. It conducted a sit-in to force the California state legislature to pass a fair housing law, launched boycotts against large chain stores to obtain more black employment, and disrupted the opening of the New York World's Fair. By 1964, however, it had begun to shift from sit-ins to community organization drives, from an integrated to an all-black membership, and from a nonviolent to a self-defense strategy. By 1966 it had become part of the black power movement and was much reduced in funds and national attention.[25]

SNCC was the organizational outgrowth of the lunch-counter sit-ins begun by black college students in the South in 1960. In 1961 its members were involved in the freedom rides begun by CORE, and large numbers of students were jailed. A bitter dispute over the future of SNCC arose as the sit-in movement began to wane, with some wishing to pursue a voter registration drive in the South and others preferring a direct action strategy of community organization and mass protests. Both groups retained, however, a commitment to nonviolent tactics. In 1964 SNCC was the leading group in a coalition of civil rights organizations, including CORE and the NAACP, that led a "Freedom Summer" in Mississippi aimed in part at challenging that state's delegation to the Democratic National Convention. The Mississippi Freedom Democratic party was formed and sought to be seated at Atlantic City, but it rejected the compromise offered by convention leaders. By the fall of 1964, the failure of many of its organizing drives, the murder of a number of black and white student workers, the rebuff, as SNCC viewed it, at Atlantic City, and the collapse of the Mississippi civil rights coalition had left SNCC unsure of its direction and embittered by its experiences. By 1966 the SNCC national chairman, John Lewis, had been replaced by the more aggressive Stokeley Carmichael, who shortly after assuming office enunciated the black power slogan while on a march through Mississippi. The few white members of SNCC were excluded. Within two years, the organization was virtually dead, having few members and almost no funds. Carmichael had been accused of inciting a riot in Atlanta; his successor as SNCC chairman, H. Rap Brown, was soon under indictment on various charges; and the organization had been eclipsed in public attention by the emergent Black Panther party. The movement that had been hailed by white liberals at its inception as a major liberating force, that had been joined in 1964 by hundreds of white northern college students, and that had raised hundreds of thousands of dollars from all over the country, was by 1965–1966 being denounced by an officer of the NAACP, a leader of the Socialist party, a key figure in the Americans for Democratic Action, a liberal southern newspaper editor, and by various union officials.[26]

All three civil rights organizations discussed here are purposive associations, but the NAACP from the first developed a structure and program that required little of the average member,[27] permitted a variety of incentives to be employed at the branch level, limited its purposes to fairly specific goals that were generally approved by blacks, and engaged in campaigns that made it possible for victories to be won in the short term. CORE and SNCC, by contrast, developed a structure that required a great deal of the average member, and so these organizations were forced to make use of powerful incentives whose appeal would inevitably be limited; furthermore, they embraced goals that were expressive of the broad and intense commitment of members, and selected strategies that offered little hope of making significant progress toward those goals and thus little prospect of winning victories that could sustain the commitment. In terms of the analysis presented in Chapter 3, the NAACP was a goal-oriented organization relying on specific purposive incentives combined with solidary and material ones; CORE and SNCC were redemptive associations relying on broadly stated purposes the achievement of which required not only a general transformation of society but also the exemplary conduct of members.

The contributions asked of NAACP members were small, and so the inducements could be correspondingly marginal; the contributions asked of CORE or SNCC activists were great—indeed, involving in some cases matters of life and death—and thus the incentives had to be appropriately large. CORE began, not as a national office, but as small chapters of whites and blacks attempting to apply nonviolent direct-action techniques to the task of converting the owners of segregated restaurants to a voluntary acceptance of an interracial clientele.[28] The first chapter in Chicago was composed of a dozen blacks and two dozen whites who were dissatisfied with the legal strategy of the NAACP and preferred direct, but nonviolent action by an interracial group. In view of CORE's later development, it is noteworthy that its early leaders explicitly rejected racial chauvinism, criticized such events as Negro History Week, and opposed Negro block voting in elections; such ethnic appeals in their view only perpetuated the cleavages in the larger society.[29]

CORE chapters bestowed voting membership only on those who fully subscribed to the CORE Action Discipline and who worked actively in direct-action projects. The average chapter was, as a consequence, small in numbers—generally having between twenty and thirty members—and intense in experience. When the national organization was formed in 1943, it was a federation of these small, largely autonomous chapters and had for many years no full-time executive and no budget supplied by assessments levied on the chapters; any money needed by the national office had to be raised by a special national fund drive aimed, usually, at white donors.[30] A paid, full-time executive was first hired in 1957; money became more plentiful and the staff numerous during the civil rights movement of the 1960s. This short-lived affluence produced neither a stable bureaucracy nor much national direction over chapter affairs.

Though the philosophical orientation of CORE, derived from the writings of Gandhi, changed over time, participation in CORE remained for many key members a "total experience," a way of life.[31] That experience differed in the North and the South. Northern black members were middle-class, often college-affiliated young people who moved easily in the white world and who gradually developed a sharp distrust of white institutions and a radical stance toward social change. Southern black members were more likely to come from working-class or farm families, to have less schooling than their northern counterparts, to have had fewer contacts with whites, and to display a more moderate political orientation.[32] By the mid-1960s, it was the northern group that took the leadership in moving CORE toward a black-power orientation and a commitment to community organizing in northern big-city ghettoes.

That the black CORE members with the most personal advantages should take this step is only superficially paradoxical. Racial progress in the South was slow at best, but it appeared slowest to northern blacks who judged a small gain in voter registration or lunch-counter integration by more exacting standards than did southern black members who had never seen any change at all. The ghetto riots of 1965–1967 also made it painfully evident to northern CORE chapters that they had no base among the urban black masses: they were unable to foment such insurrections, lead or end them once they were underway, or provide an alternative to them. Furthermore, the federal antipoverty program was beginning to spend money and create new centers of potential influence in the cities; this program offered opportunities that would be seized by somebody, and CORE leaders might as well be among the contenders.[33] The 1966 CORE convention that ratified the break with the nonviolent tradition, embraced black power as a slogan, and confirmed the community-organizing strategy, was attended primarily by black members from northern chapters. By 1966 only one white remained on the national council of CORE; by 1968 whites were formally excluded.[34] Martin Luther King, Jr. refused to address the convention, which heard instead Stokeley Carmichael of SNCC, a Black Muslim, and the leader of a New York City rent strike.[35] Though a careful reading of the resolutions adopted at the convention reveals no advocacy of violence, but only a willingness to exercise the right of self-defense, and no explicit antiwhite statements, but rather an emphasis on "negritude," liberal white attacks on CORE mounted and financial contributions dwindled.

The disillusionment that inevitably afflicts a redemptive association seeking to transform society is even more vividly illustrated in the history of SNCC. Unlike CORE, it was never active in the North and thus was never exposed to the opportunities for community organizing that CORE attempted to seize. It was born in the South and died there; during the half dozen or so years of its active existence, it changed from a communications network among black college students seeking peacefully to integrate lunch counters to a small coterie of young middle-class blacks committed to radical political action and preoccupied with what many thought was a coming race war. As it moved along this route, it attempted a variety of projects ranging from freedom marches to economic boycotts, from helping black voters to register to organizing all-black political parties. Judged by certain standards, many of the events in which SNCC was an important participant could be regarded as victories—many lunch counters were integrated, thousands of southern blacks were registered to vote, the Civil Rights Acts of 1964 and 1965 were passed by Congress, and the 1964 Democratic National Convention took the unprecedented step of offering to seat and give voting rights to two representatives of the Mississippi Freedom Democratic party even though this led the regular, all-white, Mississippi delegation to bolt the convention.

To SNCC, however, these results were at best irrelevancies and at worst defeats. An integrated lunch counter became to them only a symbolic gain; the voter registration drives exposed SNCC members to beatings, jailings, and even death, while the United States Department of Justice seemed to look the other way; the Civil Rights Acts were, in the words of SNCC chairman John Lewis, "too little and too late"; and the Democratic convention compromise was repugnant to a group that felt itself morally and politically right.[36] And though black voter registration in the South was increasing, in the areas where SNCC chose to work, such as Mississippi, it scarcely seemed to increase at all. Above all, the lot of the poor southern black, especially his economic lot, remained unchanged.

SNCC neither sought out an easily accomplished task nor developed a sustaining ideology. Quite the contrary: it deliberately chose to struggle in the most difficult and hostile regions of the Deep South and to ignore doctrinal matters except for disjointed and improvised rhetoric about the nature of society and of the movement.[37]

It is a commonplace to observe that SNCC, and to a lesser extent CORE, became radicalized out of their mounting sense of frustration. What is perhaps more important is that consciously or unconsciously, SNCC (and, to a lesser extent, CORE) *courted frustration.* After the relatively peaceful sit-ins, SNCC joined a freedom ride that ended in violence. After this incident, it began direct action and voter registration drives in the most violent and antiblack counties in the Deep South. After the registration drives, it sought to build, in such places as Lowndes County, Alabama, an all-black political party to win control of local government. At no point did SNCC retreat to the easier targets to be found in the border states or to the safer strategy of legislative and courtroom pressure.

In part, the relentless quest for the ultimate challenge reflected narrow organizational maintenance needs. After the first wave of lunch-counter sit-ins, media and national attention to a repetition of these tactics declined, and thus the members' sense of being part of a large and significant movement waned. To recover that attention, new and bolder methods were necessary, such as refusing bail when arrested after a sit-in,[38] or riding a chartered bus into the Deep South to integrate waiting rooms, or joining a march on Selma, Alabama, where local law enforcement officials were especially unyielding. In part also, the selection of the most refractory targets arose out of a desire to find a unique organizational role, one that could not easily be duplicated by the NAACP, whose local branches had been involved for some time in sit-ins, and one that would distinguish it from middle-class, "conservative" civil rights groups.

But the high-risk strategy of SNCC and CORE resulted mainly from the nature of the bond that united the members. CORE began with an elaborate view of the power of truth and nonviolence to change the hearts of the enemy; SNCC from the first saw itself as a small band of brothers united by a strong if vague commitment to the notions of community and freedom as the key elements of a new social order, the attainment of which would require great sacrifices by, and considerable danger to, those who worked for it. SNCC members thought of themselves, as Emily Stoper puts it, as "an elect group with special enlightenment" in which one might seek personal perfection as well as struggle toward social reconstruction.[39] To continue the religious metaphor, such redemptive organizations tend to govern themselves on the principle of the priesthood of all believers. CORE began by using consensual methods of reaching decisions—finding the "sense of the meeting"[40]—and SNCC distrusted organizational forms and the powers of leadership during most of its history.[41]

If an association is only a religious sect, it need test its members only with personal and inward-looking challenges. But if, as with SNCC and CORE, it seeks also the transformation of existing society, it must as a group test that society at its points of greatest resistance. For SNCC especially, proof of the worth of a member—indeed, sometimes acceptance *as* a member—required one to display commitment and courage under the most trying circumstances. Those who were most prominent in the association, such as Carmichael and Bob Moses, were those who accepted the most challenging tasks and went to the most dangerous counties. An easy victory was no victory at all, for it would mean only that society had yielded at its hypocritical periphery and not changed at its immoral core and that the members involved had proved themselves marginally involved but not totally committed. Having been in jail or having been beaten came to be a badge of honor; having avoided this was grounds for suspicion.

Because black persons in the South were more vulnerable than white ones in that they were more frequently victimized and lacked a white sanctuary to which they could retreat, SNCC became increasingly convinced that no white member could ever prove himself as fully as could a black one—the risks being less, the proof of commitment would be less—and inevitably SNCC moved toward a policy of excluding whites.

Black members were reinforced in this view when they observed that the national press devoted massive attention to the murder of white civil rights workers in the South but less, if any, attention to the murder of black ones.[42]

To any redemptive organization, the possibilities of an alliance with other associations are slim. Any other association has, in comparison, selected easier targets, has adopted less uncompromising means, or is more willing to settle for immediate gains than is the redemptive one. Given the total commitment of SNCC to a certain way of life, its hostility will be greatest toward precisely those associations that appear to share its goals without sharing its zeal. Such groups as the Southern Christian Leadership Conference (SCLC) of Martin Luther King, Jr., and the NAACP were special objects of SNCC distrust because in SNCC's view they pursued ends—racial equality, personal freedom— that were of transcendent and absolute value by means that seemed incremental and compromising.

In this, the SNCC and CORE activists resembled the more zealous advocates of abolishing slavery in 1834–1836. The American Anti-Slavery Society began in 1833 to agitate for "immediate emancipation, gradually accomplished." It was not only the apparent confusion of such a doctrine that limited its appeal, but the fact that the appeal was delivered by newspaper and pamphlet to scattered audiences who were thereby aroused to bewilderment or even hostility, but rarely to action. The transformation of the society into a movement occurred only when some students at Lane Seminary in Ohio were converted as a group, after a protracted religious and intellectual experience, into a small band of advocates, willing, under the leadership of Theodore Weld, to carry the message of immediate emancipation as a moral and religious obligation into the most hostile communities and to the most skeptical audiences.[43] The problem of planning how to emancipate the slaves and what provision to make for them once emancipated could be set aside in favor of treating slavery simply as a sin and preaching this doctrine in the language of religious revival in the small towns of America. As the South proved itself immune to its planned conversion, despair replaced hope and antisouthern hatreds supplanted the desire to win the sinner with love and patience. Within two or three years "the antislavery impulse ceased to be a missionary movement to save the slaveholders—'the bewildered Southern brethren in the Lord'—from their 'state of desperation,' and became a drive for petitions to support a sectional war."[44] By 1839 the Great Revival was over, Weld's group of student activists had disbanded, and funds for the Anti-Slavery Society were no longer forthcoming.

Just as the impact of the Great Revival on subsequent abolitionist events was more significant than its brief life would suggest, so also the impact of CORE and SNCC on the civil rights movement generally and on the NAACP in particular was more important than their inability to institutionalize themselves might imply. The influence was greatest on various NAACP branches. It has always been a strength of that association that local units could perform a wide variety of roles while remaining in the parent body, and thus, during the 1960s, many branches became, for a time at least, like CORE, if not like SNCC, in some of their activities. The NAACP Youth Council in Milwaukee, led by Father Groppi, mounted mass protests against housing segregation; the Philadelphia branch for a while became, under Cecil Moore, a militant source of picketing, boycotts, and voter registration campaigns;[45] in Mississippi, an NAACP branch became the organizational base for the political activities of Charles Evers in Adams and Wilkinson Counties. The local branches had from the earliest days of the NAACP engaged in local protest campaigns, but the civil rights movement, and the pressure exerted by rival sources of leadership such as CORE, SNCC, and SCLC, quickened that activity during the 1960s. The national office, accordingly, was not reluctant to see its branches engage in many of those protest tactics to which the spirit of the times impelled them.

But the structure of the NAACP continued to give a distinctive character to many of these branch activities. With few, if any, exceptions, the branches did not become the organizational equivalents of CORE or SNCC. The branch was to the average member an object of segmental and partial involvement, not a way of life. Leadership was of decisive importance in energizing a branch, and that leadership was supported to the extent that it generated incentives for members—a sense of solidarity, enhanced status, material benefits for those helped by a protest campaign, and, especially important in the Deep South, an enlarged sense of political competence and personal safety in the face of a decades-old pattern of exclusion from local politics. Cecil Moore in Philadelphia was a dramatic figure as NAACP branch president, gifted in the use of street-corner argot, blunt in his denunciations both of conservative blacks and of liberal whites, and dictatorial in his management of branch affairs.[46] Moore increased the membership of the branch—thousands of blacks were willing to pay at least two dollars to support his freewheeling style—but did not broaden the range of active participation in branch affairs. In Mississippi, Charles Evers mobilized several hundred blacks in counties that were largely untouched by the civil rights movement before 1964. Unlike the small, sectlike meetings of persons engaged in self-discovery characteristic of early SNCC gatherings, Evers addressed mass meetings of blacks and mobilized them by his example of outspoken courage and his ability to get away with acts of protest that many blacks had hitherto thought impossibly risky. By the fall of 1967, almost two-thirds of the eligible blacks had been registered to vote in Wilkinson County. Support for the NAACP leadership there has in part been maintained by the use of various negative inducements directed against prominent blacks unwilling to join it—public meetings at which they are denounced, and at which they are often expected to apologize publicly, and occasional boycotts or acts of minor vandalism (called a visit of "the spirits") directed at blacks who break ranks.[47]

The conventional explanation for the differences between the NAACP and the Urban League on the one hand and CORE and SNCC on the other is that the former are middle-class associations led by conservatives. Such a view is simplistic—for one thing, the active members of *all* of these associations have been middle class; for another, this theory does not specify how social class determines organizational behavior. And though in some sense a Roy Wilkins is, by the standards of contemporary race militancy, "conservative," he and his predecessors in the NAACP were in an earlier era judged by many blacks to be too radical. The views and activities of NAACP leaders are better explained, this chapter has suggested, by organizational considerations, rather than by class or ideological ones. The maintenance requirements of the NAACP —its need to fund a large national office with money raised from diverse local branches—have given to it its special style and the continuity of its viewpoint.

Similarly, the kinds of incentives used to build CORE and SNCC, and the organizational forms that those incentives implied, tell us more about the behavior of CORE and SNCC leaders than does their class position or their preorganizational ideology. But organizational factors do not explain these matters fully. Certain broad changes in American society had altered the demand for certain kinds of incentives and increased the attention given to associations that used them. These changes included the great increase in the size of the black college student population, the role of the mass media, especially television, in giving to small organizations engaged in local skirmishes a vast national audience and an enhanced symbolic significance, and the key role of Martin Luther King, Jr., with his extraordinary appeal for blacks and whites alike despite, or perhaps because of, his inability either to lead an effective civil rights organization or to win many civil rights victories.[48] The increase in the attention given to civil rights, the powerful consequences of being able to seize a leadership position in the media, and the heightened rivalry for funds and supporters all made the major civil rights groups inevitably wary of one another and unsettled the fixed resource bases of the older ones. In time, only the NAACP and the Urban League appear to have evolved an institutional form that could ensure the associations' distinctive and continuing appeal to contributors.

At no time during the 1960s did lower-class or street-corner blacks become effectively mobilized or permanently organized as part of the civil rights movement. Such persons from time to time did engage in dramatic confrontations with public officials: any such encounter, for a while, could be made to appear the result of an important organizational effort, when in fact most were ad hoc and short-lived. But these events gave to such groups as CORE and SNCC a distinctive posture—though composed of middle-class members, they cultivated a lower-class style. As Martin Kilson has put it, "lower-strata militant leaders lack the habits, values, and skills required for a durable politicization of the Negro population," but they have stamped "the politics of black ethnicity with a lower-class style," so that as middle-class Negroes participate in black politics "they must do so at least partly in terms of the lower-class criteria that legitimate politics."[49] The militant black leaders, in short, have found it necessary to differentiate their associations from the NAACP, not by real but by claimed class differences, both to satisfy the expectations of members that they prove their association to be different and closer to "the people" and to enlarge their constituency among nonmembers in the population. But such a strategy, as CORE and SNCC discovered, is vulnerable to changes in national or racial mood and in media attention; the politics of style can go out of style as quickly as it came in.

NOTES

1. Quoted in August Meier, "Booker T. Washington and the Rise of the NAACP," *The Crisis*, LXI (February 1954), 76, and in Gunnar Myrdal, *An American Dilemma* (New York: Harper, 1944), p. 832.

2. Charles Flint Kellogg, *NAACP: A History* (Baltimore: Johns Hopkins Press, 1967), vol. I, pp. 297–298.

3. Francis L. Broderick, *W. E. B. Du Bois: Negro Leader in a Time of Crisis* (Stanford, Calif.: Stanford University Press, 1959), pp. 77–78, and Elliott Rudwick, "The Niagara Movement," *Journal of Negro History*, XLII (July 1957), 177–200, reprinted in *The Making of Black America*, ed. August Meier and Elliott Rudwick (New York: Atheneum, 1969), vol. II, pp. 131–148.

4. Kellogg, *NAACP*, pp. 117–120.

5. Ibid., pp. 120–130, and personal correspondence from August Meier and Elliott Rudwick.

6. James Q. Wilson, *Negro Politics: The Search for Leadership* (New York: Free Press, 1960), p. 284.

7. These figures are taken from the annual reports of the NAACP. See also Kellogg, *NAACP*, p. 135.

8. Quoted in Broderick, *W. E. B. Du Bois*, p. 101.

9. Quoted in Elliott M. Rudwick, *W. E. B. Du Bois* (New York: Atheneum, 1969), pp. 156, 168.

10. *Guinn v. United States*, 238 U.S. 347 (1915).

11. *Buchanan v. Warley*, 245 U.S. 60 (1917).

12. The long series of what became known as the "Texas White-Primary Cases" culminated in *Smith v. Allwright*, 321 U.S. 649 (1944).

13. "When some case of discrimination occurs in a town," wrote Mary White Ovington, local Negroes "write to the National Office [of the NAACP]; we tell them how to organize; and when their case comes into court they have back of them the name and prestige of a national body." Ovington, "The National Association for the Advancement of Colored People," *Journal of Negro History*, IX (April 1924), 115.

14. Roy Nash quoted in Kellogg, *NAACP*, p. 133. Du Bois may have been himself a contender for the job of executive secretary; in any case, the board was clearly opposed to increasing his influence in the association. Ibid., pp. 96–97.

15. Data from NAACP annual reports.

16. Raymond Wolters, *Negroes and the Great Depression* (Westport, Conn.: Greenwood, 1970), pp. 270–271.

17. Ibid., pp. 256, 302–305.

18. Ibid., pp. 314–317.

19. Quoted in Wolters, pp. 325–326. The NAACP in 1933–1934 had great difficulty in raising $2,500 to begin an economic program but was able to raise many times that sum for antilynching campaigns and attacks on segregation. Ibid., p. 337.

20. Ibid., p. 356. Ralph Bunche wrote in 1939 that the "inherent fallacy" of the political strategy of the NAACP was to be found in "the failure to recognize that the instrumentalities of the state, constitution, government and laws, can do no more than reflect the political, social and economic ideology of the dominant population, and that the political arm of the state cannot be divorced from the prevailing economic structure." Bunche, "The Programs of Organizations Devoted to the Improvement of the Status of the American Negro," *Journal of Negro Education*, VIII (July 1939), 539–550, reprinted in Meier and Rudwick, *The Making of Black America*, pp. 245–256. Bunche called for a new organization that would subordinate political and racial questions to economic ones.

21. Wolters, *Negroes and the Great Depression*, pp. 362–376, and Herbert Garfinkel, *When Negroes March* (New York: Free Press, 1959), pp. 47–48.

22. Wolters, *Negroes and the Great Depression*, p. 366.

23. Garfinkel, *When Negroes March*, pp. 39–41, 112–114.

24. Elliott Rudwick and August Meier, "Organizational Structure and Goal Succession: A Comparative Analysis of the NAACP and CORE, 1964–1968," *Social Science Quarterly*, LI (June 1970), 18–22.

25. Inge Powell Bell, *CORE and the Strategy of Nonviolence* (New York: Random House, 1968), chap. 1.

26. This account of SNCC follows Emily S. Stoper, "The Student Nonviolent Coordinating Committee: The Growth of Radicalism in a Civil Rights Organization" (Ph.D. diss., Department of Government, Harvard University, 1968). The shift in liberal opinion about SNCC is documented by Stoper, pp. 87–92, *New Republic*, April 10, 1965, pp. 13–16, and Jack Newfield, *A Prophetic Minority* (New York: Signet Book/New American Library, 1966), pp. 71–82.

27. Rudwick and Meier, "Organizational Structure," p. 10.

28. August Meier and Elliott Rudwick, "How CORE Began," *Social Science Quarterly*, XLIX (March 1969), 789–799.

29. Ibid., pp. 795–796.

30. Bell, *CORE*, p. 39.

31. Ibid., p. 76, and Meier and Rudwick, "How CORE Began," p. 795.

32. Bell, *CORE*, chap. 8, esp. p. 139.

33. Ibid., pp. 178–181.

34. Rudwick and Meier, "Organizational Structure," p. 18.

35. Bell, *CORE*, pp. 187–190.

36. Stoper, "The Student Nonviolent Coordinating Committee," pp. 57–95, esp. pp. 70, 80, and Pat Watters and Reese Cleghorn, *Climbing Jacob's Ladder: The Arrival of Negroes in Southern Politics* (New York: Harcourt, Brace & World, 1967), p. 14.

37. Marxist literature was much in evidence at SNCC's Atlanta headquarters, and slogans drawn from Marx, Franz Fanon, and others were occasionally used by SNCC leaders, but there is little evidence of any serious doctrinal involvement in Marxism or any other single ideology. See Stoper, "The Student Nonviolent Coordinating Committee," chap. 5, and Gene Roberts, "From 'Freedom High' to 'Black Power': The Story of Snick," *New York Times Magazine*, September 25, 1966, pp. 27 ff. Active Communists hovered around SNCC, but while it was still a viable organization they do not seem to have been taken very seriously. Relations between individual SNCC activists and Communist nations after the organization had become moribund are another, and as yet unexplored, matter.

38. Stoper, "The Student Nonviolent Coordinating Committee," p. 3.

39. Ibid., p. 116.

40. Meier and Rudwick, "How CORE Began," pp. 794–795.

41. Stoper, "The Student Nonviolent Coordinating Committee," chap. 3.

42. The relations between northern whites and southern blacks in SNCC were probably further strained by apparent differences in levels of organizational skill and experience.

43. Gilbert Hobbs Barnes, *The Antislavery Impulse* (New York: Appleton-Century, 1933), chaps. 5–8, esp. pp. 62, 68, 77. For espousing their doctrine, the students were expelled from Lane but were quickly taken in by a moribund nearby college that was ready to do almost anything to acquire a student body. Thus, Oberlin College began by promising the Lane rebels that they could select their own president and faculty and write their own rules and that Negroes would be admitted to the college. (It later reneged on the last promise.) Even as early as the 1830s, social movements led to demands for "student power" in colleges.

44. Ibid., p. 162.

45. John Hadley Strange, "The Negro in Philadelphia Politics: 1963–1965" (Ph.D. diss., Department of Politics, Princeton University, 1966), p. 82. Strange counts twenty-four NAACP-led demonstrations in Philadelphia between April 1963 and June 1965, compared to twelve led by CORE and one by SNCC.

46. Ibid., pp. 59–61, 67, 69–72. Dissidents in the branch made efforts to impeach Moore and later to defeat him in an election, but during his heyday they were unsuccessful.

47. Lester M. Salamon, "Protest, Politics, and Modernization in the American South: Mississippi as a 'Developing Society'" (Ph.D. diss., Department of Government, Harvard University, 1971), pp. 460–466, 532–535.

48. August Meier, "On the Role of Martin Luther King," *New Politics*, IV (Winter 1965), 52–59, reprinted in Meier and Rudwick, *Black America*, pp. 353–361.

49. Martin Kilson, "Blacks in Politics: A New Power," *Dissent* (August 1971), p. 338.

PART

III

Internal Processes

CHAPTER 10

Organizational Creation and Change

Theories about how organizations behave abound; theories about how organizations come into being scarcely exist. The discrepancy is to some degree inevitable, for an organization is, by definition, a system of coordinated activity, and thus a more or less uniform pattern of behavior. Finding and explaining uniformities, both trivial and important, is the special competence, and perhaps the chief function, of social science. Creating a new organization involves discrete and perhaps unique acts representing a break in a prior pattern of behavior. Treating what is exceptional has been the special province of the narrative historian and the journalist. As a result, though organizational behavior is generally spoken of in terms of the relationship among variables, organizational creation is usually described as the fortuitous interaction of a gifted man and that fleeting moment when an idea has come of age.

It is perhaps for this reason that writers whose organizational theories derive from highly simplified assumptions about motives have so little to say about organizational formation. Mancur Olson states the terms under which persons will affiliate with economic associations producing collective goods, but does not explain how those associations came to exist in the first place. If rationally self-interested men will join only associations that offer selective inducements, why did the charter members of the group come to join when, in embryo, the group could offer them nothing at all? [1]

The problem is not peculiar to Olson, but applies to all theories of collective action that are based on a single motivational assumption. For Marx, the important collectivities were social classes, defined in terms of their members' relationship to the means of production. But though he explored at length the role of classes in political and economic struggles, he paid little attention to how a class is initially formed, except to suggest that they emerge "inevitably." Historically, capitalists replaced feudal landlords, but whence came the first capitalists and by what processes did they create the dominant form of social organization? As Joseph A. Schumpeter has indicated, Marx nowhere supplies a theory of "primitive accumulation"—that is, of the way by which capital was first formed and its value enhanced.[2]

To meet such problems, the concept of entrepreneurship is advanced. In Schumpeter's terms, an entrepreneur is a person who exploits an invention or other untried possibility by launching a new enterprise. To act in this manner is difficult because it involves risk and uncertainty and requires a willingness to defer immediate gratifications for future gains.[3] That the entrepreneurial function is as important to voluntary associations as to business firms is beyond dispute, but the attempt to develop a theory of associational entrepreneurship has been complicated by the effort on the part of some to state such a theory in ways that do not require any change in the assumptions about the behavior of organizational members generally. Specifically, the entrepreneur is conceived of as a rationally self-interested person who promises to supply some collective good—such as higher price supports for farmers, cleaner air, or lower taxes—establishes an organization to collect funds and other forms of support from members, works to produce the collective good, and retains as his personal "profit" the difference between the cost of providing, or attempting to provide, the good and the resources collected.[4] A similar view of the entrepreneur, though one less heavily encumbered with strictly economic concepts, has been advanced by Robert H. Salisbury. He notes the crucial role played by such entrepreneurs, which were sometimes other organizations rather than individuals, in the creation of farm associations such as the Grange, the Farmers Union, and the Farm Bureau.[5]

The difficulty with the more rigorous of these conceptions is that they are hard to reconcile with reality. Profit may be a suitable expression of the motives of a boss who organizes a political machine in order to win the spoils of office, but it hardly seems an appropriate description of the motives of Margaret Sanger when she organized the American Birth Control League, of Robert Welch when he organized the John Birch Society, or of James Farmer, Bernice Fisher, and others when they organized CORE. Of course, one may expand the definition of profit to embrace all manner of satisfactions, including the sense of having served a good cause, but it is difficult to understand how so broad a definition is meaningful. How does one calculate the profit rate: did Mr. Welch subtract the costs of "proving" that America was in the grip of a Communist conspiracy from the dues revenue received from John Birch Society members and place the difference on an accounting sheet? Nor does the concept of profit thus expanded have the utility for associational analysis that the narrow, monetary version of the term has for economic analysis—namely, as an explanation of why new enterprises are begun in one industry rather than in another. It is not the absolute level of profits, but profits relative to investment that is important in the theory of the firm. Comparing relative profits is possible when all are measured in money; it is not possible when, as with voluntary associations, "profits" are measured sometimes in money, sometimes in status, and sometimes in ideology.

Indeed, what is crucially important about the associational entrepreneur in so many cases is that he is, for whatever reason, a person willing to forego monetary gratifications entirely or defer them indefinitely. Salisbury notes that Oliver Hudson Kelley, founder of the Grange, managed to survive by dint of great sacrifice and generous friends until "his organizational dream began to take hold," and Newton Gresham lived off credit and handouts until the Farmers Union attracted enough dues-paying members to sustain him.[6] A study of Canadian teachers' associations stresses the vital role that small groups of enthusiastic leaders played in their formation: initially, these organizations were subsidized by zealots who traveled about the provinces to recruit members and intercede with school boards.[7]

Any explanation of the associational entrepreneur ought to begin by recognizing the fact that his motives and attitudes will be different from those of the rank-and-file members he eventually recruits: either he will respond to different rewards (purpose rather than money, and individual rather than collective status), or he will have a more distant time horizon than his followers (preferring, for example, the future possibility of a large government contract or a well-paid union office over the present certainty of a small patronage job or a modest wage increase), or both. Persons with these attitudes who also have organizational skills, personal persuasiveness, and necessary resources are few in number and idiosyncratic in behavior. They do not often appear, and many that do appear fail in their organizing efforts.

Given the crucial role and the rare qualities of the entrepreneur, one might predict that the creation of new associations would be an almost random event. To some extent this is no doubt true: many groups are formed almost by accident, the result of that fortuitous combination of personality, opportunity, and constituency about which historians so frequently speak. But the most striking fact about organizational formation is that, so far as we can tell, it is not entirely, or even largely, random. "The formation of associations," David B. Truman observes, "tends to occur in waves." [8]

There have been several such waves. In the 1830s and 1840s, the abolitionists organized in this country and the Young Men's Christian Association emerged in England; in the 1860s, the National Grange was formed to speak for farmers, a host of craft unions were created to represent workers, and the Knights of Pythias, the Benevolent and Protective Order of Elks, and countless college fraternities were launched to provide a sense of solidarity and camaraderie. In the 1880s, a new wave of organizational activity occurred: the Knights of Labor grew rapidly after 1880, the AFL was begun in 1886, scores of employers' associations emerged, the American Red Cross got underway, and the founders of the Loyal Order of Moose discovered that the demand for camaraderie had not been exhausted by their organizational rivals. But the great burst in the organization of associations, especially those of national scope, took place in the first two decades of the twentieth century. There has never been anything like it before or since. In that period were founded the United States Chamber of Commerce and the National Association of Manufacturers,[9] the American Medical Association, the American Association of University Professors, the Pennsylvania Manufacturers' Association and the National Civic Federation, the NAACP and the Urban League, the Socialist party and the Communist party, the American Farm Bureau Federation and the Farmers Union, the Boy Scouts and the Girl Scouts, the Boys Clubs of America and the Order of DeMolay, the Non-Partisan League, scores of college fraternities and sororities, the National Catholic Welfare Conference, the American Cancer Society, countless local child-labor committees and consumer leagues, the American Jewish Committee, and the Anti-Defamation League. Furthermore, many associations already in being experienced during the period their most rapid growth: a thousand new YMCAs were formed and the number of YMCA secretaries tripled during the two decades, and the average annual increase in the membership of the AFL between 1897 and 1904 was over 25 percent.[10] Daniel Bell has labeled the decade from 1902 to 1912 as the "golden age" of American socialism, and Roy Lubove has described roughly the same period as that in which federation and bureaucratization permanently reshaped the structure of American charity.[11] Finally, it was also the period of the first great national fund-raising drives: the YMCA raised \$3.5 million in 1917, Harvard University raised \$14.2 million in 1919, and the Red Cross an incredible \$100 million in 1917, in each case by means of professionalized campaigns.[12]

There are innumerable reasons that can be advanced to explain why during this period the formation of organizations was easier than had previously been the case. The completion of the railroads and the telegraph and the rise of national magazines made communication easier, and thus truly national organizations were possible. Legislation aimed at regulating business, first in the states and then at the national level, stimulated the rise of economic associations seeking to change, or cope with, the new political environment of business enterprise. Urbanization and immigration had combined to bring together a heterogeneous population in ways that produced a heightened recognition of group differences and individual needs. The increased division of labor had created more specialized occupations and thus more specialized interests, and, given the complex interdependency among these elements, when any one organized to further its interests it stimulated a countervailing organizational effort among rival elements.[13] The rapid industrialization following the Civil War produced an economy that was peculiarly susceptible to cycles of boom and bust: managing access to the jobs and influencing the wage levels made union organization attractive to workers and unattractive to employers, and thus the battle was joined.

But if all these factors facilitated, or even made necessary, the formation of large-scale voluntary associations, they did not make it inevitable. Newly defined interests do not spontaneously produce organizations, however efficient the communications or however large the cities. And some interests were not newly defined at all—agriculture, industry, and labor had all displayed a high degree of specialization since at least the 1860s, but specialized associations did not become commonplace until thirty or forty years had passed. As Salisbury notes, the rise of commercial farmers, each with a specialized crop and each at the mercy of impersonal market prices, had been going on since the Civil War, but corresponding commodity associations scarcely appeared at all—instead, there emerged broadly based farm groups or movements, such as the Grange and the Populist party. Commodity organizations and farm cooperatives flourished much later, chiefly after the turn of the century.[14] Though the spread of the county agent system helps explain the rise of county and state farm bureaus, the formation of the national organization appears chiefly to have been stimulated by political, rather than by economic, considerations: "the fear of radicalism, industrial unrest, labor disturbances." [15]

The formation of noneconomic groups during the first two decades of the twentieth century is even harder to explain by the theory that objective conditions required this. Negroes had been the object of disfranchisement and abuse since the end of Reconstruction, but the NAACP did not form and begin its decades-long campaign against lynching until 1910–1911. The Urban League, created to meliorate the problems created by the urbanization of blacks, was launched before the mass migration to the cities began during and after World War I. And the various Marxist parties came into their own long after industrialization had begun and an industrial work force had been created, and they lost their vigor long before the social problems created by these processes had been seriously addressed. In this, they were very much like the American Anti-Slavery Society, which had virtually ceased to exist twenty years before the outbreak of a civil war in which slavery was a major issue.

It is premature to attempt the formulation of a theory to account for the periods of rapid organizational formation. For one thing, different explanations account for different kinds of organizations—changes in economic conditions may explain the emergence of various labor and farm groups, perceived threats from labor or government may stimulate employers' associations, religious awakenings may result not only in pietistic revivalism but in efforts at secular perfection as well. For another, dramatic but unpredictable events—a world war, an economic depression—may play a central role in upsetting existing relationships, altering the allocation of resources, and arousing new kinds of popular demands.[16] Any theory that pretends to deal comprehensively with these phenomena will have to deal with the demand for organizational activity as well as with the supply of leadership cadres and of mobilizable resources.[17]

Whatever direction theorizing may take, however, one tentative generalization seems both warranted and crucial: periods of rapid and intense organizational formation are periods in which the salience of purposive incentives has sharply increased. Organizations become more numerous when ideas become more important. The most obvious fact in support of such a view is that widespread organizing seems always to be accompanied by numerous social movements. During the era of the 1830s and 1840s, for example, both the Antimasonic party and abolitionist organizations were formed at the same time, and out of many of the same impulses, as the Great Revival of religious fervor.[18] In 1895–1910, there was similarly an outburst of new gospels, many of them this time secular in nature though still evangelical in tone: free silver, prohibition, nativism, suffragism, the social gospel, Marxism, Taylorism, the settlement-house movement, and countless others. Theories of Christian socialism competed with theories of Christian capitalism, the former calling for reorganization and the latter for philanthropy. Robert H. Wiebe terms the period one of a "revolution in values," and though this may overstate the matter somewhat there is little doubt that more attention was then paid to values than at any time in the preceding three or four decades.[19]

Efforts to give a more precise description to the mood of the times have proliferated—the "age of enterprise," the "revolt against formalism," the "search for community," the "golden age of socialism," the "quest for utopia"—but none is very successful for the very reason that the era was one in which so many contradictory purposes were being sought. The rationalizing and bureaucratic tendencies to be found in Frederick W. Taylor were offset by the communal and neighborhood concerns of Mary Parker Follett; the realism of Arthur F. Bentley, Thorstein Veblen, or William Graham Sumner was counterbalanced by the utopian idealism of Edward Bellamy and Walter Rauschenbusch.

It is tempting to think of these new or enhanced concerns as representing simply a demand for organizations that entrepreneurs, ever alert to the emergence of new markets, were quick to satisfy in about the same way, and out of the same motives, that they were led to satisfy the demand for automobiles or electric lights. And no doubt there was much of this. But the cadres that initially responded to the entrepreneurial appeal had no realistic prospect either of personal advantage or collective gain—as cadres but not leaders, they would in most of the emergent voluntary associations get no money and little status, and they were joining their newly formed groups at the very time when the chances of political victory were most remote. The first recruits of the NAACP, the

Anti-Saloon League, or the National Association of Manufacturers were the ones on whom the heaviest burden of organizational maintenance would fall. To take up such a burden required these cadres to have either an exaggerated sense of their likely efficacy or an exceptional commitment to the purposes of the group.[20]

In fact they probably had both. And such cadres were available in the requisite numbers because structural changes in society had produced new sources for them. Richard Hofstadter notes the rise in this period of the "new middle class" of technicians and salaried professionals, by far the fastest growing stratum in the population.[21] Ministers in small towns became the local organizing agents for antisaloon leagues. Nor was the clergy only a source of reaffirmation for traditional moral standards and thus for the communal side of turn-of-the-century politics. One does not have to explain, as does Hofstadter, the shift of the urban clergy toward social and political reform as resulting from their sense of lost status to agree that the shift in fact occurred. Whereas the Protestant clergy was savage in its indictment of striking unionists in the 1870s, by 1895 the doctrines of the social gospel had given a liberal cast to the thought of many of the most articulate ministers.[22] The colleges were another source for the new cadres. The number of such institutions multiplied rapidly; by World War I two dozen major universities had firmly established themselves, and though the tone and substance of most of what was taught there served to defend traditional values, the best-known scholars were also the ones most critical of existing social arrangements —not only Bentley and Veblen, but John R. Commons, Richard T. Ely, Charles A. Beard, J. Allen Smith, John Dewey, and many others.[23] And whereas 52,000 young persons were in college in 1870, many hundreds of thousands were there by 1910. Finally, during the era the professions came to be self-regulating, clearly demarcated, and closely linked to academic training: though the American Bar Association had existed as a pleasant social club and debating society since 1878, the growth of county bar associations with licensing powers was a product largely of the early twentieth century.

Speculation on the sources of the ideas in vogue around 1900 or on the reason why such high value was given them by certain groups, especially potential organization cadres, is beyond the scope of this inquiry. It may not be going too far, however, to suggest that the same phenomena have reappeared since then—during the 1930s and perhaps again during the 1960s. For various reasons, some related to objective conditions and some not, the need to assert, define, or defend certain precarious values becomes not simply an interest of a few would-be leaders but the preoccupation of a wider circle of cadres who in turn are able either to mobilize a mass following or to persuade government officials and other audiences to take seriously certain ideas even if they lack such a following. And, clearly, the ranks of the potential cadres have swelled enormously during this century—seven or eight times as many persons are enrolled in colleges, the clergy have become increasingly secularized or at least theologically underemployed, the legal profession has increasingly been entered by persons seeking not legal practice but social and political activism, and the university faculties have been thoroughly converted from a professoriat that defends the traditional culture to one that criticizes it. Finally, the government itself has become an important source of organizing cadres. Paid members of the local Community Action Agencies of the "war on poverty" and VISTA volunteers have helped form voluntary associations, many of which have been in direct opposition to government policies. Lawrence N. Bailis found that the single most important source of organizers of the Massachusetts Welfare Rights Organization, and thus of the confrontations with government officials that it staged, were VISTA workers paid out of government funds.[24]

The rise of the organizational cadres has been a continuous process. What accounts for the episodic nature of organizational formation are the cyclical changes in opinion, and especially in the perceived value of purposive incentives. This ebb and flow of sentiment is important, not, perhaps, because it operates directly on the mass public, but insofar as it affects and motivates the potential cadres. It is to the views and actions of this group that one must chiefly look to find the link between the social structure and organizational formation and activity.

The existence of active organizing cadres and the spread of doctrines that give legitimacy to their efforts are not sufficient to explain organizational formation. In addition, there must be belief among members of a potential association that matters of concern to them are being affected by other institutions in the society whose behavior can be altered. That belief is more likely to emerge when a highly visible person or organization appears to be posing a serious threat to some value of importance to the potential members. John Mollenkopf in his study of the creation of community associations in lower-income neighborhoods emphasizes the importance of the existence of an immediate threat (for example, an urban renewal or highway land-clearance program) mounted by a visible and concrete target (for example, a city agency).[25] H. B. Davis has hypothesized that the formation of labor unions is to a great extent a defensive effort,[26] and statistical evidence seems to support this view. Orley Ashenfelter and John H. Pencavel found, for example, that much of the annual percentage change in union membership could be explained by increases in price levels and in unemployment in the preceding period, which imposed costs on workers, combined with a growth in public opinion favorable to union organizing (as measured by the Democratic percentage of the seats in the House of Representatives).[27] High-status persons, on the other hand, may be more inclined and, given their greater resources, more able to form associations in the absence of a clear threat. For example, some of them will unite to abolish capital punishment though none of them faces the prospect of being hanged. This is an example of the direct influence of ideas on organizations: in effect, a newly mobilized cadre incorporates as an association and, because it does not try to form a mass organization, need not worry about whether there exist the necessary conditions for mobilizing any particular nonelite group.

In addition to there being an organizing cadre and a widely felt problem, association building is facilitated if it can draw upon already existing networks of personal relations. John T. Dunlop has observed that unions developed first where workers occupied a strategic position in an industry—strategic in the sense that the withdrawal of their services would cripple the industry in ways that could not be easily remedied by substituting other workers, and perhaps also strategic in the sense (though Dunlop does not mention this) that they formed a natural community.[28] Neighborhood organizations are easier when they can grow upon preexisting informal social networks,—friendship, cliques, ethnic ties, political affiliations, or church membership.[29] Every politician, for example, attaches great importance when running for office to obtaining "the list," a compilation of names of persons who in the past worked for, or gave money to, candidates similar to him ideologically.

Those organizations that survive and prosper generally undergo an important transformation. The process of institutionalization, as Philip Selznick describes it, involves establishing a distinctive competence or identity, and thus a recognized jurisdiction, a process that will be discussed in later chapters; it also involves shifting to an economical incentive system. Not all new organizations rely at the outset on purposive rewards, though I would argue that most do with respect to their leadership cadres. All, however, face the problem of altered expectations: blighted hopes, reduced resources, and organized counterattacks (or worse, indifference). When the burdens of membership rise, when the resources of members decline, or when the time horizon of activists shortens, the enthusiasms accompanying the formative efforts will falter.

Some organizations act in a way that minimizes these problems. The Anti-Saloon League from the first built its organization on the foundation of local churches: each congregation that formed a local league needed to do little more than graft an additional function onto an ongoing organization with its already available religious and solidary rewards. The NAACP, with greater difficulty, accomplished much the same end, forming local branches in which a great variety of incentives could be used to raise dues for the national office. Trade unions sought union recognition guarantees, such as the closed shop or union shop. Trade and professional associations sought government guarantees and licensing powers. Various Marxist parties granted formal recognition to their foreign-language elements or, by winning municipal elections, acquired a governmental base that would endure whatever ideological disputes might divide the militants. The Non-Partisan League and the Chamber of Commerce hired traveling salesmen to sign up new members on a commission basis. As funds became available, volunteer staffs were replaced by paid staffs: the Anti-Saloon League grew from almost no paid employees in 1895 to 300 in 1903 and to more than 1,500 by 1915.[30]

The transformation of the YMCA illustrates an especially successful shift in incentives. Mayer N. Zald notes that during its formative years, the YMCA was an evangelical, proselyting organization seeking to promote Christian fellowship among young men. It raised much of its money by charitable appeals of much the same sort as, and hence often in direct competition with, the Protestant churches. Finding donors to support "fellowship" was not an easy task, and hence the resources of the organization as well as the membership rolls were affected by changes in the business cycle and by the ebb and flow of religious revivalism. The leadership soon discovered, however, that there was no reason a social movement could not also be a business enterprise. Local YMCAs rapidly developed two profitable services that could be sold on a fee-for-service basis—gymnasiums and low-rent dormitories. Between 1886 and 1900, the number of YMCA gymnasiums increased fivefold; by 1900, dormitories became the rule in all new YMCA buildings. The income generated by fees charged for these services also permitted the hiring of a large professional staff; their numbers also quintupled between 1890 and 1919.[31] This form of institutionalization—the development of an exchange economy, utilizing material incentives and administered by a professional staff—can be interpreted almost entirely in terms of Olson's theory of collective action.

But there are other voluntary associations whose process of institutionalization has followed a very different path, sometimes successfully, sometimes not. The American Red Cross has mobilized resources by a reliance chiefly on purposive and solidary incentives, not material ones. The original commitment to the cause of disaster relief was reinforced by the status and small-group interactions of the local Red Cross chapter. But an organization seeking to sustain itself by providing relief to the victims of disaster must come to terms with the fact that disasters are random and often infrequent occurrences. World War I provided an ample disaster, but peacetime left the Red Cross with a vastly expanded organization having little to do. It accordingly shifted its emphasis to public health. Just when government programs were beginning to supplant volunteer efforts in that field, World War II provided a new occasion for the Red Cross's meliorative services. With peace restored, however, the old problem reappeared: as one Red Cross worker wrote in 1946, "clouds are appearing on the disaster relief horizon." [32] A new project with wide appeal and a stable demand was selected—the blood donor program. Collecting blood was, in the words of the historian of the Red Cross, "an outlet for volunteer activity in the new period of peace." [33] A similar story of successful adaptation is the well-known shift of the National Foundation from combating polio to fighting birth defects after the Salk and Sabine vaccines had brought polio under control.

The Women's Christian Temperance Union (WCTU) and the Townsend Organization are familiar examples of associations that were unable to adapt successfully to changing circumstances. The manifest and enduring popularity of liquor consumption, and the consequent failure of Prohibition, left the WCTU with an increasingly hopeless task: to get persons to abstain totally from alcohol. The incentives for organization membership were heavily purposive, and for the most active members especially so: the lack of public response to the WCTU's efforts, by making the task of leadership more difficult, made it also attractive only to the most highly motivated. To a substantial degree, these persons were what Joseph R. Gusfield has called the "conviction-oriented" members—those who wanted to see Prohibition return, who refused to cooperate with other organizations that did not share their commitment to total abstinence, and who had no use for compromise or short-term gains. Gusfield quotes one of these women as saying: "It makes no difference to me what others think as long as I think that I am in the right." [34] The more flexible members who were willing to settle for educational campaigns to restrict the consumption of liquor had little influence in the WCTU for at least twenty years after repeal of the Eighteenth Amendment.

The Townsend Organization, formed in 1933 around the idea of giving every person age sixty or over a monthly pension of $200 as a way of ending the depression, soon attracted over two million members. The several thousand Townsend Clubs formed around the country clearly provided something more than the opportunity to help persuade the government to enact a new pension law. They also "furnished the warmth, friendship, and social activities that no longer existed for many older people" and provided opportunities for the elderly to enhance their collective and individual status in the community.[35] But if they were only social clubs, they would not have attracted the mass following they did, as evidenced by their rapid decline in membership after the New Deal and economic recovery had made the Townsend Plan irrelevant, or at best, unlikely to succeed. By 1951 the organization had lost 97 percent of its membership, and today it is virtually defunct.[36] As the organization declined, efforts were made to enhance the solidary incentives of club affiliation, but without much success. Schemes were even devised to develop material incentives by having members sell vitamin pills and other products door to door on a commission basis. The loss of a sense of purpose, and of one that in its heyday caught its adherents up in a quasi-religious fervor, made these stratagems unavailing.

Why some organizations adapt successfully and others fail is a matter about which scholars have no settled and generally accepted opinions. The social structure in which the organization is embedded exerts one constraining influence. The YMCA, the Red Cross, the Chamber of Commerce, the National Foundation, the Urban League, and countless other groups serve purposes that are held in general esteem and are able to mobilize elites that can contribute not only resources but the symbols of legitimacy. Middle-class respectability is an important resource to them. But it is not always a sufficient one: the WCTU was eminently respectable, at least in its early years, and yet it ultimately failed, perhaps because it abandoned its goal of seeking to persuade the working classes to abstain from drink and tried instead to persuade the middle classes of the wisdom of that policy. And the success of the trade unions, often organized in the teeth of entrepreneurial hostility, shows that respectability may not even be a necessary resource, though, to be sure, the unions under Gompers minimized their lack of respectability by concentrating on those purely economic issues over which bargaining was easiest. And the Welfare Rights Organization deliberately defied the ordinary canons of respectability by using confrontation techniques to win material benefits for welfare mothers, a group that ranks abysmally low in public esteem.

The influence of respectability is probably greatest over time rather than in the formative years. The problem of institutionalizing an organization—of ensuring its survival and successfully asserting its special domain—is in great part one of making the collection of its resources a routine rather than extraordinary process. This, in turn, requires the active cultivation of popular indifference, if not of popular support; minimizing hostility—of strain between organizational climate and public expectations—is an objective of all but a few ideological and redemptive associations.

This process is sometimes interpreted as the growing conservatism of voluntary associations. The original, presumably lofty, goals of the organizations are compromised to make them respectable or are displaced entirely in favor of sheer survival. Robert Michels is, of course, the foremost exponent of such a view, though to him the reason for this conservatizing trend was to be found in the "iron law of oligarchy"—namely, the maintenance needs of the leadership clique, rather than of the organization as a whole.[37] In fact, though there is a universal tendency toward organizational maintenance, there is no universal tendency toward conservatism. For example, American labor unions, at least on the national level, have espoused a wider and more far-reaching set of public policy objectives as the security of their organizations has grown. Gompers's philosophy of voluntarism was the policy of the national unions when they were struggling for survival; and now that they have won that struggle and have established expensive, well-staffed headquarters buildings in Washington, many are prepared to do battle for any number of causes—such as civil rights—not directly linked to the interests of their members.[38] The YMCA—next to various churches, perhaps the most successful voluntary association in the country and for long the very paragon of respectability—has in recent years embarked in certain cities on an ambitious and controversial program in the field of community action and work with delinquent gangs.[39] And various national religious organizations have become highly secularized political combatants in such areas as civil rights, federal communications policies, and welfare legislation.

One might almost stand Michels on his head—to judge from the few cases mentioned above, it has been precisely in those organizations with assured respectability *and* large bureaucratic staffs that one can observe the development of new objectives with wider implications. The continued interest of the Committee for Economic Development in controversial business issues has been staff led, as has been the shift in the posture of the National Association of Manufacturers from one of inflexible opposition to partial accommodation.

The reasons for this are not hard to find, yet curiously they are systematically neglected in most of the literature on organizations: the crucial role of organizational elites as instruments whereby elite opinion generally is translated into associational objectives. The role of these cadres is essential in explaining not only the formation of associations but their systematic transformation. Obviously, a staff has the freedom to explore new objectives only when organizational maintenance problems have been solved; hence, the apparent paradox that it is in associations that have managed to win obvious respectability and assured member loyalty where one often finds elites willing, indeed, eager, to take on new political tasks.

This is not the only source of organizational transformation, however. Some changes are the result of desperate efforts to revive failing associations by finding new incentives and thus new activities to generate those incentives. The leaders of the Townsend Organization were engaged in this when they tried to get members to sell vitamins door to door; so were the leaders of Tammany Hall when, during the 1950s, they sought to embrace some elements of the good government creed in order to keep in power a political machine that had been losing its patronage resources.[40]

In sum, there appear to be at least three different causes of organizational change and three corresponding strategies, each arising out of a different problem in managing the group's incentive system. The first cause is an *uncertainty* in the flow of resources—an episodic, boom-and-bust pattern of membership affiliation and resource availability. Labor unions faced with rapid decreases in membership as a result of economic recessions, the Red Cross faced with a shortage of disasters, churches faced with fluctuations in the size of congregations as religious enthusiasms wax and wane, and the early YMCAs faced with wide variations in financial contributions—all are examples of organizations attempting to cope with uncertainty. For the unions, the answer was to be found in union security agreements and the automatic dues check-off; for the Red Cross, in the blood donor program; for churches, in the development of association activities providing solidary rewards—camaraderie, sociability, organized athletics—to supplement the purposive rewards of religious devotion; for the YMCAs, in the creation of fee-for-service enterprises such as gymnasiums and dormitories. Each change exerted a stabilizing influence on resource availability. To the extent they were successful, they also had the consequence of freeing the leadership, and especially the paid staff, from managing both environmental crises and internal conflicts over the allocation of uncertain resources.

The second kind of change results from *scarcity;* not simply a condition of not having enough, which is to say, unlimited, resources, but of having a declining· resource base. This confronted the WCTU and the Townsend Organization as well as various third-party and Marxist organizations. The politics of scarcity tends to be a politics of conflict, generated by an inability to satisfy rival claims for declining resources, by criticism of existing leadership for its manifest "failures," and by challenges from rival groups for leadership positions on reform platforms. Associations undergoing a drastic decline in resources have a powerful reason for change, but change is often hardest to implement in just such circumstances. Purposive incentives are most sensitive to rapid environmental changes—shifts in the public mood, the passage of new legislation, the emergence of more appealing organizational rivals—and thus organizations experiencing a sudden decline are frequently those using these incentives. But an organization relying in its stated purposes for its reward system can only with the greatest difficulty change those purposes, or change activities that importantly implicate those purposes. Neither the WCTU nor the Townsend Organization could change its goals despite drastic declines in resources; most Marxist parties have been able to change only by a process of organizational fission that has resulted in the formation of splinter groups.[41]

Finally, organizational change can also result from a condition of *abundance,* or, as it is sometimes phrased, the existence of "organizational slack." [42] For example, secure national unions with large staffs and budgets develop new purposes and activities chiefly to satisfy staff persons with particular concerns and values. A common explanation of change in such organizations is that "a guy we wanted to keep threatened to quit if we didn't let him try out his idea." The political activism of the staffs of large church organizations, such as the United Church of Christ or the National Council of Churches, may result from a stable organization with surplus resources giving new scope for action to key personnel—or it may stem from an effort to find a new source of incentives for new groups within the organization such as inner-city blacks and central-city white liberals who demand new organizational goals as a condition of their continued membership. The beginning of new "outreach" programs by the YMCA in certain cities reflected not only the security of the existing organization but the availability of federal funds to help pay the cost of the program innovations.

The rise in recent decades of large private foundations and of massive government grant programs has provided major new opportunities for the maintenance and enhancement of organizations that, left to their own devices (which is to say, left to the interests of their members), would face decline or even extinction. CARE, for example, is a voluntary association that solicits funds from individual donors, but by far the largest part of its resources—and all that it needs to sustain itself—is obtained from government grants. The National Council of Churches has become an urban and consumer activist in part because foundation gifts have made it possible. Indeed, for some associations "members" exist only as an historical artifact, as symbols of "private" legitimacy, or as grounds for claiming a representational function. The essential contributors have increasingly become the professional staffs and their counterparts in the foundation or government agencies that provide funds, and the relevant incentives are those to which staffs and agencies respond. In the next two chapters some aspects of the roles of officers and staff will be considered.

NOTES

1. See Robert H. Salisbury, "An Exchange Theory of Interest Groups," *Midwest Journal of Political Science*, XIII (February 1969), 21; Ronald Manzer, "Selective Inducements and the Development of Pressure Groups: The Case of the Canadian Teachers' Association," *Canadian Journal of Political Science*, II (March 1969), 114; Harold E. Old, Jr., "Individual Calculus, Exchange Theory and the Logic of Collective Action: An Attempt at Synthesis," *Michigan State Political Review*, IV (Fall 1971), 55.

2. Joseph A. Schumpeter, *Capitalism, Socialism and Democracy*, 3d ed. (New York: Harper Torchbooks, 1962), pp. 15–20. Had Marx addressed the problem of primitive accumulation, he would have been required to explain it by introducing factors that would have implied an alternative conception of social structure—one based on differences in personal skill, motives, or time horizons.

3. Ibid., p. 32.

4. Norman Frohlich, Joe A. Oppenheimer, and Oran R. Young, *Political Leadership and Collective Goods* (Princeton, N.J.: Princeton University Press, 1971), pp. 26–29, 35, 57–58. The Frohlich et al. theory is ingenious and elegant, but almost devoid of empirical content.

5. Salisbury, "Interest Groups," pp. 11–15.

6. Ibid., pp. 12–13.

7. Manzer, "Canadian Teachers' Association," pp. 110–111. See also the review of Mancur Olson, *The Logic of Collective Action*, by Neil W. Chamberlain in *American Economic Review*, LVI (June 1966), 604.

8. David B. Truman, *The Governmental Process*, 2d ed. (New York: Alfred A. Knopf, 1971), p. 59.

9. The National Association of Manufacturers was originally founded in 1895, but it was a relatively unimportant organization until it was reconstituted in 1902–1903. See Chapter 8.

10. On the YMCA, see Mayer N. Zald, *Organizational Change: The Political Economy of the YMCA* (Chicago: University of Chicago Press, 1970), pp. 31, 34; on the AFL, see Truman, *The Governmental Process*, p. 81.

11. Daniel Bell, *Marxian Socialism in the United States* (Princeton, N.J.: Princeton University Press, 1967), p. 55; Roy Lubove, *The Professional Altruist* (Cambridge, Mass.: Harvard University Press, 1965), chap. 7.

12. Lubove, *The Professional Altruist*, p. 191; John R. Seeley et al., *Community Chest* (Toronto: University of Toronto Press, 1957), p. 21.

13. Truman conceives of these factors as a process of differentiation leading to unstable equilibria; new organizations emerge to reestablish a balance of political power. Truman, *The Governmental Process*, pp. 52–62. The theory is criticized in Salisbury, "Interest Groups," pp. 3–11.

14. Salisbury, "Interest Groups"; also, Theodore Saloutos and John D. Hicks, *Agricultural Discontent in the Middle West, 1900–1939* (Madison: University of Wisconsin Press, 1951), chap. 3.

15. Saloutos and Hicks, *Agricultural Discontent*, p. 258.

16. Albert and Raymond Breton, "An Economic Theory of Social Movements," *American Economic Review*, LIX (1969), 198–205.

17. In his theory of the sources of the organizational impulse, Kenneth E. Boulding argues for the greater importance of supply factors—skills, resources, communications—over demand ones, but with little evidence and considerable ambiguity. Boulding, *The Organizational Revolution* (New York: Harper, 1953), chaps. 2, 11.

18. Gilbert H. Barnes, *The Anti-Slavery Impulse, 1830–1844* (New York: Appleton-Century, 1933); William Warren Sweet, *Revivalism in America* (New York: Scribner's, 1944), chap. 7; George Hubbard Blakeslee, "The History of the Antimasonic Party" (Ph.D. diss., Harvard University, 1903); Aileen S. Kraditor, *Means and Ends in American Abolitionism* (New York: Pantheon, 1969).

19. Robert H. Wiebe, *The Search for Order, 1877–1920* (New York: Hill and Wang, 1967), chap. 6.

20. During this period, there was not only a heightened sense of collective purpose, but a deliberate and widespread effort to cultivate a stronger sense of personal efficacy. Reinhard Bendix describes the "New Thought" movement, popular in the United States between 1895 and 1915, as devoted to the cult of personal success and the belief that by willpower alone an individual could reap extraordinary (usually business) rewards. Bendix, *Work and Authority in Industry* (New York: John Wiley, 1956), pp. 259–267.

21. Richard Hofstadter, *The Age of Reform* (New York: Vintage Books, 1960), pp. 217–218; Wiebe, *The Search for Order*, pp. 112 ff.

22. Henry F. May, *Protestant Churches and Industrial America* (New York: Octagon Books, 1963), pp. 91–111.

23. Hofstadter, *The Age of Reform*, pp. 152–155; Oscar and Mary F. Handlin, *The American College and American Culture* (New York: McGraw-Hill, 1970), chap. 4. There was a considerable overlap between liberal clerics and liberal professors during this period. Twenty-three prominent ministers were among the founding members of the American Economic Association (AEA) and Richard T. Ely, who drafted the AEA's platform, devoted much of his writing to Christian social reform. Though a professor at Johns Hopkins and Wisconsin, he was in fact as much a preacher as an economist. See May, *Protestant Churches*, pp. 138–142.

24. Lawrence N. Bailis, "Bread or Justice: Grassroots Organizing in the Welfare Rights Movement" (Ph.D. diss., Department of Government, Harvard University, 1972), p. 152.

25. John Mollenkopf (doctoral diss., in progress, Department of Government, Harvard University).

26. H. B. Davis, "The Theory of Union Growth," *Quarterly Journal of Economics*, LV (August 1941), 623.

27. Orley Ashenfelter and John H. Pencavel, "American Trade Union Growth: 1900–1960," *Quarterly Journal of Economics*, LXXXIII (August 1969), 434–448. But compare R. B. Mancke, "American Trade Union Growth, 1900–1960: A Comment," *Quarterly Journal of Economics*, LXXXV (February 1971), 187–193.

28. John T. Dunlop, "The Development of Labor Organization: A Theoretical Framework," in *Insights Into Labor Issues*, ed. Richard A. Lester and Joseph Shister (New York: Macmillan, 1948), pp. 179–183.

29. See Adrian C. Mayer, "The Significance of Quasi-Groups in the Study of Complex Societies," in *The Social Anthropology of Complex Societies*, ed. Michael Banton (London: Tavistock, 1966), pp. 97–122.

30. James H. Timberlake, *Prohibition and the Progressive Movement* (Cambridge, Mass.: Harvard University Press, 1966), p. 132.

31. Zald, *YMCA*, chap. 2; Owen E Pence, *The YMCA and Social Need* (New York: Association Press, 1939).

32. Foster R. Dulles, *The American Red Cross: A History* (New York: Harper, 1950), p. 521. My review of the history of Red Cross, the WCTU, and the Townsend Organization was stimulated by the excellent brief discussion in David L. Sills, *The Volunteers* (New York: Free Press, 1957), pp. 256–264. My explanation of the adaptive process differs from his in important respects, however.

33. Dulles, *The American Red Cross*, p. 528.

34. Joseph R. Gusfield, "The Problem of Generations in an Organizational Structure," *Social Forces*, XXXV (May 1957), 323–330.

35. Abraham Holtzman, *The Townsend Movement* (New York: Bookman Associates, 1963), p. 56.

36. Sheldon L. Messinger, "Organizational Transformation: A Case Study of a Declining Social Movement," *American Sociological Review*, XX (February 1955), 3–10.

37. Robert Michels, *Political Parties*, trans. Eden and Cedar Paul (New York: Free Press, 1958).

38. See Peter M. Blau, *Bureaucracy in Modern Society* (New York: Random House, 1956), pp. 94–96.

39. Zald, *YMCA*, chaps. 8, 10, 11.

40. James Q. Wilson, *The Amateur Democrat: Club Politics in Three Cities* (Chicago: University of Chicago Press, 1962), pp. 44–49.

41. This section draws on my earlier formulation of organizational innovation, based on the concepts of abundance and scarcity outlined in James Q. Wilson, "Ne-

cessity Versus the Devil," in *American Bureaucracy*, ed. Warren G. Bennis (Chicago: Trans-Action Books / Aldine Publishing, 1970), pp. 157–160.

42. Richard Cyert and James G. March, *A Behavioral Theory of the Firm* (Englewood Cliffs, N.J.: Prentice-Hall, 1963), pp. 36–38.

CHAPTER 11

Authority and Leadership

In most voluntary associations, authority is uncertain and leadership is precarious. Because the association is voluntary, its chief officer [1] has neither the effective power nor the acknowledged right to coerce the members—they are, after all, "members" and not "employees." In a business firm, the chief officer may, within limits, hire and fire, promote or demote, his subordinates. There are, to be sure, certain kinds of "voluntary" organizations in which the head may exercise such powers—a political machine, for example, or certain trade unions—but they are the exception. In most associations, power, or the ability to get a subordinate to do what the superior wants, is limited, and authority, or the right to exercise such power as exists, is circumscribed and contingent.

This is not the way the matter is often viewed: to many, such as Robert Michels,[2] associations are inevitably oligarchical, the actions of leaders are unconstrained by the opinions of followers, and those in office tend to remain in office. This matter will be treated more fully in the next chapter; for now, it is enough to suggest that most voluntary association leaders *are* constrained by their members, but by their members' indifference rather than by their opposition. Leaders remain in office largely because the average member finds it simpler to express his disagreement or disinterest by leaving the association rather than by contesting its offices. In certain kinds of associations, an active minority—sometimes out of an ambition to supplant the officers, sometimes out of a commitment to a different set of purposes—may challenge the leadership by capitalizing on its mistakes and seeking to discredit it with the majority. The officers, knowing of their potential rivals, are usually careful to avoid taking any action that might, when suitably exploited, prove offensive to the rank and file. For the typical head of a typical association, the limits on his authority, the marginal loyalties of the member, and the possible challenges of rivals combine to ensure that whatever he does is designed to offend as few members as possible.

Though the authority of many association leaders is weak, the demands of the office are great. The chief officer of a voluntary organization must usually combine the executive task of maintaining the organization with the leadership task of defining and advancing its objectives. The chief officer of a business firm, by contrast, usually emphasizes his executive responsibilities—ensuring the continued contributions of time, energy, and money—and leaves to others the task of formulating objectives or pressing for changes.[3] The business executive presides over the process whereby competing ends and strategies are formulated and assessed, leaving himself free to adopt that policy to which the fewest important objections can be made. Ordinarily, to take sides, especially prematurely, and to become an advocate would weaken the executive's ability to perform his maintenance function—he would run the risk of cutting himself off from valuable information, of alienating important colleagues, and of becoming personally identified with an error.

The distinction between the executive function and the leadership function is common in the analysis of organizations. Social psychologists, describing how small groups behave, distinguish between "affective" and "instrumental" leadership, the former having to do with maintaining the group and good relations among its members, the latter with advancing the group in the performance of a common task.[4] Richard Neustadt, in his discussion of the presidency, compares the "President on Horseback" (the leader) with the "President in Sneakers" (the executive).[5] Even in a street-corner gang, William F. Whyte found that the acknowledged head of the group was the most popular person, but not the one who initiated suggestions for activities.[6]

The chief officer of a voluntary association is often unable to choose which task to perform; he must, like it or not, perform both, because what he does not do will not get done at all. The paid staffs of associations, if they exist at all, tend to be small, and thus duties cannot often be delegated; the "executive secretary" or "executive director" must raise the budget, persuade volunteer members to perform tasks, define particular goals, and select concrete tactics. Goal definition tends to be divisive—the more specific the objective, the greater the likelihood there will be disagreement over it within the organization. Though there are some single-issue associations that are the exception to this generalization,[7] many general-purpose civic or business associations quickly discover that maintenance needs are better served by having vague or broadly stated goals, whereas task achievement is facilitated by having explicit and concrete ones. Where such conflict exists, it is usually resolved in favor of organizational maintenance and thus in favor of having highly general purposes.[8] Put another way, when very few persons, paid or unpaid, are available to do the work of the association, they must walk a tightrope between organizational maintenance and goal achievement, but while walking they usually lean to one side, so that, if they fall, they fall on the side of keeping the association alive.

In sum, the chief officer of the typical association finds himself in a weak authority position while facing the difficult assignment of combining, in some degree, two partially incompatible tasks—that of executive and that of leader. The extent to which he confronts this problem and the manner in which he resolves it are importantly influenced by the formal structure of the organization.

There are, broadly speaking, two major kinds of voluntary association structures—the "caucus" form and the "primary" form. By "caucus" is meant an organization in which one or a few leaders carry out the work of the organization, supported by funds or other kinds of support contributed by persons who rarely, if at all, are brought together in meetings or are otherwise asked to concert their actions in cooperative ventures. A "primary" organization is one in which, whatever the role of officers, members regularly come together to act in concert and to discuss associational affairs or are otherwise mobilized to carry on group activities. The distinction made here is not the same as that between "elite" and "mass" organizations—a caucus association includes those with thousands of supporters, such as the National Association of Manufacturers (NAM) or the national office of the NAACP as well as those with only a few members, such as the National Committee for a More Effective Congress; similarly, a primary association may have very few members, such as the Student Nonviolent Coordinating Committee (SNCC) or a local PTA, or very many, such as a large union local. The distinction is rather between those associations in which the activities of significant numbers of persons are to be concerted—by getting them to attend meetings, circulate petitions, register voters, write congressmen or congresswomen, discuss issues, conduct demonstrations, or go out on strike—and those in which no such group activity is required.

A caucus organization has *contributors*, a primary organization has *members*.

Organizations that define their tasks in ways that require the application of resources to specialized, concentrated, or expert efforts will tend to assume the caucus form. The NAACP, at least the national office, hires lawyers to fight court cases, the Committee for Economic Development (CED) hires professors and others to write study papers, the National Committee for a More Effective Congress raises money to spend on favored candidates, the national AFL-CIO offices carry out lobbying, research, and publicity assignments. Organizations that define their tasks in ways that require group or mass action will assume the primary form. SNCC members sit in at lunch counters, local branches of the League of Women Voters circulate petitions and hold candidate meetings, and union locals from time to time go on strike or conduct organizing drives. A few associations combine the caucus and the primary form. Some NAACP branches have been active in local protest efforts, whereas others have merely been dues collectors for the national office.[9] The National Foundation for Infantile Paralysis publicized the threat of polio and helped care for polio victims; it also raised money with the aid of volunteers mobilized through its local chapters.[10]

The basis of authority, and thus the pattern of leadership, tends to differ in the two kinds of structures. Caucus organizations tend to have executives who are expert or professional and whose authority rests, in the phrase of Max Weber, on legal-rational grounds. Perhaps more accurately, it is thought to rest on utilitarian grounds—the executive has or can command the skills necessary to perform the specialized task of the association. There are some notable exceptions. For example, the Southern Christian Leadership Conference (SCLC), to a degree a caucus organization, was headed by a person whose authority was based on charisma, Martin Luther King, Jr. The Sierra Club has been led by an outspoken, abrasive man (David Brower) and not by a smooth, facilitative executive. But the SCLC was only in part a caucus; from time to time it actively mobilized local protest efforts, and in both these mass efforts, as well as in national fund raising, King's reputation was the association's most valuable asset. And the Sierra Club, which is both a national caucus and a collection of local clubs, was bitterly divided over the personality of Brower, its former executive. More characteristic of caucus organizations are the lawyers, human-relations specialists, business executives, and publicists who lead such organizations as the Urban League, the NAM, the CED, or the Anti-Defamation League of B'nai B'rith.

It is among associations with a primary group structure that one finds the greatest variation in the principle of legitimacy underlying the executive's authority. This is because he is attempting, often while in face-to-face contact with the members, to obtain concerted action rather than simply to raise funds. He must persuade members to attend meetings, accept responsibilities, give of their time, participate in demonstrations, perhaps even expose themselves to danger. Though mere persuasion can achieve some of these ends, it is rarely sufficient. Furthermore, though the executive can attract members to join the association by means of a variety of incentives, these often tend to be quite general—a sense of duty toward an important purpose, a feeling of kinship, or a desire for status—and thus difficult to manipulate in order to get particular persons to perform particular acts. And in any event, members will resent thinking of themselves as the objects of manipulation. Few, if any, incentives will prove effective in the long run if the members do not believe that the executive has the *right* to ask them to perform certain services. As Weber has written, "Experience has shown that in no instance does domination [*Herrschaft*] voluntarily limit itself to the appeal to material or affectual or ideal motives as a basis for its continuance. In addition every system attempts to establish and to cultivate the belief in its legitimacy." [11]

Legitimacy will to some extent arise out of the mere fact of holding office. A member can more easily be persuaded to do things by an officer than by another member. This might be called the authority of *office*. It is the most common but least powerful principle of legitimacy, for though it suffices for obtaining the performance of routine tasks, it is often insufficient to secure the performance of sustained or demanding ones. Many associations, of course, never make more than routine demands on their members, and for them no principle of executive legitimacy stronger than the authority of office is required. One thinks in this regard of a typical PTA or a businessmen's service club.

In some organizations all of the time and in many organizations some of the time the chief officer acquires, because of his personal qualities, a kind of legitimacy that is stronger than that arising from the mere fact of officeholding. *Expertise* is one such quality that can become the basis of legitimate authority. The professional executive director of a conservation society, of a legal aid organization, or of a local Urban League is deferred to by members not simply because he holds executive office but because in addition he is thought to be expert in the affairs of the association and in its substantive concerns. He is, in the term frequently employed by business civic leaders, a "pro." As indicated earlier, this form of legitimacy tends to predominate among caucus-type associations, but it is also found among primary associations.

A third form of legitimate authority is that arising out of *personal fealty*.[12] This may exist simply because the person is the most popular member of the group and his company and approval are widely sought after or because he has made himself indispensable by doing valued favors for a large number of members. The head of a street-corner gang, a college fraternity, or a newly formed political club is typically the most popular person in the group. In other kinds of associations, such as a local union or an established political club, the head may not necessarily be the most popular member (in the sense that his company and approval are esteemed above those of any other member) but may instead be the person who through unremitting efforts has succeeded in creating a network of obligations that link him to all or most members. The head of a political ward organization may not be loved, but he may be respected for his ability and willingness to "take care" of his followers.

Authority may also rest on the ability of a person to make manifest his *belief* in the purposes of the association. The legitimacy of such a person's authority may result simply from the evident sincerity of his commitment to the group's objectives, or it may result from his apparent possession of exceptional, even divine, powers and qualities. It is this extreme form of legitimacy based on belief that Weber termed "charismatic authority" (literally, authority resulting from the gift of grace).[13] This form of authority should not be confused, as in common discourse it often is, with that arising from the popularity of the leader; being liked, even adulated, is not the same thing as being honored for one's priestly or divine qualities. Sometimes both forms of legitimacy are combined in a single person: Eugene Debs, once the head of the American Socialist party, was both highly popular among his followers and, to some, an inspiring example of selfless devotion to a larger cause. Nonreligious examples of the authority of belief include the extraordinary leadership of Bob Moses in the early years of SNCC and of Cesar Chavez in the United Farm Workers' Organizing Committee.

Not all associations become invested with a principle of legitimate authority sufficient to sustain their leadership. Purposive associations lacking a leader who displays charisma or enjoys personal fealty, a coalition of organizations in which no member group is willing to concede primacy to any other, or an association composed chiefly of ambitious persons of similar status, are all familiar examples of organizations in which no person or group is granted the right to make decisions. Many do not survive; others endure only at the price of either continuous factionalism or ineffectual blandness.

The incentive system and the principle of legitimacy operating within an association obviously affect, but do not uniquely determine, one another. For example, authority based on belief is much more likely to be found in an organization relying on purposive rewards, but it is possible to imagine it operating in quite different kinds of groups. The authority of Marcus Garvey in the Universal Negro Improvement Association was chiefly that of belief, perhaps even of charisma, but many, if not most, of the members derived mainly solidary benefits—titles, uniforms, a sense of belonging—from the organization. A complete analysis of the relationship between incentives, that is, the means used to obtain compliance, and authority, that is, the right to obtain compliance by whatever means, would require a level of detail beyond the scope of this summary treatment.

The mode of executive or leadership action will be influenced by the principle of legitimacy employed. Office and expertise will ordinarily lead to an administrative style different from that resulting from either personal fealty or manifest belief. The first two kinds of legitimate authority tend to give rise to *legal-rational* administration; the latter two kinds to *patrimonial* administration. In a legal-rational administration, the chief officer of the association (and his subordinate staff, if any) will feel himself bound by a set of impersonal general rules that he cannot change in important respects except by appeal to higher authority (for example, the consent of the members, the rulings of a parent organization, or the laws of society); his task is to apply these general rules to particular cases.[14] Legal-rational administration may become bureaucratic administration if in addition to the existence of a set of general rules there is also a hierarchical arrangement of appointive offices, each with defined spheres of competence.[15] Most voluntary associations, however, are not bureaucratically administered; they are instead one-man operations, or the operations of a handful of men.

Patrimonial administration, by contrast, does not involve the application of general rules to specific cases, but rather the making of decisions on the basis of what is required by the needs of a particular person or the value of a particular purpose.[16] The patrimonial administrator will not feel himself bound by a code of impersonal rules, though he may well feel bound by the reciprocal obligations of personal loyalties or by the overriding importance of some extrapersonal goal or mission. In the extreme case of a chief with a wholly personal following or a charismatic leader with a following of true believers, the very concept of rule will be anathema. The will of the chief or the sanctity of the objective can justify virtually any act, whether or not it is consistent with prior acts.[17] The patrimonial administrator will not distinguish carefully between his personal and his official position, and if he creates a large staff, it will not be bureaucratic in form but will rather consist of a number of aides to the chief.[18]

The differences between patrimonial and legal-rational administration are illustrated by the behavior of a number of labor unions. Ralph T. Jones, in his study of city employee unions, found that the older, smaller, single-shop unions tended to display patrimonial rule, whereas the newer, larger, more comprehensive ones displayed the legal-rational style. This could be seen most clearly in the handling of member grievances. Under patrimonial authority, the employee with a grievance against management sought out his union "chief," whose decision whether and how to act would be based on his assessment of what the member deserved, and this often included his estimate of the member's loyalty to him as a leader and whether or not he owed the member a "favor." If he decided to help the member, he did so informally, using his contacts in management to get the matter "worked out." Sometimes what was done was called for in the labor contract; other times it was an extralegal settlement. The chief was part of a nexus of favors and alliances that extended into management as well as among his members. Most workers who asked for help got some; a few got a good deal more than others and a few got a good deal less. Treating equals equally was not an important consideration, though avoiding a show of obvious favoritism was.

In the legal-rational (or as Jones called them, "bureaucratic") unions, the grievance procedure was spelled out in great detail in the labor contract. Complaints went through channels—first to the shop steward, then to a grievance committee. A fairly complex common law arose as to how grievances were to be settled; occasionally an outside arbitrator was called in. Unfounded grievances were rejected, whatever the "worth" of the individual workers; well-founded ones were handled in similar ways for similar cases.[19]

Political parties provide another example. The political machine, and especially its local ward or district clubs, will rely on material incentives, but in addition will develop a principle of legitimate authority based on personal loyalty to the "boss." Sometimes the boss or club leader is popular; in other cases, he is merely effective in rewarding his followers. There will be few, if any, general rules as to how favors are to be distributed within the club or the machine. Each claimant is expected to make his own appeal, or to appeal through an intermediary, and to justify his claim by the way in which he has helped, or otherwise been loyal to, the leader and by the degree of his individual need. Such needs and loyalties may be compared with those of others on a rough scale, but few rules determining eligibility for some benefit will be promulgated, and no exact equity will be sought. In some of the reform or amateur political clubs that have in places supplanted machine-style organizations, there is not only relatively little reliance on material incentives, but, in addition, the principle of legitimate authority tends to be either that of office or of expertise and accordingly the manner of administration becomes legal-rational. Those benefits that the organization can bestow—nominations for public office or endorsement for appointive position—will be awarded on the basis of some general and impersonal procedure, an election within the club, for example. The discretion of the administrators will be closely circumscribed by rule and precedent. In the rare case, the head of the amateur club will be a charismatic or exceptional leader who will be able to exercise authority in much the same way as the leader of a machine club. In time and with the erosion of charisma, this pattern of rule will be criticized by members as an undesirable "cult of the personality."

The history of most associations shows that legal-rational rule tends to replace patrimonial rule. The principles of legitimacy necessary for the support of patrimonialism are usually short-lived or unstable. Personal loyalties weaken with the age or incapacity of the leader or with the arrival of younger members to whom the leader is simply a member of the "old guard" standing in the way of their own ambitions; alternatively, a rival leader with a different personal following will arise to challenge the established leader. Shifting the basis of legitimacy to that of office or expertise and developing a more legal-rational rule is one way for a challenged leader to buttress his weakened authority and a common way for the incompatible demands of rival leaders to be reconciled. An exemplary commitment to purposes can rarely justify for long the wielding of arbitrary power if the other members of the association believe themselves to be equally committed, and thus equally capable of making decisions. And charisma only rarely, if ever, can be transferred from a founding leader to his successor.

Changes in the social structure also encourage the replacement of patrimonial with legal-rational administration. As the middle class grows in size and affluence, it is less easily satisfied with the favors of a chief, and as it increases in education, it demands more participation in making decisions and more equity in applying them. The acquisition by an association of a larger number of tasks—as when labor unions create pension and welfare funds—and the placing of an association under more complex legal obligations—as when unions are required to comply with rules governing elections, financial accountability, and trusteeship practices—also contribute to the growth of legal-rational administration and authority based on either office or expertise.

Because voluntary associations tend to develop a legal-rational administration, it is often assumed that they also tend to become increasingly bureaucratic, that is, unresponsive, overly organized, or preoccupied with administrative means rather than organizational ends. Whatever may be true of the tendency of associations to become bureaucratic in the sense of ponderous and inflexible, it is not clear that they always and inevitably become so in the sense of proliferating hierarchically arranged offices staffed with careerists. A voluntary association, by the very fact that it *is* voluntary, ordinarily has no ready access to those money resources with which to procure an elaborate staff even if it should want to. During the latter part of the nineteenth century, when industry was becoming national in scope and bureaucratic in management, American political parties became neither centralized nor bureaucratic.[20] Though some labor unions, such as the United Steelworkers and the United Auto Workers, have developed sizable national staffs, many other unions, such as those in the building trades, still have very few full-time staff officers.

In general, voluntary associations tend to assume the form of those political or economic structures that control the resources sought by such associations. Political parties remain decentralized because they seek office in a decentralized political structure; because the local units of the decentralized party are small, few of them can mobilize the resources necessary to acquire a permanent staff of any size. Labor unions that organize workers and bargain with management in fragmented, localistic industries, such as printing or construction, tend to be composed of a large number of small locals with few, if any, paid staff members; unions that organize and bargain in nationwide industries or with a few powerful firms, such as steel and auto manufacturers, tend to have large locals and to hire staff members capable of coping with the equivalent expertise on the side of management.[21] Associations that seek to win benefits by lobbying Congress, bringing cases before the United States Supreme Court, or pressing claims before federal regulatory and administrative agencies tend to mobilize more financial and staff resources than organizations that pursue their objectives by means of local demonstrations or circulating petitions. The national NAACP office has a larger staff than any local NAACP branch or than any unit of CORE; the United States Chamber of Commerce has a larger staff than any local chamber.

Supplementing these structural reasons for greater or less bureaucratization is the effort made by an ongoing association to find the most economical incentive system possible. An organization may be formed in a burst of member enthusiasm or purposive commitment, but enthusiasm tends to wane and commitments to falter. Finding new sources of zeal is difficult and coordinating the activities of zealots is even harder. Furthermore, few associations attain their objectives quickly, and some never attain them at all. For all these reasons, the chief officers of such associations will usually seek ways of maintaining the group at a lower pitch of enthusiasm and of providing services and some sense of accomplishment in the face of slow, if any, progress toward major objectives. The association will start to issue a newsletter, will form committees to carry on routine tasks, and will seek regularized ways of meeting its budget—organizing twenty-five-dollar-a-plate banquets, setting up a dues schedule, and publishing a journal for which subscription fees are charged. To do all these things well or even at all, paid help is often required, and for this a larger budget is necessary. To raise a larger budget, more staff persons are required, and so on. What sets limits to the upward spiral of staff seeking dollars in order to hire more staff are the available resources and degree of interest of the membership base. This limit differs among associations, but in all cases the limit is reached rather quickly. The political structure may cause both the NAM and the national NAACP to be bureaucratic, caucus-style organizations, but the unequal distribution of realizable resources makes the former bigger than the latter.

To the extent that voluntary associations become bureaucratic in the sociological sense of the term, that is, to the extent that they develop a number of hierarchically arranged offices and a division of labor, they are exposed to the charge of being "bureaucratic" in the pejorative meaning of the word, namely, ponderous, undemocratic, or conservative. There is some truth in the complaint because of the nature of the staff function in an association, especially if the legitimacy of the staff rests on its legal-rational authority. The staff, rather than the lay leaders of the organization, become its executive—that is, the officers charged with maintaining the association.

Under certain circumstances, the staff responsibility for organizational maintenance will lead it to act more cautiously than many members might prefer. When an issue is of great concern to the rank and file, they are likely, in the eyes of the staff, to overvalue present action and undervalue long-term strategic considerations. Many members of the National Rifle Association (NRA), for example, may feel so strongly about gun control that they will insist that every gun-control bill be defeated, whereas some staff members of the NRA, knowing this to be politically impossible, may prefer instead to support a bill imposing weak controls. And when an issue divides the membership, the staff will at a minimum displease one faction by favoring the opposing one, or, what is more likely, it will displease both factions by taking a position stated in such general terms as to be meaningless. The larger and more diverse the association, the greater the likelihood that any specific objective will divide it. And the more the staff is directly responsible for distributing incentives to members—as will be the case if the association is of the primary form—the more the staff will be constrained by member attitudes toward those policy positions that affect the value of these incentives.

But it is a mistake to assume that the existence of a staff necessarily implies bureaucratic conservatism or the substitution of organizational, and staff, maintenance for goal attainment. In the first place, the members will be indifferent to the positions taken by the staff on many issues. But more importantly, there are many kinds of organizations—especially those of the caucus form or with a federated structure—in which the staff consistently takes positions that are either more militant or more liberal than those preferred by the membership. Henry J. Pratt has shown that as the AFL-CIO, the NAACP, and the National Council of Churches became more bureaucratic, they became more liberal and reformist. In 1931, the AFL had a single staff person; by 1972, there were sixteen departments of the national AFL-CIO, each headed by a staff professional who had many associates. The national staff of the NAACP increased from eight in 1939 to eighty-six in 1969. The number of staff members in the National Council of Churches concerned with social education and social action increased from ten in 1943 to forty-three in 1965. This increase occurred simultaneously with—and in the view of Pratt and his informants in these organizations, in fact caused

—the emergence of "a more politicized approach, involving an expansive and self-conscious progressivism" in the positions taken by these organizations on civil rights and social welfare policy. There are member constraints on staff activism, however. In 1973 many Protestant parishioners objected to the liberal social-reform policies of national church staffs and demanded that more resources be devoted to pietistic than to secular needs.[22]

There appear to be two reasons for this tendency. First, it often takes place in organizations in which the maintenance of rank-and-file membership support is not the responsibility of the national staff but of local branches (as in the NAACP), local churches (as in the National Council of Churches), or local unions (as in the AFL-CIO). These local units, sustained by locally supplied incentives, become in effect tax-collecting stations that fund the activities of a national staff. Second, the national staff in these organizations has often become an association unto itself, with its own maintenance needs. One of those needs requires that staff members be given a sense of program accomplishment. This need is especially strong when, as is often the case, the staff members of a national voluntary association are paid money wages well below what persons of comparable skill receive in government or industry. They have in effect foregone a substantial fraction of their monetary income in the expectation that they will be compensated in nonmonetary income—chiefly, by a sense of serving an important purpose.

In addition to the task of choosing goals, the staff must often recruit and train the lay leadership of the association. In some cases, this is impossible or possible only within narrow limits, as when the principal lay leader is a "founding father" or a strong personality who exercises an independent leadership role. In such instances, the staff must perform the executive function of organizational maintenance, while the lay head performs the leadership function of goal selection. The typical case, however, is for the paid staff to perform both roles and this means, in part, finding a supply of acceptable lay officers.

This recruitment and socialization process operates under two constraints—most lay officers can give only limited time to the organization and most know rather little about its inner workings. The staff will seek to turn these constraints into opportunities by helping pick lay officers who will leave effective direction of the association in staff hands and who will follow staff leadership in making public statements about the association.[23] New lay officers are inculcated with the informal rules and conventions of the association, are spoken to before and after meetings to brief them on how issues on the agenda might best be handled, and are equipped with staff-prepared speeches they can make on public occasions or in testimony before legislative committees. All this may strike the reader as cynical and manipulative; in practice, it is quite different—most lay officers want to "do the right thing" and turn to others to discover what the right thing is. A few will pursue an independent course, insisting on their own views, but usually they will find themselves isolated and ineffective in the organization.

The relationship between staff and lay officers as sketched above is most characteristic of voluntary associations involving businessmen or similar persons, usually of an upper-middle-class background, who are accustomed to working in a board-staff context and to deferring to the presumably "expert" judgment of the professionals in charge of the day-to-day affairs of the organization. A very different relationship may exist in associations made up of persons without such background or experience. In the Massachusetts Welfare Rights Organization, for example, the paid staff consisted for the most part of young, college-educated whites with a middle- or upper-middle-class background, whereas the membership consisted of women, mostly black, on welfare. In theory, the paid staff organizers saw their task as creating strong local chapters of the welfare rights movement that could then be led by lay officers chosen by the members. In practice, the staff discovered that without their organizing skills chapters tended to become dormant, and thus they tried to play a continuing leadership role. The lay officers, on the other hand, often became unhappy with what they took to be the dominant and manipulative role of the organizer and sought to increase their influence at the expense of that of the organizer. Some lay officers, unaccustomed to having status and power in any context, came to value quite highly those selective solidary rewards arising from their participation in the welfare rights organization and to resent staff efforts to ensure a rotation in leadership and the recruitment of new officers. The staff saw the perpetuation in office of one group of women as a disincentive to the continued involvement of rank-and-file members and as an impediment to new organizing efforts.[24]

When holding lay office in a voluntary association is in itself a source of substantial rewards to the incumbent, the influence of the appointed staff is likely to be lessened and that of the board members heightened. A businessman may be pleased to be the chairman or president of a civic association, but neither his income nor his social status is crucially dependent on such recognition. A blue-collar worker or a welfare mother, by contrast, may find that high office in a labor union or a welfare rights organization is a valuable source of both tangible and intangible benefits and thus work hard to win it and hold it. Appointed staff professionals, recruited from outside the organization, are likely to play a more important role in associations where lay leaders find only marginal value in their offices than in associations where they find substantial value. Indeed, in many of the latter groups, and especially among labor unions, outsiders are rarely appointed to any staff positions except to those (such as legal counsel, research director, or public-relations specialist) for which professional skills are required. Most other staff appointments are made to insiders, often on political grounds.

Organizations composed of working-class or lower-class members grant less latitude to staff members for other reasons as well. Not only do the members attach importance to the rewards of office, but they also attach great importance to selective rewards generally. They will, unlike the businessman or upper-middle-class suburbanite in a civic association, place a high value on the marginal dollar. This means that they will be cautious about hiring expensive professional staff members and will judge such staff members in great part by their success in enhancing the benefits of membership. The staff, to the extent that it consists of persons with a professional background and orientation, will often press for a broader program of association activities involving general, impersonal goals and purposive rewards. Welfare mothers, for example, were chiefly interested in larger welfare payments; staff organizers, on the other hand, were more interested in building a political movement among the poor that would play a leading role in the reconstruction of society and government.[25] Professional staff members of labor unions frequently wish to see their organizations act more aggressively on larger social issues than does the elective leadership, but the staff members are only occasionally in a position to carry out their desires.[26]

Exacerbating the cleavage between staff and lay officers in many working- and lower-class organizations is the fact that the staff is of necessity poorly paid, a fact that makes such positions attractive primarily to persons who are willing to forego some level of money income in exchange for the psychic income that derives from the sense of serving a good cause. Such staff members are attracted in part by purposive rewards and thus are highly motivated to enlarge the range and intensify the level of associational activity. The resistance they sometimes encounter from the lay officers makes staff-board relations in such groups even more frustrating for both parties than is ordinarily the case.

For all of these reasons—the differing rewards of staff and lay officer, the difficulty the staff experiences in motivating indifferent members and controlling militant ones, and the differing (and often class-based) perspectives on organization goals the staff and members bring to their task—it is not as easy as it may first appear to answer the question of whether governance by paid officers leads to the pathologies of bureaucracy. On any given issue of great importance to them, the members are more likely than the staff to be militant—the members, suddenly aroused and preoccupied with the present issue, will want to do whatever is necessary to resolve the problem, letting the chips fall where they may. The staff, on the other hand, concerned about the maintenance of the organization and of its relations with valued allies in and out of government, is likely to be much more concerned about just where (or upon whom) those chips fall. This will lead the staff to act in a way perceived by others as "cautious" or "conservative." When, on the other hand, the enthusiasms or rages of the moment have subsided, the staff will still be in business, seeking to motivate members to act on a wide range of matters that the staff thinks need to be dealt with but that have little immediate emotional appeal for the rank and file. The staff will constantly be seeking to place the organization on record as favoring a variety of matters, most of which will be important only to relatively small groups of members. At these times, the staff will be seen as "aggressive" or "political." The larger the staff, the greater the specialization of tasks and interests and therefore the greater the likelihood that under normal conditions the organization will be seeking out ways to "put itself on the record" or "make itself heard." If in addition the staff is drawn from a higher, or at least more educated, social strata than the members, the activist and cosmopolitan predilections of the professionals will further stimulate their inclination to broaden the organization's stance.

This argument is consistent with the considerable body of evidence that finds leaders to be more ideological than followers in a variety of voluntary associations. A study of the Oregon Education Association (OEA), for example, revealed that the leaders on every issue but one were more willing than the followers to have the organization get involved in a wide range of political activities, including endorsing candidates for public office, taking sides on public issues, intervening in school board elections, and "fighting attacks on educational principles and methods." The one issue on which followers were more aggressive than leaders concerned, interestingly enough, "eliminating from the

OEA staff political liberals." Furthermore, on a scale of general domestic political attitudes, leaders proved to be more liberal than followers.[27] Derek C. Bok and John T. Dunlop report that in a survey conducted in a large international union, the higher the position of white respondents in the union, the more likely they were to give a liberal answer to a question asking whether racial desegregation in schools, housing, and job opportunities was proceeding fast enough: 69 percent of the international staff, 35 percent of the convention delegates, 25 percent of the local officers, and 21 percent of the rank-and-file members said that desegregation was proceeding "too slowly." [28]

Some of the consequences of bureaucratization in voluntary associations are suggested by Seymour Martin Lipset in his comparison of staff officers in British and American trade unions. He notes that there is one paid official for every 300 members of American unions, compared to one paid official for every 2,000 members of British unions.[29] His data do not distinguish between persons holding paid offices to which they are elected and those holding ones to which they are appointed, nor between those appointed officers who are being rewarded for personal or party fealty and those who have been selected on grounds of professional competence. Elected paid officials are not bureaucrats in the strict sense of the word at all, and among the appointed ones there is probably a crucial difference between those who are part of a patrimonial as opposed to a legal-rational system of authority. Even with all these qualifications, however, the gross differences between the American and British experience are striking.

The British unions (and for that matter, many of the European ones) make much greater use of volunteer, unpaid union officers. As Lipset notes, many such persons are active because they are attracted by the purposes of trade unionism and thus have a sense of mission about being part of a "social movement." One result is that British union leaders may have less control over their subordinates than American ones. In the United States, union conventions are often meetings of full-time, local, district, and national officials. Such assemblages are less likely to create trouble for the leadership than ones composed, as is the case in Great Britain, of unpaid volunteer delegates. Indeed, in many British unions, having lay status is a *requirement* for being a convention delegate.[30]

Lay leadership may explain, as Lipset notes, "the perpetuation of serious political debate within union movements such as the British, Norwegian, or the Belgian" because these volunteer leaders are "drawn from the ranks of the more idealistic and politically motivated of the membership and are not on a union career ladder." [31] One might also suppose that such volunteer activism would lead to more militant union action, including a high frequency of strikes, but it does not—between 1955 and 1964, there were over three times as many man-days of work lost because of strikes in America than were lost in Britain.[32] The reason for this is probably to be found in the higher degree of decentralization of American trade unions, and thus the much greater number of bargaining units in which agreements must be reached.[33]

What volunteer activism in British unions does produce is a more militant and radical *political* posture. In 1960, a majority of the trade union delegates to the Labor party annual conference voted in favor of unilateral nuclear disarmament. In voting this way, they were expressing the opinions of the active, volunteer minority but not, as it turned out, the opinions of the rank-and-file trade union member. A survey taken at the same time showed that 83 percent of the union members favored retaining nuclear weapons by the British armed forces.[34] Governance by lay leaders is no more a guarantee of the accurate representation of member interests in voluntary associations than is rule by paid careerists.

NOTES

1. By "chief officer" I mean whoever exercises principal responsibility for the direction of an organization. It is a generic term, intended to include both the "executive" (who maintains the organization) and the "leader" who sets goals for it.

2. Robert Michels, *Political Parties*, trans. Eden and Cedar Paul (New York: Free Press, 1958), esp. part VI, chap. 2.

3. This view of business decision-making draws on Peter B. Clark, "The Business Corporation as a Political Order" (paper delivered to the American Political Science Association, 1961).

4. This literature is summarized in Sidney Verba, *Small Groups and Political Behavior* (Princeton, N.J.: Princeton University Press, 1961), chaps. 6, 7.

5. Richard E. Neustadt, "White House and Whitehall," *The Public Interest* (Winter 1966), p. 64.

6. William F. Whyte, quoted in Verba, *Small Groups and Political Behavior*, pp. 167–168.

7. For example, the Anti-Saloon League stuck to the single and specific issue of ending the traffic in alcoholic beverages. In this case, the league's concrete, political objective made its task easier than it would have been if it had sought to deal with the "evils of alcohol," broadly defined. See Peter H. Odegaard, *Pressure Politics: The Story of the Anti-Saloon League* (New York: Columbia University Press, 1928).

8. See Peter B. Clark, "The Chicago Big Businessman as a Civic Leader" (Ph.D. diss., Department of Political Science, University of Chicago, September 1959), chap. 5.

9. James Q. Wilson, *Negro Politics* (New York: Free Press, 1960), chap. 11.

10. David L. Sills, *The Volunteers* (New York: Free Press, 1957), chaps. 4, 5.

11. Max Weber, *Economy and Society*, ed. Guenther Roth and Claus Wittich (New York: Bedminster Press, 1968), vol. I, p. 213. The social scientist will note in this chapter both my obligation to Weber and my modification of some of his principal concepts. This reconceptualization of his insights is necessary, I believe, partly because he was writing chiefly of authority in the state rather than in the voluntary association and partly because he was not always careful to distinguish among the means used to secure compliance, the source of legitimacy for whatever means were employed, and the administrative apparatus and style that evolved. He has frequently been criticized, for example, for not discriminating between the authority of office and that of expertise; here, the two sources of legitimacy are kept distinct. Finally, I find that the concept of "traditional" authority has little application to a theory of *formal* voluntary associations, applying, as it does, largely to tribal, familial, or clan rule. I neglect, as does Weber, any consideration of illegitimate authority, or more accurately, nonauthority, such as might be found in a corrupt or coercive labor union.

12. Ibid., vol. III, p. 1006.

13. Ibid., vol. I, pp. 215–216, 241–245.

14. Ibid., vol. I, pp. 217–218.

15. Ibid., vol. I, pp. 220–221.

16. I use "patrimonial" where Weber often uses "patriarchal" only because of the gerontocratic implications of the latter. Patrimonial administration is "particularistic" in the sense of Talcott Parsons and Edward A. Shils, *Toward a General Theory of Action* (New York: Harper Torchbooks, 1962), p. 82.

17. Weber, *Economy and Society*, vol. I, p. 244.

18. Ibid., vol. I, pp. 228–241.

19. Ralph T. Jones, "City Employee Unions in New York and Chicago" (Ph.D. diss., Department of Government, Harvard University, 1972).

20. Robert D. Marcus, *Grand Old Party: Political Structure in the Gilded Age, 1880–1896* (New York: Oxford University Press, 1971), p. 252. By contrast, the German Social Democratic party at about the same time (1910) had 3,000 permanent officials, approximately one official for every 250 members. Maurice Duverger, *Political Parties*, trans. Barbara and Robert North (New York: John Wiley, 1954), p. 154.

21. Harold L. Wilensky, *Intellectuals in Labor Unions* (Glencoe, Ill.: Free Press, 1956), p. 200.

22. Henry J. Pratt, "Bureaucracy and Group Behavior: A Study of Three National Organizations" (paper delivered to the American Political Science Association, 1972), p. 18, and Pratt, *The Liberalization of American Protestantism* (Detroit: Wayne State University Press, 1972), chap. 13. The "parishioners' revolt" is reported in *Newsweek*, April 16, 1973, pp. 69ff.

23. See Clark, "The Chicago Big Businessman," chap. 5.

24. Lawrence N. Bailis, "Bread or Justice: Grassroots Organizing in the Welfare Rights Movement" (Ph.D. diss., Department of Government, Harvard University, 1972), chap. 8. A study of eight voluntary associations involved in youth programs in lower-income New York neighborhoods suggests that volunteer, that is, lay, members tended to initiate more actions than professional staff workers unless such staff constituted a large fraction of the association's membership. Marjorie H. Buckholz, "Volunteers and Agency Staff: Their Different Roles in Policy-Making Bodies," *Journal of Voluntary Action Research*, I (April 1972), 19–26.

25. Bailis, "Bread or Justice," chap. 8.

26. Wilensky (*Intellectuals in Labor Unions*, p. 183) concludes that the staff pro-

fessional in a union "typically has consistent, sustained, high influence" on problems that "don't count in the eyes of the boss"—for example, on broad political issues but not on relations with rival unions. See also Derek C. Bok and John T. Dunlop, *Labor and the American Community* (New York: Simon & Schuster, 1970), p. 174. Here and elsewhere, I use the term "professional" to refer to persons who are to an important degree trained by, and held responsible to, an occupational reference group outside the employing organization. See Peter M. Blau and W. Richard Scott, *Formal Organizations* (San Francisco: Chandler, 1962), pp. 60–74.

27. Norman R. Luttbeg and Harmon Zeigler, "Attitude Consensus and Conflict in an Interest Group," *American Political Science Review*, LX (1966), reprinted in *American Political Interest Groups*, ed. Betty H. Zisk (Belmont, Calif.: Wadsworth Publishing Co., 1969), pp. 132–149.

28. Bok and Dunlop, *Labor and the American Community*, p. 134.

29. Seymour Martin Lipset, *The First New Nation* (New York: Basic Books, 1963), pp. 191–192.

30. Ibid., p. 193; B. C. Roberts, *Trade Union Government and Administration in Great Britain* (Cambridge, Mass.: Harvard University Press, 1956), pp. 165, 288–296; H. A. Clegg et al., *Trade Union Officers* (Cambridge, Mass.: Harvard University Press, 1961), pp. 188–198.

31. Lipset, *The First New Nation*, pp. 192–193.

32. Bok and Dunlop, *Labor and the American Community*, p. 234.

33. Ibid., pp. 234–235; Lipset, *The First New Nation*, pp. 196–198.

34. Lipset, *The First New Nation*, p. 194.

CHAPTER 12

Organizational Democracy

One would suppose that the behavior of a voluntary association, including its political behavior, would always reflect, at least in general terms, the opinions and preferences of its members. After all, being a *voluntary* organization, it cannot force persons to become or remain members; it must both overcome the disinclination of persons to join any association and compete successfully against the rival inducements of other associations. A voluntary association ought to reflect in its activities the preferences of its members just as surely as a department store reflects, in the goods it offers for sale, the preferences of its customers. If this is true, then how a voluntary association is governed should be no more important to its members than how a department store is governed is important to its customers.

In fact, there are few subjects that have so preoccupied students of voluntary associations as has the question of how they are governed and, in particular, the issue of whether or not they are internally democratic. In some cases, the reason for this concern is obvious. Membership in certain associations is not entirely voluntary; to get or keep jobs in some industries, for example, one must join a union that then has the power to bargain over wages and hours. Whether the union bargains in the interests of its members, and thus whether there exist ways of keeping union leaders responsive to those interests, are matters of considerable importance to the members. In other cases, membership in the association may be entirely voluntary, but there may exist no viable alternative association to which dissatisfied members can move. A con-

235

servative or a liberal in a two-party state may well conclude that he can advance his ideological interests only within the party closest to his views, because the rival party is more hostile to his views than is his own party and there is no chance of creating a third party with any prospects for success. Accordingly, he will struggle to influence his party's leadership or even attempt to capture it for himself.

These cases involve only a fraction of all voluntary associations, yet almost all of them display a commitment to democratic procedures, somehow defined. In part this represents what David B. Truman calls the "democratic mold"—the widespread expectation in our society that collective action will be carried on only by democratic means.[1] This expectation, as Truman observes, "is a sort of hostage to other elements in the community."[2] A group that is obviously undemocratic is vulnerable to criticism from its rivals as well as to attack from dissident factions within its midst. Furthermore, the opportunity to participate in making decisions is an important part of the incentive system of some associations—a fraternal lodge that offers its members the prospect of holding fancily titled offices cannot then deny them those offices, or the decision-making prerogatives that go with them. Other associations appeal to segments of the population that insist on the formal right to be heard as a precondition for affiliation; they will support a worthy cause only if they can help decide what that cause shall be.

But these reasons for the adoption of democratic forms are all prudential ones; that is to say, they stem from the perceived *usefulness* of associational democracy, rather than from the apprehension of some *obligation* to be democratic or to acknowledge the "right" of a prospective member to be enfranchised within the group. Though social scientists who investigate the extent of, and the preconditions for, intra-associational democracy often seem to treat the issue in utilitarian terms—Does democracy exist? Why does it exist? What consequences does it have? —I suspect that the issue receives such widespread attention in part because it is, for many investigators, a moral one. Scholars are to be found disproportionately, I conjecture, among those for whom institutional legitimacy derives chiefly from explicit, regularly renewed consent, and not merely from the tacit consent that might be inferred from the fact of membership. Many would agree with Michael Walzer that "some kind of democratic legitimacy is always necessary to corporate authority."[3] And almost all associations try to act as if they accepted this judgment: even business firms hold elections for directors and conduct stockholders' meetings, even though the elections are typically uncontested and the meetings have little effect on policy. A riposte to the insistence on consent as the basis for legitimacy is the argument that whatever deference an association may show to democratic forms, the social function of such a group is to advance the interests of its members; to the extent that it does so, and provided that membership is in fact voluntary, no one can properly claim that participation in associational decision-making is a right.[4] Indeed, many associations would be hampered in the effective pursuit of their objectives by elaborate arrangements to ensure the accountability of officers to members.

This debate over how voluntary associations should be governed involves, as do most questions of value, competing perspectives on the facts. Those who feel that democratic forms are essential see the association from the point of view of its members and stress the problem of legitimacy; those who believe that forms of internal governance are less important see the association from the vantage point of society as a whole and emphasize the role of the group as one among many competitors for scarce resources. The perspective to be adopted here, however, is that of the executive of the organization for whom problems of member attitudes and environmental constraints are equally pressing: he must manage an incentive system that will satisfy members (and this often requires the sharing of decision-making authority) and he must deal with organizational rivals and government agencies (and this often requires the centralization of authority). The problem is all the more acute inasmuch as the satisfaction of member wants requires in part obtaining resources from the environment while the effective exploitation of the environment frequently requires the centralized mobilization of member action. How the executive resolves the conflicting demands of member incentives and environmental imperatives will depend in part on his skills and circumstances; it will also depend, however, on the kind of incentive system he manages and the history and structure of his organization.

There is not much agreement on how the forms of governance in an association are to be defined or measured. An organization may be said to be "democratic" if there is substantial agreement between the policies of the chief officer and the views or interests of the members, or only if elections for the chief officer's post can be regularly and effectively contested, or only if in the day-to-day decision-making of the group there is regular, extensive, and meaningful participation by the rank-and-file members. The complex issues raised by these alternative definitions will be ignored for the moment; an organization will be said to be "democratic" to the degree that it permits members freely to choose officers or policies. An association is "representative," but undemocratic, if member interests are congruent with leadership policies but the members do not, as a practical matter, choose these leaders in meaningful elections or participate in the formulation of leadership policies. An association will be considered "unrepresentative" if in its governance it meets none of the three criteria.

Incentives

The use of incentives to secure contributions of time, money, or effort involves an exchange relationship between an association and its supporters. The terms of that exchange affect the distribution of authority within the organization. The kind of incentives sought, and the value attached to them by members, influences the importance members attach to participation in making decisions, whereas the value of a member's contribution—of status, money, skill, or effort—determines the extent to which his claims to exercise authority will be honored.

The less the value to the members of the association's incentives, the less they will seek to participate in decision-making and thus the less democratic the association will be. We have all sent off our dues to a local PTA or to a National Committee for the Defense of Alchemy because we feel obliged to support the cause, and accompanying our check is the silent prayer that we will not be called upon to go to any meetings or assume any responsibilities. It is enough for us to know that the organization generally represents our opinions. Samuel H. Barnes, in studying members of the Italian Socialist party, found in one commune that about 70 percent of the "nominal" or "marginal" members subscribed to the view that a political party is democratic so long as it represents the true interests of the most numerous and needy class of the population, but only 12 percent believed that democracy required that the members be able to participate in shaping the policies of the party. Less than one-half the most active members, by contrast, were content with a representative party: over one-third believed that democracy required that they have a chance to participate in party decisions, and one-sixth thought that democracy meant that they should have an opportunity to choose the party leaders.[5] This study, as well as everyday experience, suggests that organizational incentives are differently valued by different members and that those who attach the highest value to them are likely also to prefer democratic forms of associational governance. This means that an organization that is governed democratically will be governed by those activists for whom the value of its incentives is high; in many, if not most, cases, such persons are likely to be a minority of the total membership.

The kind as well as the value of the incentive employed will affect the demand for democratic forms. Organizations that distribute primarily money benefits are less likely to be democratic than ones that distribute other kinds. At first this may seem paradoxical—material benefits may have a high value to many members, and one might suppose that this would lead to a great interest in decision-making. But the more important fact about material benefits is that they are a relatively unambiguous measure for judging the worth of the association. As long as a leader delivers money benefits that substantially exceed the costs of membership, he is not likely to be challenged. The voluntary association in these circumstances is roughly analogous to the department store—so long as its goods and services are thought to be a bargain, the customers are content. A political machine is one such organization; a cooperative store that offers goods at a discount to members is another. The analogy to the department store is not exact, however, because the voluntary association will usually retain certain democratic forms that, though rarely used, can provide the means whereby rival leaders, claiming the ability to deliver even greater material benefits to the members, can challenge the existing leadership and occasionally succeed.[6] Offsetting this possibility, and further contributing to the nondemocratic structure of many materially induced associations, is the fact that the money benefits can always be used to make secure the existing leadership by "buying off" potential rivals and staffing key lower offices with persons who are in effect the employees of those in power. For example, the International Longshoremen's Association (ILA), though nominally democratic in structure, in fact is not; daily hiring through the union-controlled shape-up is one means whereby the leadership can maintain its power over members.[7]

In the Italian Socialist party, mentioned earlier, the conception of democracy varied with the incentive to which the member responded. Members who, according to Barnes, were most ideological, that is, those who were most responsive to purposive rewards, were most in favor of party democracy—one-third defined it as member participation in decision-making and one-fourth as member election of leaders. Those who were least interested in ideology and most attracted by what Barnes calls "group benefits" or "personalities" attached the least importance to party democracy.[8]

Purposes often provide no clear basis for testing the performance of the leaders, because most goals are rarely achieved in the short run and many are never achieved at all. Unable to evaluate leader performance objectively, members of purposive associations will often insist on having a voice in how the purposes are defined and what tactics are employed to advance them. Furthermore, those motivated by a commitment to purpose are usually eager to have their version of those purposes adopted, and thus they require an institutionalized means for urging that version on the chief officers. And differences over purpose are not easily reconciled; unlike money benefits, purposes are not simply (or in the eyes of members, properly) the objects of bargaining. Thus, political decisions rather than market allocations will be made in such associations. Minorities that lose out in the definition of purposes will often defect and form new associations or dissident factions within existing ones.

Solidary incentives also contribute to membership expectations of associational democracy. Partly this is in the nature of the reward—fun and camaraderie require participation by members and an effort to please everyone by officers, and thus these incentives lead automatically to the consultation of member wishes. But partly this is the result of interaction undertaken for social reasons having consequences for organizational decisions. Lipset, Trow, and Coleman found, in their study of the International Typographical Union, that the more frequently union members saw one another off the job, the more likely they were to become interested in union affairs and to attend union meetings. Furthermore, their social involvement tended to precede their interest in union politics.[9] Because the typographers often worked nights and because they saw themselves as part of an "elite" occupational group, the rate of socializing with one another was high, and this contributed significantly to the existence of a democratic two-party system of union governance. Seidman and his colleagues found that participation by members in the affairs of a local plumber's union was also very high compared to the locals of other unions in the Midwest. One of the reasons was that for the plumbers, a union meeting offered a wide variety of attractions beyond merely the opportunity to vote on wage settlements or officers. Plumbers worked on scattered sites, and thus the union meeting was a place to see old friends, to exchange gossip, and to learn about job opportunities and trends. In the other unions, these things were done on the job in the factory, and thus meetings of the local were of less importance except at contract time.[10]

Associations will also rely more on democratic procedures when the inducements of officers and members are most similar. If the officers receive very different, or much more valuable, rewards than the members, they have a motive to hold on to their office and its prerogatives. Lipset, Trow, and Coleman observe that two-party democracy among typographers is made easier by the fact that the difference in income and status between being a union officer and a linotype operator is not great; by contrast, the absence of democracy in the United Mine Workers (UMW) is maintained in part because the income and status of a union official are very much greater than those of a coal miner.[11] The conflict between the heads of political parties who have managed to win elective or appointive office in the state and the followers who perform party chores out of a sense of duty or commitment is a familiar one in every democratic society, and this was in great part the reason why Robert Michels decided that European socialist parties, whatever their pretensions, would invariably become oligarchic.[12] To avoid such risks, reform or amateur political clubs in this country often insist that their leaders accept no appointive office, or that their service in such positions be at the pleasure of the club membership.[13]

The resistance to participation caused by the incompatible rewards of leaders and followers does not arise only when leaders come to value the perquisites of office at the expense of the followers. In the Massachusetts Welfare Rights Organization, the upper-middle-class white organizers wanted to build a mass movement with broad political objectives and worked toward this end, often at considerable material sacrifice to themselves. The members were more interested in immediate material benefits and resisted, or were indifferent to, larger goals. The conflict that resulted over decision-making procedures was only partially tempered by the ideological commitment on the part of the organizers toward associational democracy and consent as the proper basis for legitimacy.

The position in an association of the upper-middle-class liberal is especially difficult. Owing to his educational background, he is likely to have a cosmopolitan orientation and to take an enlarged view of the role of the organization in society; owing to his political inclinations, he is likely to prefer democratic procedures for making decisions. The two attitudes will often come into conflict. Attaining certain goals, such as defeating a political opponent or forming a legislative alliance, may require prompt, decisive, perhaps even secretive action; preserving the legitimacy of the association, on the other hand, may require deferring action, discussing alternatives, and protracted public debate. In reform political clubs, some leaders complain, at least privately, that the requirements of effective campaigning to win support from the electorate are partially incompatible with the requirements of legitimate decision-making to retain support from club activists.[14] Lower-status, less-educated persons are not so likely to be afflicted with this dilemma because they are more likely to value ends over means. Various measures of "authoritarianism" seem to be associated (inversely) with levels of schooling, and perhaps with social class defined more broadly.[15] At the same time, working-class individuals have a strong interest in state-provided economic benefits.[16] This suggests that a voluntary association that delivers on the focal concerns of its members, especially on their material concerns, need not be as democratically governed if its members are working class than if they are upper-middle class.

Other personal qualities, such as intelligence and ego-strength, may also influence the preference for, and the reaction to, democratic procedures. Though there are many studies of small groups claiming to show that democratic leadership patterns result in greater effort and better morale than authoritarian patterns, a careful look at the composition of many such groups suggests that in many cases it is the more intelligent and less dependent persons who chiefly benefit from democratic leadership, whereas the less able, more dependent ones are more satisfied with highly directive leadership.[17] Furthermore, the effectiveness of different leadership styles is in great part dependent on the nature of the tasks—a popular leader asking members to perform well-understood tasks can often act in an "authoritative" way and be both effective and liked, but an officer of uncertain status asking followers to perform an ambiguous or unstructured task may well discover that democratic decision-making is preferable. Finally, the appropriate way to make decisions may be influenced by culturally acquired concepts of authority that differ significantly from one society to another.[18]

A member's preferences for incentives, however determined, may shape his expectations about the proper distribution of authority in an organization, but if those expectations are not shared by others or are resisted by persons already in authority, then his ability successfully to demand a share of that authority will depend on the value of his contributions to the association discounted by the probability that those contributions will be forthcoming whether or not his demands are honored.

There will often be disagreement, of course, about how valuable a member's contribution is (for example, some will think a particular member's social status is important to the organization, others may think it unimportant, and still others may deny that he *has* any such status) and about the chances that his contribution will be withdrawn if his or her claims are not honored. Struggles for office and policy influence are often in part struggles based on differing assessments of the relative value of various resource contributions. But in many cases the relative value of resources is easily established and authority will thus be vested in, or at least members will defer to, those making the crucial contributions.

Charles Perrow has illustrated how this process operates over time in the case of voluntary hospitals (that is, hospitals that must raise from community contributions a significant part of their capital and even their operating budgets). When first organized, such hospitals will be dominated by their trustees. The trustees supply the organization with prestige, legitimate its nonprofit status, represent important class, ethnic, or religious groups in the community from whom funds and support are sought, and themselves contribute funds to the building campaign. Because their contributions are at this stage so valuable, the trustees are free to intervene, should they choose, in patient-selection criteria, the design of facilities, and the appointment of the medical staff.

As the major capital requirements of the hospital are met and its status in the community becomes secure, the value of the trustee's contributions begins to decline. At the same time, the growth in the complexity of medical technology and the proliferation of medical specialities increase the value of the contributions of the medical staff. This is further enhanced by the emergence of a sense of professional solidarity among staff doctors. The physicians soon acquire the same kind of authority that university professors have: they become self-governing, choosing their own colleagues, determining the working routines of the organization, controlling the provision of medical services, and demanding, and getting, the equipment and facilities they want. The trustees continue to raise money, but now that the reputation of the hospital's medical practice has become its most valuable asset, they must raise money on terms and for purposes set by the medical staff. Furthermore, the hospital, if successful, has itself become a *source* of community status, and thus citizens will compete for the honor of becoming a trustee rather than lay down conditions for the transfer of their own status to it.

Finally, the continued increase in the complexity and interdependence of medical services makes the need for centralized coordination of the staff greater. This tendency is given a powerful boost by the emergence of medical insurance plans (Blue Cross-Blue Shield) and government payment programs that require strong financial accountability, cost control, and planning. In addition, the level of interaction with other hospitals and community health agencies grows. For all these reasons, the hospital administrator begins to play an increasingly important role, and his contributions to the organization rise in value. The administrator will increasingly tend to be drawn from the ranks of a self-conscious profession with its own standards and norms. He thus begins to exercise authority over doctors who may still scorn him but who can no longer ignore him and to dominate the deliberations of the trustees.[19]

This mode of analysis can be applied to a variety of other organizations. Even in a supposedly monolithic business firm, the relative power of different divisions will depend on the nature of the crucial maintenance tasks facing it: accountants are dominant when cost control becomes imperative, salesmen when increasing the share of the market is important, and engineers and planners when new technologies must be introduced. Boards of directors, formally the locus of authority in most voluntary associations, are more likely actually to wield that authority when their contributions are especially valuable (as when the organization is being created), when the organization is in crisis (especially financial crisis), or when a new executive must be chosen.

Structure and Environment

In general, larger organizations seem less democratic than smaller ones, older ones less democratic than younger ones, and those created from the top down less democratic than those built from the bottom up. The evidence is not conclusive, however, and there are important qualifications to each of these generalizations.

The older, larger American labor unions hold their conventions less frequently than do smaller ones, and this has led some students, such as Philip M. Marcus, to conclude that the former are less democratic than the latter.[20] The data Marcus used were taken from the written constitutions of national unions primarily, and of course this raises the question of whether constitutional provisions are adequate indicators of actual decision-making practices and whether those practices in national unions are any indication of what they may be in the many local unions of which the national bodies are normally composed. But limiting Marcus's findings to national unions and even allowing for the possible errors arising from relying on constitutional procedures, most observers would probably agree that the *formal* checks on the leaders of many national unions—contested elections, convention reversals of leadership policies, divided executive boards—are weak or nonexistent. In one unpublished study, it was found, for example, that between 1949 and 1966, 59 percent of fifty-one large American unions of manual workers had contested elections for either the top or the second-ranking offices; in any given year, the proportion of contested elections would of course be much smaller.[21]

It is not clear what significance to attach to this finding. American unions are highly decentralized; collective bargaining and political activity are frequently carried on principally at the local level, especially in the craft unions. In some unions, the identity of the national president may be a good deal less important than the identity of the local business agent. Nonetheless, even in those unions in which the national officers do play decisive roles in bargaining, these officials often have few checks on their power other than the occasional possibility of a rank-and-file revolt stimulated by the failure to deliver on bread-and-butter issues. Such organizations as the UMW vest in their chief officer the authority to appoint and suspend most subordinate officers and the right to control union funds and policies even down to the local level.[22] Indeed, the UMW constitution explicitly forbids any member from contributing to the support of any candidate for union office or from circulating any statement "wrongfully condemning any decision rendered by any officer." [23] Former UMW president John L. Lewis put the issue squarely:

It is a question of whether you desire your organization to be the most effective instrumentally . . . or whether you prefer to sacrifice the efficiency of your organization in some respects for a little more academic freedom in the selection of some local representatives in a number of districts.[24]

Lewis left no doubt in anyone's mind that he intended to run the union in what he took to be the miners' best interests; the UMW was to be undemocratic but representative. As far as one can tell, most UMW members preferred "effectiveness" to what Lewis called "academic freedom." [25]

The substantial freedom enjoyed by leaders of many national unions in the United States is not available to persons holding similar offices in Great Britain. British unions hold conventions much more frequently than their American counterparts, and, during 1949–1966, *all* of the thirty-one large unions studied had a contested election for the first- or second-ranking office. Furthermore, there seems to be no relationship in Britain between union size or age on the one hand and convention frequency on the other.[26] There are several possible explanations for the differences between the British and American experience. One is the fact that a much higher percentage of British union officials and delegates are unpaid volunteers for whom the right to help make decisions and the opportunity to attend frequent conventions may be an important incentive. Another is the lasting impact of the formative experiences of British unions—from the first, they were preoccupied with electoral solutions to internal problems.

Local, primary organizations are more democratic than national, caucus-style ones. Seidman and his associates concluded that the six union locals they studied were "democratic" as measured by the ability of members to change leaders and influence decisions.[27] In part this is simply a result of the greater opportunity to participate afforded by local, primary associations. Almost all studies of voluntary groups have shown that involvement increases as size decreases.[28] Though small size facilitates participation and thus contributes to member influence over decisions, it does not facilitate it very much—attendance at most voluntary association and union meetings is typically but a small fraction of the membership. Furthermore, those who attend are often unrepresentative of the membership generally. For example, the active unionist tends to be better paid, to have greater seniority, to work at the more skilled jobs, and to be more satisfied with his work than the inactive one.[29] This may change over time, of course. In its formative years, an association may attract the participation of the discontented, whereas in its mature years it will enlist the efforts of those who find associational duties intrinsically rewarding rather than as a means to express and adjust grievances. And in times of crisis, as when a union is contemplating a strike, the rate of participation will be much higher and the sentiments of all its members rather than only those of activists will be decisive.

The statement that smaller associations are more responsive to member views than are large ones will seem to many a truism, especially if one has in mind a small student, civil rights, or neighborhood organization. But it is less obvious when one thinks of a small craft union, many of which have the reputation of being oligarchic. That intellectuals do not like craft unions seems beyond dispute, but that they are undemocratic is very much open to question. George Strauss in a study of thirteen building trade unions in one city during the 1950s found that most of them were quite democratic by commonsense standards—business agents frequently faced opponents at election time, meetings at which important issues were discussed were well attended, and the decisions of officers were often reversed. An able business agent could dominate his union, and many remained in office for several years, but dominance and longevity required considerable skill in dealing with members who had a high stake in the business agent's decisions; after all, the union allocated scarce jobs, and thus unjustified favoritism was quickly challenged. In the six years preceding this study, six business agents had either been defeated in elections or forced to retire.[30]

The relationship between democratic procedures in local units and those in the national units of any voluntary association is not well understood, but it is possible that it is inverse—that is, highly democratic local, primary organizations may exist in federated structures whose national leadership is not checked by democratic procedures, and vice versa. Though one can only conjecture, it seems plausible that any effective challenge to a national leader would require the effective mobilization and organization of subgroups—individuals acting alone will have as little effect on national voluntary association leaders as they would have on national political leaders. A small, highly democratic local unit, however, may well have leaders with insecure tenure, no staff, and few votes in a national convention. The locals in the best position to challenge national leaders are likely to be the largest ones, with strong leaders, large staffs, big budgets and, as a consequence, relatively little rank-and-file participation in decisions. Among unions, the smallest, and thus perhaps the most democratic, or at least most representative, locals will be most dependent on the national office for strike funds and staff assistance and least able to mount an effective opposition.[31] If this analysis is correct, efforts to increase the level of democracy at one level of any organization may well decrease it at another level.

Age is supposed to produce conservatism, in organizations as well as people. The notion has a certain intuitive appeal. An association in the process of being created arouses enthusiasms, heightens expectations, and sharpens grievances; the early recruits are those who are the true believers in its cause; its early decisions are likely to reflect the sentiments common to all members and perhaps the decisions made through the active participation of most members. If it endures, it also changes —procedures are developed, leaders are confirmed in their authority, habits become fixed, and the routine of maintenance supplants the excitement of creation. Veteran union members speak nostalgically of the "old days"; civil rights leaders recall pridefully early victories against seemingly insuperable odds. John E. Tsouderous compiled data on membership, income, meeting attendance, and size of administrative staff for ten voluntary associations over time.[32] At first membership grows rapidly, followed by a somewhat slower growth in income. As income grows, the size of the administrative staff begins to increase. But when membership and income begin to decline, the administrative component continues to grow or at least to resist reductions. Attendance at meetings begins to fall off, and the administrative staff searches for ways to stem the tide. In general it seeks to cope with problems of loss of members and of income by introducing *higher* membership dues, hiring a more professional staff, and finding incentives that will continue to attract contributors, even if they do not arouse members. The additional services, the higher dues, and the other sources of income developed—perhaps from government or foundation grants—mean that the association's total income does not decline as fast as membership, and may not decline at all; thus, fewer members can support as large a staff as before, or perhaps an even larger one.

It is not clear what impact these changes have over time on decision-making. One study, however, found that in the Saskatchewan Wheat Pool, a highly democratic Canadian farmers' cooperative, the number of contested elections for office fell more or less steadily from its formative years (1923–1930) to 1967.[33] Just as important, however, was the fact that the initial commitment to democratic procedures and the constitutional arrangements designed to ensure them meant that periodically, during the period of declining contested elections, conflict within the association could be focused on struggles for office. Thus, in 1928, 1940, 1946, 1949, and 1967, when issues arose among the members, there were sharp increases in the number of contested elections.

The continuing impact of formative experiences and organizational tradition no doubt affect more groups than just Canadian wheat farmers. As noted earlier, the United Steelworkers (USW) and the UMW were organized from the top down by strong leaders in whom the rank and file had confidence and who proved their ability to deliver. The United Auto Workers (UAW), by contrast, was organized from the bottom up as a result of intense and militant rank-and-file participation in dramatic acts; no single leader in the early years could speak for all auto workers or command their united allegiance. Despite their present size and affluence, many UAW locals experience frequent contests for office and, as we shall see, from time to time rebel against contract settlements negotiated by the national leadership.

Because voluntary associations tend to assume the form of those political or economic structures controlling the resources that they seek, those dealing with a highly centralized opponent are likely to become highly centralized themselves. Though the USW and the UAW had very different formative experiences, the needs of centralized, nationwide bargaining have led inevitably to greater authority being vested in the national leadership. To strike a bargain with the steel companies or the auto manufacturers, a union must be able to commit the rank and file to whatever collective decisions are made; no firm is likely to take seriously the demands of a union leader who is frequently repudiated by his followers over either contract ratification or contract observance. Though the USW and the UAW remain different in many respects, they face a common pressure toward centralized authority.

There are instances of large, centralized voluntary associations facing weak or decentralized opponents. The many competing truckers and shippers in the New York City ports have had to face the powerful and, by any definition, undemocratic ILA. The absence of one or a few major firms with which to bargain or against whom one could strike meant that these unions could not be created by the classic strategy of intensive organizing followed by either a summit conference or a decisive strike leading to union recognition and a contract for a single union. As a result, the ILA grew by first gaining control over the work force. This was possible because decentralized hiring as a labor practice existed together with a labor surplus. With many men seeking, often on a casual or part-time basis, relatively few jobs, any group that could control the hiring process could please management by keeping the wage rates down and at the same time build a cadre of loyal followers by selectively rewarding certain workers by giving them the best jobs. Union leaders, as in the old ILA, could profit from both sides, receiving payoffs from the companies as a reward for delivering a steady supply of labor at low cost and kickbacks from workers in thanks for getting some of the scarce jobs. So lucrative an operation naturally made it attractive to others eager to share in the profits, and thus force was often employed to maintain control over the hiring process.[34] Violence and corruption were necessary to sustain a centralized union in the face of a decentralized industry.

Consequences

The consequences for organizational behavior of varying levels of member participation in decision-making is probably the least understood aspect of voluntary association governance. There are, to be sure, any number of experimental small-group studies on the results, for morale and productivity, of "democratic" as opposed to "authoritarian" leadership styles [35] and some studies of the behavior of actual business offices or military crews under differing patterns of leadership style and group-centered decision-making.[36] But the results, and above all the interpretation, of these studies are far from clear. Some of the experiments show a relationship between participation and effectiveness but others do not,[37] the applicability of experimental findings to real-life organizations is controversial, and the measures of participation and effectiveness vary considerably from study to study. Above all, relatively little effort has been made to identify the kinds of organizations, and above all the kinds of tasks, for which participatory decisions or benevolent leadership styles are more or less effective. Though this criticism has been made repeatedly for the last decade or so by various social psychologists,[38] the relentless effort to prove the all-purpose value of organizational democracy seems to continue unabated, suggesting that ideological commitments are at least as important as scientific curiosity.

The fewest inquiries about the consequences of democracy have been made with respect to those organizations, voluntary associations, in which one would suppose that its observance is the most common and its value the greatest. Persuading a person to cooperate is not only more difficult than ordering or paying him to do so, but, in addition, the very act of persuasion implies a willingness to consider and take into account his point of view and to concede him some role in helping to determine the objects of that cooperation. The formal apparatus of democracy—contested elections or policy referenda—may or may not be present, but the consultative process, one would think, almost surely would be.

One of the few such inquiries is that of the Institute of Social Research at the University of Michigan into the behavior of local units of the League of Women Voters.[39] The effectiveness of 104 local leagues was rated by a panel of presumably expert judges—present and former national league officers—and the attributes of the leagues were measured by asking members to fill out a questionnaire. The general finding was that in the more effective as compared to the less effective leagues, the members were more likely to feel pressure to participate from fellow members, but not from the local league presidents, to believe that they had more influence over group decisions, and to think that they were better informed about league activities. Though one may quarrel with some aspects of the study (for example, "effectiveness" was subjectively defined and apparently based in part on perceptions of the size, rate of growth, and fund raising of the local associations—in short, on measures of organizational maintenance and enhancement more than on the achievement of purposes), it is likely that for *this kind* of association— that is, one recruiting middle- and upper-middle-class persons on the basis of a combination of solidary and purposive incentives to perform community-service tasks—success is in some important degree enhanced by group-centered decision-making and a strong sense of collegiality. After all, if the opportunity to associate with the group is a primary inducement, then the members will work harder the more they value that association and the more the group expects of them.

But for other kinds of associations, the willingness to work may have little to do with the opportunity to participate in decisions. Arnold S. Tannenbaum and Robert L. Kahn, themselves members of the Michigan group that conducted that league study, found in a survey of four labor union locals that the workers' loyalty to the union, as indicated by their professed readiness to walk a picket line or to help maintain the union, bore no relationship to the amount of control the workers thought they exercised over union affairs.[40] And there can be little doubt about the solidarity of coal miners in many communities even though virtually every key decision is made by officers over whom they have almost no formal control.

What may be associated with high levels of member control in unions is a broad commitment to wide social goals: the most democratic union studied by Tannenbaum and Kahn was also the one whose members were most interested in political action and in seeing the union work on community welfare issues.[41] How the members define that welfare is another matter. Union members are less likely than union officers to have liberal positions on noneconomic issues, such as racial integration, and less likely to be tolerant of political nonconformity.[42]

The officers of a democratically governed voluntary association that finds itself in conflict with another organization are likely to have less freedom of action and to feel obliged to display greater militancy on key issues than would be the case if the officers were free from potential challenges. It has been this possibility, of course, that has most concerned advocates, such as Robert Michels, of militant trade unionism and socialist politics. Internal democracy in such associations, which Michels despaired of attaining, was necessary, he thought, to keep the leaders from "selling out." But stating the alternatives as either "selling out" or "working for the best interests of the members" is too simple—there may be important differences between short-term and long-term interests, between the interests of the active minority that utilizes opportunities for constraining officers and those of the passive majority that does not, and between the dramatic choices that can be communicated to members (for example, to strike or not to strike) and the complex processes of protracted bargaining over crucial but often obscure details.

Whatever the value one places on militancy, it seems to be increased by struggles for power within the association, at least in times of crisis. One reason may be that an aroused membership is less tolerant of a compromise than an engaged leadership; alternatively, democratic procedures may allow rival elites to challenge existing ones by seeking to outbid them in their demands. Robert L. Crain and Donald B. Rosenthal found that the greater the level of competition among groups and individuals in the civil rights movement in various cities, the more militant was that leadership.[43] Arthur M. Ross and Paul T. Hartman argue that union factionalism will increase the likelihood of a strike, though obviously it is only one factor among many.[44] Plausible as such a supposition may be, it is no easy matter to find evidence that would confirm or deny it. A unique opportunity to assess the relationship between union democracy and strike activity was afforded by the passage by Congress of the Landrum-Griffin Act in 1959 that required, among other things, that union members be guaranteed the right to participate, by secret ballot, in free union elections at least every three years and that sought to confer upon the rank and file a "bill of rights." Not long after its passage, the number of wildcat strikes, that is, strikes by locals without national union authorization, increased and the proportion of tentative settlements rejected by union votes went up.[45] Some authors suggested that enhanced union democracy led to less stable bargaining relationships and more strikes.[46] And in some instances that indeed seemed to be the case. For example, a September 1961 strike at General Motors was privately described by UAW leaders as a chance for militant locals to "blow off steam" even though all major issues were settled.[47] In 1964, UAW negotiators at the last minute found themselves unable to sell the agreement they had reached to key union activists, and an unexpected strike occurred.[48] On the other hand, the early 1960s was also a period of rising prices and declining unemployment; purely economic motives—the desire to keep abreast of inflation and the recognition that workers had many other job opportunities—may have caused the increase in strikes and contract rejections.

One interesting attempt to measure the relative importance of these factors is that of Orley Ashenfelter and George E. Johnson at Princeton University. They found that between 1952 and 1967, most of the strike activity was (statistically) associated with the degree of tightness of the labor market and the previous rate of change in real wages but that a significant number of additional strikes (about eighty-eight for every three-month period) seem to be independently associated with the passage in 1959 of the Landrum-Griffin Act.[49]

Perhaps the most important organization in which to assess the consequences of democratic governance—important not only scientifically, but because of its impact on public policy—is the political party. The party is in many ways most like the department store to which we referred at the beginning of this chapter. It seeks, not only to attract and motivate members, but to win support from many nonmembers. Voters are to the party what customers are to the store. The traditional local party organization, whether a personal following or a ward machine, was prepared to offer, within very broad limits, whatever candidates or policies would prove most attractive to a majority of voters. A party organization that is democratically governed, by contrast, is more likely to select candidates and issues in order to satisfy member interests, especially if the inducements offered to the members depend crucially on the purposes of the organization. Amateur political clubs, whether Democratic or Republican, are likely to adopt positions as much to meet internal demands as to attract external constituencies.[50] The nomination of Senator Barry Goldwater in 1964 no doubt pleased enormously the many committed conservatives who had become activists in the Republican party, but it led, of course, to an electoral disaster. But disaster is neither the most common nor the most important consequence of the control of parties by men and women committed to certain political goals; indeed, to the extent that it leads to defeat, there is a built-in corrective that will probably lead, on the next occasion, to the selection of a candidate with a broader appeal. The more typical result is the problem of divided loyalties on the part of those candidates who *are* elected—whether they should serve what they take to be the interests of the majority who elected them or the sometimes very different interests of the minority who nominated them. In Great Britain, where most political workers are volunteers and local constituency associations vote either to accept or reject various candidates, candidates for the House of Commons are sometimes penalized in times of grave issues for speaking against party views even when popular views dictate a different, or at least a more equivocal, position. For example, in 1956 all ten of the Conservative Members of Parliament who opposed British intervention in Suez were either dropped as candidates or severely criticized, while none of the twenty who favored even stronger intervention lost his seat even though opinion in the country as a whole was deeply, and almost evenly, divided on the issue.[51]

NOTES

1. David B. Truman, *The Governmental Process*, 2nd ed. (New York: Alfred A. Knopf, 1971), pp. 129–139.

2. Ibid., p. 138.

3. Michael Walzer, *Obligations: Essays on Disobedience, War, and Citizenship* (Cambridge, Mass.: Harvard University Press, 1970), p. 45.

4. V. L. Allen, *Power in Trade Unions* (London: Longmans, Green, 1954), pp. 10–11, 15.

5. Samuel H. Barnes, "Leadership Style and Political Competence," in *Political Leadership in Industrialized Societies*, ed. Lewis J. Edinger (New York: John Wiley, 1967), p. 73.

6. There have been cases in which ward leaders in the Chicago Democratic organization have been deposed in part by dissatisfied precinct captains.

7. Joel Seidman et al., *The Worker Views His Union* (Chicago: University of Chicago Press, 1958), p. 206, n. 7.

8. Barnes, "Leadership Style and Political Competence," p. 74.

9. Seymour Martin Lipset, Martin A. Trow, and James S. Coleman, *Union Democracy* (New York: Free Press, 1956), pp. 72–75, 90.

10. Seidman et al., *The Worker Views His Union*, pp. 189–191.

11. Lipset, Trow, and Coleman, *Union Democracy*, p. 214.

12. Robert Michels, *Political Parties*, trans. Eden and Cedar Paul (New York: Free Press, 1958), pp. 13–14, 418.

13. James Q. Wilson, *The Amateur Democrat: Club Politics in Three Cities* (Chicago: University of Chicago Press, 1962), pp. 205–216.

14. Ibid., p. 234.

15. Seymour Martin Lipset, *Political Man* (Garden City, N.Y.: Doubleday, 1960), chap. 4; Lewis Lipsitz, "Work Life and Political Attitudes: A Study of Manual Workers," *American Political Science Review*, LVIII (December 1964), 951–962, and Lipsitz, "Working-Class Authoritarianism: a Re-evaluation," *American Sociological Review*, XXX (February 1965), 103–109; A. Kornhauser, A. J. Mayer, and H. Sheppard, *When Labor Votes* (New York: University Books, 1956), p. 266.

16. Lipset, *Political Man*, pp. 101–108; Seymour Martin Lipset and Earl Rabb, *The Politics of Unreason* (New York: Harper & Row, 1970), pp. 449–482.

17. L. G. Wispe, "Evaluating Section Teaching Methods in the Introductory Course," *Journal of Educational Research*, XLV (1951), 161–186; Victor Vroom, "Some Personality Determinants of the Effects of Participation," *Journal of Abnormal and Social Psychology*, LIX (November 1959), 322–327; A. D. Calvin, F. K. Hoffman, and E. L. Harden, "The Effect of Intelligence and Social Atmosphere on Group Problem Solving Behavior," *Journal of Social Psychology*, XLV (February 1957), 61–74.

18. Fred E. Fiedler, "A Contingency Model of Leadership Effectiveness," in *Advances in Experimental Social Psychology*, ed. Leonard Berkowitz (New York: Academic Press, 1964), vol. I, pp. 149–190; Cecil A. Gibb, "Leadership," in *The Handbook of Social Psychology*, 2nd ed., ed. Gardner Lindzey and Elliot Aronson (Reading, Mass.: Addison-Wesley, 1969), vol. IV, pp. 263–264; and Alex Inkeles and Daniel J. Levinson, "National Character: The Study of Modal Personality and Sociocultural Systems," in Lindzey and Aronson, vol. IV, pp. 448–449.

19. Charles Perrow, "The Analysis of Goals in Complex Organizations," *American Sociological Review*, XXVI (December 1961), 854–866. See also Mayer Zald, "The Power and Functions of Boards of Directors," *American Journal of Sociology*, LXXV (July 1969), 97–111, and Nicholas R. Babchuck and C. Wayne Gordon, "Men and Women in Community Agencies," *American Sociological Review*, XXV (June 1960), 399–403.

20. Philip M. Marcus, "Union Conventions and Executive Boards: A Formal Analysis of Organizational Structure," *American Sociological Review*, XXXI (February 1966), 61–70.

21. J. David Edelstein and Howard J. Ruppel, Jr., "Convention Frequency and Oligarchic Degeneration in British and American Unions," *Administrative Science Quarterly*, XV (March 1970), 48. See also J. David Edelstein, "An Organizational Theory of Union Democracy," *American Sociological Review*, XXXII (February 1967), 19–31, and Edelstein and Malcolm Warner, "The Pattern of Opposition in British and American Unions," *Sociology*, IV (May 1970), 145–163. The greater frequency of electoral opposition in British as opposed to American unions is apparently caused by a number of structural factors, including the greater power and autonomy of lesser elected officials who can organize bases of support against national leaders. (Private communication from Professor Edelstein.)

22. B. C. Roberts, *Trade Union Government and Administration in Great Britain* (Cambridge, Mass.: Harvard University Press, 1956), p. 281; Seidman et al., *The Worker Views His Union*, chap. 2, esp. pp. 25–28; Joel Seidman, "The Coal Miners: A Study of Union Control," *Quarterly Journal of Economics*, LXVIII (August 1954), 415–436.

23. Quoted in Seidman et al., *The Worker Views His Union*, p. 218.

24. Ibid., pp. 211–212.

25. Ibid., chap. 2.

26. Edelstein and Ruppel, "Convention Frequency," pp. 48–51.

27. Seidman et al., *The Worker Views His Union*, p. 185.

28. Paul H. Wilken, "Size of Organizations and Member Participation in Church Congregations," *Administrative Science Quarterly*, XVI (June 1971), 173–174, and the several studies cited therein.

29. The evidence is summarized in Arnold S. Tannenbaum, "Unions," in *Handbook of Organizations*, ed. James G. March (Chicago: Rand McNally, 1965), pp. 746–747.

30. George Strauss, "Control by the Membership in Building Trade Unions," *American Journal of Sociology*, LXI (May 1956), 527–535.

31. Seidman et al., *The Worker Views His Union*, p. 216; Lipset, Trow and Coleman, *Union Democracy*, chap. 17.

32. John E. Tsouderous, "Organizational Change in Terms of a Series of Selected Variables," *American Sociological Review*, XX (April 1955), 206–210.

33. John G. Craig and Edward Gross, "The Forum Theory of Organizational Democracy: Structural Guarantees as Time-Related Variables," *American Sociological Review*, XXXV (February 1970), 27.

34. Daniel Bell, "The Racket-Ridden Longshoremen: A Functional Analysis of Crime," in *Labor and Trade Unionism*, ed. Walter Galenson and Seymour Martin Lipset (New York: John Wiley, 1960), pp. 245–264. By contrast, on the West Coast the International Longshoremen's and Warehousemen's Union (ILWU) is notable for its lack of violence and corruption. A key organizational factor accounting for the difference appears to be the absence of a labor surplus on the West Coast docks. The ILWU, under Harry Bridges, has developed a register of full-time workers who are assigned to piers on a strict equalization-of-income basis and who are limited in numbers so that they need not compete with one another or with casual workers for jobs. As a result, the ILWU, unlike the ILA, is an organization that can generate strong feelings of mutual solidarity and leadership loyalty. See Max D. Kossoris, "Working Rules in West Coast Longshoring," *Monthly Labor Review* (January 1961), pp. 7–8; Vernon H. Jenson, *The Hiring of Dock Workers* (Cambridge, Mass.: Harvard University Press, 1964).

35. The important studies are summarized in Gibb, "Leadership," pp. 258–265, and in Stephen M. Sayles, "Supervisory Styles and Productivity: Review and Theory," in *Readings in Organizational Behavior and Human Performance*, ed. L. L. Cummings and W. E. Scott (Homewood, Ill.; Richard D. Irwin, 1969), pp. 636–642.

36. The pioneer experiment was Nancy C. Morse and Everett Reimer, "The Experimental Change of a Major Organizational Variable," *Journal of Abnormal and Social Psychology*, LI (January 1956), 120–129. The literature on participation is summarized in Victor Vroom, "Industrial Social Psychology," in Lindzey and Aronson, *The Handbook of Social Psychology*, vol. V, pp. 227–240.

37. Vroom, "Industrial Social Psychology," p. 228.

38. Ibid., pp. 239–240; Harold J. Leavitt, "Applied Organizational Change in Industry," in March, *Handbook of Organizations*, pp. 1151–1167.

39. Rensis Likert, *New Patterns of Management* (New York: McGraw-Hill, 1961), chap. 10.

40. Arnold S. Tannenbaum and Robert L. Kahn, *Participation in Union Locals* (Evanston, Ill.: Row, Peterson, 1958), pp. 178–180.

41. Ibid., pp. 174–175.

42. Samuel Stouffer, *Communism, Conformity, and Civil Liberties* (Garden City, N.Y.: Doubleday, 1955), chap. 2.

43. Robert L. Crain and Donald B. Rosenthal, "Community Status as a Dimension of Local Decision-Making," *American Sociological Review*, XXXII (December 1967), 976.

44. Arthur M. Ross and Paul T. Hartman, *Changing Patterns of Industrial Conflict* (New York: John Wiley, 1960), pp. 65–66. See also Ross, *Trade Union Wage Policy* (Berkeley: University of California Press, 1956), pp. 63–64, and A. H. Raskin, "Are Union Democracy and Responsibility Compatible?" *Challenge* (February 1962), p. 17.

45. William E. Simkin, "Refusals to Ratify Contracts," in *Trade Union Government and Collective Bargaining*, ed. Joel Seidman (New York: Praeger, 1970), pp. 110, 124.

46. See Philip Taft, "The Impact of Landrum-Griffin on Union Government," *Annals*, CCCXXXIII (January 1961), 130–140, and Ross and Hartman, *Changing Patterns of Industrial Conflict*, p. 178.

47. Raskin, "Union Democracy," p. 17.

48. *Wall Street Journal,* October 5, 1964.

49. Orley Ashenfelter and George E. Johnson, "Bargaining Theory, Trade Unions, and Industrial Strike Activity," *American Economic Review,* LIX (March 1969), 35–49.

50. Wilson, *The Amateur Democrat,* pp. 156–163, 239–257.

51. Leon D. Epstein, "British M.P.s and Their Local Parties: The Suez Case," *American Political Science Review,* LIV (June 1960), 374–390.

PART
IV

External Processes

CHAPTER 13

Competition and Coalitions

In a sense, all voluntary associations, like all retail firms, compete with one another—they struggle to obtain scarce resources from a population of prospective contributors (or customers) who in a sense are allocating their money, time, and the value of their names between associational and nonassociational uses and, within the former category, among a variety of alternative associations. If one applied to voluntary associations the same simple assumptions about motives that underlie the economic theory of the firm, one would expect organizational executives to seek to maximize the size—or wealth, or influence, or status—of their organization.

Whatever the predictive value of such assumptions with respect to the business firm, it is not clear that they have much value with respect to the voluntary association. Partly this may be because the executive of an association, unlike the executive of a firm, often does not benefit materially from the growth in the size of his organization—receiving no salary from, and having no equity stake in, an association of volunteers, he may have no incentive to maximize its size. The head of the Committee for Economic Development (CED) or the American Jewish Committee, for example, receives status by occupying that office; enlarging the membership of the organization would not enlarge that status and might, indeed, reduce it. Of course, the head of a firm may also be content with the status his office confers and thus make no effort to enlarge the firm's scale, but this possibility is discounted in economic theory by assuming that other beneficiaries of increased profitability, such as stockholders, will remove executives who tolerate declining or stagnant earnings records.

Furthermore, there are many voluntary associations that have a strong interest in deliberately restricting their membership. The business agent of a building trade union, for example, might well be turned out of office by the members if he should increase the membership of the union in ways that intensified the competition for jobs or otherwise threatened per capita wages. Similarly, the head of a sectlike civil rights organization such as the Student Nonviolent Coordinating Committee (SNCC) or of a highly ideological revolutionary or radical political party is often obliged to keep the association small in order to keep it pure—to recruit, in the case of the sect, only persons who have demonstrated their moral commitment or, in the case of the ideological party, only those who are both doctrinally sound and free of any suspicion of being a government spy.

Finally, some associations cannot increase in size because they have recruited their entire potential membership: a trade association in a small- or medium-sized industry, for example, will ordinarily have as paying members almost every firm in that line of business.

If one cannot assume that voluntary associations will in all cases seek to maximize their size, what motivational assumptions can one make that will explain their relationships with other, potentially competitive, associations? The fundamental assumption made here is that organizations seek to maintain themselves. This objective requires, in turn, that associations be able to lay claim to a more or less stable supply of resources—members, money, issues, causes, and privileged access to governmental or other relevant institutions. In principle, many associations would like to obtain as much of these resources as possible—if not more members, then at least more money and better issues. In practice, the availability of these resources is limited by the number of prospective contributors and their preferences and by the existence of rival organizational claimants. Most associations choose to attempt to obtain more resources by changing the preferences and enlarging the numbers of potential contributors by dramatizing issues or advertising causes, rather than by challenging another association for the loyalties of a given supply of contributors. Failure in the former strategy will at worst involve an expenditure of money and effort that produces no corresponding increase in resources, but failure in the latter may mean a loss of existing resources to the rival or, if worse comes to worst, the destruction of the organization altogether.

Competition

Associations, seeking to maintain themselves, are highly averse to risk and thus to active rivalry except under special circumstances. The easiest and most prudent maintenance strategy is to develop *autonomy*—that is, a distinctive area of competence, a clearly demarcated and exclusively served clientele or membership, and undisputed jurisdiction over a function, service, goal, or cause. Just as executives seek to minimize strain in managing the internal affairs of the association, so also they seek to minimize it in their relations with other organizations. Autonomy gives to an association a stable claim to certain resources and thereby reduces uncertainty and lessens threats to survival.[1] Sol Levine and Paul E. White in their study of the relationships among health organizations in a city used the term "domain" to mean essentially what is meant here by autonomy and concluded that these associations went to great lengths to ensure that there would be consensus as to what one another's domain should be. Though twenty-two such associations operated in a city of only 200,000 residents, each managed to survive by carefully distinguishing its services from those of every other association, sometimes on the basis of the disease treated, sometimes on the basis of the age or religion of the patient, and other times on the basis of the stage which the disease had reached (for example, ambulatory versus bedridden patients).[2]

Not every association can develop a high degree of autonomy—newly formed associations, for example, must often struggle to win a place for themselves among preexisting organizations that only grudgingly yield any of their domains to an upstart. Other associations are required by the nature of their activities to compete: political parties exist to contest elections, and this means to contest one another for the resources with which to win elections. Even in this case, however, the competition for resources is less than one might expect judging from campaign rhetoric, for most parties try, not to convert members of the rival party, but to mobilize their own faithful members, raise money from already committed donors, and appeal to those relatively few voters who are not firmly wedded to either party.

Associations that *oppose* one another typically do not *compete* with one another. That is, if two associations have goals that are mutually exclusive (as when, for example, a League to Abolish Capital Punishment confronts a League to Bring Back Hanging), they rarely, if ever, compete with one another for members and funds from the same list of prospects. Where competition does exist, it is in part because the two associations are *not* in opposition with respect to their objectives and therefore appeal to similar or identical contributors.

The extent to which competition will exist will depend on both the relative degree of autonomy and the relative level of resources of any pair of associations. Some groups rank high in both autonomy and resources and thus rarely compete. Solidary associations with wealthy members drawn from religiously or ethnically distinct segments of the community —the Ladies' Auxiliary of St. Luke's Church and Hadassah, for example —will not compete: each has ample resources and clear autonomy. Nor will utilitarian associations with very different functions supported by large corporations be competitive. In the electric-power industry, for example, there are at least five different trade associations, and the casual observer might suppose that they struggle furiously for the business dollar. Though they might compete marginally, in fact each has achieved a relatively high degree of autonomy—the Edison Electric Institute keeps trade statistics, the National Association of Electric Companies lobbies before Congress, the Association of Edison Illuminating Companies supplies technical information to its members, the Public Information Program handles general public relations, and the Electric Companies Advertising Program runs advertisements opposing publicly owned power sources.

A second group of associations ranks high in autonomy but has few resources. The NAACP and the Urban League, for example, have quite different functions: legal redress and protest in the case of the NAACP; research, counselling, and public relations in the case of the Urban League. Furthermore, the NAACP raises money chiefly from blacks, the Urban League, chiefly from whites. There is some competition, especially over issues and causes that have not been traditionally assigned to one or the other group—for example, residential segregation can be regarded as a legal-redress issue or as a research-and-negotiation issue. To some extent also they compete in attempting to raise funds from key black and white contributors. That competition, however, was greater during the early history of the two organizations when the domain of each was unsettled. Prominent blacks in the period from 1911 to 1920 often felt they had to choose between the NAACP and the league, for supporting both was out of the question for reasons of personal interest as well as of ideology; furthermore, each association had to contend with a host of rival groups already on the scene. The Urban League, for example, was seen as a threat by many churches and settlement houses that were already offering employment services and welfare programs. But the NAACP and the Urban League overcame their rivals and then went to considerable lengths to develop distinctive identities.[3] The clarity of their domains moderates whatever rivalry their scarce resources might prompt.

A third group of voluntary associations consists of those that have relatively abundant resources but little autonomy. Various Jewish defense and community-relations organizations are examples. The American Jewish Committee, the American Jewish Congress, the Anti-Defamation League of B'nai B'rith, and others have enjoyed, compared to other ethnic associations, sizable budgets raised from contributors who are legendary for their philanthropy.[4] They have never fully settled the question of domain, however, and the resultant rivalry has frequently been intense and on one occasion led to a major piece of self-analysis, the MacIver report.[5] This report recommended, as a solution to the problem of low autonomy, subordination to a larger coordinating agency, but of course for many agencies involved that was no solution at all, because joining such a body would only further reduce autonomy and thus intensify the problem of organizational maintenance. Another example of the same phenomenon has been the rivalry between various labor unions with overlapping jurisdictions. The early strength of the craft unions was in part the result of their defining their domain so narrowly that each had exclusive jurisdiction over a relatively homogeneous trade. Whenever jurisdictions were disputed, as they were on occasion among coal miners, meatpackers, and garment workers, the competition was bitter, the feelings aroused by "dual unionism" intense, and in time every effort was made to eliminate the competition.

A final group of associations is that with neither many resources nor much autonomy; newly formed organizations struggling to survive are often in this situation. Such associations are among the most competitive, and they will, unlike those with established domains, freely attack other groups, including, and perhaps especially, those whose goals they do not oppose but whose resources they envy. In 1885–1886, the sudden expansion in union membership intensified competition among unions for jurisdictional rights and led to the emergence of the AFL in opposition to the Knights of Labor.[6] The civil rights organizations formed in the wake of the sit-in movement of the early 1960s were more competitive than the older NAACP and Urban League because they were challenging not only those older associations but also one another for autonomy. More recently, the proliferation of feminist organizations and the revitalization of radical political groups have provided new displays of a recurring irony—because of the need for autonomy, associations lacking it appear to spend more time attacking allies than enemies.

In sum, voluntary associations not in opposition to one another are more likely to be competitive when autonomy is low than when resources are wanting. The struggle to create a distinctive identity and competence, an assured domain, seems to be the first prerequisite for maintenance; given such autonomy, aspiration levels will tend to correspond to available resources. An association can exist with a small budget or a large one; naturally it would prefer the larger one, but it rarely will seek to increase that budget if it requires making ambiguous its own autonomy or challenging that of another agency. An association lacking in autonomy and resources will devote more attention to establishing a domain than to raising a large budget.

The kind of organizational competition stimulated by conflict over autonomy differs from that arising out of resource needs. In the former case, the association will seek ways of creating an identity, and this often means attacking head-on established organizations including potential allies, especially important ones. To acquire autonomy, one must first call attention to oneself and, unless there is an organizational vacuum one can fill (a rarity), this often means picking a fight with an established group. The bigger the opponent, of course, the more attention one obtains. In their study of fourteen cities, Gerald A. McWorter and Robert L. Crain discovered nine communities in which there was a high level of permanent organization for civil rights purposes. In five of these cities, the keenest competition took place among civil rights leaders on a *personal* basis and not among the civil rights associations themselves; in three of the remaining four cities, the competition that did occur was chiefly over what has been called here autonomy rather than over resources—specifically, competition between the NAACP and the dominant local political party.[7] The party and the NAACP each claimed to speak "for" the Negroes in their city.

Competition for resources exists, but only rarely does it take the form, as the struggle for autonomy often does, of a direct challenge between two or more associations. Agencies raising private funds to combat various diseases will solicit door to door and thus compete for the public's philanthropic dollar, but it would be most unusual for one health group to claim in its sales pitch, that its disease is "more important," or its disease-fighting research more competent, than that of its rival. Its appeal is not for a reallocation of charitable funds, but for an increase. Even political parties typically instruct their precinct canvassers to identify and mobilize voters already inclined to their cause rather than to persuade opposing voters to change their allegiance. In sum, the quest for autonomy is a principal cause of competition among organizations lacking assured domains, whereas the existence of autonomy is a principal inhibitor of competition among associations having such domains.

Coalitions

By "coalition" is meant an enduring arrangement requiring that choices over some common set of interests, for example, resources, goals, strategies, or the like, be made by explicit mutual agreement among the members (in this case, the component associations). A coalition, thus, is an ongoing mechanism for explicitly coordinating some or all of the actions of the members; it is an organization of organizations. It differs from coordination that occurs implicitly—as when organizations simply take into account the actions of other organizations in planning their own moves—and from coordination that involves nothing more than sharing information or discussing, but not taking binding decisions about, common interests.[8]

Though individuals join associations in large numbers, associations rarely form lasting coalitions. There are no formal, ongoing coalitions by which business associations, farm organizations, radical political parties, Jewish defense groups, ecology enthusiasts, or municipal reformers coordinate and manage common interests. It was not until 1969–1970 that the major farm organizations tried to work together, and even then the largest one—the American Farm Bureau Federation—refused to join. The dozens of educational associations were not able to form a stable, enduring coalition until the Full Funding Committee was created in 1970. Even then the National Congress of Parents and Teachers declined to join and for a time the National Education Association withdrew.[9]

The creation of the most conspicuous permanent coalition of voluntary associations—the merger of the AFL and the CIO—took years to accomplish and became possible only after both sides were convinced that the cost of competition was excessive. The United States Chamber of Commerce began as a coalition of trade associations, but as such has never been very successful: the member associations contribute very little of the Chamber's budget and rarely, if ever, feel bound to modify their own governmental objectives to conform to agreed-upon Chamber policies. The strength of the Chamber has, almost from the first, depended on its ability to recruit individual firms rather than trade associations as members. The American Council on Education has been since 1918 a national coalition of organizations and institutions involved in higher education, but its member organizations are so diverse in interest and concern that the association has often been unable to develop and present a coalition policy on higher-education legislation except to urge that, whatever else is done, more money should be spent. Until the mid-1960s, there was no formal coalition of civil rights groups; it remains to be seen how enduring and effective the present Leadership Conference on Civil Rights will be.

Furthermore, certain kinds of coalitions are more likely to form than others. The NAACP has frequently been part of an informal coalition with the national AFL-CIO in order to lobby for civil rights legislation; its only attempt to form a coalition with CORE and SNCC (in Mississippi in 1963) collapsed after a few months. One would not expect the National Association of Manufacturers (NAM) and United Auto Workers (UAW) to be part of a coalition because their interests are so frequently opposed; one might expect that the Jewish defense agencies would form a coalition, because their interests seem identical, or very nearly so. In fact neither coalition has formed.

There are a number of theories intended to explain which coalitions out of all possible ones will form and how a coalition once formed will maintain itself. Very few of these theories have been tested adequately against the experiences of the real world, although some have been the object of laboratory experiments and simulations. All of them presuppose that the interests of the potential coalition members are not absolutely opposed—that is, there is some outcome that will give each member of the coalition something. A two-person, zero-sum game is an example of pure conflict—only one player can win, and whatever he wins is entirely at the expense of the other player. But if the game has more than two players, or if the sum of gains and losses is not zero, there is at least the possibility of a coalition because there are some rewards available for cooperative effort.

One kind of theory predicts that in these "mixed-motive" [10] situations containing elements of both conflict and coordination, the individuals involved will seek to form a coalition that is just large enough to control the outcome. "Just large enough" because that minimizes the number of parties among whom the payoffs of the coalition must be shared; "control the outcome" because without such dominance, there will be no payoffs that *can* be shared.[11] These payoffs need not be money or status incentives, but can include as well promises to modify the existing proposal so as to satisfy the ideological interests of one or more coalition members and promises of support on future issues ("log-rolling").[12] In one version of this theory, the desire to keep the coalition as small as possible is enhanced by the widely shared norm of equity, the belief that persons ought to get out of an agreement rewards proportional to the resources or power they bring to it.[13] If equity is the basis for distributing the payoffs, then obviously a member will get a larger return in exchange for his contribution of resources the smaller the total number of members of the coalition. One interesting implication of this theory is that often the largest, richest, most powerful potential member will be excluded from the winning coalition because his presence would make the coalition larger than necessary and hence larger than desirable. Because this theory says nothing about the characteristics or views of the coalition members, it is consistent with the aphorism that "politics makes strange bedfellows."

A second theory argues that in fact politics rarely makes strange bedfellows; to the contrary, "likes attract likes." In this view, though coalition members are influenced by the possibility of gain, they are also influenced by the desire to avoid conflict, to achieve certain substantive goals in which they may have no material interest, and to maintain existing social relationships.[14] In a legislature with more than two political parties, the enduring coalitions that form are likely to be among those parties closest to one another ideologically and not simply among those that constitute the smallest winning bloc. Robert Axelrod, in a study of the Italian legislature, found that between 1953 and 1969, ideologically connected coalitions were more likely to form than unconnected ones. He also found that the most common coalitions kept the number of members to a minimum.[15] Enduring coalitions generally tend to involve parties with similar attitudes and policies, especially if they are thereby able to wield influence, as when parties in a legislature combine to form a new cabinet. Coalitions formed for short periods of time or in opposition to an existing cabinet or policy may be ideologically more diverse: it is easier to agree to oppose than to agree to govern.

Leiserson has developed a combination of the minimum-size theory and the ideological compatibility theory: coalitions will form consisting of the smallest number of ideologically "adjacent" parties necessary to win. He has found that it explains many cabinet governments in Sweden and the prewar Netherlands. De Swann has modified the theory in order to account for the frequent formation of a governing coalition that is larger than the minimum size necessary to ensure victory, as has happened in Italy, France, and the postwar Netherlands. He suggests that a party will join a coalition that will adopt a policy that is as close as possible to the party's preferred policy. This will sometimes lead a party to join a coalition that is larger than that which is necessary to form a cabinet because having the "surplus" parties in the coalition increases the chance that the new government will adopt a certain policy.[16] John C. Harsanyi has generalized various studies of coalitions of individuals by stating that agreements are more likely to form when the parties share expectations about one another's behavior that lead each to believe that the other will behave "properly." Thus, coalitions will more likely form among persons who are similar with respect to age, sex, social class, and ideology.[17]

Both the minimum-size theory and the ideological compatibility theory, and their various combinations, have a defect of overpredicting the number of organizational coalitions that in fact form. They are useful in accounting for the coalitions we can observe (usually party coalitions in various parliamentary governments), but most organizations active in politics are not parts of coalitions. One reason for this is that most theories of coalition formation are based on the assumption that the outcome is certain—that is, each coalition has a probability of success of either one or zero. A parliamentary coalition can form a cabinet when it controls a majority of the seats. The number of seats controlled by each party is known in advance; thus, calculating what would be either the most profitable or the most ideologically compatible coalition that could win is a simple matter. But nonparty organizations attempting to influence a legislature or parties seeking to influence the electorate do not know precisely what their chances of success are or how much, if anything, by way of votes a prospective coalition partner could contribute to joint endeavor. And if a coalition is formed and wins (by getting the bill passed or the election won), the contribution of each member to the effort cannot be accurately measured, and thus the division of any payoffs cannot be easily settled.[18]

In those cases, by far the most common, where the probabilities of, and payoffs from, a coalition victory are uncertain, organizations are less likely to form enduring coalitions than are individuals. Individuals agree every day to allow themselves to be represented on some issue by an organization, even though it is unlikely that their views and its will coincide perfectly. Associations almost never allow another association to speak for them, and when they do, it is typically on the understanding that unanimous consent is necessary for the coalition to act, or that the coalition will have a sharply limited scope of action, or that it is an ad hoc arrangement with a brief life expectancy. Coalitions among lobbying groups designed to further a desired piece of legislation rarely last beyond the day the president signs the bill, and sometimes break up before that. There are, of course, a number of alliances among nations, but most, it would be fair to say, are not true coalitions, but treaties that have uncertain effect and are supplemented with conferences that involve only exchanges of views. The Urban Coalition, an alliance of business, labor, civic, and civil rights organizations formed after the assassination of Martin Luther King, Jr., never got off the ground in some cities, such as Boston, and is declining in importance in most other cities; furthermore, it had, despite its name, more of the characteristics of an international alliance (and one among unfriendly nations at that!) than of a true coalition.

Individuals typically are only segmentally involved in a voluntary association; for most persons, neither their existence nor their livelihood, nor even their most cherished principles, are at stake in the survival or triumphs of a voluntary association. For the association itself, and thus for its executive, involvement in a coalition may well appear threatening for all of these reasons—resources, autonomy, and purposes can be jeopardized if the organization must share the credit for victory and the blame for defeat, increase its competition for funds, moderate its commitment to a particular purpose, or weaken its distinctive identity and competence in the eyes of the members. Organizations have maintenance needs that individuals do not.

Furthermore, an organization is itself a coalition, the members of which are likely to see the costs and benefits of an even larger coalition very differently. Militant members will label any hint of compromise with coalition partners a sellout; moderate ones will criticize a refusal to compromise as being heavy-handed and rigid.

Finally, even the theories of coalition formation among individuals imply that such coalitions as form will be short-lived. The payoff theory suggests that the composition of the coalition will change as members attempt to lessen the costs or increase the benefits to themselves by threats, bluffs, and equivocations. And a coalition formed for one issue is hardly likely to remain intact for any other, inasmuch as the resources a coalition member could bring to the new conflict or the payoffs he might expect from its victorious resolution will almost certainly have changed in value. The anticompetitive or compatibility theory, if correct in predicting that coalitions will form along the lines of least resistance, also suggests that potential members who find similarity threatening will not join, or if they join, will soon resign. Among individuals, of course, likes do generally attract likes. But associations can often find similarity threatening, especially when autonomy is low. The more alike two organizations are, the greater the likelihood that they lay claim to identical causes, attempt to serve the same constituency, or compete for the same resources. Further jeopardizing one's weak autonomy by joining a coalition is not attractive to many organizations. This may help explain why ideologically similar political parties are often the most quarrelsome. In Italy, one or the other of two socialist parties (the "Nenni" and the "Saragat" socialists) were in eleven of the seventeen coalitions studied by Axelrod, but both parties were in only four.[19] The bitter rivalry among various American Marxist parties is of course well known.

An adequate theory of coalitions would probably have to integrate both the payoff and the compatibility theories as well as take into account the special characteristics of organizations as political actors.[20] In any such theory, the importance of autonomy as well as of resources would have to be recognized. A brief case history of one effort to form a very strong coalition, that is, one that would have made important demands on its members, under conditions of low autonomy will illustrate how associations evaluate coalitions that might seem, to an outsider, as "desirable." In 1951, Professor Emeritus Robert M. MacIver of Columbia University issued a report commissioned by the National Community Relations Advisory Council (NCRAC), a group that provided a forum for the discussion of matters of common interest among the American Jewish Committee, the Anti-Defamation League of B'nai B'rith, the American Jewish Congress, the Jewish Labor Committee, the Jewish War Veterans, and the Union of American Hebrew Congregations. In his report, MacIver concluded that these agencies displayed a "lack of unity, . . . active discord, [and] jealous and often quarrelsome competitiveness" that made it impossible to develop a "clear conception of a common goal." The NCRAC was of some use in encouraging negotiation among these agencies, but it could not make decisions. What was needed, MacIver felt, was a "concentration of effort" and "common planning." [21] This meant that activities that seemed to be duplicated by two or more agencies should be allocated to a single agency.[22] Specifically, he recommended that the investigations of anti-Semitism conducted by the American Jewish Committee and the Anti-Defamation League be consolidated into a single fact-finding program; that exclusive jurisdiction in the field of labor be assumed by the Jewish Labor Committee and in the field of interfaith services by the Union of American Hebrew Congregations; that the American Jewish Committee and the Anti-Defamation League give up their veterans departments and cede that responsibility to the Jewish War Veterans; that only one agency perform legal services, such as drafting legislation, in each issue area; and that the American Jewish Committee and the Anti-Defamation League allocate among themselves informational and "group appeal" programs.[23] MacIver recognized that some agencies would oppose this reallocation on grounds of ideology, "special constituency," "personality," or "distinctive mission," but he dismissed these views as "rationalization[s] of the *status quo*" and "bureaucratic special pleading." [24]

Needless to say, the agencies themselves, especially those that stood to lose functions, were far from prepared to dismiss such considerations. The American Jewish Committee, in its comment on the MacIver report, stated that its first concern was "the preservation of organizational autonomy" which was "essential," [25] because each agency was "rooted in" a "fundamental ideology or philosophy." It, of course, opposed any loss of its functions. The Anti-Defamation League complained that MacIver failed to understand "the part which constituency plays in the work of the ADL" and therefore that MacIver was unwise in his proposal to sacrifice that constituency and the staff that served it to achieve the undesirable goals of "tight and neat central control." Greater efficiency, it argued, would be achieved more by a "rounded community relations" effort, rather than by any "parcelling out of community relations functions" that would destroy the "special associations and skills" existing organizations had developed.[26] The American Jewish Congress, on the other hand, was delighted with many features of the report because it would lose no functions and might gain some, and complained only that the report did not go far enough in recognizing the importance of "ideological differences" among the agencies [27] or in assigning exclusively to the congress responsibility for legal services in the civil rights field.[28] The Jewish Labor Committee was naturally pleased to have its autonomy increased, as were the Jewish War Veterans and the Union of American Hebrew Congregations.

The Jewish defense agencies clearly had little "functional" autonomy, in that each was performing tasks similar to those performed by other agencies. In one sense, the MacIver proposals were efforts to increase that kind of autonomy by assigning each function to a single agency, thus making every agency in some sense unique. But as the agencies themselves were aware, this reassignment, while it would increase the autonomy of some groups, would lessen that of others, and in addition —though this is only hinted at in their comments—it would weaken the constituency autonomy of several associations because the reallocation of jobs would lessen their appeal to members and prospective members. The American Jewish Committee had as its principal constituency German Jews who had been in this country for several generations and were highly acculturated; the American Jewish Congress, on the other hand, had a constituency that was predominantly composed of East European Jews, many of whom were recent immigrants and were concerned about maintaining the Jewish identity. The Anti-Defamation League, in turn, was not a membership organization at all, but a specialized caucus sponsored by a fraternal association (B'nai B'rith) with chapters in many communities. Furthermore, the American Jewish Congress was established in part by those who were dissatisfied with the American Jewish Committee, and who had been more Zionist in outlook and were more willing to criticize non-Jews (by, for example, demanding that Christmas nativity scenes be removed from the public schools); the American Jewish Committee, by contrast, was more concerned with research and quiet diplomacy. A reallocation of functions would have meant that several agencies would have been required to lessen their appeal to their membership by offering fewer services in exchange for their contributions; a new equilibrium in the balance of inducements and contributions could have been restored only by finding new services to replace the reallocated ones or by reducing the expected level of contributions.

In this case, there was enough compatibility of interest to lead the agencies to form a weak coalition (the NCRAC) but insufficient autonomy to induce them to form a strong one (an NCRAC with decision-making powers). The MacIver report offered side payments to some coalition members but not to others, and hence it was resisted by the latter and accepted by the former. The intensity of the debate was probably heightened by the fact that it was the organizations with the lowest autonomy (the American Jewish Committee and the Anti-Defamation League) that were also net losers in the reallocation process, whereas some organizations (such as the Union of American Hebrew Congrega-

tions) with relatively high autonomy were net gainers in the reallocation.

Incentives for Coalition Formation

The normal tendency of formal organizations to resist coalition formation, except on an ad hoc basis, can be overcome if the existing level of
resources and autonomy for all prospective members can be significantly
threatened (a crisis) or enhanced (an opportunity). In the first case, organizations may coalesce in order to survive or to end a war of attrition
that has become too costly; in the latter, they may coalesce because a
situation has been created in which all can benefit, thereby changing a
condition of partial conflict to one of pure coordination.

A crisis may lead to the formation of a coalition because existing
money resources are suddenly jeopardized or because a dramatic event
leads to a general demand that organizations act together for the common good. The Community Chest or United Fund approach to fund
raising for health and welfare agencies was adopted, not because individual associations decided voluntarily that the payoffs to each from
joint fund raising exceeded the costs in resources and autonomy, but
rather because a principal source of these funds—large corporate
donors—announced that they would withhold their contributions unless
such a coalition were created.[29]

A crisis of opinion, as opposed to one of money, led to the formation
of a coordinated effort to reduce juvenile delinquency in Boston: a
prominent clergyman had been murdered in a public park by a youth
gang.[30] The ghetto riots and the King assassination in the mid-1960s led
to the formation of the Urban Coalition. A community disaster, such as
a flood or earthquake, will stimulate local organizations to coalesce.
Such crisis-induced coalitions are not formed out of an effort to maximize payoffs, however; there are no payoffs, except for the negative benefit of avoiding criticism about having done nothing in the face of an
emergency. When aroused public opinion subsides, the separatist tendencies of organizational maintenance needs reassert themselves, and
the coalition begins to dissolve, unless some mechanism has been de-
vised to enforce continuing cooperation. The Community Chest is one
such mechanism: agencies that desert that coalition lose their share of
the proceeds of joint fund-raising drives.

A special case of coalitions arising in order to avert costs is the merger of the AFL and CIO in 1955. The essential element of that merger was the "no raiding agreement" whereby the two groups of unions promised not to challenge each other's jurisdictions or to recruit each other's members. Raiding had proved to be too costly. In 1951–1952, there were 1,246 bargaining elections resulting from attempted raids by one union on the members of another. Over 366,000 workers were involved, but only 17 percent voted to change unions as a result of the raid. Given the cost of these organizing drives, this result made them clearly unprofitable.[31] The merger can be seen as an additional illustration of the anticompetitive tendencies of formal organizations; it is also an illustration of the weakness of those coalitions that do form in order to reduce competition. The AFL-CIO has "little power to order individual unions to do what they do not wish to do, and circumstances make it unlikely this will change in the near future." [32] It has no power over strikes and negotiations and can intervene in the internal affairs of constituent unions only to investigate them for corrupt practices or Communist influences. By a two-thirds vote of its executive committee, the AFL-CIO may suspend unions unwilling to end undesirable financial or political practices, and it has done so on a number of occasions. But suspension is hardly the kiss of death, as the prosperity enjoyed by the Teamsters' Union since its expulsion testifies, and unions which for any reason dislike an AFL-CIO decision may withdraw, as has the UAW, without incurring any important penalties. As a coalition, the AFL-CIO has two principal functions—adjudicating and, where possible, eliminating jurisdictional disputes, and carrying on peripheral activities that do not affect the internal affairs of its members—lobbying Congress, running political campaigns, and the like. The former function is accepted by most unions because experience shows that they benefit from it; the latter is accepted because they are not hurt by it.

Coalitions may also be created when the total supply of resources available to organizations is increased on condition that they join together. The antidelinquency coalition created in Boston did not endure because it conferred no benefits on many members; a subsequent effort in the 1960s, called Action for Boston Community Development, did endure because it was based on an increase in resources for many agencies made possible by grants from the federal government and the Ford Foundation.[33] In Oakland, California, various delinquency prevention agencies formed a weak coalition, largely for discussion purposes only, when the Ford Foundation made money available to such a group under the name of the Associated Agencies. Harvard University and the Massachusetts Institute of Technology have formed several coalitions (the Cambridge Electron Accelerator and the Joint Center for Urban Studies are among them), less because of any interest in cooperative effort or the joint provision of services than because the funding agency made such collaboration a condition of its support.

A coalition once formed will be more effective if it provides its organizational members with specific, divisible benefits. The "logic of collective action" of which Mancur Olson writes may be more applicable to coalitions of organizations than to those of individuals. Individuals will often contribute to large organizations without receiving any specific, material benefit from it; organizations rarely will. And when organizations do form coalitions, the largest or richest members of it tend to pay a disproportionate share of the cost. The United States, for example, pays a disproportionate share of the cost of the North Atlantic Treaty Organization and the United Nations. That is true, as Richard Zeckhauser and Mancur Olson have explained, not so much because the United States is foolish or other nations are irresponsible, as because the logic of coalition formation among rationally self-interested actors (which formal organizations are, I would argue, more so than individuals) gives the large nation an incentive to pay proportionally more than the small one. Each member of a coalition, such as the UN or NATO, gets only a fraction of the benefits of any collective good provided, such as mutual defense, but each pays the full cost of any additional amounts of the collective good. If the larger nation values defense more than the smaller one, as is typically the case, then it will spend more through the alliance to get more defense; smaller nations will have an incentive to spend less.[34] In a laboratory simulation of such an alliance, Philip M. Burgess and James A. Robinson have attempted to estimate the effect of giving to each alliance member some individual benefits (a "political and economic development fund") provided it paid its fair share of the alliance costs. As one might expect, coalitions that supplied individual benefits as well as collective ones (such as defense) were more likely to act with unanimity, to engage in cooperative activity, and to avoid major changes in alliance policies than were coalitions that supplied only collective benefits.[35]

Ad Hoc Alliances

Though coalitions are not common among political organizations, especially under conditions of uncertainty, ad hoc alliances frequently occur.

These alliances typically take the form of loose, cooperative relations between two or more associations with respect to the attainment of a particular end or the performance of a specific task. Several lobbying organizations may discuss together the testimony they plan to present, divide up lists of legislators they intend to contact, and coordinate in a general way the public posture they hope to strike. Sometimes these alliances acquire a name ("The Emergency Committee for Full Funding"), more often they do not. They represent temporary arrangements for sharing resources and especially for managing communications.

Because such alliances are more likely to form among organizations that agree, similar alliances tend to reappear frequently. The NAM, the Chamber of Commerce, and the Farm Bureau Federation are likely to be in informal contact over matters of tax and labor policy, just as the AFL-CIO, the NAACP, and the Farmers Union are likely to be in informal contact over welfare and civil rights matters. To some observers, the most important feature of interorganizational political relations is that the same groups work together over and over again. From that observation, it is not hard to move to the inference that their policies are set by joint action, and from that to the conclusion that a "power structure" (conservative or liberal, depending on which associations one dislikes) dominates policy-making in that area. In some cases the conclusion may be warranted, but it cannot be supported solely by showing that certain groups tend repeatedly to have roughly similar views and offer comparable testimony on certain issues.

The more striking fact about ad hoc alliances is that, with few exceptions, they remain ad hoc. No matter how often two organizations take the same stands on the same range of issues, no one proposes—or no one takes seriously any proposal—to merge or combine the groups into a single or larger whole. The imperatives of organizational maintenance and the need to maintain a distinctive organizational identity do not permit this.

Indeed, the reason that ad hoc alliances can form at all is that, for the most part, they are purely leadership activities in which the constituent associations are not deeply or formally implicated. Associational leaders and executives respond to a number of partially incompatible incentives: a desire to maintain the organization and one's position in it as well as a desire to acquire the support and goodwill of other key associational executives and to achieve certain policy ends, even some not much in favor with their rank and file. Furthermore, the prime currency of politics is timely and precise information, and to get information one must be prepared to give it. To act alone when confronting an important issue is to risk acting without complete information or in ways that will unwittingly antagonize a prospective ally. But to pursue the desire for information, assistance, and support too far and too systematically will weaken the distinctive competence or identity of the association and thus jeopardize its maintenance or compromise its position on those matters in which it must act for interests not shared by its ad hoc allies.

NOTES

1. Earl Latham, "The Group Basis for Politics: Notes for a Theory," *American Political Science Review*, XLVI (June 1952), 376–397, reprinted in *Political Behavior*, ed. Heinz Eulau (New York: Free Press, 1956), p. 236.

2. Sol Levine and Paul E. White, "Exchange as a Conceptual Framework for the Study of Interorganizational Relationships," *Administrative Science Quarterly*, V (March 1961), 583–601. Of the twenty-two agencies studied, fourteen were voluntary associations.

3. Arvarh E. Strickland, *History of the Chicago Urban League* (Urbana: University of Illinois Press, 1966), pp. 34–36.

4. Some of the tactics by which that philanthropy is produced are described in Norman Miller, "The Jewish Leadership of Lakeport," in *Studies in Leadership*, ed. Alvin Gouldner (New York: Russell and Russell, 1950), pp. 195 ff.

5. Robert M. MacIver, *Report on the Jewish Community Relations Agencies* (New York: National Community Relations Advisory Council, 1951).

6. Irving Bernstein, "Union Growth and Structural Cycles," in *Labor and Trade Unionism*, ed. Walter Galenson and Seymour Martin Lipset (New York: John Wiley, 1960), pp. 78–79.

7. Gerald A. McWorter and Robert L. Crain, "Subcommunity Gladitorial Competition: Civil Rights Leadership as a Competitive Process," *Social Forces*, XLIV (September 1967), 8–21, esp. 13.

8. The definition is adapted from Michael A. Leiserson, "Coalitions in Politics: A Theoretical and Empirical Study" (Ph.D. diss., Department of Political Science, Yale University, 1966), p. 112. See also William A. Gamson, "Experimental Studies of Coalition Formation," in *Advances in Experimental Social Psychology*, ed. Leonard Berkowitz (New York: Academic Press, 1964), vol. I, p. 82. Most interorganizational coordinating mechanisms are not coalitions in the sense in which the term is used here because they do not resolve conflicts over serious matters; typically a major decision can be reached only by unanimous consent. See Basil J. F. Mott, *Anatomy of a Coordinating Council* (Pittsburgh: University of Pittsburgh Press, 1968), pp. 45–46, 107.

9. *The Washington Lobby* (Washington, D.C.: Congressional Quarterly, Inc., 1971), pp. 73–74, 105–107.

10. See Thomas C. Schelling, *The Strategy of Conflict* (Cambridge, Mass.: Harvard University Press, 1960), p. 89.

11. Gamson, "Experimental Studies of Coalition Formation," pp. 86–90; William H. Riker, *The Theory of Political Coalitions* (New Haven: Yale University Press, 1962), chap. 2; Leiserson, "Coalitions in Politics," pp. 65–66.

12. Riker, *The Theory of Political Coalitions*, pp. 108–114.

13. George C. Homans, *Social Behavior: Its Elementary Forms* (New York: Harcourt, Brace, 1961), chap. 12.

14. Gamson, "Experimental Studies of Coalition Formation," pp. 90–92, 98–102; Leiserson, "Coalitions in Politics," pp. 46–56.

15. Robert Axelrod, *Conflict of Interest* (Chicago: Markham, 1970), pp. 175–183. See also E. W. Kelley, "Theory and the Study of Coalition Behavior," in *The Study of Coalition Behavior*, ed. Sven Groennings, E. W. Kelley, and Michael Leiserson (New York: Holt, Rinehart & Winston, 1970), p. 488.

16. Abraham De Swann, "An Empirical Model of Coalition Formation as an N-Person Game of Policy Distance Minimization," in Groennings, Kelley, and Leiserson, *The Study of Coalition Behavior*, pp. 424–444.

17. John C. Harsanyi, "Bargaining in Ignorance of the Opponent's Utility Function," *Journal of Conflict Resolution*, VI (March 1962), 29–38.

18. See Sven Groennings, "Notes Toward Theories of Coalition Behavior in Multiparty Systems: Formation and Maintenance," in Groennings, Kelley, and Leiserson, *The Study of Coalition Behavior*, p. 455.

19. Axelrod, *Conflict of Interest*, p. 178. Centrist parties may be less concerned about avoiding alliances with, or "contamination" by, ideologically similar parties because they rely less on purposive incentives and have in the electorate a more ambiguous image; indeed, that is why they are centrist.

20. Leiserson, "Coalitions in Politics," chap. 6, is one effort to construct such a theory.

21. MacIver, *Jewish Community Relations Agencies*, p. 53.

22. Ibid., p. 93.

23. Ibid., pp. 113–115.

24. Ibid., pp. 53–58.

25. Ibid., p. 173.

26. Ibid., pp. 224–225.

27. Ibid., p. 184.

28. Ibid., pp. 191–193.

29. John R. Seeley et al., *Community Chest* (Toronto: University of Toronto Press, 1957); and Eugene Litwak and Lydia F. Hylton, "Interorganizational Analysis: A Hypothesis on Co-ordinating Agencies," *Administrative Science Quarterly*, VI (1962), 395–414.

30. Walter B. Miller, "Inter-Institutional Conflict as a Major Impediment to Delinquency Prevention," *Human Organization*, XVII (Fall 1958), 20–23, and Miller, Rainer C. Baum, and Rosetta McNeil, "Delinquency Prevention and Organizational Relations," in *Controlling Delinquents*, ed. Stanton Wheeler (New York: John Wiley, 1968), pp. 61–100.

31. Philip Taft, *Organized Labor in American History* (New York: Harper & Row, 1964), chap. 49.

32. Derek C. Bok and John T. Dunlop, *Labor and the American Community* (New York: Simon & Schuster, 1970), p. 198.

33. Stephan Thernstrom, *Poverty, Planning, and Politics in the New Boston: Origins of ABCD* (New York: Basic Books, 1969).

34. Mancur Olson, Jr., and Richard Zeckhauser, "An Economic Theory of Alliances," *The Review of Economics and Statistics*, XLVIII (August 1966), 266–279.

35. Philip M. Burgess and James A. Robinson, "Alliances and the Theory of Collective Action: A Simulation of Coalition Processes," *Midwest Journal of Political Science*, XIII (May 1969), 194–218.

CHAPTER 14

Bargaining, Protest, and Violence

When one organization can attain its goals or carry on its activities only by thwarting the goals or impeding the activities of another organization, the two groups are said to be in opposition. Whereas organizational competition, as defined in Chapter 13 is relatively uncommon, organizational opposition is frequent, especially among political associations.

In some cases, organizations may oppose each other without dealing with each other. Two lobbies, for example, may press their cases before a legislature or an administrative agency, each hoping to win its case but neither attempting to induce the other to modify or abandon its position. Or two litigants may plead their cases before a court. In other cases, however, the associations may feel that it is necessary or desirable to deal directly with each other. This would be true if there were no third party, such as the government, whose actions would be decisive, if there were a third party, but one that was unwilling to act unless and until the contending parties had themselves reached an agreement, or if the government itself were a party to the dispute rather than simply the legislative referee.

The typical interactions between two opposed organizations can involve many kinds of behavior—a union strike against an employer, an argument between two political factions attempting to agree on a common slate of candidates for office, a sit-in of black students in a segregated lunch counter, a conference to discuss the merger of two government agencies, a televised civil rights march against the office of a school superintendent, labor-management negotiations over a wage increase, a public quarrel between two groups over the merits of an urban renewal project, or a mass meeting called to denounce a proposed tax increase.

These and other examples of struggles between partially or wholly opposed organizations can be divided into two general types—those that involve an important element of confrontation (public denunciation, showmanship, or display) and those that involve chiefly negotiation (meetings, the mutual modification of positions, the search for agreements by discussion that may involve in addition an exchange of rewards or threats of retaliation). The latter will be called *bargaining*, defined as a process by which two or more parties seek to attain incompatible ends through the exchange of compensations. The former will be called *protest*, defined as a process whereby one party seeks by public display or disruptive acts to raise the cost to another party of continuing a given course of action.[1] Obviously, there may be elements of both bargaining and protest in any given relationship, as when a picket line is formed around the office of a firm that has no black employees while negotiations go forward simultaneously over how such employees can be hired.

Protest may take place for one or more of several reasons. First, it may be a strategy designed to acquire resources with which to bargain. The protest organization wants something that another organization possesses (for example, employment opportunities) but has nothing the second organization values (for example, money, prestige, political power, or community support). Public display or disruptive acts, such as sit-ins or picketing, may create negative inducements—that is, a state of affairs distasteful to the target organization and for the cessation of which it is willing to make concessions. If so, bargaining—the exchange of compensations—results from the protest activity. Second, protest may be a strategy designed to make credible the willingness of a group to use the bargaining resources it already has. For example, an association may claim that its members will not patronize a store that follows a certain policy. If the store rejects this claim, the protest group may organize a boycott to prove the reality of its threat. The protest, in effect, raises the value of existing bargaining resources for one party. Third, a protest may be designed to activate third parties.[2] The protest organization may or may not have any resource the target organization values, but it may find it advantageous to acquire, or increase the value of, resources by enlisting the aid of third parties who are either sympathetic to its cause or who have an interest in reducing conflict and who can bring to bear on the target resources more valued than those possessed by the protestors. For example, a civil rights march may be intended, not to induce a segregationist institution to bargain with the protestors, but to awaken sympathetic public opinion or activate an agency of the federal government that in turn will exert pressure on the target. Finally, a protest activity may be carried on in order to enhance the protesting organization. This can be done by attracting new members, radicalizing old members, obtaining valuable publicity, or increasing the sense of solidarity and competence of existing members. No bargaining may ensue, no third parties may become involved, and no costs may be imposed on the target. Because it is not intended to have any effect on policy, this last case might be more accurately described as "pseudo-protest."

A single organization may on different occasions use protest for each of these purposes. Lawrence N. Bailis, in his study of the Massachusetts Welfare Rights Organization, found examples of at least two kinds of protest. Mass demonstrations in the office of a welfare administrator had as their object increasing the bargaining resources of the welfare mothers—a promise to stop the noise, confusion, and shouting could be offered in exchange for special needs grants. A rally on Boston Common featuring Dr. Benjamin Spock as a speaker and a demonstration at the Boston Army Base to demand the transfer of military funds to welfare programs were intended primarily to increase the visibility of the organization and to win it the sympathy of antiwar liberals; neither protest was aimed at a clear target that would, or even could, grant the organization's demands.[3] In the view of Michael Lipsky, the rent strikes in Harlem in 1963–1964 won some victories primarily because of the success that Jesse Gray, the rent-strike leader, enjoyed in activating other civic groups, such as the Community Service Society, the Women's City Club, and various civil rights and antipoverty organizations, and in mobilizing various ad hoc allies, including a number of law school professors, a local radio station, and reporters from the *New York Times*. Lipsky concluded that the power of Gray, though grounded in a small number of Harlem followers, was "dependent upon manipulation of communications media to project the appearance of strength and the legitimacy of rent strike concerns."[4]

Protest is sometimes described as a frequent or necessary tactic of powerless groups in a society. Bargaining occurs among groups already possessing mutually valued resources; protest occurs when one group lacks such resources. To some extent this is true, but it is not a full explanation of why one oppositional strategy rather than another is adopted. Some apparently powerless groups do bargain, relying for their "resource" on their ability to offer the other party the chance to get the petitioners "off their backs." Almost everyone has at one time or another changed his position, not because of threats or the receipt of material benefits, but because he thereby put an end to pestering. And some apparently powerful groups have on occasion lost out completely on an issue of major importance (for example, their factory has been expropriated) but have not resorted to protest tactics (for example, a sit-in). A complete account of the conditions disposing a party to adopt either a protest or a bargaining strategy must consider a number of factors in addition to the distribution of resources.

Factors Influencing the Choice of Strategies

Three kinds of factors influence the choice of strategies when two organizations are in opposition and neither pure persuasion nor coercion is possible: the nature of the issue, the social position of the organization members, and the incentive system of the organizations. Lacking any systematic empirical study of protest or bargaining, it is not possible to say which of these factors is more important or whether any single factor is of decisive importance.

Bargaining is facilitated when the two parties agree on the value premises that define their relationship; protest is more likely when that agreement is absent. The first requirement of a bargaining situation is that each party concedes to the other the right to make the decisions and demands that it is in fact making. If a firm denies that a union has the right to speak for the workers or to call a strike, or the union denies the right of management to control the enterprise, then bargaining is unlikely. Bargaining can sometimes occur when either party or both deny the legitimacy of the other, but this usually happens only when an element of coercion is involved—for example, a third party, such as a court or legislature, has ordered the parties to negotiate. Bargaining is obviously made easier if there is also agreement on the facts and objectives, but this is not essential: indeed, bargaining is necessary in the first place because the goals of the parties are at least partially in conflict. Interestingly, in many bargaining situations there is no direct confrontation of differences in goals; in the normal case, persons and organizations find it easier to dispute the facts rather than the objectives, and thus normative issues are often concealed in empirical or logical disagreement.

Bargaining is facilitated when the matter at issue is divisible—that is, when it is a matter of "more or less" rather than "all or nothing." The size of a tax increase, the amount of a wage settlement, and the price of a real estate parcel are all examples of divisible issues. Whether or not alcoholic beverages should be sold, or marijuana legalized, or abortions permitted are issues that are much less divisible. And some issues which appear divisible—such as how many blacks a firm should hire to escape the charge of being discriminatory—are in fact not divisible, because a certain number acquires important symbolic significance, as when a firm finds itself under pressure to make 20 percent of its work force black because the population of the city in which it is located is 20 percent black. Nondivisible issues require for their resolution in a bargaining situation the exchange of side payments, because the issue itself cannot be easily compromised; these side payments can include promises of future support, the making of appropriate public statements, and the granting of various preferments and perquisites. When no side payments exist, when their exchange is thought improper or immoral, or when the issue is freighted with important symbolic significance for one side, protest is more likely to replace, or supplement, bargaining.

The social structure in which the participants are embedded, as well as the character of the issue, influences the kinds of organizational strategies that will be selected. There are two elements of the social structure that are relevant—the ongoing relationships, if any, between the parties to the dispute, and the self-conception, or position in a deference hierarchy, of each party. A high level of continuing interaction among the representatives of two opposing organizations makes it less likely that the organizations will encourage their constituents to engage in protest tactics. This is partly the result of the value the representatives may attach to the existing relationship and partly the result of the value they attach to future relationships. Persons who frequently deal with each other may be embarrassed by a confrontation between their respective organizations and may fear that a protest today in a matter that divides them will reduce the chances of collaborative action in the future in matters that unite them. If the two organizations are socially segregated and have no relationships other than those occasioned by the issue of the moment, they will be less inhibited about engaging in protest tactics.

The costs of protest also vary with the status of the participants. In a society in which prestige is awarded on the basis of propriety, distinction, and occupation as well as wealth and power, persons with high status will find costly any behavior that lowers their standing in the eyes of others. Persons with little status will have correspondingly less to lose. Furthermore, the life styles associated with various status levels and subcultures reward certain kinds of behavior: normally, the older upper-status person is expected to be reasonable, dignified, accommodating, and nonviolent, whereas the younger lower-status person is expected by his peers to be tough, fun-loving, outspoken, and "sharp."

These relationships are not simple or fixed. A middle-class organizational spokesman may feel constrained to imitate the lower-class life style of his constituents. The ghetto insurrections have led middle-class black leaders to adopt lower-class rhetorical styles. On matters of great importance to them, upper-middle-class persons can be found on picket lines, though typically this occurs only in cases, as in foreign policy disputes, where they have no ongoing relationships with the target agency, and not in cases, such as arguments with the local school board, where they do have such relationships. On matters of no direct importance to them, lower- and working-class persons may express great disapproval of protest tactics, and they will thus condemn a student strike at a university, even though they would quickly join a union strike at a factory. Schoolteachers and other white-collar workers have from time to time been mobilized for protest tactics, such as strikes and mass demonstrations, but in general the salaried and professional occupational groups have resisted unionization and unionlike methods.[5] Certain groups, such as college students, though generally upper status by origin, have been placed in a social situation (the communal life of a college campus) or have embraced views (the renunciation of bourgeois standards) that have eliminated the inhibiting elements of status and in some cases provided a positive reinforcement for protest strategies. And certain acts, such as lunch counter sit-ins by middle-class black students, have broadened the range of what society defines as acceptable conduct.

The final set of factors influencing the choice of strategy is organizational. Associations that do not rely on highly valued purposive incentives will not feel obliged to attain their objective whatever the means; those that do rely on such inducements will attach such importance to their goals that not only will the results of bargaining seem unsatisfactory (a bargain by definition is an agreement in which neither party attains all his goals at zero cost) but the very idea of bargaining, with its inevitable implications of compromise, will appear objectionable. Furthermore, ideological or redemptive organizations seek to mobilize persons to perform arduous, difficult, time-consuming, and even dangerous tasks; this is made easier if the objectives are clearly and simply stated (hence the importance of slogans) and if the opportunities of the enemy to split the group are minimized (hence the reluctance to allow one or a few representatives to bargain). Opponents of such groups often make the mistake of assuming that the slogan is mere rhetoric and the refusal to negotiate a sign of disinterest in the substantive issue. These factors are better seen as the result of reconciling the intensity of feeling produced by commitment to an important goal with the organizational strains and leadership constraints produced by intense feelings of any sort.

Organizations that have resources that are valued by their opponents will be more likely to bargain than organizations lacking such resources. Protest in this case is the resource of the powerless: a negative inducement, the withdrawal of which is offered to the opponent in exchange for substantive concessions. Important as this consideration is, it is clearly not the only factor leading to the adoption of protest methods. For example, some organizations will protest, often disruptively, without having first attempted to bargain at all—not because they lack bargaining resources (they cannot know this until they have found out in greater detail what their opponent *wants*), but because protest is expressive of a life style, is less threatening than negotiation, is useful in building a movement, or is required by the symbolic nature of the objective.

Finally, the use of either protest or bargaining tactics increases as groups are rewarded for having pursued one or the other. The welfare rights organizations in various localities did not continue to conduct demonstrations in local welfare offices after it became clear that, because of a change in the law—the abolition of special needs grants—welfare officials no longer had the authority to meet the demands being made of them. Civil rights protest marches in various southern cities were often unsuccessful, in that the immediate objective was not attained, but those that were continued and attracted large support were those that received heavy attention in the media and aroused, in Lipsky's terms, "reference publics" elsewhere.[6] The rewards of protest activities are vulnerable to changing public and media concepts of what is newsworthy.

The circumstances under which either tactic is likely to succeed, and thus to stimulate its further use, are not well understood. Indeed, how one even measures "success" is an open question. A "successful" labor-management negotiation may be one that averts a strike, or that achieves a certain allocation of funds, or that enhances the position of the union and management representatives in the eyes of their respective organizational constituents regardless of the substantive outcome. A "successful" protest march may be one that produces a gain for the protestor, a gain for the target, a standoff, or some combination.

But if there is any single factor that contributes to success, somehow defined, it probably has to do with the perceived legitimacy of the demands being made. To persons or groups that have not engaged in either serious bargaining or active protest, such a view may seem strange, if not absurd. Bargaining, after all, involves the exchange of compensations, often material ones; in such a utilitarian process, whether any position is thought to be legitimate is beside the point—what counts is whether the price is right. And protest occurs typically when there is no willingness to negotiate and thus when each side can be presumed to have denied the legitimacy of the claims of the other. In fact, establishing legitimacy is the essence of organizational struggle.

In a bargaining relationship, both sides need to make their offers and threats credible and to convince their opponents that the position they advocate is one that their organizational constituents support and will defend. Neither of those objectives can be attained if one side or the other appears utterly unreasonable. An outlandish demand will not be persuasive to those who doubt that the members of the organization making it will stick by it and refuse to settle for less. What constitutes outlandishness will depend on existing norms and the state of public opinion. This does not mean that either side must reveal to the other its true or minimal position (quite the contrary—concealing that until the appropriate time is the essence of bargaining) but rather that spokesmen who are regarded as "hopelessly unreasonable" will not be taken seriously; their threats will be discounted, their promises viewed skeptically, or their reliability questioned. Making demands that are, or can be construed as, legitimate or within reason by the standards of the larger publics that will eventually learn of them is important.

This is even more the case with respect to protest. Creating the negative inducement, whether directly or indirectly, requires the development of legitimacy in the eyes of those whose actions can alter the preferences of the target organization. At a minimum, the members who are to participate in the protest event must be persuaded of the legitimacy of the demand and the actions; if reference publics or third parties are to be activated, they also must be convinced of the legitimacy of the cause and the defensibility, if not the rightness, of the act; it must be possible to find reporters and editors in the mass media who find the action legitimate; and finally, and paradoxically, the target organization itself must be brought to believe, at least in part, that the protest is not utterly illegitimate. The objective is to create the view, among at least some leaders of the target group, that "while we deplore these protest methods, and while we cannot accept all of these demands, nonetheless there is a genuine grievance here to which we must respond."

This last factor may not be apparent to those who confuse protest with coercion. If legal authority or physical force can be used in adequate measure, the beliefs of the target group are irrelevant. But that is not protest, as here defined, and protest properly understood typically does not end with the application of such direct sanctions. Protest succeeds because the target concedes. The target organization, in turn, concedes because it can neither ignore nor resist the protest. And often this is because some members of that organization prefer concessions to resistance either because such measures are right or because others will think them to be right. Though protest organizations do not always succeed, they have two advantages not always possessed by their targets: they are sure of the rightness of their cause, and, lacking in resources, they appear selfless while their opponents, having resources, do not. These sources of strength—the strengths of the weak, if you will—coupled with such legitimacy as their claims may have before the wider public, mean that protest is not always, or even usually, the hopeless strategy it may at first seem to be.

Conflict and Representation

The behavior of the representatives of two organizations locked in conflict, whether carried on by bargaining or by protest, will be strongly, perhaps decisively, influenced by the representatives' need to maintain their positions with their followers. Bargaining between individuals will be different from bargaining between organizational representatives: in the former case, the parties can more freely change their minds in response to arguments and inducements and are themselves the sole judge of the value of the bargain struck; in the latter case, the bargainer's major task is less finding a settlement satisfactory to himself and his opponent than finding one acceptable to his constituents.

What Richard E. Walton and Robert B. McKersie find of industrial bargaining is probably true of bargaining generally: "The organizations participating in labor negotiations usually lack internal consensus about the objectives they will attempt to obtain from negotiations, and this is especially true for labor organizations." [7] Disagreement about objectives may be greater on the union than the management side because, at least in industrial unions, there are many more people whose wills must be concerted (the company representative, by contrast, need please only a small group of executives and directors), and they have a greater variety of material interests in the outcome (unskilled workers want large dollar gains, whereas skilled workers want not only more money but the maintenance of a large differential between their wages and those of the unskilled group). Furthermore, there are latent cleavages that arise from the hierarchical differentiation of representatives and constituents: the union rank and file are concerned with material benefits, the union executives with organizational maintenance. Though these interests are not necessarily contradictory, they can lead to differences in emphasis—the rank and file will judge a contract by the size of the wage package and the statement of work and disciplinary rules, but the executives will judge it by the guarantees it provides for union security (for example, union-shop clauses, automatic dues check-offs) and organizational image (for example, union size and prestige). Such cleavages also exist on the management side. Finance officers are concerned about the cost of the settlement, local plant managers with the problem of administering grievance systems and work rules, and labor negotiators with problems of precedence, language, and principle.

One might suppose that confronted with a divided or uncertain constituency, an organizational representative in a bargaining situation would resolve these conflicts by taking an extreme position—ask for everything for everybody, and settle for nothing less. Occasionally, this is in fact the position taken; the difficulty with it, of course, is that bargaining, except with a very weak or incompetent opponent, is virtually impossible under these conditions. In the case of labor negotiations, such a position maintained by either party usually leads to a strike. This eventuality is often foreseen and sometimes welcomed—taking a strike is seen as a way of allowing the workers to let off steam or management to engage in punitive action; this is followed by serious bargaining on the basis of more reasonable goals and less demanding expectations from constituents. But in the typical bargaining relationship, the representative does not take positions more extreme than any given segment of his constituency, but takes rather, as Walton and McKersie find it, a "position less ambitious than that of his principals." [8] In a survey of labor-management negotiations, Herbert S. Parnes found that in a majority of cases the union rank and file is more, rather than less, "extreme" than the leadership in pressing for contract demands.[9] The negotiator is the man-in-the-middle who must find a strategy for moderating constituency pressures on him. In the case of unions, reinforcing this leadership desire to "sell" a settlement is the fact that in many cases the costs of a strike are often greater for the organization than for the members. In many unions, strikers receive strike benefits from the union treasury supplemented by what they can earn in part-time jobs or receive in the form of unemployment benefits. But what is a material benefit to the members is, in part, a cost to the organization: its treasury can be quickly depleted by a prolonged strike.

Thus, much of the actual bargaining process between organizational representatives is dominated by the need to find an outcome that can be "sold" to the respective constituencies.[10] There are a number of tactics by which this is achieved. The first is to keep control of the bargaining position in the hands of the representatives so it can be modified as circumstances may suggest. This in turn requires that the formulation of initial demands be made in a way that minimizes the chance that rigid, unattainably high goals are set. And this in turn requires that membership involvement in goal setting be minimized. If the goals are set in a mass meeting, they will almost surely be more extreme than if set by a leadership caucus: in an open forum, every speaker can attack less extreme proposals as "sellouts" or "timid," there is little opportunity for assessing feasibility and maximum opportunity for venting emotion, and political rivals can place the existing leadership in the untenable position of having either to embrace demands they know they cannot attain or to argue against them and thus appear to oppose the interests of the membership.

A second method is to make it publicly apparent that everything that could be won from the opponents was in fact won. This requires that each party describe the other's position as "rigid," "unreasonable," and "unyielding," ensure that the negotiations are protracted (if anything is settled too quickly it will appear that it was settled too cheaply), and blame any unfavorable settlement on the intervention of hostile or unsympathetic third parties. Courts, arbitrators, and government officials are prime candidates for the role of an agency that "forces" the negotiators to accept a settlement they would like to accept anyway.

A third method is to protect the autonomy of the representatives by holding the negotiations in private, by keeping information from the rank and file, by developing a pattern of authority within the organization that gives substantial discretion to the leadership (such as authority based on personal fealty or charisma rather than merely the authority of office or expertise) and by minimizing the number of groups that must ratify the proposal (in the case of unions, by having settlements adopted by the executive committee but not by the rank and file). The United Steelworkers, for example, have had contracts signed by the international union with no requirement of endorsement by the locals, but the United Auto Workers have traditionally required that the locals approve any settlement agreed to by the leadership—and on occasion, several locals have refused.[11]

Each participant in a bargaining session will be keenly aware that he is a representative of a partially divided, hard-to-please constituency, but unless he is very experienced he will forget that his opponent is in the same position. The opponent will instead be seen as an individual whose behavior is wholly to be explained by individual traits. Because his opponent will no doubt be struggling to get as much as he can for his side, he will be seen (again, except by those who are experienced at these relationships) as inflexible, power oriented, self-seeking, ruthless, and insensitive to the organizational maintenance problems of the first party. This perception is only slightly moderated by the existence of long-term personal relationships. Murray Horwitz reports of experiments in which personal friends were made the representatives of two competing groups; immediately each ceased to acknowledge the goodwill and sensitivity of the other and saw him instead as lacking in consideration.[12] This mutual perception is reinforced by the tendency of each representative to gain maximum bargaining advantage and to minimize the constituency opposition to his position by making frequent reference to the feelings of the most extreme members of his constituency ("my people are really up in arms about this"), even though such members are an unrepresentative minority. His opponent, on the other hand, is likely to assume that the representative is associating himself personally with the most extreme positions and thus is showing himself to be unreasonable.

In a protest relationship, many of the same organizational constraints operate, but they are managed by a quite different strategy. Protest, unlike bargaining, is a public act requiring the participation of the rank and file. To obtain that participation, the rank and file must be motivated; to motivate them, a strong position must be taken initially and maintained consistently. Mass involvement in ratifying, if not formulating, the demand is important if persons are to make sacrifices for its attainment; maintenance of that position in the face of demands for compromise is important if the moral or ethical quality of the position is not to be called into question. Private negotiations accompanying a protest movement are suspect; the rank and file fear that a leader who had once fired them up will now sell them out. Should negotiations occur, the protest group often insists they be done publicly, for example, by inviting the opponents to a mass meeting to debate the issue, or by a large and unwieldy delegation of members accompanying the spokesman or (a technological variant) by a leader who tapes the proceedings.

These organizational pressures frequently mean that a protest tactic originally adopted to enable a group to get into a bargaining relationship with another party can be carried out only in ways that make meaningful bargaining difficult, if not impossible. The protest group offers only one inducement, the cessation of the protest, whereas the target group may feel it requires an additional inducement, some modification in the demand. The actual bargaining that takes place may be indirect rather than direct, aimed not at getting the other party to modify its position, but at persuading such third parties as may have been aroused that either the protest group or the target group is behaving unreasonably and thus that its position is illegitimate.

The protest group will attempt to do this by claiming that the target group is self-seeking and elitist, but that the protesters are public spirited and mass based; the target group will counter with charges that the protesters are unrepresentative of the group they claim to speak for, are wrong in their facts, and are violating the accepted norms of political controversy. In this exchange, the protesters often have a powerful rhetorical advantage—they can charge the target group with seeking the wrong ends by accusing them of being racist, or antilabor, or prowar, while the target group often tries to respond by saying that it shares the ends of the protesters but disagrees only as to the means. Once an organization has conceded the moral premises to its opponent, however, it, rather than its opponent, will be expected by attentive third parties to make all the concessions—if it is only a question of *means,* then resisting change seems to be a sign of intransigence.

Such face-to-face bargaining as does occur in the aftermath of a protest activity will display in exaggerated form all the normal difficulties of negotiation. The two parties will begin in total opposition, that is, as enemies, rather than in partial opposition; the target group will see the protesters as "rigid" and "publicity oriented," and the protesters will see the target as "rigid" and "secretive"; the target group will doubt the ability of the protest leaders to bind their followers and thus to deliver on any commitments, whereas the protesters will deny that there are any limits whatever to what the target group can do provided it has the will.

Under these circumstances, it is surprising that any agreements at all emerge out of such sessions. And often they do not. A protest-induced negotiation is often conducted indirectly—by the exchange of press releases and through the intervention of intermediaries—rather than by face-to-face bargaining. The settlement that is reached is thus often nothing on which two men have shaken hands but simply an announced position that produces a diminution of pressures. Indeed, the crucial test of a proposal is not whether the protest group will accept it, but whether the attentive third parties will endorse it. If the plan strikes that third party as a step in the right direction or a reasonable suggestion, then their support, which is often crucial to the success of a protest action, will be withdrawn from efforts to continue the protest. If the protest group is dissatisfied with the proposal, it may continue the protest, but its impact is likely to be much reduced.

The relationship between leader and led in a protest activity will vary with the social class of those who are led. Lower-class members, as the experience of the welfare rights and rent-strike movements suggest, require a realistic prospect of immediate gain, coupled with the reassurance that the likelihood of sanctions, for example, being jailed, is small. Upper-middle-class members will attach less value to prospective material gains—indeed, they may value them negatively, believing that any chance of personal gain would sully the elements of sacrifice and principle involved—and more value to the ideological aspects of the activity. This does not necessarily mean that a leader of a group of lower-class protesters will make moderate and specific demands, or that the leader of a middle-class protest will offer extreme and general ones. The explanation of political rhetoric is a complex matter; much depends on the audience for which it is intended. In a small, materially induced protest group, rhetoric may be irrelevant, for the crucial problem is to persuade persons, face to face, that a group effort will confer benefits on them. In the Massachusetts Welfare Rights Organization, this process was accompanied by relatively little intense public rhetoric; in the New York City rent strikes, it was accompanied by a great deal, though it is not clear from Lipsky's account just how the rent strikers were recruited. The rhetoric that was used seems, however, to have been aimed at third parties rather than at members, and especially at newspaper reporters who had an appetite for fresh charges and new allegations.[13] Political rhetoric is more important, of course, in a protest movement that has been created with the use of purposive incentives, but the style and appeal of that rhetoric will depend crucially on whether those who employ it seek to organize a mass movement or an elite cadre. The heterogeneity of any mass grouping requires more moderate, inclusive appeals; hence the carefully controlled language of the large civil rights and antiwar marches on Washington.[14] A homogeneous ideological cadre, on the other hand, will expect the strongest possible statement of its special vision and posture.

Many protest associations fail because they cannot reconcile their organizational maintenance needs with their audience (or third party) support needs. A group will often solve the first problem by emphasizing an intense and elaborate ideology only to discover that this not only restricts its appeal among potential members but reduces its capacity to play on the benevolent, but unideological, instincts of a reference public. An attempted rent strike studied by Harry Brill failed because the organizing cadre defined the association as a radical black nationalist organization rather than an ameliorative one. These purposive appeals succeeded in holding the activists together but were of little value in recruiting tenants for whom utilitarian problems of rent levels and building management practices were paramount and to whom radicalism was faintly offensive. Further, the association was unable to enlist important third parties as allies because it insisted on confronting them with explanations of its ideology rather than with portrayals of the plight of its tenants.[15]

Protest movements rarely endure. They are victimized by both success and failure. Those seeking material objectives are vulnerable both to the granting of demands (as when the New York City government began new programs to deal with housing conditions objected to by rent strikers) and to the denial of them (as when the Massachusetts state government abolished the special needs grant from its welfare program). A mass protest activity, whether successful or unsuccessful, is hard to repeat; the larger the number of persons involved, the greater the likelihood it will be a one-shot affair. Protest by small cadres may continue in spite of apparent success, which it rejects as "co-optation," or actual failure, which it ignores as a minor reversal of the tide of history; for such groups, to abandon the protest is to abandon the organization. But any protest movement, small or large, is susceptible to the changes in interest and concern of the relevant third parties. As with all audiences, there is an important element of fashion and novelty in the collective psyche: what is a dramatic lunch-counter sit-in one year is a boring rerun the next year; an attention-getting slogan quickly becomes a dully repetitious phrase.

Given the evanescence of many protest movements and the difficulty of reconciling the organizational needs of protest with the interorganizational requirements of bargaining, a rational strategy for a group seeking political change is to have both kinds of organizations working in its behalf simultaneously. To a degree, this is what the black community in many cities has done. Jack L. Walker offers an interesting analysis of how this has worked out in Atlanta.[16] Maintaining such a dual strategy is difficult, however, for it requires that protest leaders be willing to allow bargainers to negotiate in their behalf. If the issue is sufficiently salient, or if the number of persons mobilized by it is large, it is likely that this willingness will be absent. Thus, the dual strategy will falter or collapse as protest leaders attack bargainers who in turn must either end their negotiating role entirely or commit themselves to protest goals with sufficient firmness that there is little left to negotiate over. This polarization has occurred in some cities, though for blacks a common racial identity has to a degree inhibited the public mutual criticism of leaders.[17]

Organizations and Violence

From time to time, there are outbursts of collective violence in this and other countries. Much of this violence occurs in noninstitutional settings and involves no organizations except for police or military authorities (for example, the race riots between 1919 and 1943, the ghetto riots of the 1960s, and youth riots at various resorts). Occasionally, however, the participants in collective violence are organized; the most important cases of this are to be found in the violent struggles between labor and management. Such outbursts have occurred most recently in the periods 1919–1920 and 1931–1937.

The circumstances under which members of an organization engaged in conflict with another organization will resort to acts of collective violence are not well understood. Theories abound, but as a careful analysis by G. David Garson of 226 labor disturbances suggests, no single theory is adequately supported by the facts.[18] Most theories, such as those that assert that violence results from absolute deprivation, from intransigent opposition to demands to alleviate deprivation, from the "revolution of rising expectations," or from a sense of "relative deprivation," fail to account for the central features of collective violence—namely, that it is periodic, localized, and limited. There is violence at some periods but not at others, and thus explanations based on enduring social conditions (such as class stratification, the economic system, poverty, or ethnic competition) are not especially helpful—if these conditions were the determinative ones, violence would be more or less continuous. Furthermore, violence occurs in some locales and not in others. Economic conditions turned sharply downward between 1929 and 1931, and in 1931 there were at least twenty-eight major incidents of labor-management violence, yet most of these took place in but two industries—coal and textiles. This localization might be explained in the case of coal by the fact that real wages fell among miners more sharply than among workers generally, but such an explanation is of little value in the case of textile workers because their wages fell less than the average. Sudden changes in economic conditions may well contribute to the likelihood of labor-management violence, but they do not determine it. Though unemployment was high in 1931–1933 when there was much violence, it was low in 1919 when there was even more.

Philip Taft and Philip Ross have offered an explanation of violence in the labor sector that seems to account for some of its periodic and localized character. Labor violence occurs in a specific organizational setting: a labor dispute in which organized pickets attempt to prevent struck plants from being reopened with the use of strikebreakers or in which company guards, police, or the military attempt to break a picket line.[19] The issue is typically union recognition: "the most common cause of past violent labor disputes was the denial of the right to organize through refusal to recognize the union, frequently associated with the discharge of union leaders."[20] The passage of laws guaranteeing the right to organize and bargain collectively has been responsible, in the view of Taft and Ross, for the great decline in labor violence since 1938.

This appears to be an apt description of most of the collective labor-management violence with which we are familiar, and therefore an explanation of such violence as a means of waging a struggle when effective nonviolent means are unavailable has some merit. But as Garson suggests, this explanation has a defect common to many others—it over-predicts the phenomenon in question. Before 1938, there were no doubt thousands of instances of management refusal to recognize a union, refusals that did not lead either party to resort to violence. Companies did not suddenly refuse to recognize unions in 1931, thereby leading to the sharp increase in violence; they had been refusing for many years before 1931. Nor was there a sharp increase in union demands for recognition just prior to 1931: the proportion of work stoppages in which recognition was the main issue fell from 34 percent in 1929 to 32 percent in 1931.[21] Finally, union recognition continued to be an issue after 1938, by which time collective violence had virtually ceased.

Garson suggests that several factors taken together are necessary to explain collective labor-management violence. A sharp economic reversal probably increases the susceptibility of unions to violence (if workers are locked out, or the strike is prolonged, they have fewer alternative sources of employment), whereas management has a larger pool of potential strikebreakers from which to recruit. But precipitating factors must also be present. Foremost among these is the existence of a planned organizing drive focused on particular industries. The 1931 riots occurred in coal and textiles, two industries that were in that year the major targets for union membership drives. Furthermore, they were also industries in which two or more rival unions were competing for strength—the United Mine Workers under John L. Lewis and the National Miners Union under Communist domination emerged as rivals for bargaining power in the northern coal fields, and both the United Textile Workers of the AFL and the National Textile Workers Union led by Communists were competing in the mill towns of various states. Such organizing drives are facilitated, as was seen in Chapter 7, if important national leaders confer legitimacy on them.

Once a drive is underway, the probability of violence further increases if the industries are economically unhealthy and hence unable to pass on wage increases to the public; both coal and textiles were depressed long before the depression began. And the likelihood of violence becomes greater still if there is a history of violence in the industry and its locale. Of the twenty-eight labor riots in 1925–1929, one fourth were in mining, and the textile industry had experienced twenty-two riots in the period 1917–1929.

Finally, the chances of violence increase if, with all the prior factors in play, one side or the other refuses to make concessions and seeks to destroy its opponent. Conversely, the chances decrease if third parties intervene to encourage a settlement. Though the passage of the Wagner Act no doubt helped usher in an era in which the chances of violence arising over union recognition struggles were lessened, of equal importance was the new posture of the executive branch of the government. In a variety of ways, the president and others urged negotiation on management even in cases where workers had seized management's property by sit-down strikes.[22]

Such, at least, appears to be the pattern of organized violence in the United States. A theory that sought to account for differences among societies in levels of civil violence would require a search for broader contrasts among social conditions and political legitimacy. Perhaps the best-known theory of this kind is that of Ted Robert Gurr who has shown that the familiar concept of "relative deprivation" fits the data rather well. In this view, violence becomes more likely when men become dissatisfied because their achievements fall short of their aspirations.[23]

We know very little, however, about the internal processes of organizations that systematically practice violence. Groups may create or recruit terrorists more easily when there is widespread dissatisfaction and may undermine political institutions more readily when these institutions are divided or irresolute, but as for the initial turn to violence we have no general explanations except those offered by the terrorists themselves.

Were all the facts available to us, we would probably conclude that different explanations are necessary for different organizational forms of violence. What Samuel P. Huntington calls "praetorian" violence—the *coup d'etat* or palace revolt aimed at securing office or patronage without challenging governing norms—may be thought of as a form of conventional politics in countries with traditions of violence and weak constitutional principles.[24] Labor violence arises, as Garson has shown, out of the particular conditions of industrial relations in strategic sectors. "Communal" violence between different religious, ethnic, or racial groups is an extreme form of a heightened sense of nationalism or group identity stimulated by real or imagined threats arising from the incursions or domination of another group.[25] Contemporary urban terrorism as practiced by radical political sects such as the FLQ in Quebec, the Tupamaros in Uruguay, and the Weathermen in the United States is caused by small groups of radicalized and alienated middle-class students and intellectuals who share a belief in the possibility of fundamental revolution and have concluded that systematic violence will overextend the regime, drive it to repressive countermeasures, and thus stimulate a popular withdrawal of legitimacy from it.[26]

Each kind of organized violence—praetorian, labor, communal, and ideological—has some characteristic features. Praetorian and labor violence are examples of force being used for limited, specific, and often tangible objectives—power, money, organizational recognition, institutional control—and it usually ceases when the objective is attained. Communal violence is the classic civil war in which no clear objective other than destroying the opponent may exist. It arises when feelings of group solidarity are simultaneously intensified and threatened, and, because group survival appears to be at stake, the conflict will tend to be especially bloody and protracted. Ideological violence will have specific objectives, but not the sort that can be met by wresting concessions from the state; indeed, concessions sometimes only sharpen the struggle. Broad institutional and social change is sought over the opposition of the regime and the indifference of the masses, and thus violence will be sustained but selective, aimed at delegitimizing the regime by forcing it to act in ways that will divide and arouse the larger population.

These different organizational sources of violence, and the distinctive patterns seemingly associated with each source, suggest that the analysis of organized political violence can be carried out in terms of organizational analysis generally: the nature of the incentive system of each group, the relationship between those rewards and stated objectives, and the constraints and opportunities these factors create for leaders. Clearly, violence for utilitarian ends is different from that which arises out of feelings of group solidarity, and that in turn differs from violence as a purposive, ideological strategy.

We do not have the facts with which to pursue such tantalizing possibilities. Nor can we explain the circumstances under which utility, solidarity, or purpose will lead persons to adopt violent tactics. But however violence begins, its continuance is easier to explain, for in many cases it becomes a self-sustaining process fed by its own conspiratorial life style and its appeal to certain kinds of potential recruits. Persons psychologically predisposed to violent tendencies, as well as members of the underworld, are drawn toward the terrorist organization: the Provisionals of the Irish Republican Army (IRA) have enlisted petty criminals in Belfast, as has the FLQ in Quebec and as did the FLN in Algiers.

The IRA, perhaps the oldest continuous organization practicing

political violence, offers a case study of the self-sustaining, almost autonomous nature of a commitment to force. From the Irish Civil War to the
present, the attraction of the IRA has in part depended on its willingness to fight. As explained by Tim Pat Coogan, a sympathetic observer:

The use of force is a dilemma which the movement can never solve. The guns,
the excitement and the secrecy attract new members thirsting for adventure.
The guns go off and the authorities act. Take away the guns and the excitement and how do you offer a credible possibility of achieving the IRA's object-
tives and so attract new members? [27]

NOTES

1. This definition of protest is a modification of my earlier formulation in James
Q. Wilson, "The Strategy of Protest: Problems of Negro Civic Action," *Journal of
Conflict Resolution,* III (September 1961), 291–303. The present usage is a general
conceptualization of which both my previous definition and the alternative suggested
by Michael Lipsky are special cases. See Lipsky, *Protest in City Politics: Rent
Strikes, Housing and the Power of the Poor* (Chicago: Rand McNally, 1970), pp.
1–2.
2. See Lipsky, *Protest in City Politics,* p. 2.
3. Lawrence N. Bailis, "Bread or Justice: Grassroots Organizing in the Welfare
Rights Movement" (Ph.D. dissertation, Department of Government, Harvard University, 1972), chap. 10.
4. Lipsky, *Protest in City Politics,* p. 78.
5. Organizing white-collar workers has been most successful in the public employment sector. In the private sector, the Retail Clerk's International Association has
been growing rapidly but chiefly by organizing sales workers who, though they may
wear white collars, are in fact performing routinized blue-collar jobs in large self-
service food stores. See Michael Harrington, *The Retail Clerks* (New York: John
Wiley, 1962), chap. 1.
6. Howard Hubbard, "Five Long Hot Summers and How They Grew," *The Public Interest* (Summer 1968), pp. 3–24, is an analysis of how Martin Luther King, Jr.,
and others converted a failing civil rights effort into a successful one by becoming
conspicuously victimized in Birmingham in 1963.
7. Richard E. Walton and Robert B. McKersie, *A Behavioral Theory of Labor Negotiations* (New York: McGraw-Hill, 1965), p. 281.
8. Ibid., p. 286.
9. Herbert S. Parnes, *Union Strike Votes,* Report Series No. 92, Industrial Relations Section, Department of Economics and Sociology, Princeton University (1956),
p. 61. In the sixty local unions in New Jersey that he studied, "most of the union
officers . . . were emphatic in asserting that the problem of 'selling' what they believed to be an acceptable contract to the rank and file almost always posed greater
difficulties than the problem of obtaining strike authorization" (p. 62).
10. Albert A. Blum, "Collective Bargaining: Ritual or Reality?" *Harvard Business
Review,* XXXIX (November–December 1961), 63–69, argues that "a large share of

collective bargaining is not conflict but a process by which the main terms of the agreement, already understood by the negotiators, are made acceptable not to those in charge of the bargaining but to those who will have to live with its results."

11. Walton and McKersie, *Labor Negotiations*, p. 344.

12. Murray Horwitz, "Power, Identification, Nationalism, and International Organizations" (paper, Research Center for Human Relations, New York University, 1963), p. 5.

13. Lipsky, *Protest in City Politics*, pp. 78–79.

14. The leaders of the March on Washington in 1963 were dismayed by the unwillingness of John Lewis, head of SNCC, to make a statement in support of the civil rights bill then before Congress and by what they took to be the intemperate language of his prepared speech and prevailed upon Lewis to change substantially the wording of his address. Emily S. Stoper, "The Student Nonviolent Coordinating Committee" (Ph.D. diss., Department of Government, Harvard University, 1968), pp. 69–72.

15. Harry Brill, *Why Organizers Fail: The Story of a Rent Strike* (Berkeley: University of California Press, 1971), chap. 6.

16. Jack L. Walker, "Protest and Negotiation: A Case Study of Negro Leadership in Atlanta, Georgia," *Midwest Journal of Political Science*, VII (May 1963), 99–124.

17. James Q. Wilson, *Negro Politics* (New York: Free Press, 1960), chap. 2.

18. G. David Garson, "Collective Violence Re-Examined: Alternative Theories of American Labor Violence," *Politics*, V (November 1970), 129–143, and Garson, "Collective Violence in America: 1863–1963" (Ph.D. diss., Department of Government, Harvard University, 1969). My analysis here closely follows, and is indebted to, that of Garson.

19. Philip Taft and Philip Ross, "American Labor Violence: Its Causes, Character, and Outcome," in *Violence in America: Historical and Comparative Perspective*, A Report of the Task Force on Historical and Comparative Perspectives to the National Commission on the Causes and Prevention of Violence, ed. Hugh Davis Graham and Ted Robert Gurr (Washington, D.C.: U.S. Government Printing Office, 1969), vol. I, pp. 221–301.

20. Ibid., p. 289.

21. Garson, "Collective Violence Re-Examined," pp. 136–137.

22. Alfred P. Sloan, *My Years with General Motors* (New York: Macfadden Bartell, 1965), p. 393.

23. Ted Robert Gurr, *Why Men Rebel* (Princeton, N.J.: Princeton University Press, 1970), and Ivo K. Feierabend et al., "Social Change and Political Violence: Cross-National Patterns," in Graham and Gurr, *Violence in America*, vol. II, pp. 497–542.

24. Samuel P. Huntington, *Political Order in Changing Societies* (New Haven, Conn.: Yale University Press, 1968), chap. 4.

25. Samuel P. Huntington, "Civil Violence and the Process of Development," *Adelphi Papers*, No. 83 (London: International Institute for Strategic Studies, 1971), pp. 10–14.

26. Robert Moss, "Urban Guerilla Warfare," *Adelphi Papers*, No. 79 (London: International Institute for Strategic Studies, 1971), p. 8; Jack Davis, "Political Violence in Latin America," *Adelphi Papers*, No. 85 (London: International Institute for Strategic Studies, 1972), pp. 18–20.

27. Tim Pat Coogan, *The I. R. A.* (London: Fontana, 1970), p. 50. See also J. Bowyer Bell, *The Secret Army: A History of the IRA, 1916–1970* (London: Anthony Blond, 1970), esp. pp. 376–380.

PART

V

Political Roles

CHAPTER 15

Organizational Representation

Organizations concerned about public policy represent themselves wherever politics is conducted, and sometimes, especially in the last ten years, that is as likely to be in the streets or on the picket line as before a congressional committee or an appellate judge. But mass activities do not create the problem of representation—namely, the strain produced by an organization and its representative acting, or being thought to act, in ways not consistent with each other's expectations. Organization members may suspect that their representative is not acting in their interests, or is acting either imprudently or timidly, whereas the representative may feel that his constituents are indifferent to the problem, naive about the issues, or unsophisticated about the realities of government policy-making. These strains—or the anticipation of these strains—affect organizations seeking to intervene in the complex and often obscure world of executive agencies and legislative committees.

This is, of course, the world of the "lobbyist." That term, by its origins (it refers to men who hound the lobbies of legislatures trying to buttonhole lawmakers) and its legal definition (the Federal Regulation of Lobbying Act of 1946 describes a lobbyist as someone who seeks to influence congressional legislation) is too narrow to describe what organizational representatives in fact do. Someone who speaks on behalf of a block club before a city zoning commission, who argues an organizationally sponsored *amicus* brief before a court, who appears before a state regulatory commission on behalf of an industry, or who participates by virtue of a group connection in the drafting of a piece of legislation—all these persons are performing a representational function, and each could be called a "lobbyist" in the broadest sense of that term.

But not only does the term have excessively narrow connotations, it also conveys, at least in popular usage, an image of material interest, skillful maneuver, and group influence. Indeed, for a time some scholars argued for the possibility of a "group interpretation of politics" that, though more complex and less sinister than the popular view of the rapacious lobbyist, would explain the institutions of government as "centers of interest-based power." [1]

Of late, the views put forth by the journalists and by the scholarly group theorists have undergone substantial criticism. Perhaps the most important critique can be found in a classic study of the politics of foreign trade legislation between 1953 and 1962. Expecting to find in the struggle to enact tariff revisions, with all that these revisions would imply for the material interests of hundreds of business firms, clear evidence of the decisive role of lobbies, the authors were surprised to find instead that "the lobbies were on the whole poorly financed, ill-managed, out of contact with Congress, and at best only marginally effective in supporting tendencies and measures which already had behind them considerable Congressional impetus from other sources." [2] Though the legislation would have turned out somewhat differently had no lobbies existed at all, the typical lobby that did exist had few opportunities for effective maneuver, a mediocre staff, and critical problems of organizational maintenance. Finding clients and contributors was, for many of these groups, more important than influencing Congress. Though Bauer, Pool, and Dexter do not deny the collective importance of political organizations in helping manage the communications process that is part of legislative activity, they provide substantial evidence in support of the doubts they raise about the lobbying effectiveness of any particular "pressure group."

Old legends die hard, and many persons find it difficult to accept an image of lobbyists as anything but single-minded, ruthless, and powerful. And in fact there are cases in policy areas other than tariff revision in which organized interests appear to be highly effective. One of the best known involves the generally successful efforts of the oil industry to maintain the oil import quota system by which the importation of foreign crude oil into the eastern United States was restricted to 12.2 percent of domestic production and the oil depletion allowance by which a producer is permitted to deduct a substantial fraction—before 1969, 27.5 percent, and after that, 22 percent—of the revenues from each oil well from his taxable income. Efforts, including those of presidential task forces, to end or reduce the import quotas were defeated until 1973; attempts to reduce the depletion allowance were completely frustrated before 1969, and even when it was reduced, the change was kept to a modest level. In these and related issues, various writers have claimed that the organizations representing the oil industry—the American Petroleum Institute, the Independent Petroleum Association of America, the National Petroleum Refiners Association, and the Independent Natural Gas Association of America, plus a variety of state and regional groups—effectively served the oil industry's political interests.[3] The published accounts are notably lacking in any detailed discussion of the behavior of the *organizations* as opposed to the political success of the *industry,* but the authors assume that this expensive array of associations would not be maintained were it of no value.

Even in their careful study of foreign-trade legislation, Bauer, Pool, and Dexter find examples of lobbying organizations that were effective. One of these was the American Cotton Manufacturers Institute (ACMI), representing the southern textile industry, and the other was a coalition of groups concerned about oil imports—chiefly, the National Coal Association, the United Mine Workers, and the Independent Petroleum Association of America, plus certain railroads. Beginning in about 1955, the ACMI was successful in stimulating southern congressmen, traditionally supporters of free trade, to cast votes in favor of protection of domestic industry. The passage of the 1962 reciprocal trade bill was apparently assured only after President John F. Kennedy made agreements to restrict the importation of Japanese textiles, to ban certain cotton imports from Hong Kong, and to confer a subsidy on domestic cotton growers.[4] The coalition opposing imports of foreign oil was also successful in getting the 1955 trade act amended to create the import quota system already discussed.

Other examples could no doubt be adduced. The effort to repeal or modify the treatment of capital gains in the Tax Reform Act of 1969 was defeated in part through the efforts of groups representative of the securities industry.[5] At the same time, there were a host of legislative proposals in which the role of organized groups was minimal or at best marginal—the proposed Family Assistance Plan, the Economic Opportunity Act, the auto safety act and various other consumer protection bills, anticrime bills (such as the Safe Streets Act), and legislation dealing with the space program.

There are at least two ways to explain variations in the role and effectiveness of political organizations in forcing the passage of legislation. The first is based on the differing characteristics of the organizations themselves (their activities, structure, leadership, and incentives); the second derives from the characteristics of the issues that these groups confront (the incidence of costs and benefits and the presence or absence of broad symbolic significance). The two explanations are not mutually exclusive; indeed, it is likely that organizations with certain characteristics are more effective in handling issues of a certain nature. In this chapter, we shall examine organizational explanations of variations in political representation, and in the next chapter, issue-related ones.

The Representative and His Organization

E. E. Schattschneider, writing in 1935 concerning the tariff revision of 1929–1930, concluded his analysis of pressure-group activity by observing that "equal stakes do not produce equal pressures." Though thousands of businesses stood to gain or lose from the way the new tariff schedule was written, only certain kinds of industries, and thus only certain kinds of trade associations, played an active part in the legislative struggle. In general, those favoring a new or higher duty were more active than those favoring lower duties or none at all; opposition to duties from economic groups arose only when the imposts threatened the industries' existence.[6] Schattschneider explains this pattern by the fact that a new or higher duty provides a direct, immediate, material benefit to the affected industry but imposes only an indirect, partial, and distant cost on other industries: "benefits are concentrated while costs are distributed."[7]

The tariff legislation of 1955 and 1962 studied by Bauer, Pool, and Dexter was of a quite different kind: no specific duties were enacted, but instead discretionary authority over tariffs was conferred on the president. Here the situation had a different effect on organizational incentives: there was little benefit available to the proponents of specific tariff levels, because none was to be enacted. Generalized proponents of protectionism (such as the Nationwide Committee of Industry, Agriculture, and Labor on Import-Export Policy) and generalized proponents of free trade (such as the Committee for a National Trade Policy) had an incentive to act, inasmuch as the supporters of protectionism were likely to be hurt by almost *any* exercise of presidential discretion, whereas the proponents of free trade were committed to the general idea of a liberal trade policy. But neither association was of decisive importance because both were composed of members with quite divergent interests—the Nationwide Committee included chiefly manufacturers of bicycles, glassware, and chemicals, while the Committee for a National Trade policy consisted chiefly of large multinational corporations in diverse industries. The two most effective associations were in each case those whose members had similar material stakes in the outcome and which were able to focus their political efforts on specific legislative amendments or governmental actions that would avert major threats to them—the ACMI and the National Coal Association.

In 1951 David B. Truman noted the general advantages that accrue to groups that are on the defensive. He explained these advantages, however, entirely in terms of general social and political relationships, such as the many opportunities for delay and obstruction inherent in the American legislative process.[8] Though this is true enough, it omits the internal organizational-maintenance advantages of being on the defensive. For one thing, threats to existing material or nonmaterial interests are easier to understand and less productive of disagreement than are opportunities to improve or extend those interests. Rights or income now enjoyed provide a lowest common denominator of interest and agreement; proposals for enlarging those rights or increasing that income are likely to be discounted, unless they offer the prospect of immediate and direct benefit. If the gains are in the future, if indeed they will be realized at all, there will be an unwillingness to bear present costs of programs that have no guarantee of success. Other things being equal, political activity is facilitated by the same conditions that make organizational formation easier—namely, perceived threats to existing values.

There is in addition to this rationalistic explanation for the mobilizing effects of threats a social psychological one: threats, if they arise from outside a group, tend to increase group cohesiveness and integration and heighten the attraction that group members feel toward one another. Various experiments have concluded that harsh or badgering treatment of a group by an outsider decreases hostility within the group and increases cooperativeness.[9] When a group of shopkeepers was getting organized, those who felt most threatened became most attracted to the group and its leaders.[10]

If this theoretical perspective is correct, then we can offer a better understanding of why materially induced associations are regarded so often (and so pejoratively) as vested interests. It is assumed that such groups simply prefer the *status quo* and are opposed to change. But any familiarity with the members of trade associations is sufficient to make one realize that many members, perhaps all, would greatly prefer lower taxes and less constraining labor legislation. Having a material interest in these matters, however, they realize that the size of the benefit from any feasible change—from any obtainable tax reduction or amendment of the labor code—is likely to be rather small, the chances of obtaining it not great, and thus the combined value, or expected utility, of action toward the new benefit low. From time to time, of course, such groups do strive to achieve such goals, as when various business organizations sought in the 1950s to obtain the passage of state right-to-work laws that would outlaw the union shop. They failed in most key industrial states, and the memory of that failure and its cost persist to discourage those who might otherwise think that a materially induced association can profitably become change oriented.

The advantages to the organization, or to the organization's representative, of being able to mobilize around a distinct threat or a symbolically important moral issue are likely to be greatest, of course, when the members of the organization perceive the threat or issue in similar ways, and this similar point of view is most likely to occur when the members of the organization are more or less alike in material interest or personal ideology. It is for this reason, among others, that it is frequently asserted that large organizations with diverse memberships are less likely to take positions on controversial issues than are small associations with homogeneous memberships; it is further asserted that when a large organization does take a position, it tends not to prosecute it vigorously. Bauer, Pool, and Dexter, for example, argue that "the broader and more heterogeneous the organization, the greater the probability that some subgroups will dissent on a given issue." [11] They note that the National Association of Manufacturers (NAM) took no position on foreign-trade legislation and that the United States Chamber of Commerce took a wooden and quite cautious position. Even the National Electrical Manufacturers Association, a far more narrowly based organization, was unable to take a position on the trade bill of 1955, nor was General Electric, though various departments *within* the firm did take a stand.[12]

But this generalization is supported only by a case study of a single issue. More recently, an examination of the congressional testimony of the Chamber and the NAM between 1961 and 1968 reveals that the two organizations together presented positions on an average of fifty bills each session. The Chamber testified on every bill described in its *Washington Reports,* and the NAM spoke out on every bill but one mentioned in its *NAM Reports*—the sole exception being tariff legislation.[13] Most of this testimony was on noncontroversial matters, but during this period there were seventy-nine instances when the Chamber or the NAM testified on a matter in opposition to another significant group. The Chamber or NAM position prevailed in about two-thirds of the cases, though the proportion of successes fell to about one-half when these business groups had to face the combined opposition of the White House and the AFL-CIO.[14]

This picture presented by McKean of active and successful representation by two heterogeneous business associations contrasts sharply with the more passive or timid view suggested by Bauer, Pool, and Dexter. The two views can be partially reconciled by considering the *kinds* of controversial issues on which the Chamber or NAM spoke out. In general, they tended to be bills that either affected business *as a whole* (for example, minimum-wage, tax, antitrust, right-to-work, or picketing legislation) or involved broad issues of social welfare, consumerism, or ecology (public housing, public works, social security, Medicare, Model Cities, water- and air-pollution control, women's rights, foreign aid, desalinization, and vocational education legislation). In short, the business groups testified on those matters that, though controversial in society as a whole, were not likely to divide businessmen along lines of corporate or industrial interest. The tariff bill studied by Bauer, Pool, and Dexter was, of course, deeply divisive. Interestingly enough, the Chamber-NAM position tended to prevail on matters that affected the business community as a whole, but it did not prevail on matters of broad social welfare policy.

In the light of this, it may seem anomalous that the CIO, certainly a diverse organization whose members have sharp material interests, was able at the national level to take a strong position in favor of free trade. But the incentives that hold the average member to his union have little to do with foreign trade, and thus the national leadership is relatively free to express its personal, or staff-formed, views on these matters. Those unions that *do* have a material stake in trade policy, such as those locals of the United Auto Workers involved in bicycle manufacturing, dissented from the national CIO position.

Indeed, it is only a slight exaggeration to say that among the larger, more heterogeneous political organizations, it is those whose members have *no* dominant material stake in the outcome that find it easiest to take a position. The League of Women Voters was quite active on behalf of a freer trade policy, and such purposive organizations as the Americans for Democratic Action (ADA), the Americans for Constitutional Action, and the American Civil Liberties Union (ACLU) take positions—with what effectiveness is another matter—on a vast range of issues. Because of this, broadly based organizations often tend to acquire a semipartisan status: that is, lacking any focus on a single issue of overriding importance, and having to pick a mix of issues that are consistent with, if not central to, the organization's incentive system, such associations will take positions that are consistent from the point of view of some general political outlook or ideology.

Thus, the ADA, the ACLU, the AFL-CIO, the National Farmers' Union, and the National Grange have, on the whole, taken positions that are similar to those of the liberal wing of the Democratic party, while the Chamber of Commerce, the NAM, the American Farm Bureau Federation, the American Medical Association, and the Americans for Constitutional Action have adopted a stance that places them closer to the Republican party. There are obviously exceptions to this pattern: the national AFL-CIO, which for many years had become politically indistinguishable from the national Democratic party, opposed that party's presidential candidate in 1972. And other broadly based organizations, such as the League of Women Voters, have taken great pains to maintain their nonpartisan posture, though the League's positions have almost invariably been "liberal" in the loose sense of the term.

That large associations develop a more or less coherent and consistent set of political positions may in part reflect the material interests of an occupational grouping—doctors, for example, are perhaps better off leaning toward a party that does not work for Medicare and compulsory health insurance than toward one that does. But this consistency of position also reflects the tendency of any organization to acquire, for reasons of maintenance, a "distinctive competence" or "organizational climate" of the sort described in earlier chapters. Associations, if they are to retain their attractiveness in the eyes of members, must have a reasonably clear identity, which means, in turn, a reasonably predictable posture. Whenever political issues are raised in social structures, there is a desire on the part of most persons to make their affiliations and loyalties consistent, and thus to eliminate the strain and tension that come from being involved in inconsistent social relationships. The more salient the issue, the greater the desire for affiliational consistency.[15]

Creating generalized loyalties and a distinctive organizational identity is one thing; converting these resources into effective political action is another. Groups faced with a dramatic threat to clear interests or seeking a single objective of overriding moral significance are often able to raise large sums of money or produce equivalent commitments of time and effort. But even in these cases what constitutes a "threat" or a "clear interest" is not always self-evident. Paul W. Cherington and Ralph L. Gillen interviewed nineteen Washington representatives of large American corporations. These men, most of whom spent some of their time lobbying, reported that it was not easy to get their company to take a position on an issue. As one said: "This is one of the most difficult problems of all—to get the various heads together in the company and decide: 'Is this good or bad and, if it is bad, what do we want to do about it?'" The press of routine corporate business left higher executives with little time for, or interest in, arguments from their representatives in Washington about the importance of complex pieces of proposed legislation. Most of these representatives considered their superior officers as "too provincial" and excessively preoccupied with business. These officers, in turn, often regarded lobbying as barely respectable and felt that those employees who had this responsibility were relatively unimportant members of the corporate hierarchy.[16]

Business firms prefer to leave most governmental business to their trade associations,[17] but this deference does not necessarily put the associations in a strong position. Bauer, Pool, and Dexter report that the business executive often regarded the trade association director as a man who has never been tested by the need to meet a payroll, and who is raising many issues because he has an ax to grind—namely, keeping his association, and thus his own job, alive. The association director, on the other hand, often saw the business executive as a parochial amateur who did not understand the realities of political life, who lacked the foresight and energy to deal effectively with important issues, and whose own particularistic concerns about winning a government contract or furthering personal ambitions created problems within the association with which the director must deal.[18] One response to this divergence of view is for the business firm to leave routine or industry-wide matters to the trade association but to act alone, as a firm, when its vital interests are singularly at stake.

The political representative, whether in Washington or elsewhere, is torn to some degree by the problem of reconciling what he must do to maintain his organization with what he must do to advance his cause among government officials. To mobilize his constituency, he must dramatize issues, sound the alarm, and call for help. Much of the time, this earns him at best a mild accolade for doing his job and at worst some reproach for "crying wolf" and inflating his own importance. But on occasion, an issue catches on and the alarm is heeded. Then he is likely to be regarded as too timid or perhaps even lacking in loyalty and commitment when he attempts to explain that, in politics, zeal is not enough and that politicians cannot be divided unambiguously into good guys and bad guys. The representative has built up friendships and contacts in government, and he views these as assets to be preserved; his aroused constituents may see these contacts either as no asset at all or as a valuable resource that should be "spent" immediately on the present campaign rather than conserved in part for future ones. If he tries to maintain his government contacts or otherwise seeks to temper his constituents' enthusiasm, he risks being accused of "selling out." [19]

This problem can be seen more clearly if we contrast the role of an association's political representative with that of its electoral activist. Some unions, for example, have both lobbyists and campaign directors. The lobbyist must operate within the confines of legislative and administrative institutions that are populated by a relatively small number of persons each of whom is reasonably knowledgeable about the issue and most of whom will be important to the lobbyist on future issues. Some of these officials will be men with whom the representative does not agree on many, perhaps most, matters—conservative Republicans, for example, with whom a liberal unionist is trying to work on tariff issues. The lobbyist is likely to be preoccupied with the specifics, often the minutiae, of particular bills or executive orders and may seek to trade support on one item for support on another. The electoral campaign director, on the other hand, operates within the realm of public opinion and especially the opinion of party and union activists at the local level. Few of them are familiar with the details of policy alternatives; most of them will instead respond only to bolder, more dramatic appeals, often of an ideological nature. If they are liberals, they will support only liberal candidates, and if conservatives, only conservative ones, with little regard for the bargains a lobbyist may have struck with a particular candidate or for the value of retaining access to a very senior and influential legislator with whom one can do business on some matters. A rational strategy for such an association would, of course, call for coordinating the negotiations of the lobbyist with the efforts of the campaign director so that the rewards of electoral support are calibrated rather precisely to the value of the legislative bargain. In fact, the rational strategy is seldom feasible because of the differing, and partially incompatible, roles involved and inducements employed.

There are ways by which associations can partially overcome the strains of political representation. One is by being a single-issue organization that need conserve no influence or access for other policies. The Anti-Saloon League and various antiwar groups have been of this type. This strategy is not tried as often as one might suspect, however, partly because organizations of enthusiasts tend to take on more than one issue in order to meet the demands of members (antiwar groups, for example, may have to endorse women's rights in order to retain key female members and civil rights in order to attract black supporters) and partly because organizations that are formed to deal with one issue tend to persist and thus search for other issues in order to do so. Another method of minimizing strain is not to divide the representational and the executive functions, but to have one person (the president of a corporation, the director of a voluntary association, the leader of a protest group) perform both. But this minimizes strain only to the extent that the strain arises out of disagreement between representative and executive; it obviously is no advantage at all if the strain is created by the inherently different aspects of the *roles*. If one person plays both roles, he will simply have to internalize the strain as best he can, and at the cost of sacrificing the advantages of a division of labor.

A final method is to make maximum use of the possibilities of specialization. If different persons are assigned responsibility for different issues, then each can work vigorously on behalf of his specialty with the organization executive dealing only with important conflicts. In the language of economists, this pursuit of partially independent objectives leads to "suboptimization." The growing use of lawyers as representatives may reflect the advantages of being single-minded as well as the need to have highly trained personnel working on complex issues. A corporation or a trade association, for example, may retain one firm of lawyers to handle tax issues, another to handle labor issues, and a third to handle antitrust matters. The lawyers themselves often prefer this arrangement, because it permits them to develop a specialized competence and reduces the chances of their being thought lacking in professional integrity because they have espoused a contradictory point of view.[20]

The Representative and Government

It is now well understood that what an organizational representative does in furthering his group's interests before government has more to do with his management of a communications system than with his exercise of influence. "Pressure groups" rarely "press."

The reasons for this are not hard to find, once one is prepared to accept a narrow definition of "influence." If by influence one means any action by a person that alters the probabilities of actions by other persons, then clearly there is scarcely any behavior that is not "influential." If by influence, however, we mean actions by one person that lead another person to act other than as he would freely choose to act, then most studies of organizational representation suggest that influence is rather uncommon. Most congressional representatives, for example, state to interviewers investigating the passage of a bill that they felt no "pressure," by which they seem to mean that no person with views they opposed made any serious effort to impose, by argument, sanctions, or threats, those views on them.[21]

There is, of course, a substantial gray area between the broad and narrow definitions of influence. The remembrance of past campaign contributions may be evoked by a lobbyist, though neither money nor campaigns is ever mentioned. Legislators and administrators who cherish the goodwill of celebrities, rich men, students, or newscasters may alter their own preferences, perhaps unconsciously, to accord with what they take to be the preferences of their reference group. Public officials may regard certain groups as legitimate or proper sources of opinion and facts on an issue and other groups as illegitimate, even though the legitimate group employs no technique of influence and the latter attempts to employ several. This has been referred to as the "mobilization of bias" and means that though no clear or overt acts of influence occur in making decisions, the net effect of those decisions that are made may be to favor one group or interest in society at the expense of another.[22]

Here we are interested, not in what biases may appear in policy, but rather in the activities of those who seek to produce one bias (or, as they would see it, one conception of the public interest) rather than another, recognizing that some of the biases that do occur may be the result of institutional arrangements, procedural rules, or common understanding that have nothing to do with organizational behavior. The first task of an organizational representative is to ensure that his objective is deemed a proper subject for public action and that his association is a legitimate spokesman in that debate. This requires, in turn, ensuring that the issue is regarded as a *public* matter (and not something to be left to private arrangements), that existing policy on the issue is *problematic* (and not something about which "all right-thinking people agree"), and that a particular organization has a *right* to have its views on the issue taken seriously (and is not to be regarded as the view of a collection of cranks and thieves).

At one time, prohibiting the sale of alcohol was a national public issue, and the views of various temperance groups were given respectful attention; today, such a policy is not regarded as a feasible or proper subject of national action, and temperance societies are largely ignored. At one time it was unthinkable to debate lowering the penalties for marijuana use or granting amnesty to draft resisters; today, both have become quite thinkable. In general, an organizational representative can do relatively little about putting an issue on the public agenda and cloaking his group with legitimacy; such matters depend more on broad changes in public opinion, in dramatic or critical events, and in the behavior of the organization as a whole (as protesters, for example). What he can and must do is to ensure that legitimacy once gained is never lost and that, if possible, his organization is given a privileged position in the making and administration of policy. For example, we rarely today debate the propriety of giving various subsidies to the veterans of wars, but that does not mean the American Legion is without importance; rather, it means that the Legion's influence is now institutionalized in the form of its consultative participation in the management of the Veterans Administration.

On important or divisive issues, an organizational representative can enhance his group's legitimacy if he can describe it as broadly representative of all relevant affected interests. This, in turn, often requires him to enter into coalitions with other organizations, something any given organization is not likely to relish, for reasons given in Chapter 13, especially if a coalition becomes an enduring arrangement that places constraints on the organization's own freedom of action. But an organizational representative knows that policy-makers see a broad coalition as an indication that a majority of the affected parties are behind a policy, that there is accordingly only one "right" course of action, and above all that his organization's interest in it is not narrowly self-serving.[23] Some of these coalitions persist as loose confederations with impressive-sounding names (for example, Committee for a National Trade Policy or the Leadership Conference on Civil Rights); many more fade from sight after the issue is resolved.[24]

Not only in assembling an ad hoc coalition, but even in mobilizing his own organization, the representative often plays an important role in defining the group's interest. Sometimes that interest is perfectly clear, as when the large oil companies work to prevent the revocation of the oil import quota or when the securities industry lobbies to preserve the special tax treatment of capital gains. But on many other issues, especially those where no *existing* benefit is threatened, organizational representatives often have the task of persuading their constituents of what their "self-interest" requires. The National Coal Association, for example, brought together an effective coalition of railroads, small oil companies, and coal companies to oppose oil imports in 1955. The coal industry had an obvious interest in reducing the competition from imported oil as a source of fuel for domestic and industrial purposes, but it was far from clear that the railroads had an equally unequivocal stake in the outcome. Though railroads transported coal, and thus would lose money if the demand for coal fell, they also were operating more and more diesel locomotives, and thus would suffer from an increase in the cost of fuel oil. Even some of the oil companies had investments in foreign oil fields and thus might benefit from greater sales of that foreign oil in the United States. Bauer, Pool, and Dexter recount the successful efforts by the National Coal Association to persuade railroads and oil producers that their interests lay with devising an import quota and thus in joining a coalition—the Foreign Oil Policy Committee—to further those interests. Though they joined, they were far from aggressive or even united in their posture; instead, they tended to let the spokesmen of the coal industry speak for them.[25] In a highly interdependent, complex economy characterized by firms with many lines of products and foreign as well as domestic investments, the implications of much legislation for the self-interest of a particular firm is likely to be equivocal unless, as was mentioned earlier, the law deals with business as a class rather than with a particular set of enterprises.

The clearer the apparent material stake of the organization's members in a policy issue, the more prompt, focused, and vigorous the action of the organization's representative. Small, relatively homogeneous associations have a simpler search problem and easier communications tasks. They can canvas all proposals within a defined policy area to see if any affect a concrete interest and then alert members and advise legislative friends and key administrators. Large, relatively diverse associations with purposive interests have a more difficult search problem and a more difficult communications problem. They must scan a wide range of policy areas, not to find issues that affect their members, but to find ones that will mobilize them, and then they must discover an appropriate and accessible set of public officials for the particular issue selected, explain the issue to members not previously versed in the policy area, and organize some form of associational response. Bernard C. Cohen, in examining how groups with these opposite characteristics responded to the proposed Japanese treaty in the early 1950s, found that small groups concerned with, for example, the implications of the treaty for the fishing industry, acted quickly, used all available means of communication to public officials, and intervened in the decision process sufficiently early when important provisions of the treaty were still being decided. Large, purposive organizations concerned about (for example) world peace acted more slowly, aimed their communications as much *at their own members* as at public officials, and intervened later in the decision process when the chances for altering the proposed treaty were fewer and more constrained.[26]

Whatever the timing or nature of the intervention, the experienced organizational representative will see his task as one of evoking, maintaining, and enhancing existing relationships with sympathetic or like-minded public officials. He, like the precinct captain of a political party, will devote most of his "contact" time to stimulating activity by, and providing information to, persons who he has reason to believe are in general agreement with him. Time, energy, and money are in short supply; diverting much of any of these resources to persons known, or suspected, to be opposed to you is less efficient than devoting them to persons who, once aroused and informed, will act on your behalf. And in any event, representatives are human: arguing with persons with whom one disagrees is an unpleasantness one would just as soon avoid. As a result of these factors, a representative tends to become "a service bureau for those congressmen [and other officials] already agreeing with him, rather than an agent of direct persuasion" for those who do not.[27]

The representative, indeed, can be thought of as a member of *two* organizations rather than one. The first is his constituent association; the second is that informal association of sympathetic legislators, administrators, staff assistants, and other representatives who maintain a standing interest in a certain policy area. The representative must serve the needs of both groups, needs that are similar but not always compatible.

The public official wants to build support for his proposals; he needs useful information and arguments; he seeks allies and publicity; he hopes to avoid embarrassment; and, if an elected official, he requires campaign funds. The lobbyist's association also seeks publicity, information, allies, support, and funds, but acts that will serve the officeholder's needs may not be the same as those that will serve the needs of the association. The officeholder can make a partial commitment to a policy as one of many proposals in which he is interested; the association may make a total commitment to the exclusion of all else. A public official may need to retain the goodwill of colleagues on committees and in bureaus, whatever his feelings about the issue; the lobbying association may wish to attack these colleagues as opponents. The organizational representative must mediate these differences as they arise.

In doing so, he sometimes acts as much as the agent of the public official as of the association. A legislator or his assistant, for example, may ask a lobbyist to help stimulate interest in a bill requiring automobiles to be equipped with safety devices because the legislator faces a tough reelection campaign and needs an issue that will give him visibility. A mayor may ask a civil rights leader to make certain demands on the city so that the mayor will have an opportunity to explain to the city council and the voters that he is being "forced" to submit a certain proposal for approval.

In managing these transactions, representatives may play different roles. Some will serve as "contact men" dealing with legislators; others will serve as campaign organizers drumming up grassroots support for, or pressure on, a particular legislator; others will simply gather information and alert constituencies.[28] Certain kinds of representatives may tend toward one role rather than another, though the data on this are not clear. One study suggests that labor union representatives are more likely to operate as contact men and to work with legislators as opposed to administrators.[29] Trade association representatives, by contrast, seem to dislike the contact role, especially if it involves lobbying legislators, and prefer working with officials in the executive branch.[30] This difference may be the result of the representatives' own conception of their status and function, or it may reflect the fact that labor unions are large membership organizations that are often active in electoral politics, whereas trade associations are relatively small associations that are less likely to play an active role in elections.

In choosing a role, certain legal constraints are important. The internal revenue laws deny tax exemption to any organization that devotes a "substantial part" of its activities to "attempting to influence legislation" or that participates in "any political campaign on behalf of any candidate for public office." [31] Contacting or urging the public to contact legislators in support of or opposition to a bill is proscribed for tax-exempt groups. The Committee for Economic Development, the National Congress of Parents and Teachers, the National Audubon Society, the Red Cross, the United Fund, and the Council on Foreign Relations are all tax-exempt under the law and thus are reluctant to seem to be politically involved, even though many of their interests are directly implicated in state and national legislation. Others, such as many trade associations and labor unions, must pay taxes and are free to lobby at will. Some associations, seeking both to raise money from persons who wish to claim a tax deduction for their gift and to continue their legislative activities, create parallel organizations for the specifically tax-exempt aspects of their program. Thus, the NAACP, which is not tax-exempt, has formed the NAACP Legal Defense and Educational Fund, which is; similarly, the League of Women Voters has created the League of Women Voters Education Fund. Occasionally, tax-exempt associations step over the line. In 1968, the Internal Revenue Service revoked the tax-exempt status of the Sierra Club, because it decided that the club's legislative activities went "well beyond any permissible limits of such endeavors for Federal income tax purposes." [32] At about the same time, the aggressive head of the club, David Brower, was forced out of office and formed the Friends of the Earth, which registered as a lobbying organization.

Nonorganizational Representation

Some of the strains of organizational representation can obviously be avoided if the presentation of policy positions is done by persons with no organizations to maintain, and thus with no compromises to be negotiated, no competing ambitions to be reconciled, and no incentives to be supplied.

There is a corresponding disadvantage: very few individuals have the status to be taken seriously as spokesmen for a point of view unless they can cloak themselves in some collective identity and mobilize, through concerted action, the resources of others. Because of this, almost all advocacy in politics is carried on, in fact or in theory, on behalf of some larger constituency: opinions are rarely *presented*, they are represented.

Occasionally, individuals acquire status and personal influence sufficient to enable them to speak effectively on their own behalf. One such
person has been Ralph Nader. That he acquired this position is to a
large degree an accident of circumstance—as one reporter put it: "This
town is full of guys who wander around with stacks of paper under their
arms trying to see senators or bust into magazine offices. Ralph is one
guy who got through the guards." [33]

How he "got through the guards" is, of course, a well-known story.
Nader had written a book, *Unsafe At Any Speed*, arguing that a certain
General Motors car was dangerous because of bad design. At about the
same time, he was working on a volunteer basis for the staff director of
a Senate subcommittee concerned with auto safety legislation and as a
paid consultant to Assistant Secretary of Labor Daniel P. Moynihan,
who had a long-standing interest in the prevention of highway acci-
dents. Neither the book nor his government service attracted much attention to Nader until reporters revealed that General Motors had hired
private detectives to investigate his background and personal habits.
When the story appeared, the Senate subcommittee summoned the president of General Motors before it and demanded an explanation; he
obliged by admitting the surveillance and apologizing for it.

The result of the subcommittee confrontation was to elevate Nader to
national prominence, to supply him with a responsive, but unorganized,
constituency, and to give official senatorial endorsement to his good
character and motives.

The crucial link between the man and his constituency was the press.
Nader was even more appealing to them than to the senators, for he appeared to be the quintessential journalist—a man who sought the facts
about public problems with single-minded devotion, who recounted
those facts without fear or favoritism, and who owed allegiance to nothing but his conscience. Nader, in turn, cultivated the press assiduously,
calling key reporters frequently, passing on facts and leads, and developing new investigation stories in fields other than auto safety. A senatorial hearing had found his motives to be above reproach; now reporters
were also able to learn that his facts were timely and, as far as they
could tell, accurate.

Nader has described himself as a "noninstitutional source," [34] by
which he meant that he was free of any need to advocate the interests of
others or to maintain an organization of others. In time, as students,
lawyers, and others volunteered to help him, Nader formed various

322

organizations—Nader's Raiders, the Center for Study of Responsive Law, the Public Interest Research Groups, the Center for Auto Safety, and others—but though he has retained control over the selection of personnel and the use of funds, Nader has not allowed himself to become involved in the management of these organizations. Because he retains ultimate authority but refuses to create hierarchies and procedures, there has been in many of these organizations a degree of rigidity and uncertainty that can be overcome only (if at all) by the workers' forbearance and personal devotion to Nader. Nader has undertaken some of the maintenance responsibilities for his organizations, especially fund raising, which he has accomplished by giving lectures, contacting foundations, and assigning book royalties to his centers. But the other aspects of organizational maintenance, especially the management of the incentive and communications systems and the resolution of interpersonal strain, he has left either to others or to the uncoordinated efforts of the members.

The result is a pattern of organization not dissimilar to that which Max Weber called a "charismatic community" in which the leader has disciples who serve at his call without either regular office, hierarchical relationships, or formal rules, and who are sustained by gifts from the faithful.[35] As one observer described the Nader organization, it is "not so much an administrative entity as a fellowship of the spirit. All energy is directed upward, like prayer. There is little communication among the parts. Everything must pass through Nader, and when he is not available, action is often suspended." [36]

The impact of Nader on public policy depends crucially on his identity and much less on his organization's activities: or more accurately, these activities, such as the reports of the Raiders, while of significance in themselves, acquire their public and institutional impact chiefly by virtue of Nader's name being associated with them. This identity, and the noninstitutional sense of morality that it has come to signify, is both an asset and a liability. Nader's admirers can point, as one did, to the fact that he appears to be "self-sustaining," "responsible only to his own conscience," and not required to deal with a "web of interests." [37] Those in government with whom he deals, on the other hand, see the absence of constraint as a disadvantage. As a staff member of a Senate committee put it: "Nader is assuming the role of an Ajax white knight with no reins on the horse. My instinct is to distrust anyone who doesn't have to answer to a constituency." [38]

Public officials are invariably part of an organizational and institutional nexus. One result of this is to make the actions of their colleagues predictable in some degree; another is to provide a pattern of rewards and penalties that require officeholders to assume responsibility in some measure for the consequences of their actions. The unorganized, noninstitutional advocate who has acquired public credibility is often seen by such persons—even by many of those who are in general agreement with him—as a threat because his acts, being unconstrained, are unpredictable and because his role, being noninstitutional, is devoid of any obligation to implement those policies necessary to solve a problem.

In Nader's case, the strengths or liabilities (depending on one's view) of his position can be seen in the relentless attacks he has made on the National Highway Safety Bureau, the agency created by the legislation Nader's work had helped pass, and on its first director, Dr. William Haddon, Jr. Haddon, the head of a fledgling organization with little staff, few funds, and no assured bureaucratic power, found to his surprise that Nader was not his ally, but his enemy—or as Nader would have viewed it, he found that Nader believed that the best way to help the agency was to attack it for doing too little and moving too slowly. To Haddon, beginning the process of regulating the auto industry was a difficult task for which few guidelines existed; to Nader, nothing justified any delay whatever in imposing the most rigid regulations. Haddon had an organizational view of the problem, Nader, a moralistic one. Nader explained his role to Haddon: "The best way to build government is to attack government." [39]

NOTES

1. David B. Truman, *The Governmental Process* (New York: Alfred A. Knopf, 1951), pp. 47, 506.
2. Raymond A. Bauer, Ithiel de Sola Pool, and Lewis Anthony Dexter, *American Business and Public Policy* (New York: Atherton, 1963), p. 324.
3. Robert Engler, *The Politics of Oil* (Chicago: University of Chicago Press, 1961), chap. 13, and Erwin Knoll, "The Oil Lobby Is Not Depleted," reprinted in *Introductory Readings in American Government*, ed. Robert S. Ross and William C. Mitchell (Chicago: Markham, 1971), pp. 298–310.
4. Bauer, Pool, and Dexter, *American Business and Public Policy*, pp. 359–362. It should be noted that this study offered detailed evidence only on the legislation of the 1950s.
5. Richard W. Hausler, "Inertia and Reform: Capital Gains Legislation in Congress, 1969," (senior honor's thesis, Department of Government, Harvard University, 1972).

6. E. E. Schattschneider, *Politics, Pressures and the Tariff* (Englewood Cliffs, N.J.: Prentice-Hall, 1935), pp. 106–108, 162–163.

7. Ibid., pp. 127–128.

8. Truman, *The Governmental Process*, pp. 353–354.

9. Leonard Berkowitz, "Social Motivation," in *The Handbook of Social Psychology*, 2nd ed., ed. Gardner Lindzey and Elliot Aronson (Reading, Mass.: Addison-Wesley, 1969), vol. III, pp. 65–66.

10. M. Mulder and A. Stemerding, "Threat, Attraction to Group, and Need for Strong Leadership," *Human Relations*, XIV (1963), 317–334.

11. Bauer, Pool, and Dexter, *American Business and Public Policy*, p. 339.

12. Ibid., p. 337.

13. John B. McKean, "The Legislative Success of Business Associations with Heterogeneous Memberships" (senior honor's thesis, Department of Government, Harvard University, 1970), p. 68.

14. Ibid., p. 87.

15. This is an organizational application of an argument developed about local politics in James S. Coleman, *Community Conflict* (Glencoe, Ill.: Free Press, 1959).

16. Paul W. Cherington and Ralph L. Gillen, *The Business Representative in Washington* (Washington, D.C.: The Brookings Institution, 1962), pp. 49–51.

17. Ibid., p. 50.

18. Bauer, Pool, and Dexter, *American Business and Public Policy*, pp. 330–331.

19. Lewis Anthony Dexter, *How Organizations Are Represented in Washington* (Indianapolis: Bobbs-Merrill, 1969), pp. 143–145.

20. Lester W. Milbrath, *The Washington Lobbyists* (Chicago: Rand McNally, 1963), p. 157.

21. The "communications model" of lobbying has come to dominate the literature. See Bauer, Pool, and Dexter, *American Business and Public Policy*, pp. 466–472; Malcolm E. Jewell and Samuel C. Patterson, *The Legislative Process in the United States* (New York: Random House, 1966), p. 297; Lewis Anthony Dexter, *The Sociology and Politics of Congress* (Chicago: Rand McNally, 1969), pp. 145, 171; Andrew M. Scott and Margaret A. Hunt, *Congress and Lobbies* (Chapel Hill: University of North Carolina Press, 1965), chap. 5.

22. Peter Bachrach and Morton Baratz, *Power and Poverty* (New York: Oxford University Press, 1970), p. 43; E. E. Schattschneider, *The Semisovereign People* (New York: Holt, Rinehart & Winston, 1960), p. 71. The phrase "mobilization of bias" is Schattschneider's.

23. Milbrath, *The Washington Lobbyists*, pp. 169–175.

24. See Donald R. Hall, *Cooperative Lobbying—The Power of Pressure* (Tucson: University of Arizona Press, 1969).

25. Bauer, Pool, and Dexter, *American Business and Public Policy*, pp. 363–374.

26. Bernard C. Cohen, "Political Communication on the Japanese Peace Settlement," *Public Opinion Quarterly*, XX (1956), 27–38.

27. Bauer, Pool, and Dexter, *American Business and Public Policy*, p. 353.

28. Jewell and Patterson, *The Legislative Process*, pp. 285–291.

29. Ibid., p. 286; Samuel C. Patterson, "The Role of the Lobbyist: The Case of Oklahoma," *Journal of Politics*, XXV (1963), 91.

30. Milbrath, *The Washington Lobbyists*, pp. 151–152.

31. *United States Code*, Title 26, Section 501 (c) (3).

32. *The Washington Lobby* (Washington, D.C.: Congressional Quarterly, 1971), p. 96.

33. Quoted in Charles McCarry, *Citizen Nader* (New York: Saturday Review Press, 1972), p. 107.

34. Ibid., p. 110.
35. Max Weber, *Economy and Society,* ed. Guenther Roth and Claus Wittich (New York: Bedminster Press, 1968), vol. I, pp. 243–245.
36. McCarry, *Citizen Nader,* p. 208.
37. Ibid., p. 168.
38. Ibid., pp. 168–169.
39. Ibid., p. 106.

CHAPTER 16

Organizations and Public Policy

The journalistic and scholarly mood about the importance of political organizations has varied from one of fascination with their power to one of amusement at their impotence, but whether reality has changed in accordance with the perceptions is far from clear. The plain fact is that no well-supported and comprehensive rendering of accounts about the impact of organizations on public policy is as yet possible. One of the reasons for this is that the significance of organizations will depend, in ways that are not fully understood, on the nature of both the issue and the institutional process by which it is resolved.

Issues and Organizations

Theodore J. Lowi has proposed a threefold classification of public issues and a set of hypotheses relating the kind of issue to the character of the political process ("arena of power") that it will evoke and to the extent and ways in which organized groups will participate in the decision. A *distributive* decision is one that provides, or appears to provide, specific benefits to specific groups "without regard to limited resources." Patronage is a distributive policy; so are defense contracts, government services to organized business, farm, or labor clienteles, the management of public land, and an item-by-item tariff. A *regulatory* decision involves a governmental choice as to "who will be indulged and who deprived" on the basis of some general rule: examples include awarding a television license, banning an unfair labor practice, and giving the president discretionary powers over foreign trade. Finally, a *redistributive* decision involves broad categories of citizens, "approaching social classes," to whom benefits are extended or from whom losses are taken. A progressive income tax and noncontributive welfare programs are important illustrations.[1]

Each of these policies of government has a characteristic political process associated with it. Distributive policies stimulate activity by small organizations and even by individuals, each seeking a particular benefit on the basis of "every man for himself." The government rewards all such activity so long as it does not appear that the benefits to one party are at the cost of another. "Log-rolling" is common; the legislative result is often called "pork barrel." Regulatory politics, by contrast, deal with "sectors"—industries, occupations, commodities—and thus the political process involves a higher degree of organization and coalition formation than is the case with distributive issues. These coalitions are not based on a desire for mutual noninterference but on shared interests in obtaining or defeating a regulatory proposal aimed at a sector of the economy. The trade association or local union is typically involved in regulatory matters. Redistributive policies encourage the activities of peak associations that have a broad, often ideological, interest in representing a social class: the National Association of Manufacturers and the Chamber of Commerce on one hand, the AFL-CIO and allied groups on the other. The "haves" and the "have nots," or the "money-providing" and "service-demanding" groups are decisive on these issues, and their leadership might be described as a "power elite."

Lowi's formulation is bold and imaginative but also ambiguous and incomplete. It is hard to distinguish the three arenas of power from one another except in extreme cases; there are broad areas of power that seem to fit nowhere in the scheme; and there are important changes over time in the way groups behave. Legislation to improve rivers and harbors seems clearly distributive in that it provides public facilities on a noncompetitive basis to particular areas, and thus we are not surprised to find that there is usually little legislative conflict and much mutually advantageous log-rolling in passing these bills. But the Area Redevelopment Act of 1961 also proposed to supply loans and facilities for certain regions (the "depressed" areas), and yet this act aroused the bitterest conflict and brought various peak associations into combat with one another. Four years later, the Appalachian Regional Development Act, also designed to provide aid to localities, sailed through Congress accompanied by relatively little organizational activity.[2]

There are a host of policies that could be classified under two or more categories. A bill barring discrimination in public accommodations could be seen as a measure regulating the use of hotels and restaurants or as one redistributing a benefit (access to hotels and restaurants) from one social stratum to another. The same could be said of policies concerning immigration, women's rights, or school desegregation. Urban renewal programs regulate the use of land, redistribute the housing supply, and distribute benefits to certain contractors and labor unions. Monetary and fiscal policy has both regulatory and redistributionist implications depending on whether one thinks of it as simply controlling the interest rate or as benefiting creditors at the expense of debtors (or vice versa). Calling attention to the costs and benefits of policies is helpful; classifying those costs and benefits under labels with uncertain meanings is not helpful.

Lowi suggests that the pluralist view of politics—by which he apparently means a view that argues that policy is the result of organized group conflict—is generally accurate only for the regulatory arena. This seems to be true for certain kinds of regulatory decisions, especially those that involve the competing demands of organized segments of the economy—such as struggles between labor and management over the definition of unfair labor practices, between wholesalers and retailers over the maintenance of fair-trade laws, or between two firms over the awarding of a television broadcast license. But there is a broad range of other regulatory issues in which group activity is modest, and the activity that does occur tends to be carried on by unsuccessful opponents. An example of this is the recent wave of consumer legislation. No organized interest can take credit for many of these laws, such as the National Traffic and Motor Vehicle Safety Act of 1966 and the 1962 Kefauver-Harris amendments to the Food and Drug Act. Mark V. Nadel, in his study of these and other consumer-protection bills, concludes that the "primary consumer groups are not effective" and that lobbying was far less important than the direct representation within key congressional committees of various points of view.[3] Consumer policies were often *opposed* by organized interests, but supported, at least in the ways that proved decisive, by congressmen who were aided by influential newspapermen and, in the case of auto safety, by Ralph Nader.

Lowi's fundamental insight—that the substance of a policy influences the role of organizations in its adoption—seems correct, but the conceptual scheme based on that insight requires modification in at least two ways. First, a distinction should be made between the adoption of a new policy and the amendment of an existing one, and second, the incidence of costs and benefits of a policy should not be obscured by the use of categories ("distributive," and so on) that are hard to define and to purge of misleading implications.

The most important new policies of government are adopted only after there has been a change in opinion or a new perception of old arrangements sufficient to place on the public agenda what had once been a private relationship and to clothe a particular program with legitimacy. Organized groups can rarely accomplish unaided such changes in opinion or such redefinitions of what constitutes legitimate public action; instead, these changes are the result of dramatic or critical events (a depression, a war, a national scandal), extraordinary political leadership, the rise of new political elites, and the accumulated impact of ideas via the mass media of communication. New policies born in this fashion include major social welfare measures, such as social security and Medicare, the selective service system, civil rights laws, new regulatory measures aimed at consumer protection, the creation of the Tennessee Valley Authority (TVA), the antipoverty program, the shift from an itemized tariff to a reciprocal trade policy, federal assistance to law enforcement and to education, foreign aid and various mutual security agreements, the federal interstate highway program, and some of the ecology legislation. Whether these measures are regarded as redistributive or regulatory is less important than the fact that they represent major redefinitions of the proper role and powers of government; they were controversial mainly in that people differed importantly over what it was legitimate for government to do. On some of these measures, such as social security, one social class was pitted against another; on others, such as foreign aid and aid to education, ideologies cutting across classes did battle with one another.

Sometimes political organizations assist in this process of agenda setting, as when trade unions struggled to obtain legal sanction for their conception of collective bargaining, when the NAACP demanded a federal role in civil rights, and when the Anti-Saloon League mobilized support for temperance. At other times, the new departure represented

the activities of policy entrepreneurs who, by combining personal skill, strategic institutional position, and fortuitous circumstance, managed to obtain consent for a new policy departure.[4] The development of the Economic Opportunity Act, the Family Assistance Plan (FAP), the Safe Streets Act, the tax reform act of 1969, the Model Cities program, revenue sharing, the TVA, the unsuccessful Brannan Plan for agriculture in 1949, the National Traffic and Motor Vehicle Safety Act, and the Consumer Credit Protection Act ("truth-in-lending") are illustrative of an essentially nonorganizational policy-development process.

The political locus of the key actors in these innovative policies varies. In general, legislation in the realm of social welfare and foreign policy has tended to originate in the executive branch, but consumer-protection legislation has tended to emerge from the initiatives of congressmen and their allies.[5]

Revisions to existing policies follow a different pattern that in turn depends on the extent to which the initial policy decision settled the ideological and normative issues and on the incidence of costs and benefits entailed ·by the program. Most of the new or enlarged powers acquired by government are soon taken for granted, and the debate over their propriety, if not their success, is stilled. Social security, most civil rights laws, regulatory policies, and the progressive income tax are no longer thought to be illegitimate extensions of public authority, though their administration and their efficacy are frequently questioned. Other programs retain for longer periods a controversial status and remain or become the objects of organized struggles. Welfare support of the unmarried mothers of children is one example; in the minds of many, it continually presents issues of morality and equity. Other programs remain controversial until an accommodation is reached with the groups whose interests they threaten to harm. The cessation of controversy over the TVA resulted from the adjustment of that agency, first to the organized farmers and land-grant colleges and then to the private power groups in adjacent regions.[6]

The extent and nature of organizational activity in an issue area will also depend on the incidence of costs and benefits. A cost may be widely distributed (as with the general tax burden, generally rising crime rates, the widespread practice of some objectionable act such as the sale of obscene literature) or it may be narrowly concentrated (as with a fee or impost paid by a particular industry or locality or a highway construction program that destroys a particular community). Similarly, a benefit may be widely distributed (as with social security and unemployment compensation payments or national defense) or narrowly concentrated (such as a subsidy paid to a particular industry or occupation, a tariff on a particular product, prestige conferred on a person or group, or a license to operate a television station). Note that costs and benefits may be intangible as well as tangible and that a widely distributed benefit may or may not be what economists call a "collective good"—that is, something from the enjoyment of which no one can feasibly be excluded. All collective goods, such as national defense, are a widely distributed benefit, but not all widely distributed benefits, such as social security payments, are collective goods. Policy changes can be crudely classified on the basis of whether the cost and benefits are widely distributed or narrowly concentrated from the point of view of those who bear the costs or enjoy the benefits.

DISTRIBUTED BENEFITS AND DISTRIBUTED COSTS

Policies that both confer benefits on, and spread the costs over, large numbers of persons will tend to become easily institutionalized and to produce increases in benefit levels without significant organizational intervention. In a democratic society, elected legislators have an incentive to raise the value of widely distributed benefits, especially if those benefits are material. Social security payments are usually increased in election years without the necessity of any lobbying effort; in time, Medicare benefits may also experience more or less automatic increases, as will income maintenance payments under FAP if it is ever adopted. The *initial* debate over FAP has been cast in moralistic and philosophical terms; subsequent reviews will be debated, if at all, in terms of economic and political benefits.[7] The interstate highway program is for similar reasons now *financially* noncontroversial, though insofar as its construction involves land clearance it imposes high, localized costs that render this aspect of it most contentious.

Whether a policy *has* a widely distributed benefit may not always be clear, especially if the benefit is not received in the form of individual cash payments or the equivalent. National defense may be seen as a great benefit at some periods and as a modest benefit, or no benefit at all, at other times. Increasing the number of officers in a police department may be thought to provide a greater degree of public safety even though crime rates may in fact show little sensitivity to any feasible change in the size of the police force. When the benefits are in the form of cash or of readily observable public services, such as street cleaning, governmental decisions about their magnitude rarely depend on important organizational activity. Public opinion is generally assessed directly by officials, and the electoral process generally ensures that legislators will have ample incentive to support publicly desired increases whether or not voluntary associations take an interest in the matter. Perhaps the major organization that becomes involved in issues of this type is the political party that seeks out and endorses programs with distributed benefits; cynics often call these policies "motherhood" issues.

Some organizations that represent groups for which the costs substantially exceed the benefits, such as some business and taxpayers' associations, will oppose increases in widely distributed benefits, though usually ineffectually unless they can acquire as an ally an important officeholder, such as the president or a governor, who has a stake in maintaining a general budget constraint.[8]

From time to time, the distributed costs of certain programs are seen as exceeding the value of the distributed benefits. This usually happens when there has been a sudden, sharp rise in costs—for example, large tax increases to support escalating school or welfare budgets. These increases will be felt by many persons as an insupportable new burden, the "straw that broke the camel's back"—precisely the sort of perception that offers ample opportunity for the organizational entrepreneur to create a new association. Its emergence is often described in the media as a "taxpayers' revolt." It is rarely successful because the same force—a sudden, adverse change—that stimulated the formation of the anticost group will lead to the formation of a probenefit group should politicians try to cut the budget sharply. Most officeholders, knowing that they cannot really reduce the education or welfare budget by any significant amount without precipitating an organized counterattack, rarely try very seriously to do so. Meanwhile, the anticost organization will attempt to minimize the threat it poses to the potential opposition by concentrating its fire on some budget item that can be plausibly described as a "frill." Though this may help neutralize the opposition, it rarely leads to large savings.

CONCENTRATED BENEFITS AND DISTRIBUTED COSTS

Programs that benefit a well-defined special interest but impose, or appear to impose, no visible costs on any other well-defined interest will attract the support of the organizations representing the benefited group and the opposition of none, or at best the hostility only of purposive associations having no stake in the matter. Of course, *all* programs that help a defined sector impose costs on somebody, but if the costs are widely distributed, usually in the form of generally higher taxes or prices, but the benefits narrowly concentrated, the beneficiaries will have an incentive to organize and will be able to mobilize effective political support for the policy. Veterans' benefits, agricultural subsidies, oil import quotas, and tariffs on many commodities are all examples of such programs.

Programs of this kind facilitate the emergence of voluntary associations that enter into a symbiotic relationship with the agency administering the program. There are any number of familiar examples—the National Rivers and Harbors Congress and the Army Corps of Engineers, the American Farm Bureau Federation and the Department of Agriculture, and veterans' organizations and the Veterans Administration. Some associations of this kind are in fact created by the agency or as a consequence of the agency's formation: the Soil Conservation Service stimulated the formation of the National Association of Soil Conservation Districts, and the Rural Electrification Administration helped bring into being the National Rural Electrification Cooperative Association.

Some government agencies never acquire a supportive political association (the State Department is usually cited as the leading example). By the same token, some important political associations never acquire a client agency. The NAACP, for instance, has helped pass a number of civil rights bills, but these have not led to the creation of an independent agency or bureau that the NAACP could regard as its bureaucratic counterpart. Similarly, the American Council on Education (ACE) has lobbied with some success on behalf of financial aid to colleges and universities, but there is no "Department of Higher Education" in the executive branch of government with which the ACE could enter into a mutually sustaining relationship.

DISTRIBUTED BENEFITS AND CONCENTRATED COSTS

When a specific, easily identifiable group bears the costs of a program conferring distributed benefits, the group is likely to feel its burdens keenly and thus to have a strong incentive to organize in order that their burdens be reduced or at the very least not increased. The politics of Medicare may be different from that of social security for just this reason: doctors feel that they are being asked to shoulder many of the burdens of the program (in the form of bureaucratic red tape, real or threatened control of fees, and the overcrowding of hospital facilities), and thus they fought its creation and continue to press for its modifica-

tion. The automobile manufacturers felt they were being asked, unfairly, to bear the burdens of auto safety, and other industries feel they are paying the burden of various ecological programs. Whether such objections persist, of course, will in part depend on how successful an affected group is in passing its costs on to others. Auto safety raises the prices of cars, but because all manufacturers are required to conform, all can pass the cost on to car buyers. On the other hand, a public utility required to bear the burdens of pollution control may find it difficult to pass along all the costs because the consumer has the option of substituting other forms of energy, for example, by buying more natural gas and less electricity.

Because of the organizational and tactical advantages conferred by a concentrated cost and the corresponding disadvantages imposed by a distributed benefit, it is easy to suppose that policies with these characteristics will rarely, if ever, be adopted. In fact they are, and perhaps with increasing frequency. The Sherman Antitrust Act of 1890, the Pure Food and Drug Act and the Meat Inspection Act of 1906, and the Public Utility Holding Companies Act of 1935 are early examples; the 1962 drug amendments, the auto safety act, and the various clean air and clean water bills are recent ones. Each represented, not the triumph of an organization but rather the successful mobilization of a new, usually temporary, political constituency. On occasion this was made easier by a dramatic crisis that put the opponents at a hopeless disadvantage— for example, the Depression, the thalidomide disaster, or the investigation of Nader. On other occasions the mobilization required no crisis but only the successful appeal, often through adroit use of the mass media, by a policy entrepreneur to a mass public in ways that made the goal being sought appear incontrovertibly good and the groups being opposed seem utterly self-serving. Once such legislation is adopted, however, the defeated opponents, still in being as a political association, may work hard to "capture" the agency administering the law while the victorious but unorganized supporters may turn their attention to other matters.

CONCENTRATED BENEFITS AND CONCENTRATED COSTS

Programs that benefit a well-defined group but at a cost to another well-defined group generate continuing organized conflict. Revisions and amendments and interpretations are endlessly contested and sometimes efforts are made to repeal the initial policy. The struggle between labor and management over control of the National Labor Relations

Board and the provisions of the Wagner Act is one example; the conflict over freight rates between railroads and the trucking industry before the Interstate Commerce Commission is another; the arguments over trade policy between corporations with large foreign markets and those with exclusively domestic ones is a third. Government bureaus mediating between the demands of organized competitors are less likely to be "captured" (or captured for long) by a single organized interest than are bureaus facing a single organized beneficiary.[9]

The role of the policy entrepreneur in modifying programs varies with the kind of issue. If benefits and costs are both dispersed and the former are perceived to exceed the latter, there is almost nothing one can do to effect a change other than to suggest even further increases in benefits. A radical change in social security, for example, would probably be all but impossible.

If benefits are concentrated but costs dispersed, the policy entrepreneur will seek to dramatize the costs, describe the benefits as accruing only to "vested" or "selfish" interests, and thereby call into question the motives of those public officials who support the program. He may try to organize those who pay the costs, but this will be extremely difficult, as the relative weakness of the general consumer associations suggests. The potential gain to a nonbeneficiary in taxes or prices is likely to be slight at best and thus will probably constitute no strong *material* inducement for associational activity. Organization is possible, but it will have to rely on purposive inducements. As a consequence, the leader has additional reasons for finding ways to portray the issue in moral or ethical terms.

If costs are concentrated but benefits dispersed, the entrepreneur will have a ready incentive to offer for organizational activity (that is, the possibility of reducing costs to those who pay heavily), but he will be under some obligation to portray the effort in public-spirited terms, so as not to arouse the indignation of the beneficiaries, and this means he will find it useful to supplement the material appeals with purposive ones.

Where both benefits and costs are concentrated, policy changes will generally only occur as the result of negotiating bargains among preexisting associations or of changing the political balance of power among them. The former involves a tedious process of mediation, the latter an effort to change the partisan or ideological coloration of the appropriate regulatory commission, congressional committee, or administrative bureau. This is very difficult to do (for example, commission members usually have staggered terms, and the key members of congressional committees usually come from safe districts) and will be fought every step of the way by the organized opponents.

Government Structure and Organizations

Both the locus and the strategy of representation will reflect the distribution of power within governmental structures, the general features of which were outlined in Chapter 5.

Special-interest associations are more powerful where formal political authority is weak or diffuse. Organized city employees—teachers, policemen, sanitation workers—play a more important role in cities with weak mayors and party systems (for example, Los Angeles and New York) than in cities with strong mayors and strong party systems (for example, Chicago and Albany). Where formal authority is highly centralized, as in the mayoralty of Chicago, there is little a special-interest group can do other than either petition the chief executive or enter into a coalition with him on his terms. The latter course has been followed by many of the unions, especially in the building trades, in Chicago.[10]

A similar pattern has been observed in certain state legislatures. Where the dominant political party is highly cohesive—that is, where legislative votes follow party lines very closely—lobbying organizations have been relatively weak.[11] Furthermore, if the governing party is cohesive, such lobbying efforts as do occur will be directed at the party leadership rather than at the party rank and file.[12] If the party is lacking in cohesion, lobbying will be directed at key individual legislators, especially committee and subcommittee chairmen. The often-remarked individualistic nature of group representation in Congress, with lobbyists dealing with small clusters of friendly and familiar legislators on a variety of issues, reflects in part the weakness of the congressional parties at least as compared to party systems in various state legislatures.[13]

That organized groups may be more active in political institutions where power is diffuse does not necessarily mean they will be more effective in such places. If one organization enjoys greater access in a noncohesive party system, then all organizations will enjoy greater access, and the chances of any one prevailing over the others is accordingly reduced except in those issue areas where the benefits it seeks impose small, highly distributed, or low-visibility costs on others. Furthermore, in a political system where power is fragmented, individual officeholders are freer to choose which organization, if any, to heed. It was discovered that the great majority of the 112 city councilmen holding office in twenty-two cities of the San Francisco Bay area expressed either neutral or negative attitudes toward organized groups as sources of policy direction and did not seek group support for the proposals they brought before the councils. A much smaller group of councilmen paid attention to, and actively tried to involve, such organizations in legislative politics. What determined whether a councilman would take one posture rather than another were his personal preferences—his "role orientation"—rather than any particular feature of the city in which he held office.[14]

Perhaps because organizational access to, and influence over, large numbers of legislators is uncertain, perhaps because of the weakening of the party system and the growth of judicial and other checks on executive authority, perhaps because of the increased importance of the mass media in the election of key officeholders, many political organizations emphasize influencing public opinion, or important segments of it, as much or more than influencing official behavior. There has probably been a long-term increase in the reliance on grassroots strategies, including advertising, letter writing, financing election campaigns, referenda, and securing favorable media treatment.[15] This is especially true with respect to the initiation of new policies, because of the need to develop legitimacy for a new governmental role, and perhaps most true with respect to those new initiatives that involve major extensions of the welfare state. Many of the laws of this type were passed only when there were extraordinary majorities in the legislature, as when the Democrats dominated Congress during the early New Deal and after the 1964 Johnson-Goldwater election.

Many important new pieces of legislation that failed to gain passage, such as the Family Assistance Plan of 1970, did so because there were no extraordinary majorities in Congress and public opinion was deeply divided. Statistically, the single most important factor in explaining the differences among senators' votes on this measure was public opinion within their state or region.[16]

Though there are good reasons for a political organization to direct its efforts at shaping opinion rather than influencing hostile legislators, its capacity to affect the opinion even of its members, to say nothing of nonmembers, is limited except where the organization can evoke powerful latent fears. A frequently cited example involves the efforts of labor unions to repeal the Taft-Hartley Act during the years following its pas-

sage in 1947. During the 1952 presidential election, when repeal of the act was an issue, blue-collar workers who were union members were almost three times as likely as those who were not members to support its repeal. Though this suggests substantial union influence on member opinion, its extent was limited: only 29 percent of the members favored repeal, 41 percent had no opinion at all on the matter, and curiously enough a larger proportion of members than of nonmembers favored *retention* of the law.[17] Another instance of the limits of organizational influence on member opinion comes from a poll of attitudes toward birth control conducted in 1936, when views on this matter were probably stricter than they are today. While more non-Catholics than Catholics said they favored such practices, a substantial proportion of Catholics (43 percent) said they believed in birth control.[18]

Organizational influence on the opinion of nonmembers is harder to assess. The advertising campaign against Medicare conducted by the American Medical Association may have been responsible for the decline in public support for that program revealed by polls taken during 1962 when Medicare was defeated in Congress. Nevertheless, the bill was passed three years later following the landslide Democratic victory in the 1964 elections that produced extraordinary majorities in both houses of Congress.[19]

On the other hand, when an organization can provide voters with reason to believe that they face a major threat to a widely shared benefit, they can often help evoke strong sentiments. For example, the average citizen is ordinarily inclined to favor fluoridation of municipal water supplies in order to reduce tooth decay, but if he is asked to vote on that measure in a local referendum, he will often be bombarded with organizationally inspired antifluoridation arguments that allege both the health hazards of fluoridation and the sinister motives of the proponents, with the result that his support for the proposal declines sharply, sometimes enough to defeat the measure. Similarly, the sudden rise in popular concern about the quality of the environment is apparently the result of distributing information via the media that successfully evokes latent fears about the destruction of cherished values. Between 1965 and 1970, the Gallup Poll revealed that the proportion of citizens saying that the reduction of pollution should be one of the central concerns of government rose from 17 to 53 percent.[20] The effect of such publicity has sometimes been countered effectively by organized campaigns to persuade voters that another cherished value, employment, was being threatened by efforts to curb pollution.

339

It is possible (only the almost complete lack of evidence prevents me from saying, as I suspect, that it is *likely*) that opinions can be shaped, at least at the margin, more effectively by unorganized though widespread shifts in the rhetoric and attention of the media than by publicity campaigns mounted by organizations. The attention given Ralph Nader has probably increased public sensitivity to claims of economic abuse of the consumer more than have all the efforts of the Consumers' Union or the Consumer Federation of America. The shift in attitude toward the war in Vietnam that occurred in the pages of the leading newsmagazines and national newspapers during the late 1960s probably had a stronger effect on popular attitudes toward the war, especially attitudes among the upper-middle-class readers of such periodicals, than did the efforts of antiwar protest organizations.[21]

Organizations in a Changing Society

The mood of society, the nature of public policy, and the scope of government action have changed substantially, in fact and in perception, during the twenty years since David Truman published *The Governmental Process.* The population has continued to become, as John Dollard terms it, "middle-classified," with a significant increase in the proportion of persons in white-collar occupations and having college education. Television, scarcely more than a curiosity in 1950, has become today, according to citizen surveys, the most important single source of political information. The fear of subversion and the distaste for corruption, widespread in the early postwar period, have been replaced by the clash of life styles, peace, race relations, crime, and drugs as the dominant noneconomic issues of the day. A radical critique of American institutions, unthinkable in 1950, became by 1970 commonly heard if not widely believed. And college students, who throughout the 1950s continued, even on elite campuses, to show in polls substantial support, and sometimes absolute majorities, for Republican presidential candidates and for conventional views generally, have moved substantially to the left in both attitudes and candidate preferences.[22]

The scope of governmental activity has been greatly widened. In 1950 it would have been hard to imagine that the federal government would ever pass strong civil rights bills, begin a compulsory national health insurance program, place under regulation the automobile industry, come within a few senatorial votes of adopting a guaranteed minimum income (proposed by a Republican president!), explore the surface of the moon, or require the desegregation of the southern school system. Nor would many have foreseen that federal troops would one day occupy a southern campus and a northern city, or that the open advocacy of political violence would be heard, and heard not from the lips of leaders of lower-income workers but from those of upper-income students.

Because of the great expansion in both the role of government and the size of the liberal elite,[23] a characteristic feature of the struggle of political organizations of the 1940s and 1950s is today much reduced in importance—namely, debates over the philosophical wisdom and constitutional propriety of new public initiatives. The range of government actions deemed illegitimate by some major segment of opinion is now much smaller. Quarrels over efficacy, prudence, and techniques continue, but those over the limits of government power have been greatly attenuated. Those organizations that sought to restrict the scope of government have generally lost, whereas those that have sought to enlarge it have generally won.

Viewed in this light, the argument of some that the multiplicity of interest groups would produce political paralysis seems, to put the matter charitably, rather beside the mark. Rather, it has been the rapid expansion of government policy that has produced a kind of immobilism to the extent that each new program has acquired, or even created for itself, a client association that makes it difficult to change, and impossible to abandon, the original measure. The competition of interest groups does not, in the long run, make it difficult for the government to start doing things, it only makes it difficult for the government to stop.

The expansion of the scope of government enterprise has not been solely, or even primarily, the result of the agitation of organizations. The changes that have occurred, at least with respect to major policy innovations, have been the result of broad changes in opinion, the impact of crises, and the effort of competitive officeseekers to find and attract new constituencies and satisfy new demands. But organizations have played a role in this, a role that by its nature gives an advantage to certain kinds of organizations over others. The NAACP and the AFL-CIO played a major direct role in the passage of civil rights bills, just as the early Student Nonviolent Coordinating Committee and the Southern Christian Leadership Conference played a major indirect role, and the AFL-CIO was an important actor in the events that led up to Medicare.

This suggests what may be the most important long-term consequence for political organizations of the social and governmental changes mentioned, namely, the decline in the overt political influence of associations relying on material incentives. Edward C. Banfield and I have suggested, in our study of city politics, one reason for this change—the spread of the upper-middle-class political ethos with its emphasis on the desirability of greater consumption of public, as opposed to private, goods and its repugnance at anything that smacks of narrow self-interest, political machines, or "bossism." [24] One implication of this may be to render more difficult the organization of those persons, such as lower-class ones, who respond only to highly salient incentives, of which immediate monetary benefit is one. The discussion by Lawrence Bailis of the Massachusetts Welfare Rights Organization (MWRO) is apposite: though begun by middle-class white young activists who encouraged the development of material incentives for the members, in time the white leaders became disillusioned with the "mere" search for money benefits, and the government rearranged the state welfare system so as to eliminate the special needs grants that had in effect financed MWRO. Partially offsetting this aversion to political participation out of material motives is the desire on the part of an active minority of the upper-middle class to make certain groups (currently, Negroes and members of some other ethnic groups) the object of its special benevolence and thus to overlook or excuse in them what they would never ignore or forgive in others (for example, white labor union leaders).

But in addition to the changing political ethos of the electorate, there is an institutional reason for the decline in the overt political influence of materially induced associations. So long as policy-making revolved around the question of the legitimacy of new governmental programs, organizations such as business and trade associations could claim that their opposition arose, not from self-interest, but from a philosophical commitment to the ideals of free enterprise, the libertarian state, or whatever. Once these welfare and tax policies were adopted, however, the issue of legitimacy, and constitutionality, was generally settled in the minds of policy-makers and perhaps the public generally. Arguments about amendments to these policies then had to take the form of proposed revisions based on calculations of "more" or "less," and thus apparently, and perhaps in reality, these arguments were reflective of underlying material stakes in the outcomes. Having settled, at least insofar as officeholders and the attentive public audience are concerned, the issue of whether it is right for the government to provide compulsory health insurance, to desegregate public schools, or to regulate consumer products, then the only feasible form of debate, given the general irreversibility of government action, is how much to charge for the health care, how fast and with what compensation to desegregate schools, and how burdensome to manufacturers the product control shall be. It is difficult to take negative positions on these matters without appearing to defend, out of one's own stake and without benefit of a philosophical fig leaf, private advantage.

One result of this development can perhaps be seen in the changing content of associational publicity. Business organizations in the early part of the century fought union shops under the slogan the "American Plan"; during the 1930s and 1940s, they defended free enterprise against the enlargement of government powers; today, with the earlier battles all but lost, business publicity tends to stress the "social conscience" of businessmen; thus, business groups now tend to minimize the importance, or the perceived social costs, of self-interest and to defer to some conception of public purpose.

That those representing material interests feel themselves at a disadvantage in working overtly on behalf of those interests does not mean that such work has been suspended, only that it is now more vulnerable to public exposure. The heightened scrutiny given public policy by the media and by consumer groups has reduced the area of low-visibility politics and increased the chances that any private arrangement will be converted into a public one. That private advantage is suspect does not, of course, mean it is wrong: public policy should be judged by its consequences, and not by the motives of its advocates.

Related to the suspicion of material incentives is the heightened distrust of bureaucratic organization. The bureaucratization of associational activity may or may not increase the association's effectiveness, but it reduces the extent to which the association acts as a social movement rather than as an organization, and this loss of élan is in the eyes of many a fatal defect. Organized labor and the NAACP have acquired great legislative influence in part because of the development of permanent staffs, but they have also become the objects of intellectual and activist scorn in part because such bureaucratization implies stability, limited objectives, and, again, personal material benefit.

The 1960s, like the 1900s and 1930s, was a period of social movements that were the sources of important social changes that no organizational analysis of politics alone can explain. But these movements—civil rights, black nationalism, ecology, consumerism, women's rights, party reform, the defense of neighborhood schools—had a profound effect on organizational politics, not only by spawning new associations but by giving an advantage to associations, or factions within associations, that seemed to rely on purposive incentives. In both political parties, the amateur and the ideologue made substantial gains at the expense of the "old politics"; in civil rights, purposive groups such as SNCC and CORE made (briefly) gains at the expense of the NAACP; and in industry, ecological and consumer groups gained at the expense of firms and trade associations.

If purposive organizations became more important—indeed, in a period of heightened discontent, of decisive importance—then leaders capable of producing concerted action on the basis of ideas became more influential. But only a few such leaders will succeed in institutionalizing their influence, because only a few will be able to create an enduring organizational base for their claims. Their importance in politics will thus be episodic and limited to those few policy areas that can be made the target of aroused passion. Meanwhile, other associations with their allied government agencies, immune for the moment from passion or purpose, will continue to maintain control over policy domains in ways designed to enhance, if not the interests of their constituencies, then at least those of the organizations themselves. One who wishes to describe the "policy-making process" will be free to choose either the language of stasis or turmoil, interest or ideology, depending on where he allows his gaze to fall.

In evaluating this selectively described process, American scholars have pronounced it good or bad depending on the political coloration of what they took to be the dominant challenge to interest-group politics. In the 1950s, McCarthyism, extreme conservatism, and nativism appeared to represent the most likely form of mass politics, and thus scholars, overwhelmingly liberal in their outlook, stressed the values of stability, bargaining, moderation, and pragmatism they found in interest-group politics. Even those who disliked the conservatism of such organizations would concede that the threat of "contemporary 'right' extremism" might require the maintenance of some form of interest-group politics as a barrier against "irrational mass movements." [25] When in the late 1960s the principal forms of mass politics turned out to be liberal or even radical in impulse, scholars lost no time in joining in a chorus of denunciations of group politics: it was seen as a barrier to desirable changes and an impediment to the advancement of mass movements that were now described as liberating rather than irrational and as having an impatience with bargaining that was wholesome rather than fearsome.

The scholarly fears of both chaos and impotence have proved exaggerated, but the evaluative problem will remain. There is not and there cannot be any wholly satisfactory solution to the problem of how best to aggregate political preferences and thus, as the changing opinions of American scholars should by now have revealed, we cannot expect any easy verdict on the American political system. All will depend on whose ends are being served at the moment, and scholars have their own cherished ends like everybody else.

The politics of organizational representation and interest bargaining—the politics, that is, of mobilizing small constituencies, the politics of "pluralism"—assures that organized affected parties will be heard, that the intensity of revealed preferences will be taken into account, and that the consequences of policy will be debated. But such a process also means that unorganized groups will often be neglected and that the resultant policies may reflect benefits sought by easily organized sectors rather than by broader, harder-to-organize constituencies, and perhaps only those sought by associational activists at that. The politics of mass mobilization, of media appeals and social movements, and of ideologies and personal followings will often produce a wider, public-interest debate, place new issues on the public agenda, and call into question accepted but perhaps morbid institutional arrangements. But such a process can also be the arena of the demagogue, of left or right, and can result in programs that do not work well, or work at all. And regardless of whether policies result from active organizations or mobilized publics, the adoption of any policy will in the long run usually prove easier than the modification of a policy once in effect.

NOTES

1. Theodore J. Lowi, "American Business, Public Policy, Case Studies and Political Theory," *World Politics*, XVI (July 1964), reprinted in *Public Policies and Their Politics*, ed. Randall B. Ripley (New York: Norton, 1966), pp. 27–40. See also Lowi, "Four Systems of Policy, Politics, and Choice," *Public Administration Review*, XXXII (July-August 1972), 298–310.
2. Marc K. Landy, "Group Politics and Economic Development Legislation" (paper, Department of Government, Harvard University, 1972).
3. Mark V. Nadel, *The Politics of Consumer Protection* (Indianapolis: Bobbs-Merrill, 1971), pp. 144, 210. See also Paul J. Halpern, "Consumer Politics and Corporate

Behavior: the Case of Automobile Safety" (Ph.D. diss., Department of Government, Harvard University, 1972).

4. Daniel P. Moynihan has referred to this as the "professionalization of reform" in his article of that title in *The Public Interest* (Fall 1965), pp. 6–16. Not all the individuals who are influential as policy initiators are professionals in the strict sense, however.

5. Nadel, *The Politics of Consumer Protection*, p. 242.

6. Aaron Wildavsky, "TVA and Power Politics," *American Political Science Review*, LV (September 1961), 576–590.

7. Daniel P. Moynihan, *The Politics of a Guaranteed Income* (New York: Random House, 1973).

8. Lawrence D. Longley, "Interest Group Interaction in a Legislative System," *Journal of Politics*, XXIX (August 1967), 657.

9. Roger G. Noll, *Reforming Regulation* (Washington, D.C.: Brookings Institution, 1971), p. 3–5.

10. Ralph T. Jones, "City Employee Unions in New York and Chicago" (Ph.D. diss., Department of Government, Harvard University, 1972), chaps. 4, 6.

11. Harmon Zeigler and G. Wayne Peak, *Interest Groups in American Society*, 2nd ed. (Englewood Cliffs, N.J.: Prentice-Hall, 1972), p. 148.

12. Duane Lockard, *New England State Politics* (Princeton, N.J.: Princeton University Press, 1959), p. 163; Zeigler and Peak, *Interest Groups in American Society*, pp. 148–149.

13. The greater cohesiveness of many state as opposed to national legislative parties results in part from the power of state legislative leaders to appoint committee chairmen free of a seniority rule.

14. Betty H. Zisk, Heinz Eulau, and Kenneth Prewitt, "City Councilmen and the Group Struggle: A Typology of Role Orientations," *Journal of Politics*, XXVII (August 1965), 618–646.

15. Harry M. Scoble, *Ideology and Electoral Action* (San Francisco: Chandler, 1967), p. 180.

16. John E. Jackson, *Constituencies and Leaders in Congress* (Cambridge, Mass.: Harvard University Press, forthcoming), appendix B.

17. V. O. Key, Jr., *Public Opinion and American Democracy* (New York: Alfred A. Knopf, 1961), p. 509.

18. Ibid., p. 551.

19. Gallup Poll data cited in Norman Luttbeg and Robert Erikson, *Public Opinion* (New York: John Wiley, 1973), chap. 6.

20. Ibid.

21. James D. Wright, "Life, Time, and the Fortunes of War," *Transaction* (January 1972), pp. 42–52.

22. Seymour Martin Lipset (manuscript, Department of Government, Harvard University).

23. By "liberal elite" I mean those persons ranking high in income, occupational status, and schooling who favor enlarging government-directed efforts at social melioration. They are that (I think growing) fraction of the well-to-do whose income and status have not produced political conservatism.

24. Edward C. Banfield and James Q. Wilson, *City Politics* (Cambridge, Mass.: Harvard University Press, 1963), concluding chapter.

25. Grant McConnell, *Private Power and American Democracy* (New York: Alfred A. Knopf, 1966), p. 354.

INDEX

Abel, I. W., 132
Action for Boston Community Development, 276
administration: types of, defined, 221–224; differences in British unions, 231–232
AFL-CIO: liberalizing effect of bureaucracy on, 226–227; merger of, 267, 276; political positions of, 312. *See also* American Federation of Labor; Congress of Industrial Organizations
Aid to Families of Dependent Children (AFDC), 65
Alinsky, Saul, 77n
Allen, V. L., 254n
Almond, Gabriel A., 48, 55n, 76n, 78, 90n, 117n
Amalgamated Clothing Workers, 129
Amalgamated Meat Cutters and Butcher Workmen (AMCBW), 122, 133
Amalgamated Society of Engineers (Great Britain), 124
American Academy of Arts and Sciences, 54n
American Anti-Slavery Society, 186–187, 200
American Association of University Professors (AAUP), 23, 198
American Bankers' Association, 155
American Baptist Church, 55n
American Bar Association, 80, 202
American Birth Control League, 197
American Cancer Society, 198
American Civil Liberties Union (ACLU), 312

American Communist party: Comintern leadership of, 105–106; membership in, 117n; influence of on National Negro Congress, 178; mentioned, 47, 48, 198
American Cotton Manufacturers' Association (ACMA), 149
American Cotton Manufacturers' Institute (ACMI), 307, 309
American Council on Education (ACE), 268, 334
American Economic Association, 22, 213n
American Farm Bureau Federation (AFBF), 38, 196, 198, 267, 278, 312, 334
American Federation of Labor (AFL): incentive system in, 121, 124–127; split from CIO, 129; political activity of, 134–139; Committee on Political Education, 136–139; mentioned, 7, 123, 198, 199, 265
American Jewish Committee, 198, 263, 265, 272–274
American Jewish Congress, 265, 272–274
American Legion, 42, 317
American Medical Association, 80, 198, 312, 339
American Motors Corporation, 157
American Petroleum Institute, 307
American Red Cross: process of institutionalization in, 206; mentioned, 44, 198, 199, 207, 209, 321
American Socialist party, 102, 103, 105, 198
Americans for Constitutional Action, 312

Americans for Democratic Action (ADA), 312
Ameringer, Oscar, 117n
Anti-Defamation League of B'nai B'rith, 198, 218, 265, 272–274
Antimasonic party, 201
Anti-Saloon League, 46, 202, 205, 232n, 315, 330
Appalachian Regional Development Act, 329
Area Redevelopment Act, 328–329
Arkwright Club (Boston), 147, 149
Army Corps of Engineers, 334
Arnstein, Sherry R., 77n
Ashenfelter, Orley, 204, 213n, 253, 257n
Assael, Henry, 168n
Association of Commerce and Industry (Chicago), 87
Association of Edison Illuminating Companies, 264
authority: limitations on, 215–216; legitimacy of, 219–220; and incentives, 221, 238, 242–244
autonomy: as maintenance strategy, 263, 264; as minimizer of competition, 264–267; in coalitions, 272
Axelrod, Morris, 75n, 272
Axelrod, Robert, 269, 280n

Babchuck, Nicholas, 76n, 255n
Bachrach, Peter, 325n
Bailis, Lawrence, 65, 66, 76n, 203, 213n, 233n, 283, 301n, 342
Balbus, Isaac, 52n
Baltzell, E. Digby, 53n
Banfield, Edward C., 29n, 76n, 87, 91n, 116n, 342, 346n
Baratz, Morton, 325n
bargaining: as opposition behavior, 282; factors influencing choice of, 284–289; and differing organizational goals, 289–292; as part of dual strategy, 296
Barnard, Chester I., 30, 31, 35, 52n
Barnes, Gilbert Hobbs, 191n, 212n
Barnes, Samuel H., 109, 118n, 238, 239, 240, 254n
Barss, Reitzel & Associates, 91n
Bastian, Ann V., 76n
Bauer, Raymond A.: quoted, 310; mentioned, 170n, 306–319 passim, 324n, 325n
Baum, Rainer C., 280n
Beard, Charles A., 202
Beer, Samuel H., 81, 90n
Bell, Daniel: quoted, 102; mentioned, 55n, 116n, 117n, 199, 212n, 256n
Bell, Inge Powell, 191n

Bell, J. Bowyer, 302n
Bell, Wendell, 76n
Bellamy, Edward, 201
Bendix, Reinhard, 212n
benefits, exclusive and individual: defined, 36. See also public policy: costs and benefits of, defined
Bentley, Arthur F., 4–5, 9, 15n, 29n, 201, 202
Benton, William, 163
Berkowitz, Leonard, 76n, 325n
Bernardo, Robert M., 54n
Bernstein, Irving, 279n
Black Muslims, 70
black nationalism, 70–71
Black Panther party, 26, 49, 74–75, 181
Blackstone Rangers, 72
Blakeslee, George Hubbard, 212n
Blau, Peter M., 52n, 54n, 213n, 234n
Blum, Albert A., 301n
Bok, Derek C., 140n, 141n, 142n, 231, 234n, 280n
Bolton, Charles D., 76n
Bonnett, Clarence E., 144, 168n, 169n
Booth, Alan, 76n
Boston, effect of political structure on voluntary associations, 87–89
Boulding, Kenneth E., 144, 168n, 212n
Boys Clubs of America, 198
Boy Scouts, 198
Brannan Plan, 331
Brazier, Arthur M., 77n
Breton, Albert, 212n
Breton, Raymond, 212n
Brickman, Harry, 140n
Bridges, Harry, 256n
Brill, Harry, 295, 302n
British Employers' Confederation, 81
British Legion, 81
British Medical Association, 81
Broderick, Francis L., 190n
Brook Club (London), 42
Broom, Leonard, 16n
Brotherhood of Sleeping Car Porters, 127
Brower, David, 218, 321
Brown, Edmund, 98
Brown, H. Rap, 181
Brown, Harry James, 168n
Buckholz, Marjorie H., 233n
Building Service Employees (BSEIU), 122, 139
Bunche, Ralph: quoted, 190n; mentioned, 178
bureaucracy: effect of on voluntary associations, 224, 225–227; relationship to lay officers, 227–231; British differences in, 231–232

Burgess, Philip M., 277, 280n
business associations: membership characteristics of, 144–146, 168n; incentives for, 146–148, 152, 153–158, 166; bureaucratization of, 149–150; success of, 151–152; problems of political goals of, 153; open-shop struggle in, 154–155; maintenance problems of, 165, 167

Calvin, A. D., 255n
Calvinism, 57
Cambridge Electron Accelerator, 277
CARE, 211
Carmichael, Stokeley, 180–181, 183, 185
Cataldo, Everett F., 76n
caucus organization, 217, 218, 246
Cayton, Horace R., 69, 77n
Center for Auto Safety, 323
Center for Study of Responsive Law, 323
Central Competitive Coal Operators' Association, 151
Chamberlain, Neil W., 212n
Chamber of Commerce. See United States Chamber of Commerce
Chavez, Cesar, 73–74, 220
Cherington, Paul W., 313, 325n
Chicago, effect of political structure on associations, 83–84, 87
chief officer: defined, 232n; mentioned, 215
Childs, Harold Lawrence, 170n
churches, appeal of to lower-class participants, 69–71
civic associations, effectiveness of, 87–89
Civic Federation (Chicago), 87
Civil Rights Acts, 183, 184
Clark, Peter B., 52n, 232n, 233n
Clarke, James W., 107, 117n
class: and participation in voluntary associations, 56–63, 85; Marxist views of, 56–58; lower, in voluntary associations, 64–75, 85–87, 342; and constraints on staff members, 229; and governance, 241–242; relationships in protest activities, 294
Clayton Act, 125
Clegg, H. A., 234n
Cleghorn, Reese, 191n
Cleveland, Alfred S., 169n
coalitions: defined, 267; theories of, 268–272; MacIver Report on Jewish, 272–274; incentives for, 275–277; in lobby activities, 317–318

Cochran, Thomas C., 168n
Cohen, Bernard C., 319, 325n
Cohn, Norman, 54n
Coleman, James S., 140n, 240, 241, 254n, 325n
Committee Against Legalized Murder, 35, 46
Committee for a National Trade Policy, 309, 318
Committee for a Sane Nuclear Policy, 4
Committee for Economic Development: incentive system in, 163–164; mentioned, 145, 209, 218, 263, 321
Committee on Political Education (COPE), 136–139
Commons, John R., 121, 140n, 202
Communications Workers of America (CWA), 28n
Communist party. See American Communist party
Community Action Agencies, 203
Community Action Program (CAP), 68
Community Chest, 275
Community Service Society (N.Y.C.), 283
competition: minimization of, 263; relationship to autonomy and resources, 264, 267
Conference of American Small Business Organizations (CASBO), 162
Congress of Industrial Organizations (CIO): incentive system in, 127, 129; Political Action Committee of, 133–134; political activity of, 133–139 passim, 311; mentioned, 121–122, 130
Congress of Racial Equality. See CORE
Constitution League, 171
Consumer Credit Protection Act, 331
Consumer Federation of America, 340
Consumers' Union, 340
Coogan, Tim Pat: quoted, 301; mentioned, 302n
CORE (Congress of Racial Equality): instability of, 180–181; radicalization of, 182–183, 184; redemptive quality of, 185–186; impact on civil rights movement, 187–189; incentives in, 188; mentioned, 171, 197, 268, 344
Coser, Lewis, 117n
costs. See public policy: costs and benefits of, defined
Cottrell, Leonard S., 16n
Council on Foreign Relations, 321
Craig, John G., 256n
Crain, Robert L., 252, 256n, 266, 279n
The Crisis (NAACP): success of, 175, 176; mentioned, 172, 173

Cutright, Phillips, 99, 116n
Cyert, Richard, 214n

Daley, Richard J., 101
Davis, H. B., 203, 213n
Davis, Jack, 302n
Davis, John P., 178
Dawson, William L., 100
Debs, Eugene V., 102, 103, 220
decisions (policy), defined: distributive, 327–328; regulatory, 328; redistributive, 328
Defense Mediation Board, 132
DeLeon, Daniel, 102
Democratic National Conventions: (1972), 96; (1968), 107; (1964) and Mississippi Freedom Democratic party, 180, 183
Democratic party, labor support of, 133–134, 136
De Molay, Order of, 198
Department of Agriculture, 334
De Swann, Abraham, 270, 280n
Dewey, John, 202
Dexter, Lewis Anthony: quoted, 310; mentioned, 170n, 306–318 passim, 324n, 325n
Diamond, Martin, 54n
Dollard, John, 340
Dorsett, Lyle, 116n
Downs, Anthony, 25, 29n
Drake, St. Clair, 69, 77n
Draper, Theodore, 117n
DuBois, William E. B.: role of in The Crisis, 175; role of in NAACP, 176; mentioned, 172, 173, 190n
Dulles, Foster R., 213n
Dunlop, John T., 140n, 141n, 142n, 204, 213n, 231, 234n, 280n
Dunne, John Gregory, 77n
Dutch Federation of Trade Unions, 121
Duverger, Maurice, 107, 117n, 233n

Eckstein, Harry H., 90n
economic models, problems of, 23–25
Economic Opportunity Act, 84, 307–308, 331
Edelstein, J. David, 255n
Edison Electric Institute, 264
Eldersveld, Samuel J., 111, 116n, 118n, 137, 142n
Electric Companies Advertising Program, 264
Elkin, Stephen Lloyd, 91n
Elks Club (Benevolent and Protective Order of Elks), 42, 198
Ely, Richard T., 202, 213n

Engels, Friedrich, 57, 58, 75n
Engler, Robert, 324n
entrepreneurship, 196, 197, 201
Epstein, Leon D., 257n
Equal Opportunity League, 171
Erikson, Robert, 346n
Ernst, Morris, 117n
Essien-Udom, E. U., 70, 77n
Etzioni, Amitai, 10, 15n, 16n, 52n
Eulau, Heinz, 346n
Evers, Charles, 187, 188
executives: constraints upon, 27, 215, 237; and organizational strain, 31; in purposive associations, 49; functions of, 216–219; legitimacy of, 219–221; use of incentives by, 238–239; and membership size, 261–262

Family Assistance Plan (FAP): reasons for failure, 338; mentioned, 307, 331, 332
Faris, Robert E. L., 52n
Farm Bureau Federation. See American Farm Bureau Federation
Farmer, James, 197
Farmers' Union. See National Farmers' Union
Father Divine, 70
Federal Regulation of Lobbying Act, 305
Federation of British Industries, 81, 83
Feierabend, Ivo K., 302n
Festinger, Leon, 53n
Fiedler, Fred E., 255n
Fisher, Bernice, 197
FLN (Algiers), 300
Florists' Transworld Delivery Association, 152
FLQ (Quebec), 299, 300
Foley, Henry, 77n
Follett, Mary Parker, 201
Food and Drug Act, 1962 Kefauver-Harris amendments to, 329
Ford Foundation, 276
Ford Motor Company, 129, 130, 131
Foreign Oil Policy Committee, 318
Frazier, E. Franklin, 178
"Freedom Summer" (Mississippi), 180
Frey, John P.: quoted, 125
Friends of the Earth, 321
Frohlich, Norman, 212n
Full Employment Act, 134
Full Funding Committee, 267

Gable, Richard A., 155, 169n, 170n
Galambos, Louis, 147, 168n, 169n
Galenson, Walter, 141n
Gallagher, Orvoell R., 90n

Gamson, William A., 279n, 280n
Gandhi, Mohandas, 182
gangs, 71–72
Garfinkel, Herbert, 190n
Garson, G. David, 297, 298, 302n
Garvey, Marcus, 70, 221
Gary, Elbert, 158
Gary, Indiana, 99
General Electric Company, 310
General Motors Corporation, 5, 129, 130, 131, 252, 322
Gibb, Cecil, 255n, 256n
Gillen, Ralph L., 313, 325n
Girl Scouts, 198
goal-oriented organizations: defined, 46, 50; NAACP as example of, 181. *See also* purposive incentives
Goldwater, Barry, 253
Gompers, Samuel, 125, 141n, 208
Gordon, C. Wayne, 255n
Gould, Jay, 150
Gouldner, Alvin W., 10, 16n, 54n
Grange. *See* National Grange
Gray, Jesse, 283
Great Britain, voluntary associations in, 80–83
Great Revival: abolitionist efforts of, 186–187; mentioned, 201
Green, William, 141n
Greenberg, Stanley, 76n
Green Corn Rebellion, 104
Greenstone, J. David, 84, 91n, 137, 140n, 141n, 142n
Gresham, Newton, 197
Groennings, Sven, 280n
Groppi, Father (Milwaukee), 187
Gross, Edward, 256n
Grundy, Joseph, 154
Gurr, Ted Robert, 299, 302n
Gusfield, Joseph R., 206, 207, 213n

Haddon, William Jr., 324
Hall, Donald R., 325n
Halpern, Paul J., 345n
Handlin, Mary F., 213n
Handlin, Oscar, 213n
Hanna, Mark, 97
Harden, E. L., 255n
Harrington, Michael, 301n
Harris, Abram, 176–177, 178
Harrison, Paul M., 55n
Harsanyi, John C., 11, 16n, 54n, 270, 280n
Hartman, Paul T., 252, 256n
Harvard University, 199, 276–277
Hausknecht, Murray, 75n, 76n
Hausler, Richard W., 324

Haymarket Riot, 150
Haywood, William "Big Bill," 128
Healey, James J., 141n
Heffernan, William D., 53n
Henderson, A. M., 53n
Heydebrand, Wolf V., 16n
Hicks, John D., 212n
Hodge, Robert W., 75n, 76n
Hoffman, Paul, 163
Hoffmann, F. K., 255n
Hofstadter, Richard, 202, 212n, 213n
Hofstetter, C. Richard, 117n
Holtzman, Abraham, 213n
Homans, George C., 54n, 280n
Horwitz, Murray, 292, 302n
hospitals, 243–244
Howe, Irving, 117n
Hubbard, Howard, 301n
Hudson Dusters, 71
Hunt, Margaret A., 325n
Huntington, Samuel P., 299, 302n
Hylton, Lydia, 280n
Hyman, Herbert H., 75n, 76n

ideological organizations, defined, 46–47, 48, 49. *See also* purposive incentives
ideological party: defined, 101–102; incentives in, 103–106
Illinois Manufacturers' Association (IMA), 153, 155
incentives: and rationality, 20–22; range of, 22–23; primary, 26; and constraints on executives, 27; types of, defined, 31 (*see also* material incentives; purposive incentives; solidary incentives); and class, 59–60; in lower-class organizations, 64–75; sources of in political parties, 96; in ideological parties, 103–106; in labor unions, 120–121; for business associations, 146–148, 153; in civil rights movement, 188–189; and authority, 221, 238; and governance, 238–244; for coalition formation, 275–277; negative, 282; as related to costs and benefits of public policy, 322–337 passim
Independent Natural Gas Association of America, 307
Independent Petroleum Association of America, 307
Industrial Areas Foundation, 77n
industrial unionism, 131–134
Industrial Union of Mine, Mill, and Smelter Workers, 123
Industrial Workers of the World (IWW), 47, 122, 128
influence. *See* lobbies: influence of

Inkeles, Alex, 255n
Institute of Social Research (Univ. of Michigan), 250
International Association of Machinists, 151
International Brotherhood of Electrical Workers, 124
International Ladies' Garment Workers Union (ILGWU), 129, 131, 177
International Longshoremen's and Warehousemen's Union (ILWU), 256n
International Longshoremen's Association (ILA), 239, 249
International Typographical Union, 149, 240, 241
Interstate Commerce Commission, 336
Irish Republican Army (IRA), 49, 300–301
Italian Socialist party: views of democracy in, 238, 239–240; mentioned, 109, 110

Jackson, John E., 346n
Jacobs, Bruce, 86, 91n
Jacobs, Paul, 141n
Janowitz, Morris, 51, 55n
Jenson, Vernon H., 256n
Jewell, Malcolm E., 325n
Jewish Labor Committee, 272, 273
Jewish War Veterans, 272, 273
John Birch Society, 47, 197
Johnson, George E., 253, 257n
Johnson, James Weldon, 172, 173, 176
Johnstone, John W. C., 76n
Joint Center for Urban Studies, 277
Jones, Jesse, 163
Jones, Ralph T., 91n, 222, 233n, 346n
Junior League, 41

Kahn, Robert L., 142n, 251, 256n
Karsh, Bernard, 53n
Karson, Marc, 140n, 141n
Kayden, Xandra, 52n
Kelley, E. W., 280n
Kelley, Oliver Hudson, 197
Kellogg, Charles Flint, 189n, 190n
Kelly, Alfred H., 169n
Keniston, Kenneth, 55n
Kennedy, John F., 307
Key, V. O. Jr., 346n
Kilson, Martin: quoted, 189; mentioned, 192n
King, Martin Luther Jr., 183, 186, 188–189, 218, 273, 301n
Kiwanis Club, 42
Knights of Labor, 150, 198, 265
Knights of Pythias, 198

Knoll, Erwin, 324n
Knox, Ronald A., 54n
Kolko, Gabriel, 168n
Kornhauser, A., 254n
Kossoris, Max, 256n
Koth, David, 117n
Kraditor, Aileen S., 212n
Kramer, Ralph M., 68, 77n
Ku Klux Klan, 104

Labor's League for Political Education, 134
Labor's Nonpartisan League, 133, 134
labor unions: maintenance problems of, 119, 120; union security agreements in, 119–120, 121, 129; incentives in U.S., 120–121, 124, 128, 136; incentive systems in European, 121; government support of, 131–132; political activity of, 133–139, 208; administrative styles in, 222, 231–232; democracy in, 244–249 passim; and membership loyalty, 251; effects of Landrum-Griffin Act on, 252–253; bargaining tactics of, 290–291; use of violence in, 297–299
Ladd, Everett Carll Jr., 117n
Landrum-Griffin Act, effects of, 252–253
Landy, Marc K., 345n
Lane Seminary (Ohio), and Anti-Slavery Society, 186, 191n
Latham, Earl, 279n
Laumann, Edward O., 90n
leadership: distinguished from executive function, 216; styles of and governance, 242
Leadership Conference on Civil Rights, 268, 318
League of Women Voters: decision-making in, 250–253; League of Women Voters Educational Fund, 321; mentioned, 45, 312
Leavitt, Harold J., 256n
legitimacy: as associational goal, 219; sources of, 219–220; and democratic consent, 236–237; and opposition styles, 288; of lobby groups, 317; of public policy issues, 330
Leiserson, Michael A., 269–270, 279n, 280n
Lenin, V. I., 75
Levine, Sol, 263, 279n
Levinson, Daniel J., 255n
Lewis, John, SNCC national chairman, 180, 184, 302n
Lewis, John L.: quoted, 245; mentioned, 122, 130, 131, 298

liberal elite, defined, 346*n*
Likert, Rensis, 45, 54*n*, 256*n*
Lions Club, 42, 44
Lipset, Seymour Martin: quoted, 231, 241; mentioned, 76*n*, 117*n*, 140*n*, 234*n*, 240, 254*n*, 346*n*
Lipsitz, Lewis, 254*n*
Lipsky, Michael, 283, 301*n*, 302*n*
Little, Roger W., 55*n*
Litvak, Eugene, 280*n*
Litwin, George, 52*n*
Livernash, E. Robert, 141*n*
lobbies: defined, 305–306; effectiveness of, 306–307; and incentive systems, 308–312; relationships between representatives of and organizations, 313–315; influence of, defined, 316; role of legitimacy in, 317; role of representatives, 318–321; and government structure, 337. *See also* nonorganizational lobbying
Lockard, Duane, 346*n*
London, Jack, 53*n*
London County Council, 82
Longley, Lawrence D., 346*n*
Lorwin, Lewis: quoted, 126; mentioned, 140*n*
Los Angeles, voluntary associations in, 84
Lowi, Theodore J.: public issues classification system evaluated, 327–330; mentioned, 88, 91, 345*n*
Lowndes County, Alabama: SNCC efforts in, 184
Loyal Order of Moose, 42, 198
Lubove, Roy, 199, 212*n*
Luttbeg, Norman R., 234*n*, 346*n*

McCarry, Charles, 325*n*, 326*n*
McCarthy, W. E. Jr., 140*n*
McClosky, Herbert, 118*n*
McConnell, Grant, 346*n*
MacDonald, David, 132
MacIver, Robert M., 265, 272–275
McKean, John B., 311, 325*n*
McKersie, Robert B: quoted, 290, 291; mentioned, 301*n*
McNeil, Rosetta, 280*n*
McWorter, Gerald A., 266, 279*n*
maintenance: defined, 30–31; in American Communist party, 105–106; in amateur politics clubs, 108; in solidary parties, 113–115; in labor unions, 119; in business associations, 165; in NAACP, 173, 183, 188; of SNCC and CORE, 184; in YMCA, 205; and organizational change, 205–207; in Red Cross, 206; and importance of respectability, 207–209; as executive function, 216–217; effects of bureaucracy on, 226–227; constraints upon, 237; and autonomy, 263; and bargaining, 289–292; and advantages of defensive behavior, 309, 310; in lobbying activities, 313–314; in Ralph Nader's organizations, 323
Malcolm X, 70
Mancke, R. B., 213*n*
Mann, Seymour Z., 90*n*
Mannheim, Karl, 117*n*
Manzer, Ronald, 211*n*, 212*n*
March, James G., 214*n*
March of Dimes. *See* National Foundation for Infantile Paralysis
March on Washington Movement (MOWM, 1941), 171, 178–179, 302*n*
march on Washington (1963), 7
Marcus, Philip M., 244, 255*n*
Marcus, Robert D., 97, 116*n*, 233*n*
Marshall, T. H., 58, 75*n*
Marvick, Dwaine, 108, 109, 117*n*, 118*n*
Marx, Karl: and theory of voluntary association participation, 57–58; inattention of to class origins, 196; mentioned, 14, 75*n*
Marxist parties, 102–106
Massachusetts Institute of Technology, 276–277
Massachusetts Welfare Rights Organization (MWRO): organizational history of, 65–67; staff-lay officer relationships in, 228, 241, 342; as protest organization, 283; mentioned, 203, 208, 294
material incentives: defined, 33; effects of, 36–38; use of in lower-class organizations, 65–66, 68; in political machines, 97–100; in labor unions, 124; and lobby behavior, 310–312; decline in reliance on, 342
May, Henry F., 213*n*
Mayer, Adrian C., 213*n*
Mayer, A. J., 254*n*
Meat Inspection Act of 1906, 335
media, effect of on public policy, 340
Medicare: AMA opposition to, 339; mentioned, 312, 330, 334, 341
Meier, August, 180, 189, 190*n*, 191*n*, 192*n*
Merchant Marine League, 155
Merton, Robert K., 16*n*, 76*n*
Messinger, Sheldon L., 213*n*
Metropolitan Housing and Planning Council (Chicago), 87

Michels, Robert, 55*n*, 107, 117*n*, 208, 209, 213, 215, 232*n*, 242, 252, 254*n*
Milbrath, Lester W., 76*n*, 325*n*
Miller, Norman, 279*n*
Miller, Walter B., 71, 77*n*, 280*n*
Miller, William, 168*n*
Miller, Zane, 116*n*
Mills, C. Wright, 4, 15*n*
Mineral Leasing Act, 161
Mississippi Freedom Democratic party, 180, 183
Model Cities Program, 72, 331
Mollenkopf, John, 203, 213*n*
Moore, Cecil, 187
Moore, Joan, 53*n*
Moose. *See* Loyal Order of Moose
Moratorium (1969), 7
Morlan, Robert L., 117*n*
Morland, John Kenneth, 77*n*
Morse, Nancy C., 256*n*
Moses, Bob, 185, 220
Moss, Robert, 302*n*
Mott, Basil J. F., 279*n*
movements, as political style of 1960's, 4, 14
Moynihan, Daniel Patrick, 116*n*, 322, 346*n*
Muhammad, Elijah, 70
Mulder, M., 325
Murray, Philip, 130
Muscular Dystrophy, 45
Myrdal, Gunnar, 189*n*

NAACP. *See* National Association for the Advancement of Colored People
Nadel, Mark V., 329, 345*n*, 346*n*
Nader, Ralph: nonorganizational lobbying by, 322–324; *Unsafe At Any Speed*, 322; organizations formed by, 323; charismatic qualities of, 323; quoted, 324; mentic.ied, 5, 330, 335, 340
Nader's Raiders, 323
NAM. *See* National Association of Manufacturers
Nash, Roy, 190*n*
National Association for the Advancement of Colored People (NAACP): enduring nature of, 171–173, 189; incentive systems of, 174–177, 181; Committee on Economic Activities, 177; challenged by other organizations, 178–179; by Young Turks, 179; impact of SNCC and CORE on, 187–188; as caucus organization, 217, 218, 225; liberalizing effect of bureaucracy on, 226–227; extent of competition with

Urban League, 264–265; coalition activities of, 268; NAACP Legal Defense and Educational Fund, 321; lack of client agency, 334; mentioned, 4, 7, 8–9, 26, 119, 198, 200, 201, 205, 266, 330, 341, 343, 344
National Association of Cotton Manufacturers (NACM), 149
National Association of Electric Companies, 264
National Association of Independent Businessmen, 163
National Association of Manufacturers (NAM): purposive incentives of, 154–157; maintenance constraints upon, 165, 166; as caucus organization, 217, 218; lobbying positions of, 310–311, 312; mentioned, 4, 83, 145, 158, 164, 198, 202, 209, 225, 268, 278, 311, 328
National Association of Retail Druggists (NARD), 145, 152, 161
National Association of Retail Grocers (NARG), 161
National Association of Soil Conservation Districts, 334
National Association of Wool Manufacturers, 147
National Audubon Society, 321
National Board of Trade, 158
National Catholic Welfare Conference, 198
National Civic Federation, 155, 198
National Coal Association, 307, 309, 318
National Committee for a More Effective Congress, 50, 218
National Community Relations Advisory Council (NCRAC), 272–274
National Congress of Parents and Teachers, 267, 321. *See also* Parent-Teachers Associations
National Consumers' League, 39
National Council of American Cotton Manufacturers, 149
National Council of Churches: liberalizing effect of bureaucracy on, 226–227; mentioned, 210, 211
National Education Association, 267
National Electrical Manufacturers Association, 310
National Farmers' Union, 196, 197, 198, 312
National Farmers' Union (United Kingdom), 81, 83
National Federation of Independent Businessmen (NFIB), 162
National Foundation for Infantile Paral-

ysis (March of Dimes), 44, 54n, 206, 207, 218
National Grange, 196–200 passim, 312
National Highway Safety Bureau, 324
National Industrial Recovery Act, 131, 151
National Labor Relations Board, 130, 335
National Metal Trades Association, 150, 155
National Miners' Union (NMU), 122, 298
National Negro Congress (NNC), 178
National Petroleum Refiners Association, 307
National Recovery Administration (NRA), 151, 165
National Rifle Association (NRA), 226
National Rivers and Harbors Congress, 334
National Rural Electrification Cooperative Association, 334
National Small Businessmen's Association (NSBMA), 162
National Traffic and Motor Vehicle Safety Act, 5, 329, 331
National Union of Manufacturers (Great Britain), 81
National Urban League. *See* Urban League
National Welfare Rights Organization (NWRO), 64–65
Nation of Islam. *See* Black Muslims
Nation's Business, 160
Nationwide Committee of Industry, Agriculture, and Labor on Import-Export Policy, 308, 309
Neal, Arthur, 76n
Negro History Week, 182
Neustadt, Richard, 216, 232n
New Deal: effect of on NAM, 156; black opposition to, 178; mentioned, 207
New England Cotton Manufacturers' Association, 147, 149
Newfield, Jack, 191n
New York Age, 176
New York City, effect of political structure on voluntary associations, 84–89 passim
Nexon, David, 117n–118n
Niagara Movement, 171, 172, 173
Nie, Norman H., 91n
Niebuhr, H. Richard, 90n
Nisbet, Robert, 76n
Nixon, Charles, 108, 109, 117n, 118n
Noll, Roger G., 346n
nonorganizational lobbying, 321–324

Non-Partisan League (North Dakota), 103, 104, 198, 205
Norris-LaGuardia Act, 125
North Atlantic Treaty Organization, 277
North City Area Wide Council of Philadelphia, 72

Oberlin College, 191n
Odd Fellows, 42
Odegaard, Peter H., 232n
Oklahoma Territory, socialist organizations in, 104
Old, Harold E. Jr., 211n
Olson, Mancur: on economic models, 23–25; quoted, 156; mentioned, 20, 22, 28n, 29n, 38, 53n, 120, 124, 129, 140n, 144, 159, 170n, 195, 206, 212n, 277, 280n
Oppenheimer, Joe A., 212n
opposition, organizational. *See* bargaining; protest
Optimists Club, 42
Oregon Education Association (OEA), 230–231
organizational change: and institutionalization process, 204–207; role of respectability in, 207–209; causes of, 209–211
organizational formation: entrepreneurship theory of, 196–198, 201; periods of rapid, 198–199; favorable conditions for, 199, 202–203; and purposive incentives, 201; role of organizational cadres in, 203–204
organizational representation. *See* lobbies
Orum, Anthony M., 76n
Ovington, Mary White: quoted, 190n; mentioned, 173

Packinghouse Workers, 122, 133
Packinghouse Workers Organizing Committee (PWOC), 133
Palamountain, Joseph Cornwall, 169n, 170n
Parent-Teachers Associations (PTA), 43, 44. *See also* National Congress of Parents and Teachers
Parnes, Herbert S., 291, 301n
Parsons, Talcott, 52n, 53n, 233n
participation: class characteristics of, 56–63; individual characteristics and, 58–59; and ethnicity, 61–62, 69–71; and education, 61; of lower class, 64–75, 85–87 passim; and nationality, 78–79, 91n

parties, political: administrative styles in, 222–223; consequences of democratic governance in, 253–254. *See also* ideological party; political machine; purposive party; solidary party
party organization: defined, 95–96; trends in, 115–116
Patrolmen's Benevolent Association (PBA), 121
Patterson, Samuel C., 325n
Payne, Raymond, 75n
peace groups, 63
Peak, G. Wayne, 346n
Pencavel, John H., 204, 213n
Pennsylvania Manufacturers' Association (PMA), 154, 155, 198
Perlman, Selig, 140n
Perrow, Charles, 243, 255n
Peterson, Paul E., 84, 85, 86, 91n
Philadelphia, voluntary associations in, 84, 85
Phillips, Derek L., 75n
pluralism, problems of, 14–15, 21
Political Action Committee (PAC), of CIO, 133–134
political machine: scarcity of, 95; defined, 97; patronage in, 98–101; administrative style of, 222–223
political parties. *See* parties, political
Pool, Ithiel de Sola: quoted, 310; mentioned, 170n, 306–318 passim, 324n, 325n
Pope, Liston, 77n
Populist party, 200
Port Huron Statement (SDS), 4
Powell, G. Bingham, 91n
Powell, Leona Margaret, 168n, 169n
Pratt, Henry J., 226, 233n
pressure groups, as focus of scholarly attention, 3. *See also* lobbies
Prewitt, Kenneth, 91n, 346n
primary organization: defined, 217–218; characteristics of, 219, 246
Prochaska, George E., 168n
professional societies, 80–81
profit, and organizational creation, 196–197, 201–202
Progressive Labor party (PLP), 47, 49
Prohibition, 206
protest: as opposition behavior, 282–284; factors influencing choice of, 285–289; tactics and goals of, 292–296
Protestant Reformation, 57
Public Information Program, 264
Public Interest Research Groups, 323
public policy: classification of issues of, 327–330; legitimacy of issues, 330,

331; source of issues, 331; costs and benefits of, defined, 331–333; and organizational activity, 333–337
Public Utility Holding Companies Act, 335
Pure Food and Drug Act, 335
purposive incentives: defined, 34–35; use of in organizations, 45–51; in secret associations, 49–50; in political parties, 103–110; in labor unions, 128, 138; in business associations, 155–157, 162–163; of NAACP, 173; and periods of rapid organizational formation, 201, 203; and organization creation, 204; in Red Cross, 206; and change, 210; and organizational governance, 240; and lobbying positions, 312, 319; rise in importance of, 344. *See also* goal-oriented organizations, ideological organizations, redemptive organizations
purposive party: distinguished from ideological party, 101–102; examples of described, 102–110; maintenance problems in, 108; membership types in, 109–110. *See also* ideological party

Rabb, Earl, 254n
Racquet Club (N.Y.C.), 42
Randolph, A. Philip, 127, 178–179
Raskin, A. H., 256n, 257n
Rauschenbusch, Walter, 201
Reagen's Colts, 71
Reddy, Richard D., 59, 76n
redemptive organizations: defined, 47–48, 49, 54n; CORE and SNCC as examples of, 181, 183, 185–189; use of protest by, 287. *See also* purposive incentives
Reichley, James, 98, 116n
Reimer, Everett, 256n
Renshaw, Patrick, 54n
representative. *See* lobbies
respectability: as maintenance element, 207–209; and organizational transformation, 209
Retail Clerk's International Association, 301n
Riecken, Henry W., 53n
Riessman, Frank, 77n
Riker, William H., 279n
Rivera, Ramon, 76n
Roberts, B. C., 234n, 255n
Roberts, Gene, 191n
Roberts, H. C. Jr., 29n
Robinson, James A., 277, 280n
Robinson-Patman Act, 152, 165
Rogin, Michael, 141n

Romney, George, 157
Roosevelt, Franklin D., 162, 179
Roosevelt, Theodore, 158
Rose, Arnold M., 79, 90*n*
Rosenthal, Alan, 89, 91*n*
Rosenthal, Donald B., 252, 256*n*
Ross, Arthur M., 252, 256*n*
Ross, Philip, 297, 302*n*
Rotary Club, 43
Rudwick, Elliott, 180, 190*n*, 191*n*, 192*n*
Ruppel, Howard J. Jr., 255*n*
Rural Electrification Administration, 334

Safe Streets Act, 308, 331
Salamon, Lester M., 192*n*
Salisbury, Robert H., 110, 111, 112, 118*n*, 196, 197, 199, 211*n*, 212*n*
Saloutos, Theodore, 212*n*
Salvation Army, 46
Sanger, Margaret, 197
Sapolsky, Harvey M., 83, 90*n*, 91*n*
Saskatchewan Wheat Pool, 248
Sayles, Leonard R., 53
Sayles, Stephen M., 256*n*
Schachter, Stanley, 53*n*
Schattschneider, E. E., 38, 53*n*, 143, 144, 167*n*, 168*n*, 308, 325*n*
Schelling, Thomas C., 279*n*
Schlesinger, Joseph A., 107, 117*n*
Schramek, Joseph J., 168*n*
Schriftgiesser, Karl, 170*n*
Schumpeter, Joseph, 29*n*, 73, 77*n*, 196, 211*n*
Schurmann, Franz, 29*n*
Scoble, Harry M., 54*n*, 346*n*
Scott, Andrew M., 325*n*
Scott, James C., 97, 116*n*
Scott, W. Richard, 52*n*, 234*n*
Seeley, John R., 208*n*
Seeman, Melvin, 76*n*
Seidman, Joel, 53*n*, 240, 246, 254*n*, 255*n*
Self, Peter, 90*n*
self-interest: as incentive, 23; problems of definition, 33, 52*n*; decline of as legitimate incentive, 342–343
Selma (Alabama), march on, 184
Selznick, Philip, 13, 52*n*, 105, 117*n*, 204
Sharfman, I. L., 169*n*
Shefter, Martin, 87, 88, 91*n*
Sheppard, H., 254*n*
Sherman Antitrust Act, 152, 158, 335
Shils, Edward A., 51, 55*n*, 233*n*
Shuttles, Gerald D., 77*n*
Sierra Club, 218, 321
Sills, David L., 44, 54*n*, 76*n*, 213*n*, 233*n*
Simkin, William E., 256*n*

Simmel, Georg, 135
Simon, Herbert A., 53*n*
Slichter, Sumner H., 141*n*
Sloan, Alfred P., 302*n*
Smith, David Horton, 52*n*, 59, 75*n*, 76*n*, 90*n*
Smith, J. Allen, 202
Social Democratic party (U.S.), 102
Socialist Labor party, 101, 102
Socialist party. *See* American Socialist party
Socialist Workers party, 101
Soil Conservation Service, 334
solidary incentives: specific, 33–44; collective, 34; in local parties, 110–112; in Socialist parties, 104–105; in labor unions, 124; in early business associations, 144; in Red Cross, 206; and organizational governance, 240–241; mentioned, 54*n*, 61
solidary party, 110–115
Somerset Club (Boston), 42
Sorauf, Frank, 99, 116*n*
Soule, John W., 107, 117*n*
Southern Christian Leadership Conference (SCLC): SNCC distrust of, 186; organizational structure of, 218; mentioned, 187, 341
Southern Cotton Spinners' Association, 149
Spingarn, Joel, 173
Spock, Benjamin, 283
Standard Oil Company, 146
Steel Workers Organizing Committee (SWOC), 130
Steigerwalt, Albert K., 169*n*
Stemerding, A., 325
Stevenson, Adlai, 134
Stinchcombe, Arthur L., 13, 16*n*
Stoper, Emily S.: quoted, 185; mentioned, 54*n*, 191*n*, 302*n*
Storey, Moorfield, 173
Storing, Herbert J., 90*n*
Stouffer, Samuel, 256*n*
Stove Founders' National Defense Association, 150
strain, organizational, 31
Strange, John Hadley, 191*n*
Strauss, George, 53*n*, 246, 255*n*
Strickland, Arvarh E., 279*n*
Student Nonviolent Coordinating Committee (SNCC): instability of, 180–181; radicalization of, 183–185; redemptive quality of, 185–186; impact on civil rights movement, 187–189; incentives in, 188; and Communist influence, 191*n*; as a primary association,

SNCC (*Cont.*)
217; mentioned, 4, 7, 47, 49, 171, 262, 268, 302n, 341, 344
Students for a Democratic Society (SDS): factions in, 49; mentioned, 4, 7, 47, 48
Sumner, William Graham, 201
Sweet, William Warren, 212n

Taft, Philip, 140n, 141n, 256n, 280n, 297, 302n
Taft, William Howard, 158
Taft-Hartley Act: efforts to repeal, 338–339; mentioned, 131, 140n, 156
Tammany Hall, 99, 209
Tannenbaum, Arnold S., 141n–142n, 251, 255n, 256n
Taquiri, Renato, 52n
Tax Reform Act, 307
Taylor, Frederick W., 201
Teamsters' Union, 276
Temporary National Economic Commission (TNEC), 144, 145, 152
Tennessee Valley Authority (TVA), 330, 331
Theodore, Rose, 140n, 141n
Thernstrom, Stephan, 280n
Thompson, Ralph V., 76n
Thrasher, Frederick, 77n
Timberlake, James H., 213n
Tocqueville, Alexis de: quoted, 19; mentioned, 28n, 79, 90n
Toner, Jerome L., 140n
Townley, Arthur C., 103
Townsend Organization: failure to change, 206, 207; mentioned, 209, 210
trade associations. *See* business associations
Treadgold, Donald W., 54n
Treiman, Donald J., 75n, 76n
Troeltsch, Ernst, 47, 50, 55n, 114, 118n
Trow, Martin, 140n, 240, 241, 254n
Truman, David B.: quoted, 19, 236; mentioned, 6, 15n, 28n, 198, 212n, 254n, 309, 324n, 325n, 340
Truman, Harry S, 134
Tsouderous, John E., 248, 256n
Tupamaros (Uruguay), 299
TWO (The Woodlawn Organization), 76n–77n
Typothetae, 146, 147, 149

Union of American Hebrew Congregations, 272, 273
union security agreement. *See* union shop

union shop: as maintenance device, 119–120, 121, 129; government attitude toward, 131–132; result of, 136
United Auto Workers (UAW): organization of, 130–133 passim, 224, 248–249; political activity of, 134, 137–138; strikes of, 252–253; mentioned, 122, 129, 177, 268, 276, 292, 311
United Church of Christ, 210
United Farm Workers Organizing Committee (UFWOC), 73–74, 220
United Federation of Teachers (UFT), 121
United Fund, 275, 321
United Mine Workers: political activity of, 133; alliance of with business associations, 151; absence of democracy in, 241, 245; mentioned, 122, 123, 129, 130, 177, 248, 249, 298, 307
United Nations, 277
United States Chamber of Commerce: incentive system of, 157–161; maintenance constraints on, 167; as a coalition, 267, 268; lobbying position of, 310–311, 312; mentioned, 4, 83, 145, 162, 164, 198, 205, 207, 278, 328
United States Steel Corporation, 129, 130, 146
United Steelworkers (USW): centralism in, 132, 133, 248, 249; political activity of, 139; mentioned, 122, 129, 130, 135, 224, 292
United Textile Workers Union, 148, 298
Universal Negro Improvement Association, 70, 221
Urban Coalition, 273, 275
Urban League: enduring nature of, 171, 188, 189; endorses MOWM, 178; extent of competition with NAACP, 264–265; mentioned, 4, 7, 198, 200, 207

Vall, Mark van de, 140n, 141n
Vanecko, James J., 86, 91n
Veblen, Thorstein, 201, 202
Verba, Sidney, 76n, 78, 90n, 232n
Veterans Administration, 317, 334
Veterans of Foreign Wars, 42
Vigilance Committee, 174
Villard, Oswald Garrison, 173
violence, 297–301
VISTA, 203
Vogel, Ezra F., 54n
voluntary associations: scholarly approach to, 9–13; defined, 31–32; and class, 56–64, 85–87; individual characteristics and participation, 58–61; and

nationality, 78–79; in Great Britain; 80–83; institutionalizing process in, 208; types of structures in, 217–218; legitimacy in, 219, 236–237; bureaucratization in, 224, 225; influence of goals on structure, 224–225; staff-lay relations in, 227–230; governance in, 237–248; consequences of governing styles in, 250–254; relevance of membership size in, 261–262; competition among, 263–267; coalitions among, 267–275; ad hoc alliances in, 277–279; and government structure, 337–340; in changing society, 340–345. *See also* organizational formation
Vroom, Victor, 255n, 256n

Wagner, Robert, 88
Wagner Act, 120, 131, 134, 156, 299
Walker, Jack L., 296, 302n
Walling, William English, 173
Wall Street Journal, 155
Walsh, J. Raymond, 134, 141n
Walton, Richard E.: quoted, 290, 291; mentioned, 301n
Walzer, Michael: quoted, 236; mentioned, 254n
War Labor Board, 132
Warner, Malcolm, 255n
Warner, W. Keith, 53n
Washington, Booker T.: opposition of NAACP to, 172; mentioned, 73, 176
Washington Reports (U. S. Chamber of Commerce), 311
Watters, Pat, 191n
Weathermen (SDS faction): reasons for violence of, 299–300; mentioned, 49
Weber, Max: quoted, 71, 219; author's debt to, 232n; mentioned, 14, 16n, 53n, 54n, 77n, 218, 220, 323, 326n
Wehrmacht, 51
Weinberg, Martin S., 42, 53n
Welch, Robert, 197
Weld, Theodore, 186
Welfare Council (Chicago), 87
Western Addition Community Organiza-
tion (WACO), 67–68, 74
Western Federation of Miners (WFM), 122, 128
White, Kevin, 88
White, Paul E., 263, 279n
White, Walter, 172, 178
Whitney, Simon N., 168n, 169n
Whyte, William F., 216, 232n
Wiebe, Robert H., 168n, 169n, 170n, 201, 212n
Wike, John Roffe, 169n
Wildavsky, Aaron, 346n
Wilensky, Harold L., 233n
Wilken, Paul, 255n
Wilkins, Roy: opposition to economic goals of NAACP, 177; mentioned, 8, 172, 178, 179, 188
Wilson, Bryan, 47, 54n
Wilson, H. H., 169n
Wilson, James Q., 28n, 52n, 53n, 76n, 91n, 116n, 117n, 118n, 190n, 213n, 233n, 254n, 257n, 301n, 302n
Wispe, L. G., 255n
Wolman, Leo, 168n
Wolters, Raymond, 190n
Womens' Christian Temperance Union (WCTU): failure to change, 206–207; mentioned, 46, 210
Women's City Club (N.Y.C.), 283
Wood, William W., 77n
Wootton, Graham, 90n
Wright, Charles R., 75n, 76n
Wright, James D., 346n

Young, Oran R., 212n
Young Lords, 72
Young Men's Christian Association (YMCA): maintenance in, 205; recent trends in, 208; mentioned, 198, 199, 209–211 passim

Zald, Mayer N., 205, 212n, 213n, 255n
Zeckhauser, Richard, 277, 280n
Zeigler, Harmon, 162, 168n, 169n, 170n, 234n, 346n
Zisk, Betty H., 346n